ADVANCES IN ACCOUNTING

Volume 8 • 1990

ADVANCES IN ACCOUNTING

ADVANCES IN ACCOUNTING

A Research Annual

Editor: BILL N. SCHWARTZ
Department of Accounting
Virginia Commonwealth University

VOLUME 8 • 1990

JAI PRESS INC.

Greenwich, Connecticut *London, England*

55 Old Post Road, No. 2
Greenwich, Connecticut 06830

JAI PRESS LTD.
118 Pentonville Road
London N1 9JN
England

ISBN: 1-55938-067-5

Manufactured in the United States of America

CONTENTS

LIST OF CONTRIBUTORS

Stephen F. Baginski	Department of Accounting Florida State University
Bruce A. Baldwin	School of Accounting Arizona State University
Thomas L. Barton	Department of Accounting and Finance University of North Florida
Abraham K. Charnes	Graduate School of Business The University of Texas at Austin
William W. Cooper	Graduate School of Business The University of Texas at Austin
James W. Deitrick	Department of Accounting The University of Texas at Austin
David T. Doran	School of Business Pennsylvania State University—Erie
Michael T. Dugan	School of Accountancy University of Alabama
Don E. Giacomino	Department of Accounting and Finance Marquette University
V. Gopalakrishnan	Department of Accounting and Business Legal Studies George Mason University

Adrian Harrell — School of Accounting, University of South Carolina

Anthony F. Herbst — Department of Economics and Finance, University of Texas at El Paso

Dilip D. Kare — Department of Accounting and Finance, University of North Florida

Michael C. Knapp — School of Accounting, University of Oklahoma

Wayne Label — Department of Accounting, University of Nevada, Las Vegas

James M. Lukawitz — School of Accountancy, Memphis State University

John E. McEldowney — Department of Accounting and Finance, University of North Florida

Rene P. Manes — Department of Accounting, Florida State University

Loren Margheim — Department of Accounting, University of San Diego

Charles L. Martin, Jr. — Department of Accounting, Towson State University

William Hank Moody — Peat Marwick Main & Co., Houston, Texas

Anwar Y. Salimi — Department of Accounting, California State Polytechnic University, Pomona

Thomas F. Schaefer — Department of Accounting, Florida State University

Ali M. Segaghat — Department of Accounting, Loyola College in Maryland

David L. Senteney — Department of Accounting, Eastern Michigan University

Hong-Chui Shin — Hong IK University, Korea

David E. Stout — Department of Accountancy, Villanova University

Jerry R. Strawser — Department of Accounting, Louisiana State University

Timothy F. Sugrue — Department of Finance, George Mason University

Dennis F. Togo — Department of Accounting, University of New Mexico

David W. Wright — Department of Accounting, University of Michigan

Donald E. Wygal — Department of Accounting, Rider College

Christine V. Zavgren — School of Management, Clarkson University

AIA STATEMENT OF PURPOSE

Advances in Accounting (AIA) is a professional publication whose purpose is to meet the information needs of both practitioners and academicians. We publish thoughtful, well-developed articles on a variety of current topics in financial and management accounting, accounting education and auditing.

Articles may range from empirical to analytical, from practice-based to the development of new techniques. Articles must be readable, relevant, and reliable. To be readable, articles must be understandable and concise. To be relevant, articles must be related to problems facing the accounting and business community. To be reliable, conclusions must follow logically from the evidence and arguments presented. For empirical reports, sound design and execution are critical. For theoretical treatises, reasonable assumptions and logical development are essential.

AIA welcomes all comments and encourages articles from practitioners and academicians.

Editorial correspondence pertaining to manuscripts should be sent to:

Professor Bill N. Schwartz, *Editor-in-Chief*
Chairperson, Department of Accounting
School of Business
Virginia Commonwealth University
1015 Floyd Avenue
Richmond, Virginia 23284-4000

EDITORIAL POLICY AND MANUSCRIPT FORM GUIDELINES

1. Manuscripts should be typewritten and double-spaced on 8″ x 11″ white paper. Only one side of a page should be used. Margins should be set to facilitate editing and duplication except as noted:

   a. tables, figures and exhibits should appear on a separate page. Each should be numbered and have a title.
   b. footnotes should be presented by citing the author's name and the year of publication in the body of the text, e.g., Schwartz [1981]; Reckers and Pany [1980].

2. Manuscripts should include a cover page which indicates the author's name and affiliation.
3. Manuscripts should include on a separate lead page an abstract not exceeding 200 words. The author's name and affiliation should not appear on the abstract.
4. Topical headings and subheadings should be used. Main headings in the manuscript should be centered, secondary headings should be flush with the left-hand margin. (As a guide to usage and style, refer to William Strunk, Jr. and E.B. White, **The Element sof Style**.)
5. Manuscripts must include a list of references which contain only those works actually cited. (As a helpful guide in preparing a list of references, refer to Kate L. Turabian, **A Manual for Writers of Term Papers, Theses, and Dissertations**.)
6. In order to be assured of an anonymous review, authors should not identify themselves directly or indirectly. Reference to unpublished working papers and dissertations should be avoided. If necessary, authors may indicate that the reference is being withheld for the reasons cited above.
7. The author will be provided one complete volume of the **AIA** issue in which his or her manuscript appears and the senior author will receive twenty-five off-prints of the article.
8. Manuscripts currently under review by other publications should not be submitted. Complete reports and research presented at a national or regional conference of a professional association (e.g., AAA, DSI, etc.) and "State of the Art" papers are acceptable.
9. **Four** copies of each manuscript should be submitted to the Editor-in-Chief at the Virginia Commonwealth University address. Copies of any and all research instruments also should be included.
10. A submission fee of $25.00 is required.
11. For additional information regarding the type of manuscripts that are desired, see **AIA Statement of Purpose**.

PART I

FINANCIAL AND MANAGERIAL

STOCK DIVIDEND EVENTS: EMPIRICAL SUPPORT FOR THE RETAINED EARNINGS HYPOTHESIS

David T. Doran

ABSTRACT

The purpose of this study is to conduct empirical tests of the retained earnings hypothesis (REH). The results lend consistent support to the REH. Regression analysis indicates a significant positive relationship between market reaction and requisite retained earnings capitalization (stock dividend size). Tests of market reaction to stock dividend events segmented by particular stock dividend sizes also confirm this general positive relationship. The findings are consistent across various measures of market reaction which include event period: return, abnormal return, and standardized abnormal return. The results are unchanged when controlled for event anticipation.

The appropriate accounting treatment of stock dividends and stock splits (stock distributions) is dictated by the Committee on Accounting Procedure (CAP) in *Accounting Research Bulletin* (*ARB*) *11* issued in 1941 and subsequently

Advances in Accounting, Volume 8, pages 3-23.

ISBN: 1-55938-067-5

restated in *ARB 43*. Stock dividends and splits (stock distributions) are defined by CAP [1953, p. 49] as "an issuance by a corporation of its own common shares to its common shareholders without consideration."

This study is restricted to this common-on-common type stock distribution. A shareholder's property rights to the corporation's assets do not change as a result of a stock distribution. All that changes is the number of shares held by each shareholder as evidence of his ownership interest. Thus, the shareholder received nothing of trangible worth under this type of stock distribution (actually shareholders should be negatively affected as a result of increased transaction costs [Brennan and Copeland, 1988]). However, CAP has recommended that stock dividends be treated like cash dividends in the case of "small" stock distribution announcements.

CAP recommends that small stock distributions (less than 20-25%) be accounted for by transferring from retained earnings to contributed capital (retained earnings capitalization [REC]) an amount equal to the fair value of the additional shares issues (thus reducing retained earnings by an amount equivalent to a cash dividend reduction). Conversely, the Committee recommends that large stock distributions (greater than 20-25%) be accounted for by transferring to contributed capital from retained earnings only the minimum required by law (at most par value of the shares issued in the case of large stock dividends). If no transfer is required (e.g., stock split or no par stock), none is made. Although this study does not test the cut-off point prescribed by CAP, the results do have implications for such efforts. This is discussed later.

Possibly due to differing legal requirements, REC by firms announcing large stock dividends was found to be inconsistent [see Schwartz and Monahan, 1986]. Due to this inconsistency, REH implications cannot be drawn by analyzing returns associated with large stock distribution announcements. They are, therefore, excluded from this study. In the case of small stock distributions retained earnings is capitalized for the fair market value of the shares distributed. This study is restricted to these small size stock distribution announcements (less than 25%) and will be referred to from hereon as stock dividend announcements (SDAs).

The REH argues that there is favorable market response to stock dividend announcements due to the retained earnings capitalization (REC) required under current generally accepted accounting principles (GAAP). For stock dividends, GAAP requires REC at the fair value of the shares distributed. REC reduces a firm's cash dividend paying ability. Reduction in cash dividend paying ability is the inherent cost of stock dividend events. Since this cost is self-imposed, the stock dividend announcement is generally regarded as a management signal of future firm performance. This study examines the relationship between market reaction and the amount of the self-imposed cost by analyzing market reaction while controlling for stock dividend size. Since

GAAP requires REC at fair value of shares issued; the larger the stock dividend size—the greater the number of shares issued—the larger the requisite REC.

The retained earnings hypothesis (REH) is a product of current GAAP. The inherent self-imposed "cost" of stock dividends is a reduction in a firm's ability to pay cash dividends. This "cost" is compounded given that firms generally increase cash dividends in the two quarters immediately following the stock dividend announcement [Lakonishok and Lev, 1987]. Although a firm's economic ability to pay dividends is primarily a function of cash, its legal and contractual ability to pay dividends is frequently dictated in terms of its retained earnings balance [Kalay, 1982]. Grinblatt, Masulis, and Titman [1984] state: "If the firm faces legal restrictions, stock exchange rules, or has bond covenants written in terms of retained earnings,[1] the additonal shares can further restrict a firm's ability to pay cash dividends" [pp. 463-464].

Therefore, the underlying logic of the REH is that firms announce stock dividends when management is confident that future performance will offset the self-imposed restriction caused by REC. The favorable market response generally observed in conjunction with stock dividend announcements thus is explained as an efficient reaction to a positive management signal.

Previous studies have analyzed size-segmented stock distribution event data. Although their intent was not directly to test the REH, the research of Grinblatt et al., Foster and Vickrey [1978], and Woolridge [1983] have REH implications. Each of these efforts monitored market reaction (abnormal returns) around the announcement date. The primary difficulty with these studies in drawing REH conclusions involves assignment of the sample events to size groups.

Grinblatt et al. [1984] included stock dividends and stock splits of 10 percent or more in their sample. The sample was divided into two size groups—large and small events (using a 25% cut-off). They found that the small size events generally were associated with more favorable market reaction. The other two investigations segmented the sample data into more than two groups. The size groups were partitioned so as to obtain approximately the same number of events in each size group. As a result, the span of different sizes (percentages) in each group varied considerably.

Foster and Vickrey [1978] stratified the sample into groups of 1-2.5%, 3%, 4%, 5%, 6-15%, and 20-100%. They found significant positive abnormal returns for the 3%, 4%, and 20-100% groups. Woolridge [1983] restricted his sample to stock dividend announcements (less than 25%) made by non-cash-dividend paying firms. He stratified his sample into groups of $< 3\%$, 3 percent $- < 5\%$, 5%, and $> 6\%$. Woolridge found significant positive abnormal returns associated with all but the smallest size group.

The arbitrary classification of various sizes into groups creates two difficulties: (1) the results of these previous studies are difficult to compare, and (2) the observed results are suboptimal in drawing REH inferences because the sizes included in the individual groups are not uniform. Woolridge, for example, has one group that includes only 5% SDAs, and another that includes all SDAs greater than 6%. No study to date has tested for differential market reaction to stock dividends for specific size events. This study contributes to the existing literature by analyzing individual size stock dividend events (thus avoiding the problem of arbitrary assignment to size groups); and by providing a methodological refinement through regression analysis.

This study tests the REH by monitoring market reaction to SDAs while controlling for size. Under the REH, the results should indicate the existence of a positive relationship betwen stock dividend size and market reaction because in the case of SDAs, retained earnings must be reduced by the market price of shares distributed. The larger the size of the SDAs—the greater the number of shares to be issued; given a particular market price, the greater the number of shares issued—the larger the requisite REC.

The data and the empirical methodology are described in the next section. The paper concludes with a section which presents and discusses the results.

DATA AND METHODOLOGY

Empirical Methodology

This study involves the analysis of market reaction to SDAs. This market reaction is monitored by observation of returns during the event period (day of and day following stock dividend announcement). Three measures of return will be monitored: raw return, abnormal return, and standardized abnormal return. Raw return (RAW) is the average daily event period return from the Center for Research in Security Prices (CRSP). Abnormal return (ABNL) is defined as the difference between "normal" return and actual event period return where "normal" return is generated under the mean-adjusted returns model. ABNL is divided by the comparison period daily return standard deviation to yield the standardized abnormal event period return (STD).

The daily returns sample data were obtained for all stock dividends announced during the period November 11, 1971, to December 31, 1982, from the CRSP daily returns file. The daily return on a stock is defined by CRSP as

$$R_{it} = \frac{(P_{it} + D_{it}) - P_{it-1}}{P_{it-1}} \tag{1}$$

where: R_{it} = return on stock i for day t.
P_{it} = closing price of stock i on day t.
D_{it} = cash dividend per share on stock i when day t is the ex-dividend date.

The event period is the day the stock dividend was announced and the day after. The day after the announcement date is included as part of the event period because it is the date the announcement usually appears in the *Wall Street Journal* and becomes publicly available. Appearance in the *Wall Street Journal* is assumed to meet the public availability assumption under the semi-strong form of the efficient market hypothesis [Fama, 1976]. RAW is the average daily event period return from CRSP.

$$\text{RAW} = \sum_{t=0}^{1} R_{it} \ / \ 2 \tag{2}$$

Various models have been used to generate expected returns that are compared with actual returns to measure abnormal returns. Brown and Warner [1985] have found that the mean adjusted returns model is at least as good as other models when analyzing nonclustered daily returns data. Time series analysis of the events included in the study indicated no evidence of clustering (see Table 1). Note that the events conclude in September 1982 due to the lack of daily return data needed in calculating the comparison period return under the mean adjusted returns model. Other studies of market reaction to stock distribution announcements [Woolridge, 1983; Grinblatt et al., Brennan and Copeland, 1988] have used the mean adjusted returns model.

Under the mean adjusted returns model, the mean return for a comparison period is assumed to be the normal (or expected) return for a given sercurity. This normal return is compared with the actual return of the particular security for the event period. The difference is the abnormal return. The comparison period used in this study is similar to that used by Grinblatt et al. [1984]; days 3-42 (with the date of announcement = 0) relative to the announcement date of the stock distribution.

ABNL is the average daily event period abnormal return.

$$\text{ABNL} = \sum_{t=0}^{1} A_{it} \ / \ 2 \tag{3}$$

where: A_{it} is the abnormal return on stock *i* for event day *t*.

$$A_{it} = R_{it} - \bar{R}_i \tag{3a}$$

where: R_{it} is the return on stock *i* for event day *t*, and
$\bar{R}_i$ is the mean return of the comparison period.

$$\bar{R}_i = \sum_{t=3}^{42} R_{it} \ / \ 40 \tag{3b}$$

Table 1. Data Clustering

Month/Year	*Percent of Sample*	*Month/Year*	*Percent of Sample*	*Month/Year*	*Percent of Sample*
11/71	2.0	7/75	.1	3/79	.4
12	1.4	8	.3	4	.4
1/72	1.0	9	.7	5	.5
2	.5	10	.9	6	.2
3	1.4	11	.8	7	.5
4	1.1	12	1.2	8	.8
5	1.3	1/76	.4	9	.5
6	1.0	2	.6	10	.5
7	.1	3	.7	11	1.1
8	.7	4	.7	12	.6
9	1.2	5	.8	1/80	1.2
10	.6	6	.6	2	1.2
11	1.6	7	.6	3	.8
12	1.7	8	.5	4	.4
1/73	.3	9	.4	5	1.3
2	.7	10	.7	6	.6
3	.9	11	1.0	7	.3
4	.8	12	.7	8	.4
5	1.6	1/77	.7	9	.7
6	.9	2	.8	10	.9
7	.6	3	.7	11	1.0
8	.5	4	1.1	12	1.0
9	.6	5	.7	1/81	.8
10	1.0	6	.4	2	.9
11	1.4	7	.5	3	.2
12	1.3	8	.2	4	1.0
1/74	.8	9	.5	5	.9
2	.6	10	1.2	6	.7
3	.7	11	.8	7	.4
4	.7	12	.5	8	.6
5	1.2	1/78	1.1	9	.8
6	.2	2	.7	10	.9
7	.3	3	.3	11	1.4
8	.7	4	.5	12	1.0
9	.7	5	.9	1/82	.8
10	1.0	6	.4	2	1.0
11	1.8	7	.6	3	.6
12	2.1	8	.4	4	.7
1/75	.9	9	.3	5	.9
2	.4	10	.8	6	.5
3	.8	11	.9	7	.1
4	.9	12	.3	8	.6
5	.9	1/79	.7	9	.4
6	.4	2	.5		

Each event day abnormal return (A_{it}) is divided by its estimated standard deviation to yield a standardized event day abnormal return (A'_{it}). These standardized abnormal event day returns are averaged to yield STD.

$$\text{STD} = \sum_{t=0}^{1} A'_{it} \; / \; 2 \tag{4}$$

$$A'_{it} = A_{it} \; / \; S'(A_i) \tag{4a}$$

$$S'(A_i) = S(A_i) \sqrt{(1/40 + 1)} \tag{4b}$$

$$S(A_i) = \sqrt{\sum_{t=3}^{42} (A_{it} - \bar{A}_i)^2 \; /39} \tag{4c}$$

where: $S(A_i)$ is the standard deviation of the comparison period daily returns
$S'(A_i)$ reflects the appropriate adjustment to $S(A_i)$ for the out of sample prediction point.
$\bar{A}_i$ is the mean abnormal return of the comparison periods.

The *t*-test used to determine the significance of the mean return of a particular size group is similar to that used by Brown and Warner [1985]:

$$\text{t} = \overline{\text{MktReact}} \; / \; (s_g \; / \sqrt{n}) \tag{5}$$

$$\overline{\text{MktReact}} = \sum_{i=1}^{n} \text{MktReact}_i \; / \; n \tag{5a}$$

where: MktReact_i = the particular market reaction measure (RAW, ABNL, or STD) on stock *i*,
n = the number of sample events in group *g*, and
S_g = standard deviation of MktReact for group *g*.

In the case of the *t*-test of STD the standard deviation of a particular size group is assumed to equal one since STD is a standardized variable.

Data

The CRSP daily returns file for the period November 1971 to December 1982 was used in this study. The initial criterion for sample selection is that the stock distribution announcement be included on CRSP's stock master file within the specified time constraints. There were 2,037 such events.

The next sample selection criterion required that CRSP have sufficient daily return data to accommodate calculation of the normal return under the mean

Table 2. Sample Reduction

Size (%)	*A*	*B*	*C*	*D*
.42	1	1	1	—
.75	7	7	7	1
1.00	39	39	39	7
1.50	2	2	2	—
2.00	204	201	200	53
2.50	46	46	46	26
2.60	1	1	1	—
2.80	1	1	1	—
2.90	1	1	1	1
2.95	1	1	1	1
2.99	1	1	1	1
3.00	253	248	247	96
3.20	1	1	1	1
3.50	1	1	1	1
4.00	232	227	226	86
4.50	1	1	1	—
5.00	604	587	586	297
6.00	61	58	58	23
7.00	11	11	11	4
7.14	2	2	2	2
7.50	19	18	18	15
8.00	9	9	9	3
8.50	1	1	1	1
9.00	1	1	1	1
10.00	431	415	413	181
12.00	6	6	6	—
15.00	28	28	28	8
20.00	72	70	70	26
Total	2037	1985	1979	835

Notes: A = Entire sample per CRSP.
B = Comparison period returns available.
C = Event period returns available.
D = Pure events sample.

adjusted returns model. This criterion reduced the sample size to 1,985 events. Those SDAs with missing daily return data for the event period (day of announcement and day following) were eliminated. Six events were missing event period returns data.

Finally, in an attempt to assure that the observed results were attributed to the SDA event, contaminated events were eliminated from the sample. The *Wall Street Journal Index* was examined for a three day period. The simultaneous event period is defined as days 0, +1, and +2 with day 0 the stock distribution announcemenet date. Any news announcement concerning

Table 3. Simultaneous News Announcements

	Number of Events	*Percent of Sample*
Cash dividend related	825	41.7
Earnings related	416	21.0
Contract	9	.5
Appointment of officers	77	3.9
Miscellaneous	240	12.1
Pure evetns	835	42.2

the stock distribution announcing firm (other than the stock distribution itself) was recorded. This final sample selection criterion reduced the sample substantially. The remaining "pure" event sample includes 835 events. Reduction of the sample due to application of selection criteria by stock dividend size is illustrated in Table 2.

Due to the high incidence of simultaneous events (58%), additional information concerning the nature of the contaminating announcements is documented in Table 3. Dividend-related announcements include actual cash dividend declarations and any other cash dividend related announcements (e.g., announcement that regular quarterly cash dividend will be omitted). The earnings-related announcements include actual earnings announcements as well as management announcements of earnings projections. Contract announcements are indications that the firm has been awarded a large contract. Appointment of officers is self explanatory. These four types of announcements are documented individually because they occurred most often. Miscellaneous news announcements include all announcements not included in one of the specifically defined categories. Pure events had no simultaneous news announcements per the *Wall Street Journal Index.*

The high incidence of contaminating simultaneous events indicates that the market reaction analysis should be restricted to the "pure events" sample. In the case of "contaminated events," the observed market response may be attributed to the contaminating event (events) rather than the SDA event. The resulting pure sample descriptives are contained in Table 4.

Empirical Tests of REH

A minimum number of events required for analyzing a particular size SDA was set arbitrarily at twenty. As indicated in Table 4, there are eight different stock dividend sizes that have the requisite 20 events. These are: 2%, 2.5%, 3%, 4%, 5%, 6%, 10%, and 20%. For these particular size SDAs, a numeric and graphic analysis of market reaction measured in terms of RAW, ABNL, and STD is presented. Evidence supporting the REH should reveal more favorable market reaction to larger size SDAs.

Table 4. Pure Sample Descriptives

Percent (Size)	*N*	*n*	*NYSE*	*AMEX*	*Percent NYSE*	*Percent AMEX*
.75	1	1	0	1	0	100
1.00	7	3	7	0	100	0
2.00	53	33	34	19	64	36
2.50	26	9	19	7	69	31
2.94	1	1	1	0	100	0
2.95	1	1	1	0	100	0
2.99	1	1	1	0	100	0
3.00	96	40	41	55	43	57
3.20	1	1	1	0	100	0
3.50	1	1	1	0	100	0
4.00	86	45	43	43	50	50
5.00	297	139	91	206	31	69
6.00	23	13	8	15	35	65
7.00	4	4	2	2	50	50
7.14	2	1	0	2	0	100
7.50	15	1	15	0	100	0
8.00	3	3	2	1	67	33
8.50	1	1	1	0	100	0
9.00	1	1	1	0	100	0
10.00	181	103	73	108	60	40
15.00	8	7	2	6	25	75
20.00	26	21	11	15	42	58
Total	835	434	355	480	43	57

Notes: N = Number of sample events.
n = Number of firms.

In order to test the REH directly simple regression analysis is performed using all 835 pure events. The analysis includes RAW, ABNL, and STD as dependent variables individually regressed on the continuous independent variable stock dividend size. Finding a significant positive relationship will result in rejection of the null hypothesis that there is no differential market reaction to SDAs conditional upon the requisite REC. This result combined with the observation of larger positive mean market reaction to larger size SDAs lends consistent support to the REH.

Doran and Nachtmann [1988] note the correlation of the stock distribution size and the level of market anticipation of the event. They note that small size announcements generally tend to be anticipated by the market while large size events tend to be unanticipated. In an attempt to assure that the observed regression results are not due to size serving as a proxy for anticipation, the regressions are repeated controlling for market anticipation.

Table 5. Expectation and Size

Size (%)	*Exp*	*Unexp*	*Neither*	*Exp* (%)	*Unexp* (%)	*Neither* (%)
.75	1	0	0	100	—	—
1.00	7	0	0	100	—	—
2.00	33	6	14	62	11	27
2.50	19	3	4	73	12	15
2.90	1	0	0	100	—	—
2.95	1	0	0	100	—	—
2.99	1	0	0	100	—	—
3.00	69	14	13	72	15	13
3.20	1	0	0	100	—	—
3.50	0	0	1	—	—	100
4.00	58	8	20	68	9	23
5.00	176	51	70	59	17	24
6.00	13	1	19	57	4	39
7.00	1	2	1	25	50	25
7.14	0	1	1	0	50	50
7.50	13	1	1	86	7	7
8.00	0	1	2	—	33	67
8.50	0	0	1	—	—	100
9.00	0	0	1	—	—	100
10.00	91	52	38	50	29	21
15.00	3	3	2	37	37	26
20.00	4	9	13	15	35	50
Total	492	152	191	59	18	23

Notes: Exp = Expected event.
Unexp = Unexpected event.
Neither = Neither expected nor unexpected event.

A classification rule segmented the data into three groups. The first group comprised "expected" events. This group includes all SDAs for which the same size distribution was announced by the firm within the immediately preceding 13 month period. The additional month allows for variation in the announcement date for firms announcing annual stock dividends. The second group includes "unexpected" events. These are identified as SDAs by firms that had no SDAs (regardless of size) within the preceding three year period. The final group includes the remaining events that cannot be classified as "expected" or "unexpected" and is thus termed the "neither" group. This classification scheme recognizes that market expectation is a matter of relative degree and attempts to capture the ambiguous middleground.

Table 5 documents the sample data categorized by market expectation. Smaller SDAs (less than 10%) are primarily comprised of expected events; whereas the larger SDAs are not. Given the high incidence of expected events in the case of smaller SDAs, the regressions were performed on the sample data controlled for expectation.

Table 6. Market Reaction by Size

	2%	2.5%	3%	4%	5%	6%	10%	20%
N	53	26	96	86	297	23	181	26
RAW	-.001	.004	.005	.009	.009	.015	.020	.025
SD	.019	.021	.023	.029	.028	.021	.028	.025
t-Stat	-.30	1.06	2.06*	2.95*	5.72*	3.26*	9.47*	4.96*
ABNL	-.001	.006	.004	.009	.008	.015	.019	.025
SD	.019	.021	.023	.029	.028	.022	.028	.025
t-Stat	-.53	1.46	1.48	2.87*	4.92*	3.22*	8.76*	5.04*
STD	-.025	.251	.113	.327	.294	.496	.756	1.357
SD	.922	.995	.886	.914	.908	.669	1.101	2.002
t-Stat	-.18	1.26	1.10	2.97*	5.01*	2.35*	10.17*	6.92*

Notes: *N* = Number of sample events.
RAW = Mean average event period daily return.
ABNL = Mean average event period daily abnormal return.
STD = Mean average event period daily abnormal standardized return.
* Significant at 5% level.

RESULTS AND DISCUSSION

Results of Empirical Tests

Table 6 presents the results of market reaction to SDAs by size. As indicated previously, there are eight individual stock dividend sizes with the minimum twenty events stipulated for separate identification. As the table indicates, there is a general tendency for the mean market reaction to increase with stock dividend size. This result is robust across all measures of market reaction (RAW, ABNL, and STD). However, the results are not consistent across all size groups (e.g., none of the market reaction metrics associated with 5% SDAs are larger than those of the 4% group). One would not expect to obtain perfectly linear results because an efficient market is cognizant of all firm-specific information conveyed through the SDA signal. The entire information set cannot be captured by monitoring stock dividend size.

The market reaction metrics become significantly positive at particular levels of stock dividend size (3% for RAW and 4% in the case of ABNL and STD) and maintain significance for all larger sizes. Graphic depiction of the levels of mean market reaction for RAW, ABNL, and STD is provided by histograms in Figures 1 to 3, respectively. The positive relationship between market reaction and size is particularly obvious when monitoring the general market response without methodological adjustments—RAW.

Table 7 provides the results of the regression analysis. Panel A reports the results of the full sample tests. The intercept term is consistently near zero and

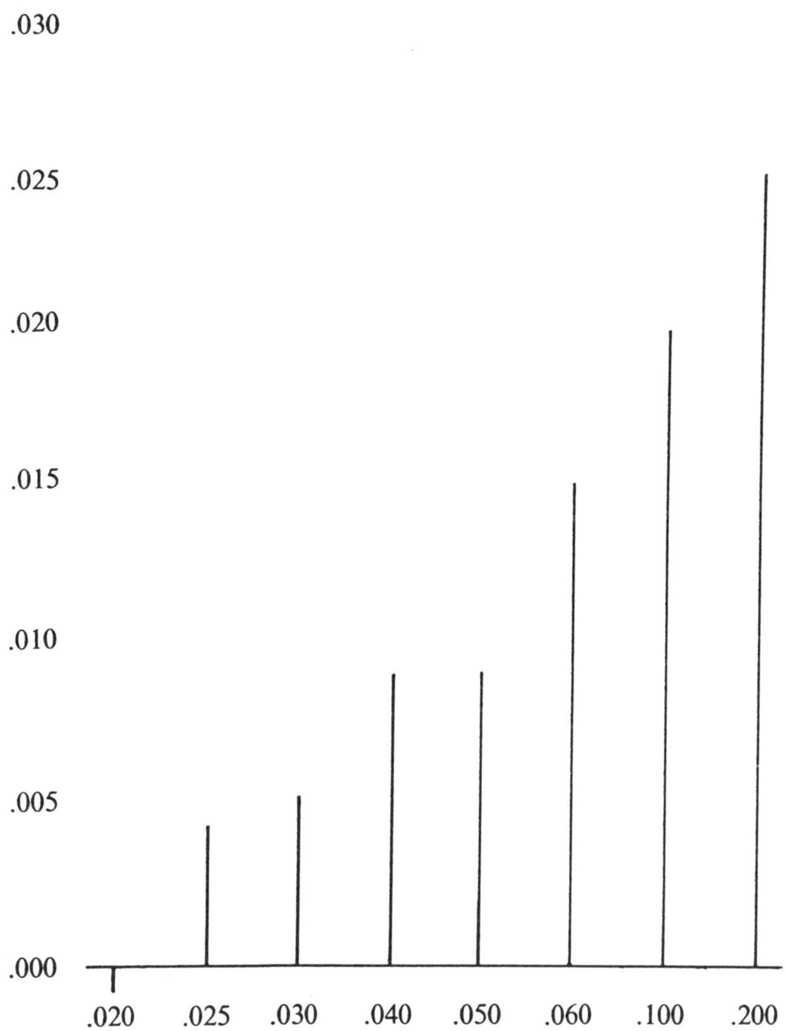

Figure 1. RAW

insignificant. The slope is consistently positive, and stock dividend size is found to be significantly related to market reaction across all measures of performance (RAW, ABNL, and STD). The same regression analysis was performed on the entire sample (including all contaminated events). Other than higher *t*-statistics (which is not surprising given the larger sample size), the results are very similar and are not reported.

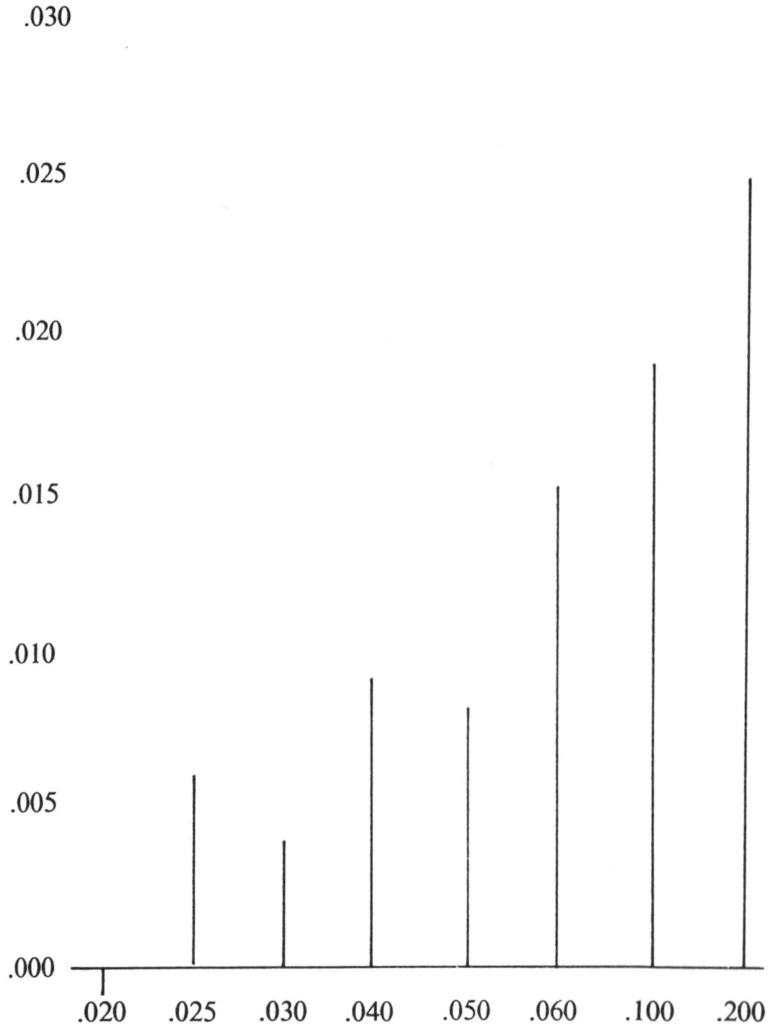

Figure 2. ABNL

In panel B of Table 7, market expectation is controlled for, and regressions were performed for each subsample: "expected," "unexpected," and "neither." The results are unchanged. Except for RAW in the case of the "neither" group, the intercept term is insignificant. The relationship between stock dividend size and market reaction also is consistently positive and significant across all performance measures.[2]

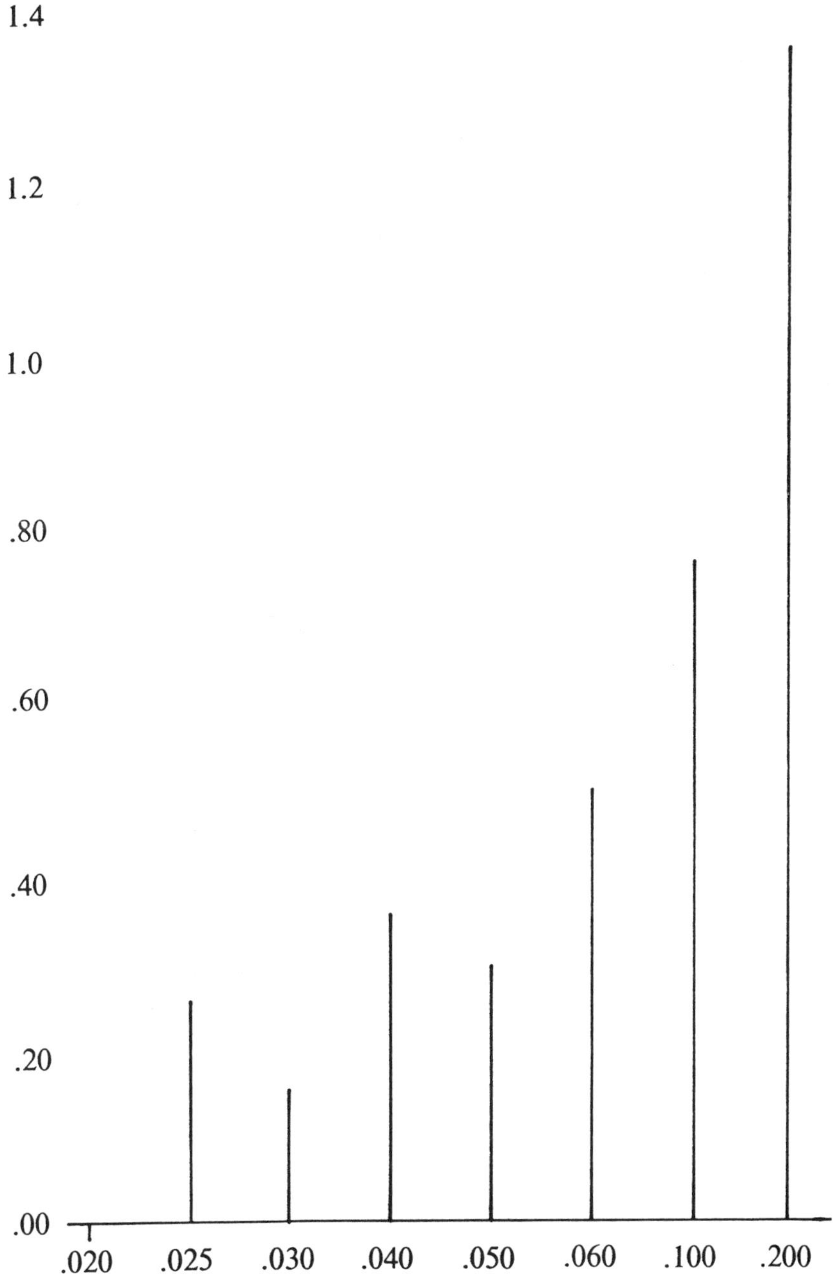

Figure 3. STD

Table 7. Regression

	Intercept	*t-int*	*Slope*	R^2	*MSR*	*MSE*	*t-slope*
			Panel A: All Events ($N = 835$)				
RAW	.001520	.880	.155282	.04724	.02801	.00068	6.427*
ABNL	.000644	.367	.155850	.04618	.02821	.00070	6.351*
STD	-.054241	-.822	7.589731	.07512	66.90656	.98892	8.225*
			Panel B: Market Anticipation Subsamples				
			Expected ($N = 492$)				
RAW	-.001195	-.532	.165618	.04088	.01201	.00058	4.570*
ABNL	-.001848	-.802	.163171	.03778	.01166	.00061	4.386*
STD	-.079415	-.950	6.791732	.04980	20.20141	.79879	5.029*
			Unexpected ($N = 152$)				
RAW	.004071	.936	.156273	.06040	.00698	.00072	3.105*
ABNL	.000311	.710	.152413	.05680	.00664	.00074	3.006*
STD	.094031	.601	5.932996	.06682	10.06655	.93725	3.277*
			Neither ($N = 191$)				
RAW	.008862	2.265*	.097820	.02117	.00362	.00089	2.022*
ABNL	.007548	1.919	.107457	.02519	.00437	.00089	2.210*
STD	.040283	.250	8.514189	.08828	27.43095	1.49887	4.278*

Notes: *t*-int = The *t*-statistic for the intercept.
MSR = Mean square regression.
MSE = Mean square error.
t-slope = The *t*-statistic of the slope.
* Significant at the 5% level.

These results provide consistent support for the notion that the market reacts to SDAs in relation to the requisite retained earnings capitalization. The larger the stock dividend size (and the larger the requisite REC), the more favorable the observed market response. Therefore the null hypothesis is rejected in favor of the REH. Thus, the differential market response to SDAs depends upon the associated requisite REC—the larger the requisite REC, the more favorable the general market response.

Discussion

It is interesting to note that a discretionary management signal with absolutely no direct economic consequence can have capital market ramifications caused by GAAP. Stock dividend events have no direct cash flow consequences to a firm or its owners. The only direct effect of stock dividends is to increase the number of shares held by owners as evidence of their ownership interest. Their relative ownership interest remains unchanged. However, since GAAP requires REC, and since this cost is self-imposed, a signaling mechanism has been put into place. Due to the asymmetric information sets of ownership and management, the market reacts favorably to stock dividends because they signal management confidence in future performance of the firm. In this study the degree of favorable market response was found to be directly related to the amount of the self-imposed cost that results from current GAAP—REC.

Tucker [1985] provides an interesting perspective on the motives of the Committee on Accounting Procedure (CAP) in issuing *ARB 11*. It seems that there may have been little (if any) conceptual motivation for current GAAP in accounting for stock dividend announcements. At the time the committee drafted *ARB 11* there was a feeling that stock "dividends" were generally misleading and unethical. CAP only had been in existence for three years and had yet to establish its credibility and sphere of influence and authority. George May, then vice-chairman of CAP, indicates in a 1952 letter that a primary motivation of *ARB 11* was to gain acceptance by the SEC and NYSE in order that CAP (the first such private sector authoritative body) establish itself as a legitimate entity for promulgation of GAAP.

The Committee tried to justify the requirements of ARB 11 by citing a review of then recent stock dividends and stock splits. Supposedly their review revealed different market "action" [CAP, 1953, p. 52] in the case of large (greater than 20-25%) as opposed to small (less than 20-25%) stock distribution announcements. They rationalized the differential accounting treatment based upon size due to this observed difference in market "action." The Committee never defined market "action."

Researchers have attempted to test the assertions of the Committee by monitoring abnormal returns associated with stock dividends and stock splits [see Choittiner and Young, 1971; Foster and Vickrey, 1978]. The results of this study would indicate that their efforts are inappropriate. The data used in their analyses are post *ARB 11,* and as such are subject to *ARB 11* accounting requirements. Livermore [1930] monitored the market reaction associated with various size SDAs but, due to his sample selection criteria, limited the analysis to distributions of 25% or more. Therefore, his is not an appropriate test of the supposed observations of CAP. Given the relationship of current GAAP (under *ARB 11*) and market reaction observed here, the only appropriate test of the supposed observations of CAP in 1941 is by using pre *ARB 11* data.

Future Research

If a replication of the Committee on Accounting Procedure's review of market "action" associated with stock distribution announcements is appropriate, it should be undertaken using pre *ARB 11* data. Using post *ARB 11* events confuses the results because the data are contaminated by the REC effect.

This study attempted to monitor the REC cost of SDAs by controlling for stock dividend size. The stock distribution signal should be a function of firm affordability as well as the amount of REC cost. A refinement of the empirical method in future efforts would be to include firm specific variables that attempt to capture firm affordability,[3] such as the retained earnings position at the time of the event. For example, two firms, identical except for retained earnings composition within stockholders equity, announce stock dividends that require REC of $1,000,000. Assume that firm A has $1,000,000 of retained earnings available to absorb the REC whereas firm B has only $1,500,000. Even though the requisite REC cost is $1,000,000 for each firm, it is a more imposing signal for firm B than for firm A.

Therefore, future research could be conducted that includes in the analysis such additional firm specific information as: retained earnings position at the time of the event, dividend restrictive covenants, cash dividend policy, etc. These refinements in monitoring the SDA signal would accommodate interesting tests of the REH and market efficiency on a more discriminating firm specific basis.

ACKNOWLEDGMENTS

The author would like to recognize the valuable comments of Jacob Birnberg, Frank McCarthy, Bob Nachtmann, Pandu Tadikamalla, and Neil Wilner.

NOTES

1. Indeed this is frequently the case; see Henn [1970, pp. 650, 672], Simmons [1972, p. 196], and the American Bar Foundation [1971, p. 414] for a discussion.

2. As another means of controlling for event expectation the entire pure sample was pooled and expected and unexpected events were identified as dummy variables (EE and UU respectively). The various measures of market reaction served as dependent variables (RAW, ABNL, and STD) while stock dividend size (SIZE), EE, and UU were the independent variables. The results follow (*t*-statistics in parenthesis with * indicating significance at the 5% level):

									R^2
RAW	=	.00602	+	.13992(SIZE)	−	.00073(UU)	−	.00582(EE)	.05716
		(2.397*)		(5.664*)		(-0.257)		(-2.604*)	
ABNL	=	.00527	+	.14126(SIZE)	−	.00132(UU)	−	.00593(EE)	.05545
		(2.064*)		(5.628*)		(-0.460)		(-2.609*)	
STD	=	.13170	+	7.1602(SIZE)	−	.12940(UU)	−	.23111(EE)	.08332
		(1.373)		(7.584*)		(-1.199)		(-2.705*)	

The multiple regression results indicate market reaction is positively related to stock dividend size and that the market reacts less favorably to expected events. Unexpected events are not significantly different from neither expected or unexpected events (measured in the intercept term which is consistently positive and significant).

3. In an attempt to monitor firm affordability in the study, earnings per share (EPS) data was included in the analysis. The rationale for including EPS is that firms with high EPS expectations provide a lesser constraining stock dividend signal than firms with low EPS expectations. Therefore, market reaction to SDAs should be negatively related to EPS expectation level.

The source of the EPS expectation data is *The Value Line Investment Survey*. The one year forecast issued the week preceding the SDA event was obtained from *The Value Line Summary and Index*. Not all firms are tracked by Value Line. As a result there was a severe sample reduction to 258 pure events. A multiple regression was performed with the market reaction measures again serving as the dependent variables. The independent variables include stock dividend size (SIZE) and the one year earnings forecast of Value Line (EPS). The results follow (*t*-statistics in parenthesis with * indicating significance at the 5% level):

							R^2
RAW	=	-.00055047	+	.160629(SIZE)	+	.000032218(EPS)	.06439
		(-0.211)		(3.935*)		(0.046)	
ABNL	=	-.001199	+	.163032(SIZE)	−	.000192880(EPS)	.06213
		(-0.454)		(3.958*)		(-0.272)	
STD	=	-.006189	+	6.16608(SIZE)	−	.008135(EPS)	.05937
		(-0.061)		(3.872*)		(-0.297)	

To assure the results indicating insiginficance of EPS was not due to severe sample reduction, the regressions were repeated using the entire sample set (including contaminated events). There were 770 SDA events by Value Line tracked firms and therefore included in this analysis. The results follow (*t*-statistics in parenthesis with * indicating significance at the 5% level):

								R^2
RAW	=	-.00010637	+	.199788(SIZE)	−	.00013958(EPS)		.08839
		(-0.061)		(8.506*)		(-0.275)		
ABNL	=	-.00038608	+	.195861(SIZE)	−	.00026836(EPS)		.08393
		(-0.220)		(8.307*)		(-0.528)		
STD	=	-.004045	+	8.724768(SIZE)	+	.001574(EPS)		.08799
		(-0.052)		(8.421*)		(0.070)		

The results are unchanged when the regressions were performed on the entire sample, There is no differential market reaction dependent upon Value Line's earnings expectations at the time of the stock distribution announcement. The implications that may be drawn are either the market does not discriminate for firm affordability; or more likely, the variable used here does not sufficiently characterize affordability.

REFERENCES

American Bar Foundation, *Commentaries on Indentures* [ABF, 1971].

Brennan, M.J. and T.E. Copeland, "Stock Splits, Stock Prices, and Transaction Costs," *Journal of Financial Economics* 22 [1988], pp. 83-101.

Brown, S.J. and J.B. Warner, "Using Daily Stock Returns in the Case of Event Studies," *Journal of Financial Economics* 13 [1985], pp. 3-31.

Choittiner, S. and A. Young, "A Test of AICPA Differentiation Between Stock Dividends and Stock Split," *Journal of Accounting Research* 9, 2 [Autumn 1971], pp. 367-374.

Committee on Accounting Procedure, *Accounting Research Bulletin Number 43* [AICPA, 1953].

Doran, D.T. and R. Nachtmann, "The Association of Stock Distribution Announcements and Earnings Performance," *Journal of Accounting, Auditing, and Finance* 3, 2 [Spring 1988], pp. 113-132.

Fama, E.F., *Foundations of Finance* [Basic Books, 1976].

Foster, T.W., III and D. Vickrey, "The Information Content of Stock Dividend Announcements," *The Accounting Review* 53 [April 1978], pp. 360-370.

Grinblatt, M., R. Masulis, and S. Titman, "The Valuation Effects of Stock Splits and Stock Dividends," *Journal of Financial Economics* 13 [1984], pp. 461-490.

Henn, H., *Handbook of the law of corporations and other business enterprises* [West Publishing, 1970].

Kalay, A., "Stockholder-Bondholder Conflict and Dividend Constraints," *Journal of Financial Economics* [July 1982], pp. 211-233.

Lakonishok, J. and B. Lev, "Stock Splits and Stock Dividends: Why, Who and When," *Journal of Finance* [1987], pp. 913-932.

Livermore, S., "Value of Stock Dividends," *American Economic Review* 20, 4 [December 1930], pp. 687-691.

May, G.E., Letter to John B. Inglis, Dated August 5, National Office Library of Price Waterhouse and Co., [1952].

Schwartz, B. and T. Monahan, "Accounting for Stock Dividends and Stock Splits," *National Public Accountant* [March 1986], pp. 24-26.

Simmons, R., "Drafting of Commercial Bank Loan Agreements," *Business Lawyer* 28 [1972], pp. 179-201.

Tucker, J.A., III, "The Role of Stock Dividends in Defining Income, Developing Capital Market Research and Exploring the Economic Consequences of Accounting Policy Decisions," *Accounting Historians Journal* 12, 2 [Fall 1985], pp. 73-94.

Woolridge, J.R., "Stock Dividends as Signals," *Journal of Financial Research* 5, 3 [Spring 1983], pp. 1-12.

THE INFLUENCE OF PROFITABILITY ON A FIRM'S LEASE-OR-BORROW DECISIONS

Dilip D. Kare and Anthony F. Herbst

ABSTRACT

Even though leasing accounts for nearly one-third of all new assets put into use every year by businesses, very little is known about the financial determinants of leasing. Based on the cost of leasing an asset is substantially higher than the cost of borrowing to purchase the asset, this paper presents and tests the hypothesis that highly profitable firms, because of their easy access to low cost debt, would prefer debt to leasing; firms with poor profitability, on the other hand, would be unable to borrow money on favorable terms and would, therefore, resort to leasing. This hypothesis is tested using financial data on firms belonging to 46 industries, over an 11-year period from 1976 to 1986. A direct comparison of operating profit margin (EBIT/Sales, representing profitability) of leasing and nonleasing firms shows that there is a significant difference in average profitabilities of the two groups of firms, with leasing firms, on average, having lower profitability. A 2×2×2 analysis of variance design was used to eliminate the effects of two confounding factors: the operating risk and the firm size. The results of the analysis of variance show that even after removing the effects of varying operating risk and the differential firm size, leasing practices of firms associate with profitability.

Advances in Accounting, Volume 8, pages 25-36.

ISBN: 1-55938-067-5

THE INFLUENCE OF LEASING ON A FIRM'S LEASE-OR-BORROW DECISION

During the last decade, leases have gained an immense popularity as a source of financing. According to an estimate published by the leasing industry in the November 24, 1986 issue of *Fortune Magazine,* leasing accounted for nearly one third of all new capital raised by businesses.

In spite of the popularity of leasing as an alternative source of funds, some fundamental questions about the leasing remain unanswered. Practitioners as well as academicians maintain that leases and debt are substitutes, but empirical research on this issue fails to support this view. Studies by Bowman [1980], and Ang and Peterson [1984] address the issue of the relationship between leases and debt. Bowman found a significant association between firm leasing and systematic risk, but the question about the substitute relationship between leases and debt was not conclusively answered by his research.

Ang and Peterson attempted to estimate the displacement ratio between debt and leases, that is, the amount of debt displaced by a dollar in leases. They used financial data on nearly 550 firms between 1976 and 1981. If leases and debt are indeed substitutes, then one would expect this displacement ratio between leases and debt to the positive. But Ang and Peterson found the ratio to be negative for all six years. If debt and leases are not substitutes, then the question that arises is: Why do firms employ leases? The choice between leases and debt is unlikely to be random; therefore, one might expect to find a pattern in firms' choices between leases and debt.

HYPOTHESIS

This paper presents the hypothesis that the profitablity of firms is a major financial determinant in their lease-or-borrow decisions. We suggest that highly profitable firms will resort to debt, while firms with low profitability are more likely to employ leases in their capital structure.

Theoretical support for this assertion is derived from Long [1977], who demonstrated that the cost of leasing a dollar in assets is substantially higher than the cost of borrowing to purchase those assets. Empirical studies by Sorenson and Johnson [1977], and Crawford, Harper, and McConnell [1981] provided support for Long's assertion. The Crawford et al. study, using leasing data from Houston banks, showed that, on average, the yield from a lease was approximately twice as large as the yield on a corporate BBB bond. A question that arises is: Why should firms opt for leasing an asset, if they could borrow funds to purchase the asset? If a firm has a choice, it should employ the lower cost source of funds, namely debt.

Moreover, firms enjoying high profitability should be more able to raise debt at a low cost. This should be the case because:

1. Firms with high profitability produce greater equity capital (through retained earnings) that supports additional debt. Firms with low profitability need to sell additional equity to support the new debt burden. This will drive up their cost of capital. In comparison, the lease option might seem less expensive.
2. Firms with lower profitability are likely to be deemed less creditworthy by lenders, because these firms will have less favorable debt service ratios. Because of this, these firms may find themselves unable to borrow funds at a reasonable cost.
3. The tax shelter hypothesis of leasing [see Copeland and Weston, 1988] suggests that firms with large existing tax shelters choose to employ leases in preference to debt, because they are unable to use the additonal tax shelters generated through the ownership of new assets (such as the interest on new debt, the depreciation of the new asset, and the investment tax credit if applicable). These firms trade away these tax shelters to lessors in return for favorable lease payments. Empirical data presented in Table 2B show that, on average, the tax shelter ratio (the sum of depreciation, the investment tax credit (ITC) and operating loss carryforward divided by the earnings before depreciation, interest and taxes) for leasing firms is significantly higher than that for nonleasing firms. It is not strictly correct to add ITC to the other items in the numerator, because ITC is a tax credit, but such a ratio has been used in prior financial research [see Boquist and Moore, 1984].

Once again, the link between tax shelter ratios and firm profitability is clear. Firms with high profitability will be able to make use of their tax shelters to shield their income and, therefore, reduce their tax liabilities. These firms are more likely to resort to borrowing and acquiring assets because they can utilize the tax shelters generated through the ownership of the new assets to reduce their tax liabilities futher. On the other hand, firms with low profitability will not be able to use the existing tax shelters, and, therefore, would be more interested in trading away any new tax shelters to get favorable payments on their lease contracts and reduce their expenses.

The foregoing discussion suggests that firm profitability is a major financial determinant in the lease-or-borrow decisions of a firm.

DATA AND RESULTS OF DATA ANALYSIS

Financial data on firms belonging to 46 different industries were collected from the COMPUSTAT Annual Industrial Tape Library for the period 1976-1986.

Table 1A. Industries From Which the Sample Firms Are Drawn

No.	*SIC*	*Industry*	*Nonleasing*	*Leasing*	*Total*
1	1311	Crude Petro & Nat'l Gas	28	6	34
2	1381	Drill Oil & Gas Wells	5	2	7
3	1382	Oil Gas Expl Svcs	0	0	0
4	1389	Oil, Gas Fld. Services	4	0	4
5	2000	Food & Kindred Products	9	3	12
6	2010	Meat Products	2	4	6
7	2020	Dairy Products	3	0	3
8	2030	Can, Pres. Fruit, Veg.	3	4	7
9	2082	Malt Beverages	2	1	3
10	2085	Distill. Rect. Blend Liq.	3	1	4
11	2086	Bottled & Can Soft Drinks	2	1	3
12	2800	Chem & Allied Products	9	6	15
13	2810	Ind'l Inorganic Chemicals	2	2	4
14	2830	Drugs	7	1	8
15	2841	Soap & Other Detergents	8	1	9
16	2844	Perfume, Cosm., Toilet Prep.	10	0	10
17	2850	Paints, Varnish & Lacquers	6	0	6
18	2860	Ind'l Organic Chemicals	1	1	2
19	2870	Agriculture Chemicals	1	0	1
20	2890	Misc. Chemical Products	8	2	10
21	2911	Petroleum Refining	25	7	32
22	3310	Blast Furnaces & Steel Works	14	9	23
23	3330	Prim Smelt, Refin Nonfer Metl	7	2	9
24	3350	Rolling & Draw Nonfer Metal	1	1	2
25	3410	Metal Cans, Ship Containers	3	3	6
26	3429	Hardware	4	5	9
27	3460	Metal Forgings & Stampings	8	2	10
28	3510	Engines and Turbines	4	0	4
29	3520	Farm & Garden Machinery & Eq.	2	4	6
30	3530	Const, Mining, Matl Handle Eq.	4	1	5
31	3531	Const Machinery & Equipment	1	4	5
32	3533	Oil Field Machinery & Eq.	5	1	6
33	3540	Metl Working Machinery & Eq.	6	4	10
34	3550	Spcl Industry Machinery	9	1	10
35	3558	Pollution Control Machinery	0	1	1
36	3560	Genrl Ind'l Machinery & Eq.	14	8	22
37	3570	Office, Comp, Acctng Mach	2	0	2
38	3580	Refrig & Service Ind'l Mach	4	2	6
39	3711	Motor Vehicles & Car Bodies	7	1	8
40	3713	Truck & Bus Bodies	0	1	1
41	3714	Motor Vehicle Parts & Acc	8	12	20
42	3716	Motor Homes	2	1	3
43	3720	Aircraft & Parts	2	2	4
44	3721	Aircraft	8	3	11
45	3728	Aircraft Parts, Aux Eq.	4	1	5
46	4830	Radio & TV Broadcasting	2	3	5
		Total	259	114	373

Table 1B. Profitability Ratios—Industry Averages

		EBIT/Sales		*EBIT/TA*	
No.	*SIC*	*Nonleasing*	*Leasing*	*Nonleasing*	*Leasing*
1	1311	.277	.203	.101	.427
2	1381	.234	.204	.132	.146
3	1382	.153	.163	.215	.194
4	1389	.169	.163	.170	.095
5	2000	.090	.112	.147	.158
6	2010	.047	.084	.122	.121
7	2020	.079	.118	.155	.151
8	2030	.084	.065	.125	.148
9	2082	.130	.110	.118	.241
10	2085	.151	.107	.125	.162
11	2086	.122	.102	.159	.153
12	2800	.090	.089	.101	.101
13	2810	.101	.134	.206	.143
14	2830	.178	.092	.180	.091
15	2841	.114	.083	.186	.140
16	2844	.131	.040	.187	.082
17	2850	.068	.058	.133	.119
18	2860	.095	.106	.108	.116
19	2870	.099	.198	.093	.104
20	2890	.125	.119	.164	.166
21	2911	.084	.096	.123	.124
22	3310	.079	.084	.097	.102
23	3330	.100	.065	.092	.064
24	3350	.050	.067	.073	.114
25	3410	.059	.072	.091	.124
26	3429	.135	.111	.177	.162
27	3460	.078	.088	.133	.125
28	3510	.095	.070	.146	.098
29	3520	.059	.087	.058	.108
30	3530	.121	.082	.155	.101
31	3531	.093	.061	.124	.089
32	3533	.149	.156	.153	.159
33	3540	.107	.082	.139	.101
34	3550	.081	.090	.114	.131
35	3558	.096	.072	.123	.100
36	3560	.087	.091	.120	.118
37	3570	.093	.123	.129	.124
38	3580	.086	.068	.131	.108
39	3711	.066	.053	.121	.094
40	3713	.138	.060	.207	.085
41	3714	.098	.087	.160	.117
42	3716	.146	.032	.138	.042
43	3720	.096	.099	.113	.109
44	3721	.078	.064	.110	.114
45	3728	.121	.091	.136	.129
46	4830	.206	.010	.133	.213

Note: The averages are calculated over the 11-year period.

Table 1C. Break-Up of the Sample

	Year										
Firms	*76*	*77*	*78*	*79*	*80*	*81*	*82*	*83*	*84*	*85*	*86*
Nonleasing	259	215	199	194	190	201	193	214	226	232	217
Leasing	114	159	184	187	184	178	158	144	161	142	143
Total	373	374	383	381	374	379	351	358	387	374	360

Table 1D. Lease/Assets Ratios for Leasing Firms

	Year										
	76	*77*	*78*	*79*	*80*	*81*	*82*	*83*	*84*	*85*	*86*
Mean	0.13	0.030	0.072	0.033	0.035	0.049	0.033	0.030	0.027	0.026	0.10
SD	0.38	0.064	0.450	0.040	0.042	0.170	0.041	0.039	0.036	0.034	0.27

The number of firms in the sample varies from year to year because the search for data on the Compustat tapes is made using the 4-digit SIC number as the key for search. Some firms may have ceased to exist during the eleven years because of bankruptcies or mergers. It is also likely that some new entrants appear from year to year.

FASB Statement No. 13 made the disclosure of leases mandatory in 1976. Therefore, the post-1976 data are assumed to be more representative of leasing practices. Eighty-six percent (323 firms) of the firms in 1976 belonged to manufacturing industries—those industries with a Standard Industrial Classification (SIC) between 2000 and 4000. Care was exercised to ensure that firms classified in the retail industry were not included in the sample, because retail firms employ relatively standard assets versus the specialized assets used by manufacturing firms. The market for leasing these standardized assets is likely to be well developed in contrast to the market for leasing specialized, one-of-a-kind assets used by manufacturing firms. Therefore, one might suggest that retail firms employ more leases than manufacturing firms. At the same time, retail firms suffer from low profitability (EBIT/Sales). Thus, the inclusion of retail firms would bias the sample data in favor of the hypothesis being tested in this study. For similar reasons, firms in the transportation industry (e.g., Trucking, Airlines, Water Transportation, and Railroads) were also omitted. The list of industries from which firms in the sample are drawn is presented in Table 1A. (Note that the number of firms listed for each industry is valid only for 1976, and will change slightly from year to year because of the reason cited above.) The sample of firms was then classified into two categories: (a) Firms which employ leases in their capital structures, and (b) Firms which do not employ leases in their capital structure. Table 1B shows the average EBIT/

Table 2A. Comparison of Debt-Equity Ratios

	Year										
Firms	*76*	*77*	*78*	*79*	*80*	*81*	*82*	*83*	*84*	*85*	*86*
Nonleasing	0.44	0.43	0.41	0.44	0.42	0.40	0.46	0.51	0.48	0.51	0.64
Leasing	0.52	0.55	0.61	0.56	0.52	0.53	0.55	0.50	0.58	0.74	0.61
t-statistic	1.43	1.65	2.23*	1.90*	1.92*	2.21*	0.92	0.03	1.98*	2.21*	0.14

Note: * Indicates that the *t*-statistic is significant at the 95% confidence level.

Table 2B. Comparison of Tax-Shelter Ratios

	Year										
Firms	*76*	*77*	*78*	*79*	*80*	*81*	*82*	*83*	*84*	*85*	*86*
Nonleasing	.330	.324	.310	.313	.322	.355	.396	.463	.432	.511	.531
Leasing	.317	.358	.372	.383	.434	.451	.563	.609	.577	.684	.714
t-statistic	-.416	1.138	2.17*	2.14*	2.83*	2.92*	3.25*	2.4*	2.81*	2.86*	2.89*

Note: * Indicates that the *t*-statistic is significant at the 95% confidence level or better.

Table 2C. Comparison of Firm Size

	Year										
Firms	*76*	*77*	*78*	*79*	*80*	*81*	*82*	*83*	*84*	*85*	*86*
Nonleasing	5.50	5.27	5.30	5.49	5.60	5.77	5.87	5.89	5.88	5.99	6.11
Leasing	5.37	5.88	6.05	6.14	6.22	6.29	6.28	6.46	6.40	6.57	5.41
t-statistic	-.58	3.06*	3.96*	3.37*	3.22*	2.70*	1.98*	2.76*	2.58*	2.78*	-1.69

Note: * Indicates that the *t*-statistic is significant at the 95% confidence level or better.

Sales and EBIT/Total Assets ratios for leasing and nonleasing firms by industry. Table 1C presents the break-up of the entire sample into these categories for each of the eleven years. In calculating a firm's lease commitments, only financial leases (i.e., the capitalized value of financial lease obligations) were taken into consideration.[1]

Leasing practice of the firms under investigation was measured using the ratio of the firm's lease commitments to its total assets. The average values of the lease-to-total assets ratio for leasing firms over each of the eleven years under investigation are provided in Table 1D. Tables 2A, 2B, and 2C provide average values of some relevant ratios for leasing and nonleasing firms for each of the eleven years. The *t*-statistics provided in these tables test the null hypothesis that the difference in the average values of respective ratios for leasing and nonleasing firms is not significant. Results in Table 2A indicate that, on average, leasing firms had significantly higher debt-equity ratios

Table 3A. Comparison of Operating Profit Margin: Financial Leases Only

	Year										
Firms	*76*	*77*	*78*	*79*	*80*	*81*	*82*	*83*	*84*	*85*	*86*
Nonleasing	.134	.139	.141	.152	.163	.138	.129	124	.125	.121	.102
Leasing	.096	.097	.099	.101	.097	.096	.085	.087	.087	.079	.070
t-statistic	4.57*	4.90*	4.94*	5.79*	5.35*	4.58*	4.72*	4.24*	5.03*	5.62*	4.85*

Note: * Indicates that the *t*-statistic is significant at the 99% confidence level.

Table 3B. Comparison of Operating Profit Margin: Financial and Operating Leases

	Year										
Firms	*76*	*77*	*78*	*79*	*80*	*81*	*82*	*83*	*84*	*85*	*86*
Nonleasing	.142	.146	.142	.152	.156	.138	.129	.124	.123	.120	.101
Leasing	.102	.101	.104	.104	.108	.096	.090	.090	.092	.084	.078
t-statistic	4.15*	4.73*	4.31*	5.38*	3.83*	4.57*	4.04*	3.50*	3.69*	4.03*	3.11*

Note: * Indicates that the *t*-statistic is significant at the 99% confidence level.

Table 3C. The Results of 3-Factor ANOVA *F*-Statistics

	Year										
Effects	*76*	*77*	*78*	*79*	*80*	*81*	*82*	*83*	*84*	*85*	*86*
Lease	9.99*	17.3*	25.6*	31.9*	20.1*	18.3*	17.2*	14.3*	20.0*	24.5*	20.5*
Size	0.11	0.25	1.07	1.79	0.06	0.66	0.17	0.36	0.34	0.18	2.17
Risk	1.95	2.84	3.52	11.6*	6.8*	12.9*	0.02	0.04	1.94	8.9*	11.7*
Lease*Size	0.07	0.13	0.06	0.64	2.57	0.00	1.28	1.21	1.66	4.63	1.66
Lease*Risk	0.06	1.71	3.43	1.34	1.95	3.01	0.35	1.26	1.67	0.06	0.38
Size*Risk	0.11	0.70	0.47	1.56	1.27	0.49	0.44	3.20	1.35	0.75	6.16*
(L*S*R)	0.05	0.43	1.17	0.04	1.54	0.01	1.18	0.73	0.41	0.21	0.02

Notes: L*S*R is the interaction effect lease*size*risk.
* Indicates significance at the 99% confidence level.

compared to nonleasing firms for six of the eleven years. This finding supports the finding in the Ang and Peterson [1984] study about the complementary relationship between leasing and debt. Table 2b represents the comparison of the tax-shelter ratios between leasing and nonleasing firms. The difference in the respective tax-shelter ratios is statistically significant for nine of the eleven years. These results lend some support to the conventional wisdom that much leasing is tax-driven. Table 2C shows that, on average, firms employing leases have a larger asset base (measured by the logarithm of total assets) compared to those not employing leases, and that the difference in asset sizes between these two groups is statistically significant.

Firm profitability was represented by the firm's operating profit margin. For the initial investigation, the profitability was measured by the ratio of the earnings before interest and taxes to sales—EBIT/Sales.

The most direct test of the hypothesis presented in this paper is to measure the profitability of the firms under investigation and compare them. If there is indeed a difference in the profitability of firms employing leases and those not employing leases, then this comparison would reveal it. Table 3A presents the results of such a comparison. The results of this rather simple test are supportive of the hypothesis that the profitability ratios are indeed significantly different. Moreover, the profitability of firms employing leases is significantly lower for all of eleven years under study.

It may be suggested, however, that differences in the operating profitability may be caused by: (a) differences in operating risk, and (b) differences in the size of firms. The higher the operating risk, the higher will be the profitability. If more risky firms are also more likely to use leases, then the risk effect may be confounding the findings of the t-test. Data presented in Table 2C show that for nine of the eleven years, larger firms are more likely to resort to leasing. If there is also a difference in profitabilities of larger firms and smaller firms, then the t-test presented above simply may be an indication of the size difference and not the difference in profitability. To eliminate the effect of varying operating risk and firm size, and to compare the operating profitability of the two groups of firms on a matched sample basis, analysis of variance was performed on the sample of firms in our study, using a three-factor 2X2X2 analysis of variance (ANOVA) design. The three factors, namely the lease variable, the risk variable and the firm size variable each have two levels. The dependent variable is the operating profit margin as measured by EBIT/Sales.

Because the presence or the absence of a financial lease commitment in the balance sheet of a firm can be easily detected, there is no problem in representing it as a categorical or discrete variable as required in the above design.

The coefficient of variation of a firm's operating earnings over the preceding ten years was used as a proxy for the operating risk (or the unlevered beta) of the firm. Similar measures have been used in capital structure investigations by Bradley, Jarrel, and Kim [1985] and Chaplinsky [1982]. This variable, however, is a continuous variable and, therefore, cannot be used directly for the purpose of the analysis of variance. Therefore, the firms having a coefficient of variation greater than the median coefficient of variation of the entire sample were classified as 'high-risk' firms; others were classified as 'low-risk' firms. A similar procedure was used to convert the continuous firm size variable into a discrete variable with the two levels.

The results of the three-factor analysis of variance based on the financial data from our sample of firms spanning an 11-year period from 1976 to 1986

Table 4A. Comparison of Return on Assets

Firms	76	77	78	79	80	81	82	83	84	85	86
	Year										
Nonleasing	.139	.139	.145	.151	.150	.132	.112	.108	.112	.114	.098
Leasing	.134	.132	.131	.137	.127	.123	.104	.105	.111	.102	.087
t-statistic	0.69	1.12	2.02*	2.13*	3.20*	1.31	1.16	0.48	0.94	1.96*	1.55

Note: * Indicates that the t-statistic is significant at the 95% confidence level.

Table 4B. Comparison of Capital Intensity Ratios

Firms	76	77	78	79	80	81	82	83	84	85	86
	Year										
Nonleasing	1.09	1.26	1.25	1.23	1.28	1.44	1.39	1.46	1.38	1.30	1.36
Leasing	0.75	0.81	0.81	0.77	0.79	0.81	0.86	0.88	0.92	0.86	0.94
t-statistic	3.92*	3.14*	2.87*	4.34*	3.96*	3.21*	4.65*	5.54*	3.99*	4.79*	3.79*

Note: * Indicates that the t-statistic is significant at the 99% confidence level.

are provided in Table 3C. It is evident that the lease effect for the entire eleven year period is significant at the .01 level. Moreover, over the entire 11-year period interaction effects are not significant except in one instance. The risk effect contributes significantly in 5 of the 11 years to the variation in profitability. These results suggest that the differences in operating profitability between firms which employ leasing and those which do not employ leasing are statistically significant, even after removing the effect of the differential operating risk and the difference in firm sizes.

As an extension of the study, the EBIT/Total Assets (ROA) ratio was used next to represent the profitability of firms under investigation. The average values of ROA for both leasing and nonleasing firms as well as the t-statistic testing the null hypothesis that the average ROA is the same for both the groups are provided in Table 4A. The results are startlingly different from those using the operating profit margin. The average ROA values are not significantly different for the leasing and nonleasing firms in seven of the years (specifically, 1976, 1977, 1981-1984, and 1986). Thus, it appears that if ROA is used as a measure of profitability, the strong association between leasing and profitability found earlier dissipates.

In order to find an explanation for this puzzling result further tests were carrried out on the data. The operating profit margin and ROA, the alternate measures of profitability used in this study, have a common numerator. So the only reason why the results of a test using these alternatives are different must be that asset utilization efficiency must be different among the two groups of firms. This explanation was statistically tested using a new ratio, the capital intensity ratio (Total Assets/Sales). This ratio is often used in economic research. The average values of the capital intensity ratio for the two groups of firms and the *t*-statistic testing the hypothesis that the average values are not significantly different from each other are presented in Table 4B. Clearly, for all the eleven years under investigation the capital intensity ratio for leasing firms, on average, differs significantly from that for nonleasing firms. It appears that, for whatever reasons, leasing firms employ fewer assets to generate a dollar in sales compared with nonleasing firms. Further exploration into this aspect of leasing is necessary to explain why the use of two different profitability ratios should provide two different findings.

Based on the results presented in Tables 3A and 3C, we conclude that the financial data on the sample of firms used in this study strongly support the hypothesis: The operating profit margin is a determinant in a firm's lease-or-borrow decision. Firms with higher operating profit margins are more inclined to borrow funds to acquire an asset, while firms with low operating profit margins tend to resort to leasing. When ROA is used as the profitability measure, the average values of ROA are still higher for nonleasing firms compared to those for leasing firms, but the difference between the two is statistically significant in only four of the eleven years. These results are provided in Table 4A.

CONCLUSION

We presented a hypothesis relating a firm's lease-or-borrow decisions and its operating profit margin. We suggested that firms with poor operating profitability are more likely to employ leases, while firms with good profitability are more likely to use the debt alternative. This hypothesis is based on the results of the Long [1977] study which demonstrated that the cost of leasing is higher than the cost of borrowing. Empirical studies by Sorenson and Johnson [1977] and Crawford, Harper, and McConnell [1981] have shown that result to be valid.

The hypothesis was tested using financial data on firms belonging to 46 different industries over an eleven year period between 1976 and 1986. When profitability is measured as EBIT/Sales, results of all the statistical tests strongly support the hypothesis. Alternatively, when profitability is measured as EBIT/Total Assets, the difference in profitability ratios between leasing and nonleasing firms is not significant in most of the years under investigation. We suggest that this stems from the difference in the efficiency of asset utilization found to be present between the leasing and nonleasing firms.

We hope these analyses provide insight in a firm's lease-or-borrow decision process, however, much uncertainty still exists. Further research is necessary to determine the role of other financial considerations like the tax shelters and debt service coverage in leasing decisions of a firm. Also needed is an explanation for the observed difference in capital intensity between leasing and nonleasing firms.

NOTE

1. Table 3B presents the comparison of operating profit margins between leasing and nonleasing firms when both capital and operating leases are taken into account. The results are similar to those obtained when only capital leases are considered (Table 3A).

REFERENCES

Ang, J. and P. Peterson, "The Leasing Puzzle," *Journal of Finance* [September 1984].

Boquist, J. and W.T. Moore, "Inter-industry Leverage Differences and DeAngelo-Masulis Tax Shield Hypothesis," *Financial Management* [Spring 1984].

Bower, R.S., "Issues in Lease Financing," *Financial Management* [Winter 1973].

Bowman, R., "The Debt Equivalence of Leases: An Empirical Investigation," *Accounting Review* [April 1980].

Bradley, M., G. Jarrel, and E.H. Kim, "On the Existence of an Optimal Capital Structure: Theory and Evidence," *Journal of Finance* [July 1984].

Chaplinsky, S., "The Economic Determinants of Leverage: Theories and Evidence," Ph.D. dissertation, University of Chicago [September 1983].

Copeland, T. and J. Weston, *Financial Theory and Corporate Policy,* 3rd ed. [Addison-Wesley, 1988].

Crawford, P.J., C.P. Harper, and J.J. McConnell, "Further Evidence on the Terms of Financial Leasing," *Financial Management* [August 1981].

Johnson, R. and W. Lewellen, "Analysis of the Lease or Buy Decision," *Journal of Financial* [September 1972].

Long, M., "Leasing and Cost of Capital," *Journal of Finance and Quantitative Analysis* [November 1977].

Sorensen, I. and R. Johnson, "Equipment Financial Leasing Practices and Costs: An Empirical Study," *Financial Management* [September 1977].

THE IMPACT OF FINANCIAL STATEMENT EFFECTS ON THE ADOPTION OF ACCOUNTING PRONOUNCEMENTS:

THE CASE OF SFAS 87

David L. Senteney and Jerry R. Strawser

ABSTRACT

Statement of Financial Accounting Standards No. 87 (*SFAS 87*) prescribes new methods of accounting for defined benefit pension plans. Adoption of *SFAS 87* was required for fiscal years beginning after December 15, 1986; however, the Financial Accounting Standards Board (FASB) encouraged implementation of its provisions prior to this date. This paper examines the impact of *SFAS 87* on the financial statements of those companies adopting *SFAS 87* in 1985, 1986, and 1987. The results of our analysis indicate that *SFAS 87* generally (1) did not appear to have a significant balance sheet impact and (2) resulted in decreased pension expense in the year of adoption. Differences noted in comparisons by year of adoption indicate that the financial statement impact of *SFAS 87* appears

Advances in Accounting, Volume 8, pages 37-60.

ISBN: 1-55938-067-5

to have influenced the timing of its adoption. These results suggest that the FASB's practice of allowing a transition period for adoption of its pronouncements may result in systematic financial statement effects as certain firms elect early adoption while others postpone adoption until the required implementation date.

The method used to account for defined benefit pension plans has been a controversial issue for some time. In 1985, this controversy resulted in the issuance of *Statement of Financial Accounting Standards No. 87* (*SFAS 87*) [Financial Accounting Standards Board (FASB), 1985] which affected: (1) the deferred pension charge (pension obligation) reported in the balance sheet; (2) the amount of pension expense reported in the income statement; and, (3) the disclosures provided in the footnotes accompanying the financial statements. While implementation of *SFAS 87* was required for fiscal years beginning after December 15, 1986, the FASB encouraged the adoption of its provisions prior to the mandatory date.

SFAS 87 resulted from a 10-year examination of accounting for single-employer, defined-benefit pension plans. During this period, the potential effects of revising the method of accounting for pension plans were widely debated.[1] Preliminary investigations of the impact of *SFAS 87* on financial statements [Norton, 1988; Stone and Ingram, 1988] examined the pension disclosures of companies adopting *SFAS 87* in 1985 and 1986. These studies concluded that *SFAS 87* (1) decreased reported pension expense and (2) did not substantially impact the balance sheets of adopting companies (in the form of disclosing a minimum liability for unfunded pension benefits).

A limitation of prior research is that it considered only those companies electing to implement *SFAS 87* prior to the required date. The possibility exists that early adoption was elected because *SFAS 87* had favorable (or did not have highly unfavorable) effects on financial statements. Therefore, these results may not represent the impact of *SFAS 87* on those firms electing later adoption. To date, no attempt has been made to compare the financial statement effects of *SFAS 87* for companies adopting the pronouncement in different years.

This study examines the pension disclosures of companies adopting *SFAS 87* both prior to and after the mandatory implementation date. Our purpose is twofold. First, comparison of companies adopting *SFAS 87* prior to the mandatory implementation date with those adopting it at this date may indicate that the financial statement effects of an accounting pronouncement impact management's decision as to the timing of adoption. Second, a more representative assessment of the effects of *SFAS 87* on corporate financial statements may be made by including companies whose adoption of *SFAS 87* is involuntary.

BACKGROUND ON PENSION PRONOUNCEMENTS

Prior to the issuance of *SFAS 87,* employer accounting for defined benefit pension plans was based on the provisions of Accounting Principles Board (APB) *Opinion No. 8* (*APB 8*) [APB, 1966] and *Statement of Financial Accounting Standards No. 36* (*SFAS 36*) [FASB, 1980]. *SFAS 87* altered the requirements for reporting defined benefit pension plans in the: (1) balance sheet; (2) income statement; and, (3) footnotes accompanying the financial statements. These changes are discussed below.

Balance Sheet Disclosures

Under the provisions of *APB 8,* a deferred pension charge (pension obligation) was recorded in the balance sheet when the pension costs funded (cash paid) during current and past periods exceeded (was less than) the pension expense recorded during those periods. Thus, the pension charge (obligation) recognized under *APB 8* represented differences between the pension cost funded and the expense recognized. It should be noted that the funded status of a pension plan (i.e., the relationship of the obligation owed to participants and the assets available to satisfy that obligation) was not reflected in the pension obligation recognized under *APB 8.*

In contrast, *SFAS 87* requires the disclosure of a minimum liability for unfunded pension benefits when the accumulated benefit obligation (ABO) exceeds the fair value of pension plan assets. The ABO represents the present value of the vested and nonvested pension benefits earned to date based on current and past compensation levels. When a minimum liability for unfunded pension benefits is recognized, a corresponding intangible asset is also recorded. The minimum liability is the excess of the ABO over the fair value of pension plan assets.

As a result of *SFAS 87,* a liability for unfunded pension benefits related to defined benefit pension plans may be reported. While information concerning the funded status of a pension plan has not been reported in the body of the financial statements prior to *SFAS 87,* it has been disclosed in the footnotes under the provisions of *APB 8* and *SFAS 36.* Therefore, the minimum liability required under *SFAS 87* does not represent the disclosure of additional information concerning the funded status of a pension plan.[2] However, as discussed in a subsequent section of this paper, footnote disclosure of additional information concerning the funded status of a defined benefit pension plan is made under the provisions of *SFAS 87.*

Pension Expense

In addition to the disclosure of a minimum pension liability, *SFAS 87* reduces the flexibility allowed in determining periodic pension expense. *APB 8* permitted the use of any acceptable actuarial method to compute pension expense as long as the computed pension expense fell between specified minimum and maximum amounts. As a result of the flexibility permitted by *APB 8,* various actuarial methods were used to calculate periodic pension expense.

SFAS 87 standardizes the calculation of pension expense by requiring the use of a single actuarial method. The actuarial method selected must directly reflect the terms of the defined benefit pension plan (the benefit/years-of-service approach). In addition, *SFAS 87* requires that footnote disclosure be made of the components of pension expense. While the amount of pension expense reported is affected, the a priori impact is indeterminate. Pension expense may either increase or decrease as a result of implementing *SFAS 87,* depending on the actuarial method previously used.[3]

Footnote Disclosures

In addition to its effect on an entity's financial statements, *SFAS 87* expands the footnote disclosures concerning the funding of defined benefit pension plans. Under *APB 8,* only the amount of unfunded vested pension benefits was disclosed. Unfunded vested pension benefits represented the difference between (1) the present value of vested pension benefits earned to date based on current and past compensation levels (the accumulated vested benefit obligation) and (2) the amount of assets currently available to satisfy these benefits (plan assets). Under the provisions of *APB 8,* the unfunded vested pension benefits were commonly presented as a single net amount in the footnotes accompanying the financial statements.

SFAS 36 expanded and modified the footnote disclosure requirements of *APB 8.* Unlike *APB 8,* which required only that net unfunded vested benefits be disclosed, *SFAS 36* required separate disclosures of: (1) the accumulated vested benefit obligation; (2) the accumulated nonvested benefit obligation; and (3) the plan assets. Thus, footnote disclosures were expanded to include a provision for the present value of nonvested pension benefits earned. These disclosures contain the same information concerning the funded status of the entity's pension plan as the minimum liability subsequently required by *SFAS 87.*

In addition to the disclosures required by *APB 8* and *SFAS 36, SFAS 87* requires disclosure of the projected benefit obligation (PBO). The PBO reflects the present value of vested and nonvested pension benefits earned to date based on expected *future* compensation levels. *SFAS 87* also requires reconciliation of the difference between the PBO and the fair value of plan assets to the deferred pension charge (pension obligation).

A consequence of disclosing the PBO is that it provides additional information concerning the funded status of a pension plan. Since, in almost all cases, future compensation levels exceed past and current levels, the PBO

Table 1. Major Reporting Requirements Under Pension Pronouncements

	APB 8	*SFAS 36*	*SFAS 87*
Balance Sheet	Asset or liability based on difference between (1) amounts funded and (2) amounts expensed	Same as *APB 8*	Minimum liability if ABO exceeds the fair value of plan assets
Pension Expense	Use of any actuarial method is acceptable. Amount of expense is subject to minimum and maximum thresholds	Same as *APB 8*	Must use an actuarial method which reflects the terms of the pension plan. No maximum and minimum thresholds
Footnotes	1. Accumulated vested benefit obligation 2. Pension plan assets (*Note:* Could show as a net disclosure)	1. Accumulated vested benefit obligation 2. Accumulated nonvested benefit obligation 3. Pension plan assets	1. Accumulated vested benefit obligation 2. Accumulated nonvested benefit obligation 3. Projected benefit obligation 4. Pension plan assets 5. Components of pension expense

will exceed the ABO. Therefore, the relationship of the PBO to pension plan assets provides a less favorable indication of the funded status of a pension plan than the relationship of the ABO to pension plan assets. These indications concerning the funded status of a pension plan could ultimately lead to less favorable perceptions of the overall financial condition of the firms. The reporting requirements under the various pension pronouncements are summarized in Table 1.

THE FINANCIAL STATEMENT EFFECTS OF ACCOUNTING PRONOUNCEMENTS

Previous Research

Previous examinations of the financial statement impact of *SFAS 87* [Norton, 1988; Stone and Ingram, 1988] were limited to its voluntary adopters. However, the financial statement effects of *SFAS 87* for this group of companies may differ from the effects for those adopting *SFAS 87* at a later date. Companies adopting *SFAS 87* prior to its required implementation date may have done so because it had favorable (or did not have highly unfavorable) effects on their financial statements. Arguably, adverse financial statement impacts would make it unlikely that *SFAS 87* be adopted prior to the required implementation date.

The decision to adopt *SFAS 87* prior to the required implementation date may be viewed as the choice between two competing accounting principles. This decision is the choice of accounting for pensions under the provisions of *APB 8* and *SFAS 36* or those of *SFAS 87*. Beginning with Gordon's [1964] research, several studies have attempted to identify the economic factors that influence management's selection of accounting procedures.[4]

Choices examined by this research have been management's decisions to: (1) expense or capitalize interest associated with capital expenditures [Bowen, Noreen, and Lacey, 1981]; (2) adopt full cost accounting or successful efforts accounting (for firms in the oil and gas industry) [Dhaliwal, 1980; Lilien and Pastena, 1982; Johnson and Ramanan, 1988]; (3) select straight-line or accelerated depreciation methods [Holthausen, 1981; Dhaliwal, Salamon, and Smith, 1982]; (4) capitalize or expense research and development costs [Daley and Vigeland, 1983]; and, (5) select from a series of accounting principles [Hagerman and Zmijewski, 1979; Zmijewski and Hagerman, 1981]. These studies conclude that the financial statement effects of a particular accounting principle (especially the impact on net income) have a significant effect on selection among competing accounting principles.

To date, only a single study examined the factors influencing management's decision to adopt an accounting pronouncement prior to its required implementation date. Ayres [1986] concluded that management's decision to adopt *SFAS 52* prior to the mandatory implementation date was influenced, in part, by its financial statement effects. Ayres' results, as well as the accounting choice research discussed above, indicate that the effect of an accounting principle on a company's financial statements may influence management's decision to (1) select from among competing accounting principles and (2) adopt a mandatory pronouncement prior to the required implementation date. These results imply that it is unlikely that the disclosures examined by Norton [1988] and Stone and Ingram [1988] are representative of the financial statement effects of *SFAS 87* for later adopters as contrasted with earlier adopters.

If, ceritus paribus, the financial statement impact of *SFAS 87* does not differ among firms, there should be no differences in the adoption date. This study compares the financial statement effects of *SFAS 87* for companies adopting *SFAS 87* in 1987 (mandatory adoption), 1986 (voluntary adoption), and 1985 (voluntary adoption). This comparison may provide further evidence that the timing of the adoption of a particular accounting pronouncement is influenced by its financial statement effects.

Sample

The pension disclosures examined in this study were obtained from the annual reports of a total of 189 publicly-traded companies. Forty-two of these companies are those examined by Norton [1988]. This group represents the population of adopters in 1985 as identified by the FASB.

A sample of 1986 and 1987 adopters was selected from the population of annual reports of publicly-traded companies available in our university library. This sample resulted in a total of 92 companies that adopted *SFAS 87* in 1986 and 55 in 1987.[5] The latter group represents companies that did not voluntarily choose to implement *SFAS 87* prior to its mandatory implementation date.

Table 2 summarizes the industry membership and firm size by year of adoption for the firms included in our sample. A complete listing of the sample firms along with the two-digit S'andard Industrial Classification (SIC) code is contained in the Appendix to this paper. Analysis of variance procedures indicate the firm size does not significantly differ across adoption years. However, a chi-square test of independence indicates that the sample adopters are not independent with respect to industry membership.[6] Thus, the adoption decision may be influenced, in part, by industry membership.

Table 2. Descriptive Statistics for Sample of Firms by Year of Adoption

Panel A: Size (Sales or Operating Revenues in Thousands of Dollars

Percentile	*1985* (*n* = *42*)	*1986* (*n* = *92*)	*1987* (*n* = *55*)
10	76,353	762,147	528,313
20	272,518	1,107,100	742,845
30	624,546	1,430,036	1,048,151
40	808,300	1,934,937	1,332,109
50	913,600	2,778,132	1,770,329
60	1,625,428	3,720,400	2,699,300
70	2,408,502	4,639,486	3,365,785
80	5,650,558	6,440,871	4,166,100
90	15,636,000	10,047,000	5,647,460
100	91,620,000	34,276,000	16,680,400
Mean	5,660,548	4,651,718	3,218,421
SD	15,402,250	5,534,008	3,170,003

Panel B: Industry Membership (Single Digit SIC Code)*

Code	*1985* (*n* = *42*)	*1986* (*n* = *92*)	*1987* (*n* = *55*)
0000	0	1	0
1000	5	3	1
2000	9	32	14
3000	7	27	12
4000	7	11	18
5000	3	9	0
6000	10	8	8
7000	0	0	1
8000	1	0	0
Not located	0	1	1
Total	42	92	55

Note: * All sample firms and their two-digit SIC Codes are listed in the Appendix.

RESULTS

The results of our examination of the effects of *SFAS 87* on the (1) balance sheet/footnote disclosures and (2) income statement disclosures for each group of companies adopting *SFAS 87* are summarized in this section.

Balance Sheet/Footnote Disclosures

Under the provisions of *SFAS 87,* a minimum liability will be recognized in the balance sheet when the accumulated benefit obligation exceeds the fair value of plan assets. Unlike the other provisions of *SFAS 87* discussed earlier in this paper, disclosure of this minimum liability is not required until 1989. However, the minimum liability that will eventually be recognized in the balance sheet (the excess of the ABO over the pension plan assets) is disclosed in the footnotes.

In addition to this requirement, *SFAS 87* extends prior footnote disclosures of information concerning the funded status of an entity's defined benefit pension plan by requiring disclosure of the PBO. Because disclosure of a minimum liability for unfunded pension benefits in the balance sheet is not required until 1989, the primary effect of *SFAS 87* prior to 1989 is the disclosure of the PBO.

The balance sheet/footnote disclosures of the sample companies adopting *SFAS 87* in 1985,[7] 1986, and 1987 are summarized in Table 3. Table 4 summarizes the funded status of these pension plans based on the relationship of (1) ABO to pension plan assets and (2) PBO to pension plan assets.

Comparing the balance sheet/footnote disclosures of adopters over the three-year implementation period reveals a number of interesting differences. As indicated in Table 3, the ratio of both (1) ABO to pension plan assets and (2) PBO to pension plan assets increases each year as the year of adoption selected by the company approaches the mandatory implementation date (1987). Analysis of variance (ANOVA) procedures indicate that the differences in the ratio of ABO to pension plan assets ($p < 0.0001$) and the ratio of PBO to pension plan assets ($p = 0.001$) between adopters are statistically significant. The results are identical using nonparametric Kruskal-Wallis procedures (at $p < 0.001$ for both ratios).

Since overall differences exist among adopters, multiple comparison procedures (Newman-Keuls tests) [Montgomery, 1984] are performed in order to identify which adopters differ with respect to the ratio of (1) ABO to pension plan assets and (2) PBO to pension plan assets. These procedures reveal that companies implementing *SFAS 87* at the earliest possible date (1985) have significantly lower ratios than either 1986 or 1987 adopters. While the ratios for companies adopting *SFAS 87* in 1986 are lower than those for 1987 adopters, the differences are not statistically significant. The results of these tests indicate that the funded status of pension plans deteriorates (that is, the ratio becomes larger) as the date of adoption approaches the mandatory implementation date. Identical results are obtained using nonparametric, two-sample, Mann-Whitney U tests [Daniel, 1978].

In addition to the ratio of ABO and PBO to pension plan assets, an additional indicator of the funded status of a defined benefit pension plan is a dichotomous measure of whether the plan is overfunded (plan assets exceed the future obligation) or underfunded (plan assets are less than the future obligation). As indicated in Table 4, panel A, the percentage of firms with pension plans that are underfunded based on ABO ranges from 7.1% (1985

Table 3. Summary of Balance Sheet/Footnote Disclosures and Tests of Significance

	ABO[a]	*PBO*[a]	*Plan Assets*[a]	*ABO/Plan Assets*[b]	*PBO/Plan Assets*[b]
1987 Adopters					
Mean	576,299.47	686,753.09	867,087.31	0.7530	0.9388
SD	1,176,528.69	1,291,969.35	1,859,579.46	0.2386	0.2776
1986 Adopters					
Mean	740,128.07	887,435.36	1,012,078.01	0.7423	0.9231
SD	1,803,857.76	2,119,149.53	2,495,232.63	0.2304	0.2330
1985 Adopters					
Mean	367,158.69	436,803.15	622,940.69	0.5717	0.7567
SD	944,790.17	1,101,961.69	1,638,464.78	0.2280	0.2746
Ovevall Significance Between Years				0.0001	0.0010

Notes: Means connected by a bracket are significantly different using Newman-Keuls procedures ($\alpha = 0.005$).

[a] Amounts are stated in thousands of dollars.

[b] These values are based on the ABO/Plan Assets and PBO/Plan Assets for each individual firm and not on the mean ABO, PBO, and Plan Assets over the sample of adopters. Therefore, these results will differ from the results obtained by dividing the columns in this table representing the mean ABO and PBO by the column representing the mean Plan Assets for any given year of adoption.

Table 4. Funded Status of Sample Companies' Pension Plans

Panel A: Funded Status Based on ABO

	Overfunded ($ABO < Assets$)		*Underfunded* ($ABO > Assets$)		
	N	%	*N*	%	*Total*
1987 Adopters	41	74.5	14	25.5	55
1986 Adopters	82	89.1	10	10.9	92
1985 Adopters	39	92.9	3	7.1	42
Overall	162	85.7	27	14.3	

Chi-square = 8.23 ($p < 0.01$)

Panel B: Funded Status Based on PBO

	Overfunded ($PBO < Assets$]		*Underfunded* ($PBO > Assets$)		
	N	%	N	%	Total
1987 Adopters	38	69.1	17	30.9	55
1986 Adopters	59	64.1	33	35.9	92
1985 Adopters	37	92.5	3	7.5	40
Overall	134	71.7	53	28.3	

Chi-square = 11.30 ($p < 0.01$)

adopters) to 25.5% (1987 adopters). These results are consistent with those presented in Table 3.

Panel B of Table 4 presents the funded status of pension plans based on the PBO. The percentage of firms with pension plans that are underfunded based on PBO ranges from 7.5% in 1985 to 35.9% in 1986. For both ABO and PBO, the differences in percentages of underfunded and overfunded pension plans by year are statistically significant using nonparametric Chi-square tests of association.

Taken together, the results presented in Tables 3 and 4 indicate that companies adopting *SFAS 87* earlier (especially in 1985) have pension plans which are funded to a greater extent than later adopters based on both the ABO and PBO. A possible explanation for the differences in the year of adoption relates to *SFAS 87's* requirement of disclosing the PBO. Regardless of the timing of adoption, disclosure of the ABO and the fair value of pension plan assets is required. Companies with pension plans funded to a lesser extent may be reluctant to adopt *SFAS 87* because the excess of the PBO over the fair value of plan assets may be perceived as a liability by financial statement users.[8] The larger ratio of PBO to pension plan assets for later adopters in Table 3 and the larger percentage of adopters with underfunded pension plans based on PBO shown in panel B of Table 4 for later adopters (1986 and 1987) reflect this possibility.

Examining the results in Tables 3 and 4 also indicates that, although disclosure of a minimum liability is not required until 1989, *SFAS 87* does not appear to have a significant balance sheet impact. As indicated in Table 3, the average ratio of ABO to plan assets for adopters in all three years is less than one. This indicates that, on average, the pension plans examined in this research are generally overfunded. As a result, recognition of a minimum liability does not appear to affect a large number of companies. In addition, Table 4 indicates that, if the minimum liability is recognized as of the date of adoption of *SFAS 87*, a relatively small number of companies (14.3%) would be required to recognize such a liability for unfunded pension benefits in the year of adoption.

In summary, the conclusions drawn from examining the pension disclosures of the sample companies indicate that *SFAS 87* does not appear to have a substantial balance sheet impact (based on the minimum liability for underfunded pension plans). A comparison by year reveals that those companies electing adoption of *SFAS 87* in the earliest available year have pension plans which are funded to a greater extent (lower ratio of ABO and PBO to pension plan assets and lower percentage of underfunded plans) than do later adopters. These differences are statistically significant and suggest that companies electing the earliest available adoption of *SFAS 87* may do so, in part, because its adoption does not have adverse implications for perceptions of the company's financial condition.

Income Statement Effects

In addition to expanding the footnote disclosures and requiring the future recognition of a minimum liability, *SFAS 87* standardizes the methods used to compute periodic pension expense by requiring explicit consideration of the terms of the plan in the computation of pension expense. Under the provisions of *APB 8* and *SFAS 36*, the use of any acceptable actuarial method was allowed with the resulting pension expense constrained by minimum and maximum limits. While *SFAS 87* should affect the amount of pension expense recognized in the income statement, the a priori overall impact of *SFAS 87* on pension expense is not determinable.[9] *SFAS 87* may result in either an increase or a decrease in reported pension expense, depending on the actuarial method used to determine pension expense under *APB 8* and *SFAS 36*.

Table 5 summarizes: (1) the pension expense in the year of adoption of *SFAS 87*; (2) the pension expense in the year prior to adoption; and, (3) the percentage change in pension expense in the year of adoption. The percentage change is measured for each firm as the difference between (1) and (2) above, divided by pension expense in the year prior to adoption.

Table 5. Summary of Income Statement Disclosures and Tests of Significance

	Expense in Adoption Year[a]	*Expense in Prior Year*[a]	*Percentage Change*[b]
1987 Adopters			
Mean	21,562.59	38,265.62	-66.64
SD	81,783.48	118,955.28	154.73
1986 Adopters			
Mean	11,131.27	39,635.68	-100.02
SD	87,603.33	105,465.27	137.27
1985 Adopters			
Mean	4,231.93	29,138.15	-140.82
SD	28,035.47	86,908.80	180.93
Overall Significance			
ANOVA			0.0632
Kruskal-Wallis			0.0002

Notes: Means connected by a bracket are significantly different from one another using Mann-Whitney U tests (at $\alpha = 0.05$).

[a] Amounts in thousands of dollars.

[b] The percentage change is based on the ratio of (1) the difference between the pension expense in the year of adoption and the pension expense in the year prior to adoption to (2) the pension expense in the year prior to adoption for each individual firm and not the ratio for the mean values presented in the above table. Therefore, these results will differ from the results obtained using the mean values presented above.

Based on the results presented in Table 5, *SFAS 87* appears to result in a mean decrease in pension expense compared to the amount recognized in the year prior to adoption. Expressed as a percentage of the prior year's pension expense, this change ranges from a reduction of 140.82% (1985 adopters) to a 66.64% reduction (1987 adopters).[10] The differences in the percentage reduction in pension expense between years of adoption are statistically significant using nonparametric Kruskal-Wallis procedures (at $\alpha = 0.05$). Two-sample Mann-Whitney *U*-tests indicate that the percentage reduction in pension expense is significantly different for each year. The use of parametric analysis of variance procedures does not reveal any significant differences (at $\alpha = 0.05$).

A second measure of the impact of *SFAS 87* on pension expense is the net effect of *SFAS 87* on pension expense in the year of adoption. This measure is the difference between (1) pension expense reported in the year of adoption using *SFAS 87* and (2) the pension expense that would have been reported in the year of adoption using pre-*SFAS 87* actuarial methods. The disclosure of the impact of *SFAS 87* on pension expense in the year of adoption is not required by *SFAS 87* but is provided by 112 of the 189 sample companies (by

Table 6. Descriptive Statistics and Tests of Significance—
Effect of *SFAS 87* on Adoption Year Pension Expense[a]

	Effect of SFAS 87[b,c]	*Effect of SFAS 87/ Prior Year Expense*
1987 Adopters ($n = 25$)		
Mean	-12,052.76	-1.23
SD	21,942.62	2.02
1986 Adopters ($n = 56$)		
Mean	-27,979.11	-1.04
SD	55,163.49	1.72
1985 Adopters ($n = 31$)		
Mean	-14,966.87	-1.54
SD	33,558.79	2.33
Overall Significance Between Years		
ANOVA		0.5315
Kruskal-Wallis		0.3505

Notes: [a] Results in this table reflect the 112 companies in our sample who disclosed the effect of *SFAS 87* on adoption year pension expense.
[b] Amounts in thousands of dollars.
[c] The effect of *SFAS 87* is measured as the difference between (1) the amount of pension expense recognized in the year of adoption using *SFAS 87* and (2) the amount of pension expense that would have been recognized in the year of adoption using pre-*SFAS 87* methods.

footnote disclosure). Descriptive statistics relating to the effect of *SFAS 87* on pension expense in the year of adoption as well as this effect divided by pension expense in the year prior to adoption are presented in Table 6.

The results in Table 6 indicate that *SFAS 87* has a substantial impact on the pension expense reported in the year of adoption, since the average reduction for all three years of adopters is greater than the pension expense reported in the year prior to adoption. Of the 112 companies providing this information, only three indicated that *SFAS 87* actually increases the pension expense reported in the year of adoption. While the effect of *SFAS 87* in relation to prior year's pension expense is largest for companies adopting in 1985 (-1.54), the difference between adoption years is not statistically significant at $\alpha = 0.05$ using either parametric ANOVA procedures or nonparametic Kruskal-Wallis procedures.

To determine whether the effect of *SFAS 87* on pension expense in the year of adoption is statistically significant, the net effects reported in Table 6 are examined using paired-differences *t*-tests. For all three years of adoption, the difference between pension expense reported in the year of adoption based on *SFAS 87* is significantly lower than the amount that would have been reported using pre-*SFAS 87* actuarial methods (largest $p = 0.0188$). Thus, the impact

Table 7. Effect of *SFAS 87* in Adoption Year Compared to Prior Year

	Increase in Pension Expense		*Decrease in Pension Expense*		
	N	%	*N*	%	*Total*
1987 Adopters	11	20.00	44	80.00	55
1986 Adopters	11	11.96	81	88.04	92
1985 Adopters	1	2.38	41	97.62	42
Total	23	12.17	166	87.83	

Chi-square 6.933 ($p < 0.05$)

of *SFAS 87* on pension expense in the adoption year pension expense appears to be fairly large.

Table 7 provides frequency counts of changes in pension expense in the year of adoption as compared to the prior year. As indicated in Table 7, only 12.17% of the entire sample report higher expense in the year of adoption than in the prior year. The percentage of companies whose adoption of *SFAS 87* increases pension expense from the prior year ranges from a low of 2.38% (in 1985) to a high of 20% (in 1987). A Chi-square test of association indicates that the percentage of adopters whose pension expense increases in the year of adoption vis-à-vis the prior year's expense differs significantly by year of adoption ($p < 0.05$). The results of this test indicate that companies adopting *SFAS 87* earlier are more likely to experience a reduction in pension expense than later adopters.

Taken together, the above findings indicate that firms electing to adopt *SFAS 87* prior to the mandatory implementation date may do so in order to benefit from the reduction in periodic pension expense (and, thus, increase in net income) associated with *SFAS 87*.[11] A possible explanation of these findings is that companies may be more likely to adopt a particular accounting pronouncement if the benefits of adoption increase. In this case, for both measures of the effect of *SFAS 87* on adoption year pension expense in comparison to pension expense in the prior year (Tables 5 and 7), the benefits (in the form of lower pension expense) are greatest for 1985 adopters, followed by 1986 adopters, and with the least benefit accruing to 1987 adopters.

The greater benefits resulting from early adoption could, in part, account for management's decision to adopt *SFAS 87* prior to the mandatory implementation date.[12] However, as noted in Table 6, the actual impact of *SFAS 87* on adoption year pension expense (compared to the expense that would have been recognized under previous pronouncements) is not significantly different between adoption years. In addition, as discussed in the following section, these results could be influenced, in part, by industry membership.

LIMITATIONS AND CONCLUSIONS

Certain limitations should be considered in evaluating the results of this research. First, we examined only the financial statement effects of *SFAS 87* on a company's decision as to the timing of *SFAS 87* adoption. Other firm-specific factors not explicitly considered herein, such as the size of the company or industry membership, may affect the likelihood of a company adopting an accounting pronouncement prior to is required implementation date.[13] In addition, this research is restricted to examining the financial statement effects of *SFAS 87* in the year of adoption. Therefore, any attempt to extrapolate the results to years subsequent to the adoption of *SFAS 87* should be done with caution.

A final limitation of this research is that it examines only the impact of the financial statement effects of a single accounting pronouncement (*SFAS 87*) on the timing of a company's decision to adopt that pronouncement. The relationships observed for *SFAS 87* in this research may not exist for the decision to adopt other accounting pronouncements. Future researchers may wish to consider whether differences exist between companies adopting other accounting pronouncements at various times.

The results presented indicate that companies electing early adoption of *SFAS 87* have pension plans that are funded to a greater extent (based on both ABO and PBO) than those electing to postpone adoption until the mandatory implementation date. In addition, the percentage reduction in pension expense in the year of adoption is greater for early adopters than that for those adopting *SFAS 87* at the mandatory implementation date. The above differences are especially pronounced when comparing companies adopting *SFAS 87* in the initial available year of adoption (1985) to other adopters.

For example, as indicated in Table 4, the three 1985 adopters with underfunded pension plans based on the PBO also have underfunded pension plans based on the ABO. The remaining 37 firms are overfunded using either the ABO or PBO definition of a pension obligation. As a result, these 37 companies may choose to adopt *SFAS 87* because it reduces pension expense (and, thus, increases net income) as shown in Tables 5 and 6. Based on these findings, companies adopting *SFAS 87* in 1985 appear to do so because (1) they experience a relatively substantial reduction in pension expense and (2) are not underfunded based on the PBO.

While the pension plans of the 1986 adopters are not funded to the same extent as those of the 1985 adopters, an explanation for their decision to adopt *SFAS 87* is the relatively large reduction in pension expense from the prior year. As noted in Table 5, companies adopting *SFAS 87* in 1986 had a mean decrease in pension expense of approximately 100% from the year prior to adoption. This large reduction in pension expense results from the fact that many companies reported pension income (negative pension expense). As a result, these companies may have decided that the benefits of adopting *SFAS 87* (the reduction in pension expense) more than offset the disadvantages associated with reporting the PBO.

The above discussion indicates that the financial statement effects of a particular accounting pronouncement may induce companies to accelerate (delay) the adoption of that pronouncement because of the perceived advantages (disadvantages) of implementation. As shown in the case of *SFAS 87,* the FASB's practice of allowing early adoption of an accounting pronouncement can result in systematic financial statement effects as certain firms elect early adoption while others postpone adoption until the required implementation date. As an alternative, the FASB could consider providing a delayed adoption date which must be adhered to by all firms.

APPENDIX: SAMPLE FIRMS AND INDUSTRY CODES

1985 Adopters

Company	*Code*	*Company*	*Code*
Acme United Corp	38	Kay Corp	51
Alexander & Alexander	64	M Corp	60
American Petrofina	29	Manufacturers Hanover	60
Asarco	10	Marine Midland	60
Big Three Industries	35	Monarch Machine Tool	35
Butler International	89	Morrison-Knudsen	16
Centel	48	Munsingwear	22
Chemical Bank	60	Phelps Dodge	10
Chubb Corp	63	Phillips Petroleum	29
Comerica Inc	60	Quanex	33
Dayton-Hudson	53	Rowan Corp	13
Development Corp	65	Sealed Power	35
Dexter Corp	28	Sea-Land Inc	44
Dupont Corp	28	Shell Oil	29
Edison Brothers	56	Stanadyne	35
Emery Air Freight	47	Stone Container	26
Emhart	35	Transcoenergy Co	49
Exxon Corp	29	Turner Corp	48
First Chicago	60	United Air Lines	45
Homestake Mining	10	Washington National	63
Johnson & Johnson	28	Waste Management	49

1986 Adopters
(N/L = Industry Code Not Located)

Company	Code	Company	Code
A.O. Smith	N/L	Georgia Pacific	24
Abbot Laboratories	28	G. Heilman Brewing	20
Allegheny Ludlum	34	Houston Industries	49
Allied-Signal Corp	28	H.J. Heinz Company	20
Amway Inc	20	International Business Machines (IBM)	36
Arvin	37	International Paper	26
Avon	28	Irving Bank Corp	60
Bank America	60	ITT Corporation	36
Bausch & Lomb Inc	38	JC Penney	53
Bechan, Dickinson and Co.	38	Johnson Controls	38
Borden Inc.	20	Kraft, Inc	20
Burlington Industries	22	Lockheed Corporation	37
Campbell Soup Co.	20	Louisiana Land and Exploration	29
Carter Hawley Hale Stores	53	Lubrizol	28
Castle & Cooke Inc	01	Lucky Stores	54
Caterpillar Inc	35	MapCo	29
Cincinnati Milacron	35	Martin Marietta	37
Columbia Gas	49	McDonnell Douglas	37
Crown Cork & Seal	34	Melville Corporation	56
Culbro Corporation	51	Monsanto	28
Dans Water and Waste	49	Murphy Oil	29
Dominion Resources Inc	49	National Distillers & Chemical	28
Dorsey Corporation	30	Norton	32
Dover Corportion	35	Norwest	60
Eaton Corporation	38	Panhandle Eastern	49
Eli Lilly	28	Penwalt Corporation	28
Fairchild Industries Inc	37	Piedmont Aviation	45
Farmland	20	Raytheon	36
Federated Department Stores	53	Reynolds Metals	33
First Bank System	60	RJR Nabisco	20
FPL Group	49	Santa Fe Southern Pacific Railroad	40
Gannett Inc.	27	Sara Lee	20
Geico	63		
General Electric	36		
General Re Corp	63		
GEO International	13		

(*continued*)

1986 Adopters (continued)

Company	Code	Company	Code
Singer Company	36	Union Texas Petroleum	13
Southwestern Bell	48	Unisys	36
Square D Corp	36	United Merchants & Manufacturers	22
Squibb Pharmaceuticals	28	Upjohn Company	28
Stop and Shop	54	USX	29
Sun Oil Company	29	Valley National Corporation	60
Sunstrand	37	Washington Post Company	27
Supermarkets General	54	Westmoreland Coal	12
Tenneco	49	Whirlpool Corporation	36
Texas Commerce Bankshare	60	Wickes Companies Inc	52
Texas Eastern	49	Williamette Industries	35
Time, Inc.	27		
Union Camp	26		

1987 Adopters
(N/L = Industry Code Not Located)

Company	Code	Company	Code
A H Robbins	28	Consolidated Papers	26
Aetna	63	Contel	48
American Cyanamid Co.	28	Cooper Tire and Rubber Co	30
American Electric Power	49	Dana	37
American Information Tech	48	Dennison	26
Ameritech	48	Diamond Shamrock	29
BF Goodrich	30	Duke Power Co	49
Ball Corporation	34	Equitable of Iowa	63
Baltimore Gas	49	Farmers Group Inc	63
Baxter-Travenol	38	Gibraltor Financial	61
BDM International	73	Gould Electronics	36
Belding Hemingway	22	IC Industries	20
Clark Equipment Co	35	Illinois Light & Power	49
Cliffs	10	Interlake Corp	34
Coca Cola Company	20	J P Morgan	60
Colgate-Palmolive	28	Kellogg's	20

(continued)

1987 Adopters (continued)

Company	*Code*	*Company*	*Code*
Kerr-McGee Corp	29	Pacific Enterprises	N/L
Manufacturers National	60	Pennsylvania Power & Light	49
McDonnell Douglas	37	Philadelphia Electric	49
Mereck	28	Potomac Electric Power	49
Michigan National	60	Public Service Electric and Gas	49
Mississippi Power Co	49	Ralston Purina Co.	20
National Cash Register (NCR)	36	Schering-Plough	28
New England Electric Service	49	SooLine	40
Northern Indiana Public Service	49	Southern Northeast Telecommunications	48
Northern States Power	49	The St. Paul Companies	63
Owens-Corning Fiberglass Corp	32	United Telecom	48
		Wyman-Gordan	35

ACKNOWLEDGMENTS

The authors acknowledge the helpful comments and suggestions of Robert M. Harper, Jr., William G. Mister, Robert H. Strawser, and the two anonymous reviewers.

NOTES

1. See, for example, Lucas and Miller [1983], Liebtag [1986], "Will Pension Liabilities" [1983], and "Accounting Proposal Troubles Firms" [1985].

2. Under the requirements of *SFAS 87*, companies are not required to recognize this minimum liability until 1989. However, the same information will continue to be disclosed in the footnotes. Throughout the remainder of this paper, the phrase "balance sheet effects of *SFAS 87*" or "the effects of *SFAS 87* on a company's balance sheet" refer to the relationship between the ABO and the fair value of pension plan assets.

3. This conclusion results from a field test conducted by the FASB [1983] on the effects of a proposed method of accounting for pensions prior to *SFAS 87* (*Preliminary Views*) [FASB, 1982]. Prior to the issuance of *SFAS 87*, companies could use any number of actuarial methods to determine pension expense. Under *SFAS 87*, companies must use the benefits/years-of-service approach, which only considers pension benefits attributable to employee service provided to date in its determination of service (normal) cost. Since this approach generally results in delayed expense recognition in comparison to actuarial methods permitted under *APB 8*, *SFAS 87* may result in decreased pension expense for many companies.

4. Reviews of this research are provided by Ball and Foster [1982], Holthausen and Leftwich [1983], Kelly [1983], Foster [1986], and Watts and Zimmerman [1986].

5. Because of the timing of our examination, not all 1987 adopters' reports were available for inclusion in our sample. Specifically, some 1987 adopters' annual reports were not issued by the company at the time our sample was selected. Since there is no reason to believe that companies issuing their reports later in 1988 are systematically different from those issuing their reports earlier in 1988, the unavailability of these reports does not appear to represent a prohibitive limitation. Any differences between these two groups of 1987 adopters represent a possible limitation of this research.

6. One problem associated with the use of chi-square tests in this instance is the small number of expected values for given industry codes. The use of a single digit industry code indicated that statistically significant differences exist; however, many cells had expected values of less than five firms, which generally reduces the appropriateness of using the chi-square test [Ott, 1977], To generate expected call frequencies of five or more firms, several classification schemes based on the SIC code were utilized to represent industry membership. The resulting chi-square tests provided mixed evidence. Based on this finding, as well as the lack of a priori justification for combining various one digit industry codes, the differences across adoption years for industry membership should be interpreted accordingly.

7. The disclosures reported by Norton's [1988] sample of 42 companies adopting *SFAS 87* in 1985 are used in this research, since his sample included all adopters identified by the Financial Accounting Standards Board with available annual reports. However, Norton did not report the amount of the PBO for his sample companies. The annual reports of Norton's sample companies were examined to obtain the PBO for use in this research. Of the 42 companies examined by Norton, the amount of the PBO could be determined for 40 companies. The following statistical tests use the pension disclosures for all 42 1985 adopters except for tests involving the PBO. These tests use the 40 companies for whom information about the PBO could be located.

8. While no liability is required to be recognized in this situation, these perceptions are not altogether unusual. In its *Preliminary Views* [FASB, 1982], the FASB initially advocated that a liability be recognized in an entity's balance sheet when the PBO exceeded the fair value of pension plan assets. Previous research has determined that, prior to *SFAS 87*, the market viewed the excess of ABO over the fair value of plan assets as a corporate liability in its determination of: (1) stock prices [Oldfield, 1977; Gersovitz, 1980; Feldstein and Selgiman, 1981; Feldstein and Morck, 1982; Daley, 1984]; (2) the equity value of the firm [Landsman, 1986]; and, (3) systematic risk [Dhaliwal, 1986]. Therefore, the capital market's use of footnote disclosures relating to a company's pension plan is found to exist in the accounting literature.

9. However, *SFAS 87* is likely to decrease reported pension expense, since this pronouncement requires use of the benefits/years-of-service approach (see note 3).

10. While these percentages seem fairly large, an examination of the footnote disclosures indicates that many companies actually reported pension income (negative pension expense) in the year that they adopted *SFAS 87.* For firms electing adoption in 1985, 1986, and 1987, the number of companies reporting pension income is 20 (approximately 48%), 30 (33%), and 9 (16%). Since any company reporting pension income in the year of adoption has a minimum percentage change of greater than 100 percent, these high percentages are not altogether surprising.

11. Previous accounting choice research notes that, in certain cases, companies would prefer to select accounting procedures which result in a *decrease* in net income. These studies (see Holthausen and Leftwich [1983] and Watts and Zimmerman [1986] for a review) hypothesize that "large" firms may select income-decreasing accounting principles to reduce their visibility to consumers, employees, unions, and politicans. This hypothesis is referred to as the "political costs" hypothesis. Zimmerman [1983] notes that the political costs hypothesis may only hold for the very largest firms. Examination of the political costs hypothesis is beyond the scope of this paper.

12. See Holthausen and Leftwich [1983] and Watts and Zimmerman [1986] for a discussion of how the effect of an accounting principle on net income can influence management's decision to select from among competing accounting principles.

13. To determine whether industry membership and size influenced firms' decisions to adopt *SFAS 87,* the impact of these characteristics on the financial statement effects examined in this research was examined. Industry membership and size were included along with the adoption date as main effects in separate two-way analysis of variance (ANOVA) designs. If either characteristic (or its interaction with the year of adoption) has a significant impact on a financial statement effect, the relationship observed between the year of adoption and that financial statement effect may be influenced by either industry membership or size.

To measure the effect of size, firms were separated into both quartiles and deciles based on sales or operating revenues. The results of the ANOVA indicate that size did not significantly affect the financial statement effects examined in this research (lowest $p = 0.13$). Thus, it did not appear that our results were influenced by the size of the companies.

We were unable to use two-digit SIC codes for industry classification because of the lack of observations for all years of adoption for many of the industries represented in our sample. Two alternative classifications for industry were used: (1) classification based on the first digit of the SIC code; and, (2) groupings within each first digit of the SIC code. For both classifications, the effect of industry membership on (1) the ratio of ABO to plan assets and (2) the percentage reduction in pension expense in the year of adoption was statistically significant ($\alpha = 0.05$). Examination of these relationships for the ratio of ABO to plan assets revealed that the significance resulted from the magnitude of the ratio (i.e., some industries had larger ratios across all adoption years than others) and not the relationship between adoption years (i.e., for all industries, the ratios were lowest for 1985 adopters, then 1986, and finally 1987). Thus, our results for the ratio of ABO to plan assets do not appear to be influenced by industry membership.

Alternatively, further examination of the relationship between industry membership and the percentage reduction in pension expense indicates that the results may reflect the averaging of different effects. That is, for some industries, the companies having the greatest reduction adopted *SFAS 87* in 1986; for others, the greatest reduction occurred for 1985 adopters. Thus, the results in Table 5 may reflect limited industry differences in addition to difference between year of adoption, and should be interpreted accordingly.

REFERENCES

Accounting Principles Board, *Opinion No. 8,* "Accounting for the Costs of Pension Plans" [AICPA, 1966].

"Accounting Proposal Troubles Firms: Pension Rule Would Boost Reported Liabilities," *Wall Street Journal* [December 6, 1985], p. 6.

Ayres, F.L., "Characteristics of Firms Selecting Early Adoption of SFAS 52," *Journal of Accounting and Economics* 8 [1986], pp. 147-158.

Ball, R. and G. Foster, "Corporate Financial Reporting: A Methodological Review of Empirical Research," *Journal of Accounting Research* [Supplement 1982], pp. 161-234.

Bowen, R.M., E.W. Noreen, and J.M. Lacey, "Determinants of the Corporate Decision to Capitalize Interest," *Journal of Accounting and Economics* [August 1981], pp. 151-179.

Daley, L.A., "The Valuation of Reported Pension Measures for Firms Sponsoring Defined Benefit Plans," *The Accounting Review* [April 1984], pp. 177-198.

Daley, L.A. and R.L. Vigeland, "The Effects of Debt Covenants and Political Costs on the Choice of Accounting Methods: The Case of Accouting for R&D Costs," *Journal of Accounting and Economics* [December 1983], pp. 195-211.

Daniel, W.W., *Applied Nonparametric Statistics* [Houghton Mifflin, 1978].

Dhaliwal, D.S., "The Effect of the Firm's Capital Structure on the Choice of Accounting Methods," *The Accounting Review* [January 1980], pp. 78-84.

________, "Measurement of Financial Leverage in the Presence of Unfunded Pension Obligations," *The Accounting Review* [October 1986], pp. 651-661.

Dhaliwal, D.S., G. Salamon, and E. Smith, "The Effect of Owner Versus Management Control on the Choice of Accounting Methods," *Journal of Accounting and Economics* [July 1982], pp. 41-53.

Feldstein, M. and R. Morck, "Pension Funding Decisions, Interest Rate Assumptions and Share Prices," Working Paper [National Bureau of Economic Research, 1982].

Feldstein, M. and S. Seligman, "Pension Funding, Share Prices, and National Savings," *Journal of Finance* [September 1981], pp. 101-124.

Financial Accounting Standards Board (FASB), "Disclosure of Pension Information," *Statement of Financial Accounting Standards No. 36* [FASB 1980].

________, *Preliminary Views of the Financial Accounting Standards Board on Major Issues Related to Employers' Accounting for Pensions and Other Postemployment Benefits* [FASB 1982].

________, *Preliminary Views–A Field Test: Employers' Accounting for Pensions* [FASB 1983].

________, "Employers' Accounting for Pensions," *Statement of Financial Accounting Standards No. 87* [FASB 1985].

Foster, G., *Financial Statement Analysis* [Prentice-Hall, 1986].

Francis, J.R., "Lobbying Against Proposed Accounting Standards: The Case of Employers' Pension Accounting," *Journal of Accounting and Public Policy* [Summer 1987], pp. 35-57.

Gersovitz, M., "Economic Consequences of Unfunded Vested Pension Benefits," Working Paper [National Bureau of Economic Research, 1980].

Gordon, M.J., "Postulates, Principles and Research in Accounting," *The Accounting Review* [April 1964], pp. 251-263.

Hagerman, R.L. and M. Zmijewski, "Some Economic Determinants of Accounting Policy Choice," *Journal of Accounting and Economics* [August 1979], pp. 141-161.

Holthausen, R.W., "Evidence on the Effect of Bond Covenants and Management Compensation Contracts on the Choice of Accounting Techniques: The Case of the Depreciation Switch-Back," *Journal of Accounting and Economics* [March 1981], pp. 73-109.

Holthausen, R.W. and R.W. Leftwich, "The Economic Consequences of Accounting Choice: Implications of Costly Contracting and Monitoring," *Journal of Accounting and Economics* [August 1983], pp. 77-117.

Johnson, W.B. and R. Ramanan, "Discretionary Accounting Changes from 'Successful Efforts' to 'Full Cost' Methods: 1970-76," *The Accounting Review* [January 1988], pp. 96-110.

Kelly, L., "Positive Theory Research: A Review," *Journal of Accounting Literature* [1983], pp. 111-150.

Landsman, W.L., "An Empirical Investigation of Pension Fund Property Rights," *The Accounting Review* [October 1986], pp. 662-691.

Liebtag, B., "Adverse Effects Expected from New Pension Rules: Greater Role Seen for CPAs," *The Journal of Accountancy* [April 1986], pp. 53-57.

Lilien, S. and V. Pastena, "Determinants of Intramethod Choice in the Oil and Gas Industry," *Journal of Accounting and Economics* [December 1982], pp. 145-170.

Lucas, T.R. and P.B.W. Miller, "Pension Accounting: Impacting the Financial Statement," *Journal of Accountancy* [June 1983], pp. 90-106.

Montgomery, D.C., *Design and Analysis of Experiments* [Wiley, 1984].

Norton, C.L., "Pension Accounting: Effects of Early Adoption," *CPA Journal* [March 1988], pp. 46-51.

Oldfield, G.S., "Financial Aspects of the Private Pension System," *Journal of Money, Credit and Banking* [February 1977], pp. 48-54.

Ott, L., *An Introduction to Statistical Methods and Data Analysis* [Duxbury Press, 1977].

Stone, M. and R.W. Ingram, "The Effect of Statement No. 87 on the Financial Reports of Early Adopters," *Accounting Horizons* [September 1988], pp. 48-61.

Watts, R.L. and J.L. Zimmerman, *Positive Accounting Theory* [Prentice-Hall, 1986].

"Will Pension Liabilities Hurt Corporate Balance Sheets?," *Institutional Investor* [October 1983], pp. 219-221.

Zimmerman, J.L., "Taxes and Firm Size," *The Journal of Accounting and Economics* [August 1983], pp. 119-149.

Zmijewski, M. and R.L. Hagerman, "An Income Strategy Approach to the Positive Theory of Accounting Standard Setting/Choice," *Journal of Accounting and Economics* [August 1981], pp. 129-149.

MODELING THE DIFFERENCE BETWEEN DOLLAR-VALUE LIFO AND UNIT LIFO:

A SIMULATION

Thomas L. Barton and John E. McEldowney

ABSTRACT

The Last-In, First-Out (LIFO) inventory method is used extensively by businesses. Two implementation methodologies are generally utilized: Unit LIFO and Dollar-Value LIFO (DVL). While DVL has long been considered an acceptable inventory valuation method, no generally accepted accounting principles (GAAP) have been established to govern its implementation. Various indices, both internal and external, may be used to compute DVL. Companies may make use of external indices sanctioned by the Internal Revenue Service, or may develop their own internally generated indices. Results generated under DVL may vary markedly from those derived from Unit LIFO, yet both are acceptable. This paper addresses those differences through the use of a simulation model. The model was developed to identify both the nature and extent of these variations and also to isolate factors which significantly impact these differences.

Advances in Accounting, Volume 8, pages 61-78.

ISBN: 1-55938-067-5

The results of this study indicate that inflation, inventory turnover and the difference between external and internal indices can be significant predictors of the differences between Unit LIFO and Dollar-Value LIFO. The study also found that the distributions of differences were approximately normal for the simulated data, and that when an external index is used for DVL, the variability of the distribution can increase significantly.

INTRODUCTION

The Last-In, First-Out (LIFO) inventory method is widely used by businesses to counter the effects of inflation and the accompanying "inventory profits" generated by higher replacement costs. There are two choices available concerning the LIFO election: Unit LIFO and Dollar-Value LIFO. Unit LIFO accounts for every unit in the firm's inventory separately and for many inventories is excessively cumbersome and costly to implement. Unit LIFO also proves to be quite inflexible when old products are phased out and new items are stocked. Even though the overall inventory level may increase, a temporary reduction in an isolated inventory item could partially liquidate the original, lower-cost base layer, thus permanently eliminating a portion of the LIFO tax benefit.

The use of the simpler Dollar-Value LIFO (DVL) method eliminates many of the disadvantages of Unit LIFO while preserving the important benefit of tax savings in periods of rising prices [Schwartz and Diamond, 1980, p. 33]. DVL uses "dollars" as the primary measurement unit instead of "quantities" of goods. Overall price indices related to pools of inventory items replace unit costs.[1] Through these indices, dollars of inventory are deflated to costs in effect when DVL was instituted (base year costs). These base year costs are then compared to the beginning inventory value (also at base costs) to determine the change in inventory for the period. The change is expressed in terms of layers, and the layers are converted, again using indices, to historical cost to arrive at the total inventory valuation.

At present, there are no generally accepted accounting principles (GAAP) which specifically address the calculation and presentation of DVL inventories. The only standards currently available are the minimal guidelines established by the Internal Revenue Service (IRS). Yet, there is a strong potential for DVL to generate inventory and cost of goods sold amounts that differ significantly from those under Unit LIFO [Bainbridge, 1984, p. 335]. Currently, little is known about the extent of these variations and the factors that cause them.

This has led to extensive use of a method for financial reporting that possesses only indirect authoritative support. Coupled with this is the valuation problem that arises when published price indices are used to generate DVL inventory values under the tax regulations. Using these potentially unrepresentative external indices, instead of internally calculated indices for an inventory pool, may generate even wider variations in Unit LIFO and DVL results.

This study uses a simulation model to examine the differences between Unit LIFO and DVL inventory values. The model is designed to identify both the degree and nature of these differences, as well as isolate significant factors affecting the differences.

The remainder of this paper addresses the basic research methodology used in this study and the findings of the study. Variables used in the research effort will be discussed and the regression model specified. The techniques used to generate the data for this simulation and the manipulation of the data sets will also be addressed. Finally, the research results and conclusions will be presented.

RESEARCH QUESTIONS AND METHODOLOGY

Research Questions

The literature on the LIFO inventory method is rich in analytical discussions of the mechanics of the method itself, its variants (such as DVL), the advantages and disadvantages of its use, and the external factors that can impact LIFO inventory values and, therefore, cost of goods sold. To date, however, no empirical work (and little analytical work) has addressed the Unit LIFO-DVL difference.

The research questions addressed in this study are as follows:

A-1. What are the statistical characteristics of the distributions of differences between Unit LIFO and DVL?
A-2. How do inflation rates tend to affect these distributions?
A-3. How do the differences between internal and external indices tend to impact these distributions?
B-1. What factors tend to have a significant effect on the differences between Unit LIFO and DVL for individual inventory pools?
B-2. How are the effects of individual factors influenced by inflation rates and differences between internal and external indices?

Certain factors seem to be logical candidates for research questions B-1 and B-2. These were developed on an a priori basis with guidance from the literature. To avoid possible bias in the research conclusions, once selected, none of these factors were excluded from the final analyses. The following factors (independent variables) have been cited in the literature as having significant impact on the LIFO calculation:

1. Inflation [Schwartz, 1982, p. 42].
2. Inventory Turnover [Firmin, 1963, p. 274].
3. Inventory Mix [Firmin, 1963, p. 274; Stark, 1978, p. 184]: With the diversity of items usually present in an inventory pool, this problem becomes even more relevant [Bainbridge, 1984, pp. 336-337].
4. Erosion of the Base Layer under DVL: One of the most serious problems facing a LIFO firm is the potential for erosion of the base layer. When this happens, old inventory costs are released to cost of goods sold in place of higher costs from more recent layers. Under these conditions, LIFO tends to yield unreliable and unpredictable results. It should be expected, then, that erosion of the base layer when DVL is used will introduce serious instabilities when compared to Unit LIFO.
5. Index Difference [Wolff, 1981, p. 170]: The IRS permits firms to use published external indices under certain conditions. While external indices may be thought of as surrogates for internally computed indices based on the actual composition of LIFO pools, it is reasonable to assume that potentially large differences between the external and internal indices can exist. Since Unit LIFO is based on actual internal costs, these index differences are likely sources of inventory valuation differences between Unit LIFO and DVL.

Significant interrelationships between these variables may also exist. It is possible, for example, that higher turnover rates mitigate the effect of inflation on the differences between Unit LIFO and DVL. The literature in the area supports this premise, and often alludes to these possible interaction effects [Moonitz, 1953, p. 685]. Various interaction effects were included in the model, and will be addressed in the next section.

The issue of interaction effects is a complex area that has received only minimal attention in the literature to date. Also, while existing research indicates that these effects probably exist, little work has been published which addresses the rationale for these interactions. Without an empirical or thorough analytical study, any explanation posed for these interaction effects would be primarily conjectural in nature.

Methodology

There are obviously no real-world data for inventories valued under both Unit LIFO and DVL simultaneously. Accordingly, it was necessary to base the research effort on simulated data. Simulated data for three products and two time periods were generated to allow for multiproduct and some time series complexities, and yet maintain a reasonable level of computational complexity.

To analyze the research questions relating to distributional differences, a series of data sets was generated under various assumptions as to average inflation rates, first without the presence of external indices (Group 1), and then, for certain data sets, with external indices (Group 2). The distributions of Unit LIFO-DVL differences were plotted using the technique of density tracing,[2] and their means and standard deviations were analyzed and compared.

Multiple regression analysis was used to examine the research questions relating to factors affecting the Unit LIFO-DVL differences. The factors cited previously and their interactions, except for index difference interactions,[3] were used as independent variables. The dependent variable was the percentage difference between the Unit LIFO and DVL inventory amounts at the end of the second period.

The process of operationalizing the factors was straightforward in every case except inventory mix. Here, the standard deviation of the beginning inventory of the three products (in dollars) was used.[4] For erosion of the base layer, a value of +1 was assigned if the deflated dollar ending inventory (period 2) was greater than the base layer (beginning of period 1). It was set equal to -1 if the deflated ending inventory was less than or equal to the base layer. This variable is referred to as "direction" in subsequent discussions.

The regression model may be expressed as follows:

$$Y = \beta_0 + \beta_i X_i + \beta_{ij} X_i X_j$$

where Y represents the percentage difference between Unit LIFO and DVL; β_i ($i = 1 \ldots 5$) represents the five main effects (inflation, inventory turnover, standard deviation of beginning inventories, direction, and index difference); and β_{ij} (for all $i \neq j$, $i, j \neq 5$) represents the six interaction effects.

DATA GENERATION

Nine data sets were generated synthetically under a variety of inflation and external-internal index scenarios. Each data set consisted of 100 observations, with every observation containing three inventory products under two consecutive time periods. Figure 1 provides a summary of the differences in data sets.

Each observation contained the following eight variables for each of the three products (a total of 24 variables):

Variable 1:	Beginning Inventory in units
Variable 2:	Unit Purchases—Period 1
Variable 3:	Unit Sales—Period 1
Variable 4:	Unit Purchases—Period 2
Variable 5:	Unit Sales—Period 2
Variable 6:	Base Cost
Variable 7:	Purchase Cost—Period 1
Variable 8:	Purchase Cost—Period 2

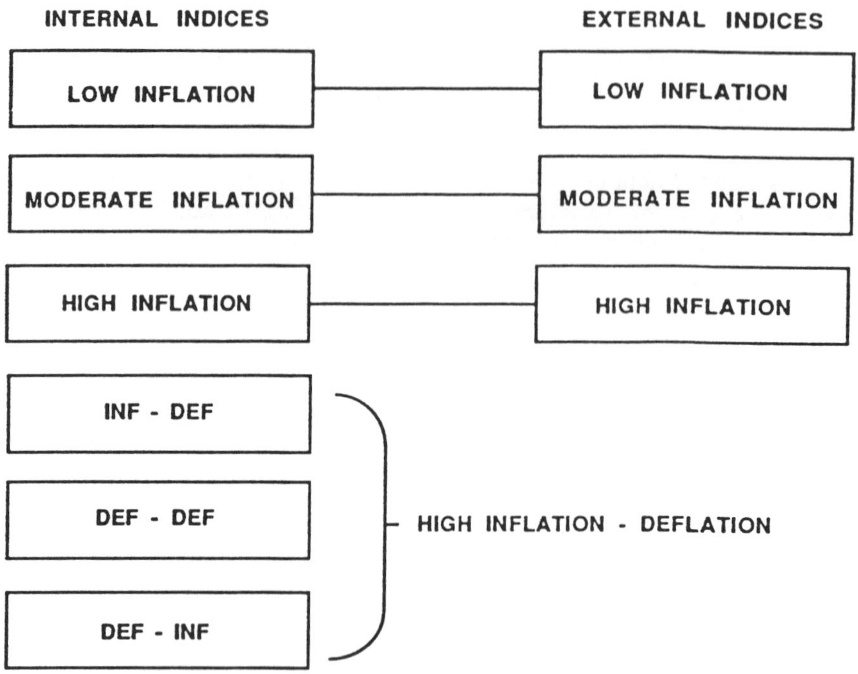

Figure 1. Summary of Differences in Data Sets

Data were generated from a set of basic parameters with specific observations drawn from random number generators.[5] All data sets contained the same basic observations except for unit costs (inflation rates differed) and the presence of external indices.

The overall intent in the generation of observations was to allow a high degree of variability in the observations, yet force the observations for individual variables to be mound-shaped and within certain predefined ranges. The double-extension approach was used in the calculation of internal indices.

For six of the nine data sets (Group 1), it was assumed that the external and internal indices were identical. The Group 1 data sets were formed under various inflation assumptions:

a. Low inflation averaging 5% for all products in both time periods.
b. Moderate inflation averaging 10.3% and 11.5% in periods 1 and 2, respectively, but with average inflation rate varying between products and between time periods.
c. High inflation averaging 20% for all products in both time periods.

d. High inflation (+20%) in period 1 followed by high deflation (-20%) in period 2.
e. High deflation (-20%) in period 1 followed by high inflation (+20%) in period 2.
f. High deflation averaging -20% for all products in both time periods.

The Group 2 data sets incorporated an external index different from the internally calculated index. They used only the low, moderate and high inflation scenarios (*a, b,* and *c* above).[6] The average internal index was computed for all observations in each data set. Then, each observation in the data set was randomly assigned an external index from a normal distribution of indices with a mean equal to the *average* internal index for that observation and a standard deviation equal to 10% of the average internal index for all observations.[7] The difference between the internal and external indices was calculated for each observation.

RESULTS

Distributions of Differences

Table 1 summarizes the means and standard deviations of the Unit LIFO-DVL difference distributions for the nine data sets. All of the difference distributions were approximately normal (determined by examining their normal probability plots).

The standard deviation comparisons are particularly significant. For all three internal-external comparisons, the standard deviations increased significantly when the external index was introduced. Apparently, the use of external indices (current DVL practice) can raise the variability of the Unit LIFO-DVL differences. This is highlighted in the increased range and altered shape of the difference distributions.

These points are illustrated graphically in Figures 2 and 3. Here the density traces for the low and high inflation distributions are shown for the internal and external index scenarios.

Multiple Regression

The regression results are summarized in Tables 2 through 6. Table 2 displays the results for the low, moderate, and high inflation scenarios in parallel columns to facilitate comparison of the results among data sets. Table 3 displays the results for the high inflation-high deflation scenarios. Finally, Tables 4, 5, and 6 compare regression results for the internal and external scenarios under the assumptions of low, moderate, and high inflation.[8]

Table 1. Parameters of Difference Distributions: All Data Sets

	Inflation						*High Inflation/Deflation*		
	Low		*Moderate*		*High*				
	Internal	*External*	*Internal*	*External*	*Internal*	*External*	*INF–DEF*	*DEF–INF*	*DEF–DEF*
Mean	0.50	0.87	2.26	0.26	2.16	-0.04	-0.44	-0.67	-2.99
	Test of Equal Means: $t = -0.346$ (df = 128.4), $p = 0.73$		Test of Equal Means: $t = 1.84$ (df = 147.5), $p = 0.07$		Test of Equal Means: $t = 1.90$ (df = 153.7), $p = 0.06$				
SD	3.85	9.99	4.90	9.69	5.53	10.20	3.72	5.52	5.33
	Test of Equal Std. Deviations: $F = 6.72$ (df = 99,99), $p = 0.00$		Test of Equal Std. Deviations: $F = 3.91$ (df = 99,99), $p = 0.00$		Test of Equal Std. Deviations: $F = 3.40$ (df = 99,99), $p = 0.00$				

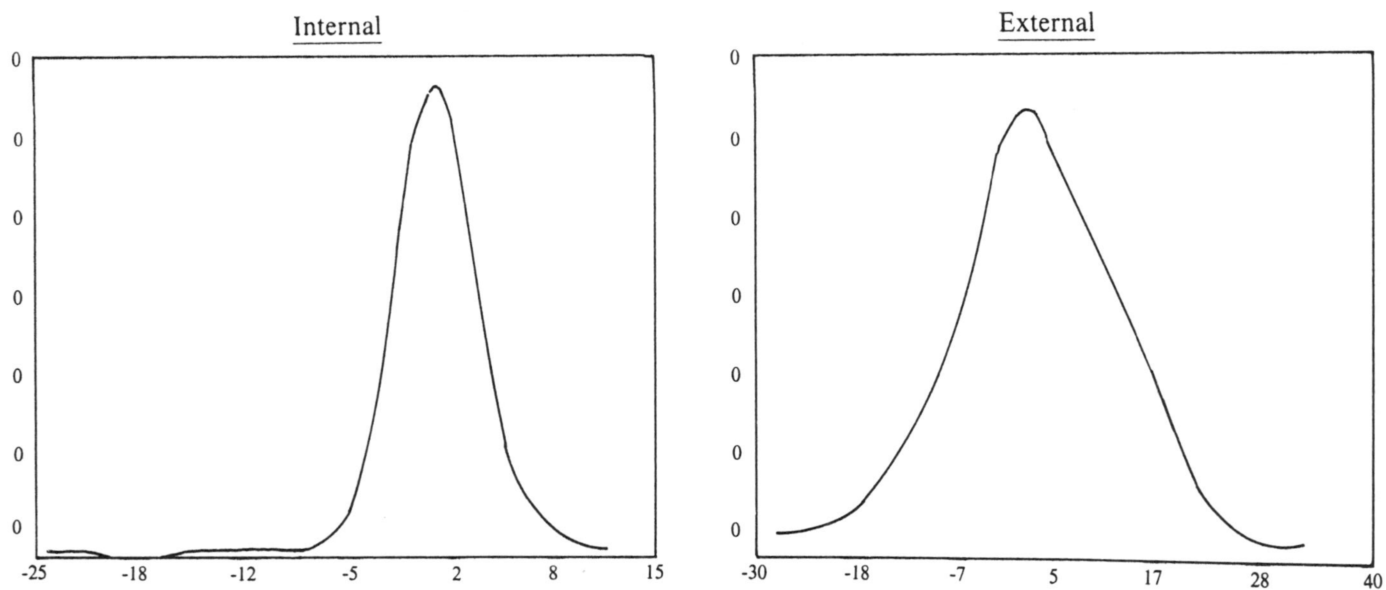

Figure 2. Density Traces for Difference Distributions: Low Inflation

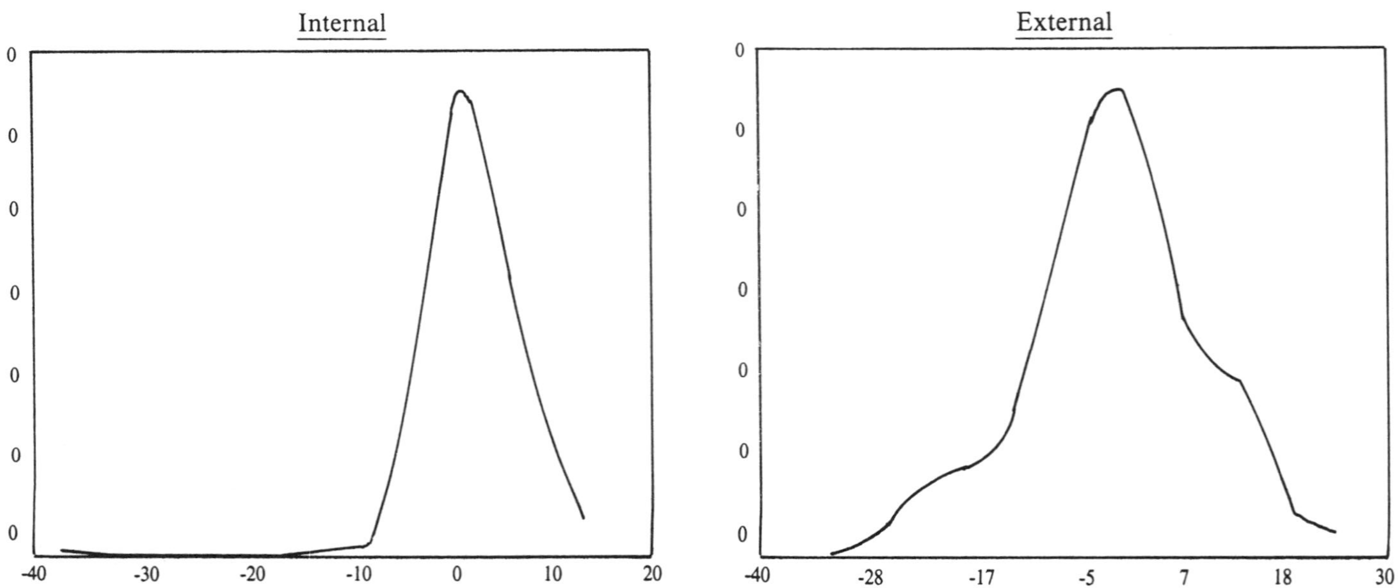

Figure 3. Density Traces for Difference Distributions: High Inflation

Table 2. Low, Moderate, and High Inflation Comparison
Levels of Significance and Direction for Main Effects and Interactions

Independent Variable	*Data Sets* Low[a]	Moderate[b]	High[c]
Main Effects			
Inflation	** +	** +	** +
Turnover	*** +	* +	*** +
Beginning Inventory—STD Deviation	·	·	·
Index Difference	N/A	N/A	N/A
Interactions			
Inflation X Direction	·	·	·
Inflation X Turnover	*** —	·	*** —
Turnover X Beg Inv SD	** —	·	·
Turnover X Direction	*** —	·	·
Beg Inv SD X Inflation	*** +	·	·
Beg Inv SD X Direction	·	·	·
R^2 (%)—All	70.8	52.7	63.4
R^2 (%)—Significant Variables Only	69.5	39.1	58.1

Notes: [a] Data Set constructed assuming average annual inflation for all products of 5% in Period 1 and 5% in Period 2.
[b] Data Set constructed assuming average annual inflation for product A of 12% in Period 1 and 5% in Period 2; product B, 12% and 20%; product C, 5% and 0%.
[c] Data Set constructed assuming average annual inflation for all poroducts of 20% in Period 1 and 20% in Period 2.
*** Significant at 0.01 level.
** Significant at 0.05 level.
* Significant at 0.10 level.
· Not Significant ($p > 0.10$).

The regression models for all nine data sets were highly significant ($p < 0.01$). Individual R^2 values ranged from 52.7% ($F = 9.93$, $DF = 10$ and 89) to 93.3% ($F = 110.86$, $DF = 11$ and 88). Inflation and turnover were highly significant in most data sets,[9] as was their interaction. The inflation effect was consistently

Table 3. High Inflation Versus High Deflation
Levels of Significance and Direction for Main Effects and Interactions

	Data Sets			
Independent Variable	*INF–INF*[a]	*INF–DEF*[b]	*DEF–INF*[c]	*DEF–DEF*[d]
Main Effects				
Inflation	** +	*** +	*** +	*** +
Inventory Turnover	*** +	*** –	·	*** –
Beginning Inventory—STD Deviation	·	* –	* +	·
Index Difference	N/A	N/A	N/A	N/A
Interactions				
Inflation X Direction	·	·	** –	·
Inflation X Turnover	*** –	*** –	*** –	** –
Inflation X Beg Inv SD	·	** –	* +	·
Turnover X Beg Inv SD	·	* +	·	·
Turnover X Direction	·	*** +	·	*** +
Beg Inv SD X Direction	·	·	** –	·
R^2 (%)—All	63.4	77.4	73.9	62.2
R^2 (%)—Significant Variables Only	58.1	74.4	72.0	51.3

Notes: [a] Assumes average annual inflation for all products of 20% in Period 1 and 20% in Period 2.
[b] Assumes average annual inflation for all products of 20% in Period 1 and average *deflation* of 20% in Period 2.
[c] Assumes average annual deflation for all products of 20% in Period 1 and average *inflation* of 20% in Period 2.
[d] Assumes average annual deflation for all products of 20% in Period 1 and average deflation of 20% in Period 2.
*** Significant at 0.01 level.
** Significant at 0.05 level.
* Significant at 0.10 level.
· Not Significant ($p > 0.10$).

Table 4. Internal Index Versus External Index
Levels of Significance and Beta Estimates for Main Effects and Interactions: Low Inflation Scenario

	Significance		*Beta Estimates*	
Independent Variable	*Internal*[a]	*External*[b]	*Internal*[a]	*External*[b]
Main Effects				
Inflation	**	*	+0.647	+0.687
Turnover	***	**	+5.124	+4.017
Begining Inventory STD Deviation	·	·	·	·
Index Difference	N/A	***	N/A	−79.975
Interactions				
Inflation X Direction	·	***	·	+0.264
Inflation X Turnover	***	**	−0.362	−0.298
Inflation X Beg Inv SD	***	*	+0.018	+0.013
Turnover X Beg Inv SD	**	·	−0.089	·
Turnover X Direction	***	**	−0.828	−0.753
Beg Inv SD X Direction	·	·	·	·
R^2 (%)—All	70.8	93.3	70.8	93.3
R^2 (%)—Significant Variables Only	69.5	92.9	69.5	92.9

Notes: [a] Average inflation for all products of 5% in Periods 1 and 2. Internally generated index used for dollar value LIFO computations.
[b] Average inflation for all products of 5% in Periods 1 and 2. External index used for dollar value LIFO computations. External index for each observation taken randomly from normal distribution around internal index for that observation.
*** Significant at 0.01 level.
** Significant at 0.05 level.
* Significant at 0.10 level.
· Not Significant ($p > 0.10$).

positive and its beta estimate was stable across data sets (see Table 4). The importance of this stability cannot be overstated. It indicates that the effect of inflation is positive *over the continuum of differences* from minus (DVL > Unit LIFO) to plus (DVL < Unit LIFO). Turnover was generally positive except when there was high deflation in Period 2. Higher turnover, therefore, was associated with *greater* Unit LIFO values in normal situations.[10]

The significance of the index effect in each of the three "external index" data sets (Group 2) was very strong. This index effect was correlated with inflation but its effect was much stronger. It is interesting to note that inflation's beta estimate was not significantly influenced by its correlation with the index effect.

Table 5. Internal Index Versus External Index
Levels of Significance and Beta Estimates for Main Effects and Interactions: Moderate Inflation Scenario

	Significance		*Beta Estimates*	
Independent Variable	*Internal*[a]	*External*[b]	*Internal*[a]	*External*[b]
Main Effects				
Inflation	**	·	+0.887	·
Turnover	*	·	+5.200	·
Beginning Inventory STD Deviation	·	·	·	·
Index Difference	N/A	***	N/A	−72.058
Interactions				
Inflation X Direction	·	·	·	·
Inflation X Turnover	·	·	·	·
Inflation X Beg Inv SD	·	·	·	·
Turnover X Beg Inv SD	·	·	·	·
Turnover X Direction	·	·	·	·
Beg Inv SD X Direction	·	·	·	·
R^2 (%)—All	52.7	84.1	52.7	84.1
R^2 (%)—Significant Variables Only	39.1	74.4	39.1	74.4

Notes: [a] Average inflation for product A of 12% in Period 1 and 5% in Period 2; product B, 12% and 20%; product C, 5% and 0%. Internally generated index used for dollar value LIFO computations.
[b] Average inflation for product A of 12% in Period 1 and 5% in Period 2; product B, 12% and 20%; product C, 5% and 0%. External index used for dollar value LIFO computations. External index for each observation taken randomly from normal distribution around internal index for that observation.
*** Significant at 0.01 level.
** Significant at 0.05 level.
* Significant at 0.10 level.
· Not significant ($p > 0.10$).

As shown in the tables, many of the interactions were significant, but there was little pattern to their significance across data sets. This implies that the process generating the Unit LIFO-DVL differences is very complex and not susceptible to simple modeling. The inflation-turnover interaction was consistently negative, indicating that higher turnover tends to offset the effect of inflation.

Table 6. Internal Index Versus External Index
Levels of Significance and Beta Estimates for Main Effects and Interactions: High Inflation Scenario

Independent Variable	*Significance*		*Beta Estimates*	
	Internal[a]	*External*[b]	*Internal*[a]	*External*[b]
Main Effects				
Inflation	**	**	+1.275	+1.210
Turnover	***	***	+13.058	+11.874
Beginning Inventory STD Deviation	·	·	·	·
Index Difference	N/A	***	N/A	−64.108
Interactions				
Inflation X Direction	·	·	·	·
Inflation X Turnover	***	**	−0.479	−0.403
Inflation X Beg Inv SD	·	·	·	·
Turnover X Beg Inv SD	·	·	·	·
Turnover X Direction	·	·	·	·
Beg Inv SD X Direction	·	·	·	·
R^2 (%)—All	63.4	87.0	63.4	87.0
R^2 (%)—Significant Variables Only	58.1	86.4	58.1	86.4

Notes: [a] Average inflation for all products of 20% in Periods 1 and 2. Internally generated index used for dollar value LIFO computations.

[b] Average inflation for all products at 20% in Periods 1 and 2. External index used for dollar value LIFO computations. External index for each observation taken randomly from normal distribution around internal index for that observation.

*** Singificant at 0.01 level.

** Significant at 0.05 level.

* Significant at 0.10 level.

· Not Significant ($p > 0.10$).

LIMITATIONS

This study used synthetic inventory data over two time periods in the examination of Unit LIFO-DVL differences. Although an attempt was made to perform the analysis over a wide range of possible scenarios, the use of synthetic data represents the primary limitation of the study. One could not conclude, for instance, that the study has shown that there are large differences between Unit LIFO and DVL inventory values in the *real world* because the study never used *real world* data.

Related to this problem is the study's process of generating the differences between internal and external indices. As indicated in note 7, the variability of the Unit LIFO-DVL differences seems to be linearly related to the standard deviation parameter used in the generation of the external indices. The *real world* standard deviation may be considerably smaller that the one used in the study, allowing the possibility that any Unit LIFO-DVL differences caused by the use of external indices may be negligible.

Also, the study did not directly address possible *time series* properties of the Unit LIFO-DVL differences. It may be the case that the Unit LIFO and DVL results further diverge, or even converge, over more time periods. Obviously, consideration of more than two time periods, entailing much greater computational complexity, would be needed to explore this aspect.

There seems to be little doubt that some interaction effects occur in the generation of Unit LIFO—DVL differences. The literature in the area refers to the possibility and the results of the study consistently point to various forms of interaction. But there is considerable difficulty in explaining specific interactions. For example, why would higher inventory turnover reduce the effect of inflation on Unit LIFO-DVL differences? Without thorough analytical work in explaining the *overall* process of generating the Unit LIFO-DVL differences, attempts at explaining the interaction effects by themselves are likely to be mere speculation. Such analytical work is beyond the scope of this research effort and will be left to future studies.

CONCLUSIONS

This study attempted to identify variables which could generate significant differences between Unit LIFO and Dollar-Value LIFO, and to examine the distribution of those differences. A mathematical model was developed which incorporated a broad range of scenarios to test the significance of variables that have been outlined in the accounting literature as possibly affecting the LIFO calculation. The mathematical model incorporated one dependent variable and five main independent variables and exhibited strong predictive power. Ancillary significance tests were also performed for each of the independent variables and interaction effects included in the model.

The research results demonstrated that a number of key factors could significantly impact the DVL calculation. Differences between the results generated by Unit LIFO and DVL can be attributed to various factors normally present in the business environment (inflation, turnover, product mix, etc.). Also, when coupled with other variables, the impact of the factors can often become even more pronounced. This seems to imply that the process causing the Unit LIFO-DVL differences is likely to be quite complex. The study has shown that materially different results could be obtained under DVL versus Unit LIFO especially when there is divergence in internal and external indices.

Unfortunately, little guidance has been forthcoming from the accounting profession concerning the proper application of DVL. It is apparent that important differences can exist between the results obtained by the two methods. Yet, the profession's standard-setting bodies seem to have overlooked these potential differences for the sake of operational expediency. In fact, DVL is one of the few widely used accounting methods garnering its authoritative support almost exclusively from tax law and historical use.

This research has helped to isolate those variables which the Financial Accounting Standards Board would need to address in formulating any standards in the area. And, given the possible divergence of results between the two methods, it appears to be an area that warrants closer scrutiny.

NOTES

1. Two methods commonly employed in practice to generate the indices are the double-extension and link-chain methods. The link-chain approach is permitted only in those cases where the double-extension method is not practical.

2. Density tracing is a method of graphically depicting the distribution of a set of observations using a smoothing methodology. It avoids the "raggedness" caused by discontinuities in the data. See Chambers, Cleveland, Kleiner, and Tukey [1983, pp. 32-37].

3. Preliminary multiple regression runs showed interactions involving the index differences to be consistently non-significant when inflation interactions were also present in the model. This is apparently due to the correlation between the index difference and inflation. In the regression models, the inflation interactions captured any underlying significant effects, causing the index difference interactions to have little incremental explanatory power.

4. In the two-product case, mix can be represented as the percentage of total inventory accounted for by one of the two products. But in the three-product case, this expands to two separate percentages. To specify a model as parsimonious as possible, a surrogate measure of mix expressible in one statistic was sought. This resulted in the use of the standard deviation measure.

5. For example, Variable 1 (unit beginning inventory, Product A) for each observation was selected from a normal random distribution with mean set equal to:

$$500 \times [\mathrm{RND(V)/RND(W)}]^{0.25}$$

and standard deviation set equal to:

$$300 \times \mathrm{NOR(X)} \times [\mathrm{RND(Y)/RND(Z)}]^{0.25}$$

where RND(X) is a uniform random number seeded by the value of X and NOR(X) is a unit normal random number seeded by X. Each observation of Variable 1 was forced to be a positive integer. The mean of Variable 1 over all 100 observations was 530.3 and the standard deviation was 331.9. The range was 15 to 1526. Other variables were generated in a similar fashion.

6. The distributions of differences for the various heavy inflation and deflation scenarios were very similar. It was felt that little insight would be added by incorporating the additional scenarios into the external-internal index analyses.

7. This process was intended to emulate a real-world scenario in which external indices can be thought of as the expected value of the pool's internal index ± a residual, where the residuals are normally distributed.

The generation of the external indices is obviously critical to the generalizability of the results. For instance, one may suppose that 10% is too high in the computation of the standard deviation, and would be unrealistic in practice. To examine the sensitivity of the results to the 10% assumption, the low inflation data set was re-generated under assumptions of 1% and 3% standard deviations for the external indices. Comparing the results showed a strong linear relationship ($R^2 = 98.9\%$) between the standard deviation percentage used and the standard deviation of the Unit LIFO-DVL difference distribution. When the standard deviation percentage is zero, the external and internal indices are equal. For every standard deviation percentage point above zero, the standard deviation of the Unit LIFO-DVL difference distribution increased by 16%. For a 10% standard deviation, the total increase was approximately 160%.

8. Erosion of the baser layer under DVL ("Direction') was consistently *not* significant as a main effect. It was not included in the tables for simplicity.

9. A notable exception was the moderate inflation scenario. Here the index difference effect apparently overwhelmed the other variables.

10. For certain industries where *deflation* is a major concern (some high technology industries, for example), this reversal of direction for turnover could be important.

REFERENCES

Bainbridge, D.R., "Is Dollar-Value LIFO Consistent With Authoritative GAAP?," *Journal of Accounting, Auditing, and Finance* [Summer 1984].

Chambers, J.M., Cleveland, W.S., Kleiner, B., and Tukey, P.A.,*Graphical Methods for Data Analysis* [Duxbury Press, 1983].

Firmin, P.A., "Dollar-Value LIFO: Legitimate or Not?," *The Accounting Review* [April 1963].

Moonitz, M., "The Case Against LIFO as an Inventory Pricing Formula," *Journal of Accountancy* [June 1953].

Schwartz, B.N., "Dollar-Value LIFO—Evaluating One Experience," *CPA Journal* [April 1982].

Schwartz, B.N. and Diamond, M.A., "Is 'Dollar-Value' LIFO for You?," *CPA Journal* [July 1980].

Stark, M.E., "A Survey of LIFO Inventory Application Techniques," *The Accounting Review* [January 1978].

Wolff, L.W., Jr., "LIFO Layer Valuations Under the Dollar-Value Index Method," *The Tax Adviser* [March 1981].

AN ASSESSMENT OF THE LIABILITY CLASSIFICATION OF NONCURRENT DEFERRED TAXES

James M. Lukawitz, Rene P. Manes, and Thomas F. Schaefer

ABSTRACT

This paper provises an analysis of whether reported noncurrent deferred tax credits are considered by the market as a form of debt. A market criterion related to financial leverage is employed in evaluating the liability classification of taxes which accountants claim to be incurred, but the payment of which is deferred. The theoretical relationshiop between accounting measures of debt and market risk measures provides a basis for measuring the market's assessment of the contribution of noncurrent deferred taxes to financial leverage. The evidence indicates that recently reported noncurrent deferred taxes, classified as long-term liabilities, are significantly associated with market risk measures for a cross-section of firms.

Advances in Accounting, Volume 8, pages 79-95.

ISBN: 1-55938-067-5

The recent issuance of *Statement of Financial Accounting Standards No. 96,* "Accounting for Income Taxes" (*SFAS 96*) [FASB, 1987] reflects the increased attention regarding the disclosure of firms' tax liabilities. Of particular importance is the retention of the "comprehensive allocation" method which records and reports as liabilities taxes which are measured by accountants as incurred, but for a variety of reasons the payment of which is deferred. This allocation procedure and debt classification of deferred taxes has been criticized [e.g., Wheeler and Outslay, [1986] because many corporations appear to defer these tax payments indefinitely. The purpose of this paper is to address the issue of the liability classification of deferred taxes by providing a basic empirical test of the account's possible effects on investors.

First, the nature of deferred taxes is discussed and placed in an historical perspective. Recent accounting treatment of the deferred tax account is described and then tested regarding its ability to explain market measures of financial relationships. In particular, the classification of deferred taxes as a liability is assessed in terms of its contribution to a measure of risk as established through theoretical and empirical relationships. The employment of a market-determined measure to assess alternative accounting treatments is viewed as an important criterion for analyzing the usefulness of accounting classifications and techniques. Finally, our results are discussed with reference to the current pronouncement (*SFAS 96*) which mandates a "liability method" of deferred tax reporting.

AN HISTORICAL PERSPECTIVE ON THE DEFERRED TAX PROBLEM

During the Eisenhower administration, Federal revenue laws were recodified into the Internal Revenue Code of 1954. In response to Japanese and Western European practices, Section 167 of the Code provided a choice of depreciation methods which for the first time permitted accelerated depreciation for tax reporting. The materiality and significance of timing differences which resulted from the accelerated depreciation option led to a decade-long debate on interperiod tax allocation.

In 1966 the Accounting Research Division of the AICPA published H. Black's *Accounting Research Study* (*ARS*) No. 9 "Interperiod Allocation of Corporate Income Taxes." Taking the position that taxes are not distributions of corporate profit but rather expenses which should be allocated or matched to revenues of appropriate periods, this study recommended comprehensive allocation. One year later the Accounting Principles Board (APB) in its Opinion 11 [AICPA, 1967], also came out in favor of the deferred method of comprehensive allocation with classification of deferred taxes into a net current and a net noncurrent amount. Critics, however, argued that the resulting noncurrent deferred tax credit in the balance sheet was not an obligation to pay the federal government, was uncertain in amount, undiscounted, and part of the amounts might be deferred indefinitely.

Early on, Price Waterhouse [1967] reported that a survey of 100 firms showed that deferred taxes recognized because of the acceleration of long-lived assets were not reversed over the life cycle of those assets. Fifteen years later, Beresford et al. commented on "the ever increasing 'bulge' of deferred tax credits on the corporate balance sheet" [1983, p. 6]. The delayed impact of the Accelerated Cost Recovery System (ACRS), introduced in the Recovery Tax Act of 1981, further contributed to increases in deferred tax credits. Not only did 85% of the 600 firms reported on by *Accounting Trends and Techniques* [AICPA, 1987, pp. 206-207] present captions for deferred tax but the amounts reported have swelled steadily both in absolute terms and as a percentage of total corporate debt.

More recently, *SFAS 96* replaces the deferred method with the liability method and provides that deferred taxes be adjusted for tax rate changes. During the same period of time Congress passed the Tax Reform Act of 1986 reducing future tax rates. It is premature to anticipate investor reaction to these changes but the approach taken here for the 1982 to 1985 interval should permit an approach for measurement and tracking investor reactions to the deferred taxes account for subsequent periods.

THE DEFERRED TAX LIABILITY ACCOUNT

The balance in the deferred tax account of corporations under *APB 11* has been described as an "accumulation of annual adjustments that defied simple explanation" [Price Waterhouse, 1987]. The lack of a straightforward, intuitive explanation of the deferred tax account may be attributable to the emphasis which was placed on the calculation of tax expense for periodic income determination. Another reason making it difficult to provide a direct interpretation of the account is the fact that a variety of "timing differences" (and their reversals) often contribute to its balance. Furthermore, these timing differences affect both current and noncurrent deferred tax balances.

In this study attention will be focused on noncurrent deferred taxes only, current deferred taxes being included with current liabilities. For noncurrent deferred taxes, timing differences can result both from revenue and expense recognition. The completed-contract versus percentage-of-completion method provided enormous credits for some defense contractors [see Wheeler and Outslay, [1986]. Although the Tax Equity and Fiscal Responsibility Act of 1982 (TEFRA) limits the contract's life, such limits affected only new contracts leaving continuing timing effects in the deferred tax account. Other revenue differences involved the use of the equity method for accounting for investees and subsidiaries that did not qualify as affiliates (less than 80% ownership) for tax purposes.

However, the most common timing differences result from expense acceleration (e.g., depreciation, interest capitalization, intangible drilling costs, and so on) for tax purposes relative to book amounts. For the year 1984 an analysis of the breakdown of entries in the deferred tax account for 38 firms shows that depreciation and other accelerated expenses accounted for over 95% of the total net deferred tax credit.[1] The significance of the depreciation component of deferred taxes is underscored by the expectation of increased depreciation from application of quicker writeoffs allowed under the ACRS provided in the Economic Recovery Tax Act of 1981. Despite the large effect of depreciation on the deferred tax account balance, other included timing differences may limit is interpretive usefulness.

The FASB's *Statement of Concepts No. 1* [1980a] points as a primary objective of financial reporting that reported information be useful to investors. That information is to be useful "both (to) those who desire safety of investment and those who are *willing to accept risk* to obtain high rates of return" (para. 35, emphasis added). In general the degree of the investor's risk is believed to be directly and functionally related to the extent of debt of the firm and this belief has been tested both for reported and unreported components of debt (e.g., leases, pensions, and consolidation of finance subsidiaries) but no empirical studies have attempted to measure the extent to which investors identify the billions of dollars of deferred taxes as a corporate liability. Stated otherwise: Does the market believe that the federal government is a major, long-term creditor of corporate America or has there been steady and growing misstatement of income and debt? This is the question which our statistical tests attempts to answer for the years 1982-1985 inclusive by use of a cross-sectional analysis of each of those four years.

THE RELATIONSHIP BETWEEN RISK AND THE DEBT-TO-EQUITY RATIO

As preparation for an empirical test, we review that part of financial literature which establishes the theoretical relationship between the amount of debt in a firm's capital structure and its expected return to owners.

We start with a definition of the rate of return of the unlevered firm:

$$E(R_{ut}) = \frac{E(X_{ut})}{S_{ut}} \tag{1}$$

where: u = totally debt-free or unlevered firm.
R_{ut} = return on equity of the unlevered firm in period t.

X_{ut} = earnings of the unlevered firm devined as $S_{u(t+1)} - S_{ut} + C_{ut}$
S_{ut} = market value of equity at begining of period t.
C_{ut} = dividends paid to equity in period t.

If, without in any way changing their operations or the composition of assets, the owners of S_u replace a part of their investment by borrowing an amount D, expected earnings become (without time subscripts):

$$E(R_L) = \frac{E(X_u) - iD}{S_L} \tag{2}$$

where the subscript L indicates that levered firm and i is the cost of borrowing. Substituting $E(X_u) = E(R_u) \cdot (S_L + D)$ from Equation (1) into Equation (2) we have

$$E(R_L) = E(R_u) + D/S_L\,[E(R_u) - i] \tag{3}$$

Equation (3) can be recognized as the Modigliani and Miller [1958] proposition II result for the cost of capital when i is the risk free rate. In its expected value, ex ante form, Equation (3) models the relationship between the expected rate of return and a given amount of debt in the capital structure.

Next, using the capital asset pricing model (CAPM) [Sharpe, 1964], we can make a parallel analysis of the impact of debt on the risk measure of the levered and the unlevered firm. According to the CAPM, the returns of levered and unlevered firms are given by the following equation:

$$E(R_u) = i + \beta_u\,[E(R_m) - i] \tag{4}$$

$$E(R_L) = i + \beta_L\,[E(R_m) - i] \tag{5}$$

where: β = the systematic risk of a firm
R_m = the return on the market portoflio
$\beta_L > \beta_u$, reflecting favorable leverage effects.

Substituting Equations (4) and (5) into (3) we obtain

$$\beta_L = \beta_u + D/S_L\,[\beta] \tag{6}$$

Equation 6 describes β_L as a function of both β_u and D/S_L and thus relates the systematic risk of a firm to its debt/equity ratio. Later in the paper, we explicitly introduce the tax effects of debt (due to interest deductions) when testing the relationships in Equation (6).[2]

Note, however, that Equations (1) to (6) are market value equations and that the debt/equity ratio, D/S_L, must be evaluated in market terms. The value, S_L, that is, the market value of outstanding common shares, is readily enough observable but there is no easily calculated value of D, the totality of the firm's debt. True enough, bonds, mortgages, notes, and most current liabilities have measurable market values, but many liabilities do not. Among these latter obligations are pensions, warranties, contingencies, and, of course, deferred taxes.

A major area of investigation by accounting researchers [e.g., Beaver et al. 1970] is the extent to which annual report, accounting data can be used as surrogates for market values to approximate true measures of market return and risk. Bowman [1980] points out that accounting measures of debt are highly correlated with market values of debt when both of these sets are known. When market values are not clearly known, studies have evaluated accounting footnote disclosure of "debt-like" items such as leases [Bowman, 1980] and pensions [Dhaliwal, 1986] in terms of their ability to reflect the market's assessment of debt and thus contribute to the explanation of systematic risk as theoretically defined above. If accounting information is used to measure D in D/S_L, we should remember that D includes all sources of financing on the right hand side of the balance shet other than equity; D thus includes not only clearly defined, long-term obligations such as bonds, notes, and mortgages but also current liabilities, contingent liabilities, minority interests, preferred stock, and deferred credits, such as deferred taxes and the investment tax credit. The purpose of the next section is to use and disaggregate Equation (6) to determine whether or not the deferred tax, dt, component of debt, D, as measured in accounting reports, does make a significant contribution toward the assessment of systematic risk. Although the same question could be asked with respect to the investment tax credit or to other noninterest bearing debt or to preferred stock we shall focus our attention on the deferred tax account.

METHOD OF ANAYLSIS

The Empirical Model

To operationalize the theoretical relationships in Equation (6), our model disaggregrates total reported debt into two components, noncurrent deferred taxes and all other reported debt. This separation allows for the estimation of the incremental contribution of the deferred tax component to the assessment of systematic risk, beyond that of all other noncommon shareholder sources of capital. If deferred tax disclosures, as reported during the period of anaylsis, are considered a component of debt, we would expect the deferred tax component of the model to be positive and significantly different than zero.

On the other hand, if market participants do not regard deferred taxes as debt, we should not find a significant contribution toward the explanation of β_L, the systematic risk of the firm.

Cross-sectional ordinary least squares analysis was used to provide for coefficient estimates of the parameters in Equation (6). Equation (6), however, was derived in the absence of taxes. As Bowman [1979] points out, the presence of taxes lessens the effect of leverage on systematic risk by a net of tax adjustment. Accordingly a net of tax adjustment was incorporated the regression model as follows:

$$\beta_L = \alpha + \lambda_1\beta_u + \lambda_2\beta_u\,[D^*(1-t) + d - dt]/S_L + \lambda_3\beta_u dt/S_L + e \qquad (7)$$

where: β_L, β_U, and S_L are as previously defined
α = intercept term
λ_i = regression slope cofficients for $i = 1, 3$
D^* = long-term debt
d = all other debt items
dt = balance in the deferred tax account (long-term)
t = tax rate
e = error term; $E(e) = 0$

The tax rate was defined as total tax expense divided by pre-tax income, D^* represents long-term debt (e.g., bonds payable) and d represents all other debt items (e.g., short-term payables, preferred stock, etc.). The purpose of the further disaggregation of debt was to allow for tax effects on those debt items which produce tax deductible interest.

Our use of Equation (7) closely parallels analyses by Bowman [1980] and Dhaliwal [1986] with one important distinction. A major limitation of previous studies was that the accounting beta, β_u, had to be estimated over a very long time period (e.g., 20 years) prior to the period when its estimate was used as an independent variable. Estimation error for the β_u parameter, however, is likely to be a major concern as the length of time between estimation and use in empirical testing increases. Because we employed the recently available expanded Compustat II quarterly data base, our study was able to reduce substantially the time period of estimation (from 20 years to 20 quarters) without sacrificing the number of observations. Quarterly estimation also allowed a closer alignment of estimation and test periods, thus minimizing this source of parameter estimation error. Another benefit to quarterly estimation of β_u was that our sample size was much larger than if annual estimation had been used. This is presumably due to the higher likelihood of complete data over a shorter time horizon.

Table 1. Sample Selection Criteria

12-31 year end firms listed on the COMPUSTAT Industrial Database and CRSP Monthly Stock Returns file for which the following data were available:

COMPUSTAT Annual, 1982-1985
1. Non-Current Deferred Tax Liability
2. Total Assets
3. Total Common Equity
4. Long-Term Debt
5. Common Stock Price
6. Common Shares — 388 firms

CRSP, 1978-1985
1. Stock return — 246 firms

COMPUSTAT Quarterly, 1978-1985
1. Interest Expense
2. Total Liabilities
3. Preferred Stock
4. Dividends
5. Common Stock Price
6. Common Shares

Total number of firms available for analysis — 213

Further reductions were made in each year based on marginal tax data availablility and Chapter 11 bankruptcies.

	1982	1983	1984	1985
Underlying sample	213	213	213	213
Marginal tax rate data restriction*	18	9	14	17
Firms in bankruptcy**	5	4	5	5
Ending Sample	190	200	194	191

Notes: * Reductions in the sample were made for missing tax data or when the computed tax rate was greater than 100% or less than zero.

** Examining each firm's debt/equity ratios showed some unusually high values (e.g., 30). Retrieval of the actual annual reports revealed these firms to be involved in Chapter 11 bankruptcy proceedings, thus obscuring any theoretical relationship between financial leverage and systematic risk.

Sample Data Retrieval and Selection

Standard and Poor's *COMPUSTAT* industrial tape was used to identify a sample of firms which reported deferred tax credits in their balance sheets. The period 1982-1985 was chosen to highlight the relatively large amounts of deferred taxes in recent years. The annual and quarterly *COMPUSTAT* databases provided the data for all debt and deferred tax items as well as income and market values used in computing the unlevered beta, β_u.

Table 2. Industry Classification

Industry	*S&P 2-digit code*	*No. of Firms*
Metal Mining	10	5
Coal	12	2
Oil and Gas	13	8
Nonmetal Minerals	14	2
Construction, Not Building	16	1
Food	20	9
Tobacco	21	1
Textiles	22	3
Apparel	23	1
Lumber and Wood	24	2
Furniture	25	2
Paper	26	8
Printing/Publishing	27	6
Chemicals	28	25
Petroleum	29	10
Rubber	30	4
Leather (footwear)	31	1
Glass/Concrete	32	7
Smelts (steel)	33	8
Fab metals	34	5
Machinery	35	15
Electric Machines	36	16
Motor Vehicles	37	12
Instruments	38	5
Miscellaneous Manufacturing	39	2
Railroad	40	5
Trucking	42	3
Water Transport	44	1
Air Transport	45	3
Transport Services	47	2
Communication	48	4
Natural Gas	49	7
Wholesale parts	50	5
Retail Variety	53	1
Retail Grocery	54	3
Retail Apparel	56	2
Retail Eating	58	3
Insurance Brokers	64	2
Real Estate	67	2
Hotels	70	1
Service Personnel	72	1
Motion Picture	78	1
Service Amusement	79	1
Service Engineering	89	3
		213

The Center for Research in Security Prices (CRSP) tape provided monthly security return data for estimating the levered beta, β_L. Each firm was required to have a December 31 year-end to allow for the estimates of β_L to reflect comparable time periods. Additionally reported results were restricted to nonregulated firms. Due to the reduction in operating risk provided by rate regulation, this group was viewed as sufficiently different in terms of its relationship between market risk and accounting measures of debt to warrant exclusion. After application of these restrictions and deletion of firms with missing data, 213 firms remained available for further analysis. Table 1 shows details of the sample selection criteria. Table 2 provides an industry breakdown of the firms selected for analysis and indicates a well-diversified selection of firms at the 2-digit industry level.

Variable Definitions

To estimate the parameters in Equation (7) definitions of each of the variables were constructed. Debt ($D^*+d\text{-}dt$) consisted of long term liabilities, current liabilities (including the current deferred taxes), all convertible debt, preferred stock, and minority interest. Noncurrent deferred taxes (dt) were intentionally excluded from the overall definition of debt to allow for an estimation of a separate effect. Equity, S_L, consisted of the market value of the common shares outstanding.

The measures of systematic risk, unlevered β_u and β_L were computed for each firm using ordinary least squares regressions to estimate the traditional market model. Because β_u represents a risk measure for a pure equity firm, interest expense (net of tax) was added back to capital gains and dividends in the computation of the quarterly rate of return of the firm using the approach of Hamada [1972]. For each firm the following model provided the β_u measure:

$$R_{uit} = \alpha + \beta_u(R_{mt}) + e \tag{8}$$

where: R_{uit} = [Capital gains + dividends + Interest (net of tax)]/[S + D (net of tax)].

R_{uit} is the rate of return on firm i in quarter t adjusted for interest plus preferred dividends to yield a rate of return as if the firm had converted to all equity financing. R_{mt} represents the return on the market for quarter t. Equation (8) was estimated over a 20 quarter horizon prior to each test period. Quarterly data wer used here to parallel the time horizon for which the levered β_L risk measure was computed.

The dependent variable from Equation (7), β_L, was also estimated using the market model. For each year of analysis, the previous 60 months of return data was used in the regression of R_{uit} on R_{mt}.

Table 3. Results of Regression Analysis of Equation (7) Relating Debt and Deferred Taxes to Market Risk

$$\beta_l = \alpha + \lambda_1\beta_u + \lambda_2\beta_u\,[D^*(1-t) + d - dt]/S_L + \lambda_3\beta_u dt/S_L + e$$

Variable	*coefficient*	*t-ratio*	r^2
	1982		
Constant	.52	9.76*	46.5
Unlevered beta (β_u)	.44	8.91*	($n = 190$)
β_u · Debt/equity	.39	7.39*	
β_u · Deferred tax/equity	.38	1.45	
	1983		
Constant	.45	10.03*	55.6
Unlevered beta (β_u)	.45	10.14*	($n = 200$)
β_u · Debt equity	.45	7.89*	
β_u · Deferred tax/equity	.62	2.72*	
	1984		
Constant	.46	10.04*	54.7
Unlevered beta (β_u)	.41	8.86*	($n = 194$)
β_u · Debt/equity	.42	8.62*	
β_u · Deferred tax/equity	.56	2.94*	
	1985		
Constant	.44	8.53*	45.8
Unlevered beta (β_u)	.49	8.80*	($n = 191$)
β_u · Debt/equity	.41	6.24*	
β_u · Deferred tax/equity	.65	2.39*	

Notes: * Significant at .01 level.

Results of the Analysis

Table 3 shows the results of the regressions using Equation (7) to explain the systematic risk of the firm for each of the four years of analysis. The results clearly substantiate the theoretical relationships indicated by Equation (6). Both the unlevered beta and the debt/equity ratio significantly contribute toward the explanation of systematic risk. The effects are consistent in direction and magnitude across all four years. The results for the deferred tax component are significant in each of the last three years uner study. This significance indicates that the effect ofthe deferred tax component on the firm's systematic risk measure is distinguishable from zero at conventional significance levels.

In examining the results in Table 3, there is the possibility of some impact from residual cross-sectional (RCC) correlation on the reported significance levels. Research concerning the use of cross-sectional regressions in the presence of RCC has shown that the standard errors of the regression

Table 4. Descriptive Statistics for Selected Variables

Variable	*Mean*	*Median*	*SD*
1982			
Levered Beta	1.134	1.103	.382
Unlevered Beta	.86	.792	.420
Debt	1149m	331m	2531m
Debt/Equity	1.036	.773	1.065
Deferred Tax	195m	39m	727m
Deferred Tax/Equity	.109	.064	.120
Deferred Tax/Total Debt*	.119	.095	.106
1983			
Levered Beta	1.086	1.068	.381
Unlevered Beta	.868	.798	.415
Debt	1265m	336m	2788m
Debt/Equity	.811	.645	.765
Deferred Tax	210m	34m	753m
Deferred Tax/Equity	.097	.053	.108
Deferred Tax/Total Debt*	.127	.092	.124
1984			
Levered Beta	1.066	1.072	.381
Unlevered Beta	.846	.780	.410
Debt	1491m	403m	3398m
Debt/Equity	.950	.671	.908
Deferred Taxes	239m	40m	788m
Deferred Tax/Equity	.116	.067	.126
Deferred Tax/Total Debt*	.130	.094	.123
1985			
Levered Beta	1.034	1.011	.358
Unlevered Beta	.775	.470	.348
Debt	1597m	409m	3670m
Debt/Equity	.886	.686	.806
Deferred Taxes	721m	43m	959m
Deferred Tax/Equity	.098	.055	.104
Deferred Tax/Total Debt*	.123	.094	.120

Notes: m = Millions of dollars
* Total Debt includes Deferred Tax.

coefficients may be underestimated [e.g., Bernard, 1987; Christie, 1987] thus leading to overstated t-values. Bernard observes that for monthly market model regressions the largest source of RCC correlation results primarily from intra-industry effects. To the extent that the β observations are characterized by intra-industry clustering, RCC may be a problem in this study. Our sample (see Table 2), however, appears to be well diversified (45 different industries) with most industries containing a relatively small number of firms.

Table 5. Correlations Among the Independent Variables

	Unlevered Beta (β_u)	*β_u · Debt/ Equity*	*β_u · Deferred Tax/Equity*
	1982		
β_u · Debt/equity	.075		
β_u · Deferred tax/equity	.131	.515	
β_u · Debt*/equity	-.010	.873	.450
	1983		
β_u · Debt/equity	.148		
β_u · Deferred tax/equity	.137	.489	
β_u · Debt*/equity	.142	.876	.446
	1984		
β_u · Debt/equity	.166		
β_u · Deferred tax/equity	.184	.380	
β_u · Debt*/equity	.167	.956	.344
	1985		
β_u · Debt/equity	.143		
β_u · Deferred tax/equity	.163	.271	
β_u · Debt*/equity	.139	.920	.294

Note: * Debt after tax adjustment.

Table 3 presents also the adjusted coefficients of determination (R^2) for each cross-sectional regression model estimated. These R^2, which represent the proportion of variation in the dependent variable explained by the set of independent (explanatory) variables, adjusted for degrees of freedom, compare favorably with those reported in previous studies in which systematic risk was the dependent variable [e.g., Bowman, 1980; Dhaliwal, 1986]. The Equation (7) model thus appears to provide empirical validation to those relationships which, it is hypothesized, explain systematic risk.

Table 4 provides descriptive statistics for each of the variables included in the regression equation. Although deferred taxes increase throughout the time period studied, their percentage of equity fluctuates. Most of the other variables show consistency or moderate increases across time although 1982 is marked by a somewhat higher debt/equity ratio. Next, Table 5 reports the correlation coefficient between each of the independent variables. The levels of the correlations coupled with the significant t-statistics in the regression models suggest that the dta are not characterized by a multicollinearity problem.

Given that a significant association bewteen deferred taxes and market risk was found, a logical extension of the research was to search for the possibility of different debt classes within the firm capital structure. Specifically, the question of whether deferred taxes were of the same risk class as ordinary debt was addressed. This analysais was undertaken using the approach of Dhaliwal

Table 6. Results of *F*-Test Analysis to Determine If Deferred Taxes and Debt Are of Same Risk Class

Comparing Equation (7) Full and Restricted (7a) Models

Year	*F*-ratio
1982	.000
1983	.464
1984	.458
1985	.574

F-statistic at .05 significance level = 3.840

[1986]. The statistical test involves the comparison of two regression equations. The first is Equation (7) which was used as a basis for tests of individual coefficients. The second is a restricted version of Equation (7) where deferred taxes and debt are *not* disaggregated but instead are combined and represented by a single tax adjusted variable (D^1) as follows:

$$\beta_L = \alpha + \delta_1\beta_u + \delta_2\beta_u(D^1/S_L) + z \tag{7a}$$

In comparing the error sum of squares of Equations (7) and 7a), the increase in explanatory power from dichotomizing debt into deferred tax and all other debt can be explicitly measured. If there is no increase in explanatory power, then it is presumed that the λ_2 and λ_3 coefficients from Equation (7) are essentially equivalent. To measure the change in explanatory power the following *F* statistic was computed.

$$F = \frac{SSE(R) - SSE(F)}{(n-3) - (n-4)} \div \frac{SSE(F)}{n-4}$$

where $SSE(R)$ and $SSE(F)$ represent the error sum of squares for the restricted (7a) and full (7) models, respectively. As can be seen from Table 6, the inclusion of a deferred tax component produces a coefficient which is not significantly different (.05 level) from the coefficient for all debt. Thus, although the deferred tax credits appear to be viewed by the market as a significant explanatory component of risk, we are unable to identify that contribution as being significantly different from that of all other debt.

CONCLUSIONS

To anyone addressing the issue of the liability classification of deferred taxes, it is clear that many of the early criticisms have yet to be resolved. In particular, as evidenced by the increasing amounts on balance sheets, the charge that deferred tax disclosures appear uncertain and perhaps indefinite as to repayment is being resurrected by both professionals and academics.

In this paper, we appeal to a market criterion to shed some light on this issue and examine a large sample of firms over four recent years. We use the theoretical relationship between the debt/equity ratio and a firm's market risk to assess whether including the recently reported deferred tax balances contribute to the explanatory ability in this relationship. Our results show that they do. The recently reported values of noncurrent deferred taxes as liabilities has had both a significant and consistent effect in its ability to explain measures of market risk of firms. These results are consistent with the view that the firms' postponement of taxes is an indirect financing source.

Our results, however, were unable to show that the deferred tax liability is considered differently than other debts, even though unlike other debt the deferred tax balance does not carry an effective interest rate. Because of this lack of an effective interest rate, the leverage effect would be expected to be greater than interest bearing debt, ceteris paribus. Possible reasons for this empirical finding include the uncertainty involved with changing tax laws and their impact on the deferred tax liability.

How are we to interpret these findings? At least two groups of accountants, with dramatically opposed views of the intrisic value of standards, will not be very impressed by them. In one group will be those who may not question the results but who do question the suitability of allowing the market place to influence accounting standards for what is reported and how it is reported. These "global" or "normative" theorists believe that methods for expressing the "true" concepts and axioms by resorting to what the market thinks or does, can only debase the currency of accounting principles.

A second group believes that accounting reports are of little use in explaining market values ("whatever information value annual reports contain is already impounded in the value of securities by the time the reports are published"). For them disaggregation of D (in Equation [6]) is of little value unless it can be shown that D/S_L in Equation (7) is an accurate surrogate for all other claims on the assets of the firm beyond those of common stock equity. To that extent, they would agree that the deferred taxes account is a component of debt.

Our own conclusion is that if a market criterion for assessing debt classification and measurement is accepted as useful, a deferred tax debt classification and current efforts by the FASB to standardize a "liability" method are appropriate. Our results suggest that noncurrent deferred tax credits are an identifiable debt component across a wide variety of firms and over several time periods. Future research in the area should be able to contribute to the ongoing debate by examining the new deferred tax disclosures under *SFAS 96*.

ACKNOWLEDGMENTS

The authors wish to thank workshop participants at Georgia Tech, Baruch College, and Florida State. Special thanks are due to Ron Woan for his valuable suggestions. The comments of the anonymous reviewers are also gratefully acknowledged.

NOTES

1. This 95% figure must be discounted somewhat because in some cases, expense recognition and revenue realization credits were offset by early statement expensing of pension, facility writedowns and other reserves. A sample of 71 of the over 200 in the later-to-be reported sample was used for this breakdown. Firms did not provide sufficient detail on timing differences but many indicated the deferred tax provision was "mostly due to depreciation."
2. The analysis was replicated on a before tax basis. The results were similar to the ones presented herein.

REFERENCES

American Institute of Certified Public Accountants, Accounting Principles Board, *APB Opinion 11,* "Accounting for Income Taxes" [AICPA, December 1967].

———, *Accounting Trends and Techniques,* 41st ed. [AICPA, 1987].

Beaver, W., P. Kettler, and M. Scholes, "The Association Between Market Determined and Accounting Determined Risk Measures," *The Accounting Review* [October 1970], pp. 654-682.

Beresford, D., L. Best, P. Craig, and J. Weber, "Accounting For Income Taxes: A Review of Alternatives," *FASB Research Report* [1983].

Bernard, V.L., "Cross-Sectional Dependence and Problems in Inference in Market-Based Accounting Research," *Journal of Accounting Research* [Spring 1987].

Black, H., "Interperiod Allocation of Corporate Income Taxes," *Accounting Research Study No. 9* [AICPA, 1966].

Bowman, R., "The Theoretical Relationship Between Systematic Risk and Financial (Accounting) Variables," *Journal of Finance* [June 1979], pp. 617-630.

———, "The Debt Equivalence of Leases: An Empirical Investigation," *The Accounting Review* [April 1980], pp. 237-253.

Christie, A.A., "On Cross-Sectional Analysis in Accounting Research," *Journal of Accounting and Economics* [December 1987].

Dhaliwal, D., "Measurement of Financial Leverage in the Presence of Unfunded Pension Obligations," *The Accounting Review* [October 1986], pp. 651-661.

FASB, *Applicability of Indefinite Reversal Criteria to Timing Differences* [FASB, 1978].

———, *Financial Accounting Concepts Statement No. 1,* "Objectives of Financial Reporting by Business Enterprises" [FASB, 1980a].

———, *Financial Accounting Concepts Statement No. 3,* "Elements of Financial Statements of Business Enterprises" [FASB, 1980b].

———, *Statement of Financial Accounting Standards No. 96,* "Accounting for Income Taxes" [FASB, 1987].

Foster, G., *Financial Statement Analyses,* 2nd ed. [Prentice-Hall, 1986].

Hamada, R., "The Effect of the Firm's Capital Structure on the Systematic Risk of Common Stocks," *Journal of Finance* [1972], pp. 435-452.

Modigliani, F. and M. Miller, "The Cost of Capital, Corporation Finance and the Theory of Investment," *The American Economic Review* [June 1958], pp. 235-284.

Price Waterhouse and Co., *Is Generally Accepted Accounting for Income Taxes Possibly Misleading Investors? A Statement of Position on Income Tax Allocation* [Price Waterhouse and Co., 1967].

Sharpe, W.F., "Capital Asset Prices: A Theory of Market Equilibrium Under Conditions of Risk," *Journal of Finance* [September 1964], pp. 425-442.

Wheeler, J.E. and E. Outslay, "The Phantom Federal Income Taxes of General Dynamics Corporation," *The Accounting Review* [October 1986], pp. 760-774.

INFORMATION TRANSFER ASSOCIATED WITH MANAGEMENT FORECASTS:

EVIDENCE OF ATTENTUATING FACTORS

Stephen P. Baginski

ABSTRACT

This paper documents information transfer for a sample of management forecasts issued in isolation. Subsamples of forecasts are identified based on a proxy for economic relations between forecasters and nonreleasers. The information transfer relation exists for the entire sample and for forecasters whose quarterly sales are highly associated with nonreleaser sales. Information transfer is not documented for lower sales associations. Within the high sales association groups, stronger results are observed for smaller forecasters. These results imply that 4-digit Standard Industrial Classification code co-membership is not sufficient to conclude that an information transfer relation exists between any two firms.

Advances in Accounting, Volume 8, pages 97-111.

ISBN: 1-55938-067-5

INTRODUCTION

In discussing the interdependencies of disclosure decisions, Benston [1979] identifies information externalities as a limitation of voluntary disclosures, noting that in the presence of externalities, "the resulting quantity and quality of disclosure need not be optimal" [pp. 1477, 1479]. Therefore, empirical evidence of externalities in voluntary reporting is useful to information producers and to individuals involved in regulating such disclosures. Foster [1981, p. 224] states that one form of empirical evidence that is relevant to this type of argument is identification of the "sub-set of logically possible information transfers that are empirically significant." Baginski [1987] examines intraindustry information transfers associated with voluntary disclosures of management earnings forecasts, and documents relations between the news conveyed by the forecasts and the unexpected share price reactions of certain firms.

The purpose of this study is to examine an additional issue related to documentation of information transfers associated with voluntary disclosure of management earnings forecasts. This issue relates to the identification of the subset of logically possible information transfers. Baginski [1987] documents the existence of information transfers for firms that are highly similar to the forecasting firm. The subset of firms for which the information transfer is documented is defined by statistical partitions of 4-digit SIC code industries into small homogeneous groups. This result does not, however, preclude the documentation of information transfer for a broader subset of firms. In addition, assuming that information transfer is lessened as the subset of firms expands, it is necessary to identify economic relations among firms that attenuate information transfer. This study identifies and examines the effects of these economic relations among firms on the documentation of information transfer at the 4-digit level. Information derived from quarterly sales is used to proxy the economic relations. This method of identifying firms with expected positive information transfer is simpler and more intuitive than the clustering approach used in Baginski [1987].

The results indicate the existence of information transfer at the 4-digit level for management forecasts issued in isolation. The results are strongest for the subset of forecasters whose changes in sales covary highly with nonreleasers' changes in sales. The information transfer relation does not exist for forecasters whose sales changes have a low association with nonreleasers' sales changes. Thus, the economic factors indicated by sales change association are determinants of the existence of information transfer.

Within the subset of forecasters for which sales change association is high, the stronger information transfer relation is documented for forecasts made by smaller firms. This inverse relation between firm size and security price reaction is consistent with results provided by Atiase [1985], Freeman [1987], and Ro [1984].

ATTENUATING FACTORS: BASIS FOR THE HYPOTHESES

Within a given industry, firms may be different in (1) structure for a given project (product) and (2) the projects (products) undertaken. Each of these differences may result in weak or negative associations of revenue changes across firms in the industry and reduce the likelihood that information releases that convey a change in cash flow expectations for one firm will result in a change in cash flow expectations for other firms.

With respect to the first type of difference, Flaherty [1980] examines structuring decisions for homogeneous goods industries. Flaherty shows that the only stable long-run industry structure involves firms with different market shares.[1] This movement from equal to different market shares implies less than perfect positive correlation of changes in sales even for homogeneous goods industries. It also raises the possibility of within-industry negative correlations of changes in sales across firms. In constant-sum game models of industrial organization, differences in firms' cost functions are often used to generate within industry output choices (and hence, sales changes) which are inversely related cross-sectionally.[2] The notion of a likely impact of weak or negative within-industry sales correlations on information transfer detection is not new. Foster [1981, pp. 202-203] suggests market share shifts of an information releaser as an attenuating factor in detecting directional information transfer.

The second difference across firms within industries is the choice of projects. In an attempt to diversify risk, new projects may be chosen with little or no revenue association with projects normally identified with the industry. To the extent that firms have obtained different diversification levels relative to each other, the detection of directional information transfer may be confounded. Foster [1981] presents some evidence for earnings releases that is consistent with this idea. Foster detected information transfer effects for homogeneous line-of-business firms more often than for SIC-code firms.

The correlation of changes in quarterly sales is used in this study as a summary measure of the structural relations of firms within an industry. This is consistent with the modeling of firm relations via reaction functions. In the industrial organization literature [see Friedman, 1977], reaction functions describe the change in output for one firm in the industry with respect to changes in output for another firm. As illustrated in Bresnahan [1982], specific assumptions about the relations among firms (cost structure, leader-follower relations, and so forth) determine the strength and direction of the slope of the reaction function. An empirical measure of this output relation among firms through time is the correlation of their changes in sales.[3] Low correlation of changes in sales is hypothesized as attenuating the information transfer relations.

The above arguments suggest rejection of the following null hypotheses for the full sample of firms and for the subsample of firms where forecasters and nonreleasers have the higher correlation of sales changes:

H_{01}: There is no relation between the *sign* of changes in earnings expectations conveyed by management earnings forecasts and the unexpected share price revisions of nonreleasing firms in the same 4-digit SIC code as the forecaster.

H_{02}: There is no relation between the *sign and magnitude* of changes in earnings expectations conveyed by management earnings forecasts and the unexpected share price revisions of nonreleasing firms in the same 4-digit SIC code as the forecaster.

Rejection in the positive direction is expected given positive sales change correlation. For the subsample with low correlation of changes in sales, the rejection of the null hypotheses in the positive direction is not expected because the economic relations among firms are not sufficiently strong.

Also, holding sales change correlation at a high level, research by Atiase [1980, 1985] suggests that firm size plays a role in the determination of security price reaction. Atiase argues that the amount of private predisclosure information production and dissemination is an increasing function of firm size and thus, other things being equal, that unexpected information is inversely related to firm size. In the context of information transfer, a larger forecaster having a high correlation of changes in sales with nonreleasers should convey less information than a smaller forecaster having a high sales change correlation with nonreleasers. Size would be expected to have little effect if the potential for information transfer is low already (low sales change correlation). **H_{01}** and **H_{02}** are tested for size partitions and partitions of the data based on combinations of sales change correlation and size.

FORECAST AND NONRELEASER SAMPLES

Management earnings forecasts for the 1974-1982 period were obtained by combining portions of two samples, both identified by reference to the *Wall Street Journal Index*. The final sample of 113 forecasts possessed the following attributes:

1. released within the first eleven months of the company's fiscal year;
2. attributed to a corporate official;
3. point or interval estimate;

Table 1. Distributions of Management Earnings Forecasts and Nonreleasing Firms

Distribution of Forecasts and Nonreleasers by Year

Year	*Forecasts*	*Nonreleasers*
1974	6	108
1975	22	138
1976	21	286
1977	18	103
1978	12	115
1979	7	45
1980	14	72
1981	6	58
1982	7	114
Total	113	1,039

Distribution of Forecasts by Firm

	Firms	*Forecasts*
Firms issuing one forecast	81	81
Firms issuing two forecasts	13	26
Firms issuing three or more forecasts	2	6
Total	96	113

4. issued in isolation (no earnings reports, dividends, or other significant announcements in a plus or minus one day period);
5. forecasting firm had sufficient data on *COMPUSTAT* Quarterly Tape for estimate of sales change correlation with industry (described later);
6. at least one nonreleasing firm in the forecasting firm's 4-digit SIC code had sufficient data on the *COMPUSTAT* Quarterly Tape for estimating sales change correlation with forecaster and sufficient data on the CRSP daily returns tapes for estimating unexpected returns (described later): and
7. at least one analyst forecast issued within a five-week period prior to the management forecast was reported in the Standard and Poor's *Earnings Forecaster* (for purposes of estimating the change in earnings expectations conveyed by the management forecast).[4]

With the exception of item 4, these sample filters correlate highly with extant management forecast and information transfer research. The requirement that forecasts be issued in isolation is added for two reasons. First, intra-industry information transfer has been documented for a number of other significant releases.[5] Second, Waymire [1984] documents a positive association between types of disclosure packages issued with management forecasts (e.g., good news) and signs of forecast deviation computed from the forecasts.

For each of the 113 forecasts, nonreleasers belonging to the same 4-digit *SIC* code during the forecast year were chosen. To estimate the sales change correlation variable, each nonreleaser had to have complete sales data on the *COMPUSTAT* quarterly tape. Table 1 provides the distribution of forecasts and nonreleasers by year and the distribution of forecasts across firms. The 113 forecasts and 1039 nonreleasers are well distributed in calendar time. Relatively few repeat forecasters entered the sample. Eighty-one of 96 firms issued only one forecast that was included in the final sample.

VARIABLE MEASUREMENT AND METHOD

Unexpected Returns

Standardized unexpected returns were estimated for each of the 1039 nonreleasing firms:

$$UR_{ik} = [R_{ik} - (\hat{\alpha}_i + \hat{\beta}_i R_{mk})] / \hat{\sigma}_e \quad (1)$$

where: UR_{ik} = standardized unexpected return for firm i on day k during the event period;

R_{ik} = return for firm i on day k during the event period;

R_{mk} = equally-weighted market return on day k during the event period;

$\hat{\alpha}_i$ = market model intercept for firm i estimated using Scholes-Williams [1977] adjustment;

$\hat{\beta}_i$ = market model beta for firm i estimated using Scholes-Williams adjustment;[6] and

$\hat{\sigma}_e$ = standard deviation of market model residuals over the estimation period.

Defining day zero as the date of the management forecast, the market model estimates were generated over days −215 to −16. UR_{ik} were computed from days −15 to +15. For certain tests, the UR_{ik} were summed over days −1 and 0 to capture the often documented one day lead reaction to events:

$$CUR_i = \sum_{k=-1}^{0} UR_{ik} \quad (2)$$

Han, Wild, and Ramesh [1989] construct an unexpected return metric by controlling for both market and industry effects. They motivate this procedure as a purge of the effects of intraindustry cross-sectional correlation of security prices from the measure of information transfer. They find evidence of positive information transfer associated with the sign of management forecast news before, but not after, subtracting the industry index.

The unexpected returns in this study are derived without controlling for the industry return. Such a control, by construction, removes any positive information transfer effect in the cases where the effect is most likely. Industry indices should be significant most often in homogeneous industries where information about unexpected earnings for one firm conveys information about similar changes in earnings expectations for other firms (information transfer). The information is reflected in the comovement of returns. If these returns are aggregated into an industry index and subtracted to remove commonalities in price movements, then any attempt to associate a given piece of earnings related information of one firm to the industry controlled security returns of another yields a finding of no relation. This occurs even though the releaser's earnings information is precisely what determines the movement in nonreleaser returns and hence, the cross-sectional correlation. Baginski [1987, section 6.3] provides evidence of firm releases as a major determinant of industry return covariability. Further, Han et al. [1989, p. 8] suggest that *if any* relation exists between a releaser's forecast news and market *and* industry controlled nonreleaser returns, then it is probably negative. These arguments suggest that controlling for industry returns is not valid in the context of this study since the interest is in factors that attenuate the entire information transfer relation among firms (the sum of positive and negative transfers).

Changes in Earnings Expectations

An accounting-based measure of changes in earnings expectations conveyed by a management earnings forecast was computed by comparing the forecast to an analyst forecast of earnings collected from the *Standard and Poor's Earnings Forecaster*. The most recent analyst forecast for each firm within a 5-week period preceding the management forecast was selected. An equally-weighted forecast was calculated if more than one analyst released on the same day. The change in expectations (CIEE) is as follows:

$$CIEE_i = (MF_i - AF_i) \,/\, AF_i \tag{3}$$

where: $CIEE_i$ = change in earnings expectations caused by the i'th forecast.
MF_i = the i'th management forecast of earnings, and
AF_i = the analyst forecast for the firm preceding the i'th forecast by management.

Given that the smallest denominator was \$.58, large values of $CIEE_i$ did not occur regularly in the sample, and thus, no truncation rule was employed.

There were no negative forecasts in the sample. In addition, the management and analyst forecasts were consistent as to whether they conveyed forecasts of primary or fully diluted earnings per share. The use of AF_i as a deflator is consistent with prior research into the information content of management forecasts, both in terms of information content to the releaser [Waymire, 1984] and information content to nonreleasers [Baginski, 1987; Han et al. 1989].

A security market-based metric (standardized unexpected return of the forecaster) is also available as a measure of changes in earnings expectations. The security market-based measure avoids the use of a specific earnings-based expectation model and is, ceteris paribus, a direct measure of the market's assessment of the discounted cash flow consequences of the forecast. A disadvantage of the measure is that it is, by definition, associated with other news events having cash flow implications for the firm. Thus, association of this measure with the unexpected price reaction of a nonreleasing industry co-member may occur absent a management forecast in the presence of other industry-level announcements. This measure is used extensively in the literature examining information transfer associated with earnings releases [Foster, 1981; Clinch and Sinclair, 1987].

To compute the accounting earnings-based measure, the management forecast is compared with a preceding analyst forecast to determine the sign and magnitude of the changes in earnings expectations conveyed by the forecast. This measure, used in studies dealing with the information transfer associated with management forecasts [Baginski, 1987; Pownall and Waymire, 1987], is not as likely to be associated with any other news event released during the period having cash flow implications for the firm. However, it requires a specific source of earnings expectations (financial analysts) and is not a direct measure of the discounted cash flow implications of the forecast.

Sales Association Measure and Size

As described earlier, the correlation of changes in forecaster sales (FS_i) and changes in nonreleaser sales (NRS_j) is used as a surrogate for the economic relations among firms. This correlation (RHO_i) is computed using 20 quarterly sales observations immediately preceding the forecast year:

$$RHO_i = \rho\,(FS_{it} - FS_{it-1}\,,\, NRS_{it} - NRS_{it-1}) \qquad (4)$$

There are 839 (200) positive (negative) values of RHO. This is consistent with the notion that industry demand shifts dominate market share shifts.

The size variable is computed as follows for each forecaster (i=1,...,113):

$$SIZE_i = \sum_{t=13}^{20} FS_{it}/8 \qquad (5)$$

Table 2. Descriptive Statistics

	Variable			
	SIZE	*RHO*	*CIEE*	*CUR*
Number of observations	113	1039	113	1039
Mean	334.519	.363	.0046	-.043
Median	185.060	.437	.0000	-.047
Standard deviation	466.344	.418	.1261	1.406
Maximum	3256.150	.988	.7750	5.536
Minimum	16.699	-.826	-.4736	-6.058

Notes: *SIZE* = Average quarterly sales over the eight quarters preceding the forecast year described in Equation (5) (in millions).

RHO = Correlation of changes in forecaster and nonreleaser quarterly sales over the 20 quarters preceding the forecast year described in Equation (4).

CIEE = Change in earnings expectations conveyed by the forecast as measured by the difference between management and preceding analyst forecast divided by the analyst forecast (Equation [3]).

CUR = Unexpected return for the two-day period beginning one day before the management forecast date calculated using the market model with the Scholes-Williams adjustment (Equation [2]).

where t = the last eight of the 20 quarters preceding the forecast year. The use of eight quarters should reduce the effects of seasonality in sales and the potential effect of an unusual year on the size measure.

Partitions of the sample based on *SIZE* and *RHO* are based on the median values of the variables. Table 2 provides descriptive statistics on each variable used in the study.

RESULTS

Table 3 presents the results of the binomial test of a sign relation between forecast news and nonreleaser security returns.[7] Under the null hypothesis for the binomial test, the sign of the change in earnings expectations conveyed by the management forecast (*CIEE*) is unassociated with the sign of the cumulative unexpected return of the nonreleaser (*CUR*). That is, the signs agree or disagree with equal probability.

The actual percentage of times sign agreement was observed ($\hat{P}_A$) and probability level for the binominal test are reported in the last two columns of the table for the full sample and various partitions. The sign null is not rejected for the full sample of 113 forecasters and 1039 nonreleasers ($\hat{P}_A$ = .513, p = .203).[8] When the sample is partitioned based on *RHO,* the null is rejected for the high sales correlation sample ($\hat{P}_A$ = .542, p = .026) but not for the low sales correlation sample ($\hat{P}_A$ = .484, p = .770). When the sample is partitioned by size, neither subsample percentage is significantly different from that expected under the null.

Table 3. Binomial Test of Information Transfer Related to Sign of News Conveyed by Management Earnings Forecasts

Null Hypothesis for Binomial Test (H_{01})

There is no relation between the *sign* of changes in earnings expectations conveyed by management earnings forecasts and the sign of unexpected returns of nonreleaing firms ($P_A = .50$).

Forecaster Characteristics	*Forecasts*[a]	*Nonreleasers*	$\hat{P}_A$[b]	P[c]
All Firms	113	1039	.513	.203
High Rho	84	520	.542	.026
Low Rho	98	519	.484	.770
Large Firms	57	408	.527	.138
Small Firms	56	631	.504	.421
High Rho				
Large Firms	45	229	.541	.104
Small Firms	39	291	.543	.071
Low Rho				
Large Firms	48	179	.508	.413
Small Firms	50	340	.471	.859

Notes: [a] When splitting the sample on "Rho" (the correlation of forecaster and nonreleaser changes in sales), it is possible for a forecaster to be represented in both the "High Rho" and "Low Rho" groups. This is caused by a forecaster having high correlations with some industry comembers and low correlations with others. Thus, the number of forecasts in any subsample based on a "Rho" partition will sum to more than 113.

[b] $\hat{P}_A$ = Sample proportion of nonreleasing firms' unexpected returns that have signs which agree with the sign of the news conveyed by the management forecast (*CIEE*)

[c] p = Significance level (one-tailed test).

The final two partitions in Table 3 examine the size effect with sales change correlation held constant. The highest $\hat{P}_A$ value is observed for smaller, high sales correlation forecasters ($\hat{P}_A = .543$, $p = .071$). However, a high value is also obtained for larger firms with high sales correlation ($\hat{P}_A = .541, p = .104$). Note that neither of the p-values are less than .05. Also, the null is not rejected for large or small firms when sales correlation is low ($\hat{P}_A = .508$ and $\hat{P}_A = .471$, respectively).

Although not reported in Table 3, the Kolmogorov-Smirnov (KS) test is performed for each subsample. This test examines the strength of the sign relation at days −1 and 0 vis-à-vis the other 30 days surrounding the forecast. To construct the KS statistic for the test, the sign of the changes in earnings expectations conveyed by the forecast (*CIEE*) is observed. If the sign is positive (negative) the unexpected returns (*UR*) of the nonreleasers for the 31 days in the test period are ranked from largest positive (negative) to largest negative

Table 4. Spearman Rank-Order Correlation Test of Information Transfer Related to the Sign and Magnitude of News Conveyed by Management Earnings Forecasts

Null Hypothesis for Spearman Test (H_{02})

There is no relation between the *sign and magnitude* of changes in earnings expectations conveyed by management forecasts of earnings and unexpected returns of nonreleasing firms ($r_s = 0$).

Forecaster Characteristics	*Forecasts*	*Nonreleasers*	$\hat{r}_s$	*p*
All Firms	113	1039	.079	.005
High Rho	84	520	.110	.005
Low Rho	98	519	.061	.083
Large Firms	57	408	.042	.201
Small Firms	56	631	.091	.011
High Rho				
Large Firms	45	229	.047	.242
Small Firms	39	291	.098	.047
Low Rho				
Large Firms	48	179	.014	.429
Small Firms	50	340	.074	.087

(positive). The distribution of the ranks is complied for the days −1 and 0 individually. Under the alternative hypothesis, the strongest positive sign relation with the changes in earnings expectations (a rank of one) occurs during the forecast holding period. Under the null, ranks of 1 through 31 occur with equal probability on days −1 and 0 individually.[9] The KS test is significant at the .05 level or better in only one case. For the "High Rho" subsample, the null is rejected at the .05 level at day zero. In summary, the sign hypothesis (H_{01}) is rejected only for the high sales correlation case. In the low sales correlation sample, the economic relations among firms attenuate the information transfer relation.

Table 4 presents evidence on the sign and magnitude hypothesis. The Spearman rank-order correlation is calculated for the full sample and each subsample. The correlations are between the ranks of the change in earnings expectations ($CIEE_i$) and the ranks of unexpected returns of nonreleasing firms (CUR_i) calculated in Equations (1) and (2).[10]

For the full sample, the Spearman rank correlation is positive, as hypothesized, and significantly different from zero ($r_s = .079, p < .005$). Thus, the sign and magnitude null hypothesis (H_{02}) is rejected. The partition based on *RHO* indicates a stronger and significantly positive correlation ($r_s = .110$,

$p < .005$) for the high sales change correlation group. For the low sales correlation group, the correlation is weaker and insignificantly different from zero ($r_s = .061, p < .083$) at the .05 level.

Smaller forecasters appear to be associated with the stronger information transfer effect ($r_s = .091$, $p < .011$). Larger firms have an insignificant information transfer effect ($r_s = .041$, $p < .201$). Also, when examining the consequences of size and sales change correlation together, only the high RHO, small firm group has a significant Spearman correlation at the .05 level ($r_s = .098$).

In summary, Tables 3 and 4 document information transfer except where economic relations among firms attenuate the relation (low sales relations). Also, the information transfer relation appears stronger for smaller forecasters. Only the more powerful sign and magnitude test (in which no information is ignored) is able to reject the null for the full sample.

LIMITATIONS AND IMPLICATIONS FOR FUTURE RESEARCH

A significant internal/external validity trade-off is made in this study. To investigate the information transfer effects of management forecasts alone, only forecasts issued in isolation are included in the sample. Thus, the ability to generalize these results to other time periods and populations is lessened. Also, given the significant data requirements for each firm (e.g., complete quarterly sales series, and analyst following), smaller firms, newer firms, or firms traded in smaller markets may be underrepresented in the sample.

Sales change correlation is chosen as the proxy for the economic characteristics of heterogeneous cost functions and relative diversification. This proxy is sufficient to identify information transfer attenuation. This does not preclude the identification of other, more discriminating economic factors and proxies based on other economic arguments. In addition, the discriminating power of this proxy must be interpreted with respect to the voluntary nature of management forecasts. It is possible that firms not issuing forecasts may bear different economic relations with firms in their industry.

The primary implication of this study's results for future information transfer research is that documentation of intraindustry information transfer appears to be a function of the economic differences between the releaser and nonreleaser within industries. Thus, the assumption that all firms within 4-digit *SIC* codes are sufficiently homogenenous to infer an information transfer relation may lead to weak tests of the null hypothesis. Specifically, nonreleasers similar to the releaser may need to be identified to maximize the probability of rejecting the null. This study fails to reject the null for low sales association subsamples. Also, the stronger results for small forecasters implies that dominant (large) firm partitions of the data may not yield stronger results in the absence of a high sales change correlation between releasers and nonreleasers.

ACKNOWLEDGMENT

Comments received from participants at The Florida State University Colloquium and from anonymous referees are gratefully acknowledged.

NOTES

1. Firms in the model face initial symmetric conditions (except for possibly different marginal costs at time zero). They choose their cost structure by undertaking cost reducing investment. The result of the model is an equilibrium path on which all firms' outputs (which are not equal) and investments do not change.

2. See Friedman [1977] for a review of these models, and Bresnahan [1982] for an example of the zero-sum game in the context of a duopoly.

3. There are other ways of measuring the factors that drive sales change correlation. For example, direct measures of diversification are possible. Berry [1971] and McVey [1972] derive a measure of diversification using the weighting system of the Herfindahl Summary Index of Concentration [see Adelman, 1969]. Other measurements include the number of nonprimary industries in which an enterprise operates, the ratio of nonprimary to total output, and combinations of the two [Gort, 1962]. Gorecki [1974] discusses problems associated with each of these measures. Barnea and Logue [1973] propose another measure of diversification based on the market model. Amihud and Lev [1981] use this measure to proxy corporate diversification. The problem with all of the aforementioned methods is that they do not measure the diversification of one firm relative to another, and more importantly, the effect of that relative diversification on information transfer.

4. Portions of this sample have been used by Baginski [1987], Beshara [1981], and Ajinkya and Gift [1984]. Each observation meets the sample criteria listed. In addition, certain of the observations may meet slightly more restrictive criteria. An example is the requirement that analysts have issued a forecast within five weeks prior to the management forecast. Observations taken from the Ajinkya and Gift sample have a three week requirement. This should have little effect on the results since the studies listed above report consistent results.

5. Aside from the studies that have documented information transfers for earnings releases [Foster, 1981; Firth, 1976; Clinch and Sinclair, 1987], information transfers for a variety of other significant announcements have been documented. These include Bowen, Castanias, and Daley [1983] and Hill and Schneeweis [1983] (news of a nuclear accident); Eckbo [1983] and Stillman [1983] (horizontal merger announcements); and Boim [1977] (the announcement of a dividend omission).

6. Use of this method is justified by the potential for nonsynchronous trading [Scholes and Williams, 1977].

7. Nonparametric tests were chosen due to the tenuous assumption of normality for daily stock return data required for parametric tests.

8. All statistical tests are one-tailed given the hypothesized directional alternative of positive association of forecast news and nonreleaser returns.

9. The *KS* test is run for -1 and 0 individually given the usual uncertainty about the exact date of the forecast release.

10. This is similar in spirit to the parametric regressions on individual firms run in Han et al. [1989].

REFERENCES

Adelman, M., "Comment on the H Concentration Measure as a Numbers Equivalent," *The Review of Economics and Statistics* [1969], pp. 99-101.

Ajinkya, B. and M. Gift, "Corporate Managers' Earnings Forecasts and Symmetrical Adjustments of Market Expectations," *Journal of Accounting Research* [Autumn 1984], pp. 425-444.

Amihud, Y. and B. Lev, "Risk Reduction as a Managerial Motive for Conglomerate Mergers," *Bell Journal of Economics* [Autumn 1981], pp. 605-617.

Atiase, R., 'Predisclosure Information Asymmetries, Firm Capitalization, Financial Reports, and Security Price Behavior," Ph.D. dissertation [University of California, Berkeley, 1980].

———, "Predisclosure Information, Firm Capitalization, and Security Price Behavior Around Earnings Announcements," *Journal of Accounting Research* [Spring 1985], pp. 21-36.

Baginski, S., "Intra-Industry Information Transfers Associated with Management Forecasts of Earnings," *Journal of Accounting Research* [Autumn 1987], pp. 196-216.

Barnea, A. and D. Logue, "Stock-market Based Measures of Corporate Diversification," *Journal of Industrial Economics* [September 1973], pp. 51-60.

Benston, G., "Required Periodic Disclosure Under the Securities Act and the Proposed Federal Securities Code," *University of Miami Law Review* [September 1979], pp. 1471-1484.

Berry, C., "Corporate Growth and Diversification," *Journal of Law and Economics* [1971], pp. 371-383.

Beshara, R., "Newness and Imputed Accuracy of Management Forecasts: An Empirical Investigation," Ph.D. dissertation [University of Florida, 1981].

Boim, N., "The Effects of Consolidated Edison's 1974 Divident Omission upon the Common Stock Returns of the Utilities Industry," *The Chicago MBA* [Spring 1977], pp. 85-117.

Bowen, R., R. Castanias, and L. Daley, "Intra-Industry Effects of the Accident at Three Mile Island," *Journal of Financial and Quantitative Analysis* [March 1983], pp. 87-111.

Bresnahan, T., "Duopoly Models with Consistent Conjectures," *American Economic Review* [1982], pp. 934-945.

Clinch, G. and N. Sinclair," Intra-Industry Information Releases: A Recursive Systems Approach," *Journal of Accounting and Economics* [April 1987], pp. 89-106.

Eckbo, B., "Horizontal Mergers, Collusion, and Shareholder Wealth," *Journal of Financial Economics* [1983], pp. 241-273.

Firth, M., "The Impact of Earnings Announcements on the Share Price Behavior of Similar Type Firms," *Economic Journal* [June 1975], pp. 296-306.

Flaherty, M., "Industry Structure and Cost-Reducing Investment," *Econometrica* [July 1980], pp. 1187-1209.

Foster, G., "Intra-Industry Information Transfers Associated with Earnings Releases," *Journal of Accounting and Economics* [December 1981], pp. 201-232.

Freeman, R., "The Association Between Accounting Earnings and Security Returns for Large and Small Firms," *Journal of Accounting and Economics* [July 1987], pp. 195-228.

Friedman, J., *Oligopoly and The Theory of Games* [North-Holland, 1977].

Gorecki, P., "The Measurement of Enterprise Diversification," *The Review of Economics and Statistics* [August 1974], pp. 399-401.

Gort, M., *Diversification and Integration in American Industry* [Princeton University Press, 1962].

Han, J., J. Wild, and K. Ramesh, "Managers' Earnings Forecasts and Intra-Industry Information Transfers," *Journal of Accounting and Economics* [February 1989], pp. 3-34.

Hill, J. and T. Schneeweis,"The Effect of Three Mile Island on Electric Utility Stock Prices: A Note," *Journal of Finance* [September 1983], pp. 1285-1292.

McVey, J., "The Industrial Diversification of Multiestablishment Firms,," *Canadian Statistical Review* [1972], pp. 4, 6, 112-117.

Pownall, G. and G. Waymire, "Information Transfer Via Earnings Disclosure: Hypotheses and Tests," Working paper [Washington University, 1987].

Ro, B.T., "Firm Size and the Information Content of Annual Earnings Announcements," Working paper [Purdue University, March 1984].

Scholes, M. and J. Williams, "Estimating Betas From Nonsynchronous Data," *Journal of Financial Economics* [1977], pp. 309-328.

Stillman, R., "Examining Antitrust Policy Toward Horizontal Mergers," *Journal of Financial Economics* [1983], pp. 225-240.

Waymire, G., "Additional Evidence on the Information Content of Management Earnings Forecasts," *Journal of Accounting Research* [Autumn 1984], pp. 703-718.

THE DEBT EQUIVALENCY OF UNFUNDED ACCUMULATED AND PROJECTED PENSION OBLIGATIONS

V. Gopalakrishnan and Timothy F. Sugrue

ABSTRACT

This study examines the debt equivalency of three measures of unfunded pension liabilities of a firm: (1) vested, (2) accumulated, and (3) projected, using the model proposed by Hamada and extended by Dhaliwal relating the systematic risk of a firm to its operating risk, financial risk and the effective tax rate. Evidence on the debt equivalency of these three measures of pension obligations can provide valuable input into the accounting policy-making process on pensions. *SFAS 87* on pension accounting calls for the recognition of a minimum pension liability on the balance sheet of a firm, when accumulated benefit obligation exceeds the fair value of plan assets. If market participants regard the unfunded projected pension liability similar to debt, then it is justifiable to recognize and report pension liability based on the projected liability measure. The results indicate that market participants treat the above three measures of unfunded pension liabilities as similar to debt in assessing the systematic risk of a firm.

Advances in Accounting, Volume 8, pages 113-129.

ISBN: 1-55938-067-5

INTRODUCTION

The issue of accounting for pension liabilities has received detailed attention in the academic literature. Recently, the Financial Accounting Standards Board (FASB) issued *SFAS 87,* "Employers' Accounting for Pensions," mandating some radical changes in accounting for pensions. Among other things, the standard requires the disclosure of a minimum liability on the face of the balance sheet itself when accumulated benefit obligations exceed the "fair value" of plan assets.[1] Accumulated benefit obligation is the actuarial present value of benefits accrued to date based on current salary levels. On the other hand, projected benefit obligation is the actuarial present value of benefits accrued to date based on future salary levels. In a nonpay-related or flat-benefit pension plan, the projected and the accumulated benefit obligations are the same. The issue of whether unfunded pension liabilities are the liabilities of the employer has not been fully resolved. Dhaliwal [1986] posits that if unfunded vested pension liabilities of a firm constitute a liability, one would expect market participants in an efficient capital market to treat pension liabilities in the same manner as debt in determining the market value and the market-perceived risk of the firm. Bulow, Morck, and Summers [1987] suggest that if investors treat pension liabilities differently from other forms of debt in valuing firms, then managers should recognize these differences and modify their pension funding decisions accordingly. Using cross-sectional valuation models, a number of empirical studies examined the market valuation of unfunded pension liabilities [see Oldfield, 1977; Feldstein and Seligman, 1981; Feldstein and Morck, 1983; Bulow et al., 1987].[2] Dhaliwal [1986] examined the debt equivalency of unfunded vested pension liabilities using a model developed by Hamada [1972] which relates the systematic risk of a firm to its financial risk and business risk (operating risk). Specifically, he examined the effect of unfunded vested pension liabilities on the systematic risk of the firm and concluded that market participants treat unfunded vested pension liabilities as similar to debt in assessing the firm's systematic risk. This paper attempts an important extension of Dhaliwal's work by including three forms of pension liabilities: (1) unfunded vested liabilities, (2) unfunded accumulated liabilities (both unfunded vested and unfunded unvested), and (3) unfunded projected liabilities.

ACCUMULATED VERSUS PROJECTED LIABILITY

Two definitions of pension obligations are frequently discussed in the financial press and academic literature: accumulated and projected liabilities. Accumulated liability is essentially a "shutdown" liability in the sense that it represents a hypothetical plan termination calculation. On the other hand, projected liability represents the actuarial present value of benefits payable to current plan participants taking into account the future service and earnings of the plan participants. In other words, projected liabilities are future based whereas the accumulated liabilities are solely based on past experience.

Kotlikoff and Smith [1983] argue that for ongoing plans, projected benefit obligations represent implicit, if not legal claims, on the employer. The concept of projected liability is consistent with the implicit contractual arrangements between employers and workers that link future service to future pension compensation. They posit that if the employer is committed to a long-term level of worker compensation, then it is the projected not the accumulated liability that represents a claim on the employer's nonpension assets and future profits.

Only a few studies have attempted to estimate the projected liabilities and empirically evaluate their significance over accumulated liabilities. Selling and Stickney [1986] examined the time series correlations between three measures of the unfunded pension liability and an economic measure of a firm's pension obligation using computer simulated data. The results indicate that the unfunded projected benefit obligation is more highly correlated with the economic measure than the unfunded accumulated benefit obligation.

The issue of debt equivalency of the unfunded projected liability is of particular interest because of its implications for accounting standard setting. *SFAS 87* [FASB, 1985, para. 40] requires that the amount of pension expense to be reported on the income statement be based on the projected liability concept. The standard also calls for the disclosure of the amount of projected liability in addition to the accumulated liability and the vested liability in the footnotes to the financial statements [FASB, 1985, para. 54]. However, for the purpose of determining the "minimum" pension liability to be reported on the balance sheet, firms need to consider only the accumulated benefit obligation rather than the projected benefit obligation. Prior to issuing *SFAS 87,* FASB issued *Preliminary Views* [FASB 1982] which called for the recognition of a net pension liability or an asset based on the difference between the projected benefit liability and the fair value of plan assets. The financial community in general was bitterly opposed to the Preliminary Views and finally the FASB backed off its views on the liability recognition issue when the Exposure Draft was issued in 1985. For instance, some respondents to the Preliminary Views objected to the recognition of any liability based on estimates of future compensation levels because of the uncertainties inherent in predicting future interest rates and salary levels [FASB, 1985, para. 99-100). Lorensen and Rosenfield [1983] posit that a firm does not have pension liabilities to employees before the employee's benefits vest and strongly rejected the projected liability measure of pension liability. However, FASB concluded that the projected benefit obligation provides a more realistic measure of the employer's obligations on a going concern basis [para. 149] and this view is shared by some corporate pension plan sponsors.[3] If market participants regard the unfunded projected pension liability as similar to debt in assessing the firm's systematic risk, then it is justifiable to recognize and report unfunded pension liability based on the projected liability measure. This paper attempts to empirically examine the debt equivalency of the unfunded accumulated liability and the unfunded projected liability.

The remainder of this paper is organized as follows. First, the model developed by Dhaliwal [1986] is presented, followed by a discussion of the procedure used to derive the projected benefit liability. Second, the models are described, the hypotheses are developed, and the sample selection procedures are discussed. Third, the results are reported and analyzed, followed by the summary, conclusions, and limitations of the study.

DEBT EQUIVALENCY OF UNFUNDED VESTED PENSION LIABILITIES

Based on the work of Hamada [1972], Dhaliwal [1986, p. 654] proposed the following model to examine whether unfunded vested pension liabilities are considered as equivalent to debt.

$$\beta_i = b_0 + b_1\beta_{ai} + b_2\beta_{ai}(1-t_i)(D/E)_i + b_3\beta_{ai}(1-t_i)(\Delta D/E)_i + e_i \tag{1}$$

where:

β_i = systematic risk for firm i

β_{ai} = accounting beta for firm i

$(D/E)_i$ = debt to equity ratio for firm i

$(\Delta D/E)_i = (D/E)_{ai} - (D/E)_i$ and

$$(D/E)_{ai} = \frac{D_i + (1 - t_i)\text{ (Unfunded vested pension liabilities)}}{E_i - (1 - t_i)\text{ (Unfunded vested pension liabilities)}}$$

In the above model, accounting beta was used as a surrogate for the operating risk for firm i. The unfunded vested pension liabilities were multiplied by $(1 - t_i)$ to determine the after-tax debt equivalence of a firm's unfunded vested pension obligations. Dhaliwal hypothesized that if the market participants regard unfunded vested pension liabilities as a form of debt then the coefficient b_3 should be statistically significant and positive. The second hypothesis was that if the unfunded vested pension liabilties affect the market-perceived risk in the same manner as debt and other liabilities, then $b_3 = b_2$. His estimates of Equation (1) are given below (t-statistics in parentheses).[4]

$$\beta_i = \underset{(4.13)}{0.891} + \underset{(1.77)}{0.160}\,\beta_{ai} + \underset{(1.86)}{0.241}\,\beta_{ai}(1 - t_i)(D/E)_i + \underset{(1.91)}{0.227}\,\beta_{ai}(1 - t_i)(\Delta D/E)_i$$

($N = 55$ observations, adjusted $R^2 = 0.24$)

The coefficient b_3 is statistically significant and is positive. Based on the above results, Dhaliwal [1986, p. 658] concluded that the market participants regard the unfunded pension liabilities as a form of debt. He did not reject the second null hypothesis $b_3 = b_2$ and concluded that the market participants treat unfunded vested pension liabilities as similar to debt and other liabilities in assessing the systematic risk of a firm.

ESTIMATION OF PROJECTED LIABILITIES

Currently there are no published data available on the projected liabilities of corporations. *SFAS 87* calls for the disclosure of the projected liability beginning 1987. Kotlikoff and Smith [1983] report that the ratio of projected to vested liabilities ranges from 1.77 to 2.70 for governmental pension plans for the year 1980. This study makes use of the following exponential adjustment procedure developed by Ippolito [1986a,b] in estimating the projected liabilities for the years 1980 through 1983. This procedure was also used by Francis and Reiter [1987].

$$PBO_A = (ABO)(0.85)e^{(-0.077)(\text{economic rate}-\text{reported rate})}$$

$$PBO_R = (ABO)(0.15)e^{(-0.057)(\text{economic rate}-\text{reported rate})}$$

where: PBO_A = Projected benefit obligations for actives
PBO_R = Projected benefit obligations for retirees
ABO = Accumulated benefit obligations

Economic rate is the post-retirement discount rate and reported rate is the rate used in determining the present value of the accumluated benefit obligations.[5] The sum of PBO_A and PBO_R represents the total projected benefit obligations of a firm. Ippolito [1986b] and Francis and Reiter [1987] assume that the ratio of active to total particpants is 85% and that there is homogeneity across firms in the expected growth of future wages. We incorporate the above two assumptions in estimating the projected pension liabilities.

MODEL DEVELOPMENT, HYPOTHESES, AND SAMPLE SELECTION

Following the model developed by Dhaliwal [1986], the following three models were run to examine the debt equivalency of unfunded pension liabilities.

Models

Model (1)

$$\beta_i = b_0 + b_1\beta_{ai} + b_2\beta_{ai}(1-t_i)(DEBT_i) + b_3\beta_{ai}(1-t_i)(\Delta DEUVL_i) + e_i \quad (2)$$

Table 1. Definition and Measurement of Variables

1. Systematic risk (β_i) was estimated from the market model using daily returns for January 1979 through December 1983. Daily returns were obtained from the CRSP tapes.
2. Accounting beta was used as a surrogate for operating risk. Accounting beta (β_{ai}) was estimated by regressing the accounting return (AR_{it}) for firm i in period t, on the accounting return for the market portfolio (AR_{mt}). The AR was defined as income before interest and tax expense over total assets at the beginning of the year. Both AR_i and AR_m (S&P 400) were measured over the period of 20 years (1967 through 1986). This measure of accounting beta is identical to the one used by Dhaliwal [1986].
3. Effective tax rate (t) is total tax expenses divided by pretax income and is averaged over the years 1980 through 1983. This definition of tax rate is identical to t_2 used by Dhaliwal. Dhliwal used three measures of tax rates: t_1 was income tax expense (excluding changes in deferred taxes) over pretax income; t_2 was total tax expense over pretax income and t_3 was the marginal tax rate equal to the maximum federal tax rate. We believe that total tax expense over pretax income is the appropriate measure of tax rate for our study. We reject the marginal tax rate for the reason it ignores the cross-sectional differences (due to state taxes for example) in tax rates across firms. A comparison of the effective tax rates obtained from the 10-K reports (measure t_1) with the tax rates calculated using measure t_2 shows that they were very similar for most of the firms. However, regression analyses were performed using all the three measures of tax rates and results indicate that all the variables in Models (1) through (6) were significant. There were no significant differences in the coefficients obtained based on the three tax rates. The results of the regression analysis presented in Tables 3, 4, 6, and 7 are based on the definition t_2 (total tax expense/pretax income). Note 9 reports the estimates of the coefficients obtained based on the definition t_1.
4. $DEBT$ is the firm's average debt to equity ratio.
5. $DEUVL$ is the firm's average debt to equity ratio adjusted for unfunded vested pension liability. This ratio is calculated as follows:

$$(D + (1-t)(UVL)) \,/\, (E - (1-t)(UVL))$$

where D = book value of debt; E = market value of equity; t = effective tax rate; and UVL = unfunded vested pension liability defined as the excess of vested benefits over net assets available for benefits.

6. $$\Delta DEUVL = (DEUVL) - (DEBT)$$

7. $DEUAL$ is the firm's debt to equity ratio adjusted for unfunded accumulated pension liability. This ratio is calculated as follows:

$$(D + (1-t)(UAL)) \,/\, (E - (1-t)(UAL))$$

where UAL = unfunded accumulated pension liability defined as the excess of accumulated benefits over net assets available for benefits.

8. $$\Delta DEUAL = (DEUAL) - (DEBT)$$

9. $DEUPL$ is the firm's debt to equity ratio adjusted for unfunded projected pension liability. This ratio is calculated as follows:

$$(D + (1-t)(UPL)) \,/\, (E - (1-t)(UPL))$$

where UPL = unfunded projected pension liability defined as the excess of projected pension liability over the assets available for benefits.

10. $$\Delta DEUPL = (DEUPL) - (DEBT)$$

11. Standard deviation of the Price/Earnings ratio ($PERSD$) was used as a second surrogate for the firm's operating risk. $PERSD$ was calculated using annual data over the period 1974 through 1983.

Model (1) is similar to the Equation (1) presented earlier. The definition and measurement of variables *DEBT* and *DEUVL* and other variables used in this study are described in Table 1.

Dhaliwal did not adjust for the cross-sectional differences in the interest rate assumptions across firms. Feldstein and Morck [1983, p. 201] indicate that the choice of the interest rate can have a powerful effect on the value of vested benefits. We standardize actuarial interest rates in order to facilitate cross-sectional comparisons.[6] As reported in Table 1, *DEBT* is the debt to equity ratio for firm i and *DEUVL* is the debt to equity ratio adjusted for the unfunded vested pension liability. *DEUVL* is identical to (D/E_a) described earlier.[7] Dhaliwal's sample of 55 firms included only firms with 'material' unfunded vested pension liability during the years 1976 through 1979. In other words, he looked at firms which had an average adjusted debt to equity ratio $(D/E)_a$ of at least 110% of the average debt to equity ratio. We adopted a similar approach in designing the study and focused on firms with a (*DEUVL*)/(*DEBT*) ratio of 1.10 are greater. Model (1) was run to examine the stability of the coefficients reported by Dhaliwal [1986].

Model (2)

$$\beta_1 = b_0 + b_1\beta_{ai} + b_2\beta_{ai}(1-t_i)(DEBT_i) + b_3\beta_{ai}(1-t_i)(\Delta DEUAL_i) + e_i \quad (3)$$

Model (2) is similar to Model (1) except for the third independent variable. In Model (1), *DEUVL* represents the average debt to equity ratio adjusted for unfunded vested pension liability. In Model (2), *DEUAL* represents the average debt to equity ratio adjusted for both unfunded vested and unfunded unvested pension liabilities (i.e., unfunded accumulated pension liability).

Model (3)

$$\beta_i = b_0 + b_1\beta_{ai} + b_2\beta_{ai}(1-t_i)(DEBT_i) + b_3\beta_{ai}(1-t_i)(\Delta DEUPL_i) + e_i \quad (4)$$

DEUPL is the average debt to equity ratio for firm i adjusted for the unfunded projected pension liability estimated using the exponential procedure developed by Ippolito [1986b]. The definition of the unfunded projected pension liability is described in Table 1.

Hypotheses

The principal research question examined in this study focuses on the debt equivalency of the three measures of a firm's unfunded pension liabilities. The following two hypotheses will be tested to examine the debt equivalency issue of unfunded pension liabilities.

Table 2. Industry Membership

Two Digit SIC	*Type of Industry*	*Number of Firms*
10	Mining	1
17	Construction	1
20	Food	3
21	Tobacco	1
22	Textile	1
23	Apparel	2
26	Paper	1
27	Printing & Publishing	1
28	Chemicals	4
30	Rubber & Plastics	4
32	Glass	3
33	Steel	7
34	Hardware	5
35	Machinery	7
36	Electrical & Electronics	7
37	Motor Vehicles	4
38	Machinery	2
39	Precious Metals	1
40	Railroad	1
47	Transportation	1
48	Telecommunications	1
51	Groceries	1
53	Retail (department stores)	1
62	Security & Commodity services	1
73	Data processing services	2
	Total	63

H$_o$: 1. The market participants do not regard the three measures of unfunded pension liabilities (unfunded vested, unfunded accumulated and unfunded projected) of a firm as forms of debt in assessing the systematic risk of a firm.

If the market participants regard these three measures of pension liabilities as forms of debt, in assessing the systematic risk of a firm, then the coefficient b_3 in Models (1), (2), and (3) should be > 0 and statistically significant.

H$_o$: 2. The market participants do regard unfunded vested, unfunded accumulated and unfunded projected pension liabilities as similar to debt in assessing the systematic risk of a firm.

A rejection of **H$_o$**: 2 would mean that the above three measures of pension liabilities do not affect the systematic risk of a firm in the same manner as debt in Models (1), (2), and (3).

Table 3. Descriptive Statistics
(Number of Observations = 63)

Variable	*Mean*	*Standard Deviation*	*Range*
Beta	0.62	0.34	0.17- 2.78
OPERISK	0.97	0.77	0.34- 4.37
DEBT	0.94	0.86	0.10- 5.50
DEBTUVL	1.14	1.08	0.18- 7.93
DEBTUAL	1.32	1.22	0.27-11.44
DEBTUPL	1.89	1.94	0.48-37.50
PERSD	2.14	1.61	0.53- 7.63
TAX RATE	0.35	0.22	0.17- 0.59

Sample Selection

The years 1980 through 1983 were chosen as the time period for this study. The sample of firms included in this study were chosen subject to the following conditions: (1) the average debt to equity ratio adjusted for unfunded vested pension liabilities (*DEUVL*) should be at least 110% of the unadjusted debt to equity ratio (*DEBT*); (2) the firms should have been listed on the COMPUSTAT (Industrial) tape; (3) data on income before interest and tax expense and total assets should have been available for the years 1967 through 1986; (4) the firms should also be on the CRSP (daily version) tape over the period January 1979 through December 1983. This process resulted in a sample of 63 firms. The industry classification of these firms is presented in Table 2. The data on pension related information such as vested benefits accumulated, nonvested benefits, net assets available for benefits and interest rate assumptions were obtained from the footnotes to the annual reports. Information pertaining to the effective tax rates were also obtained from annual reports and 10-K reports. Some basic descriptive statistics about the sample are presented in Table 3.

RESULTS

Results of the regression analysis using Models (1), (2), and (3) are presented in Table 4. The estimates of Equation (1) obtained by Dhaliwal [1986] are also presented for the sake of comparison. The estimates of Model (1) in general are consistent with the estimates obtained by Dhaliwal. The adjusted R^2 values for the three models range from 57% to 59% which are considerably higher than the R^2 values reported by Dhaliwal.[8] In all the three models, the sign of the coefficient b_3 is positive as predicted and the coefficient is statistically significant. These results suggest that the market participants treat the three

Table 4. Results of Regression Analysis (Systematic Risk is the Dependent Variable and Accounting Beta is the Surrogate For Operating Risk)

	b_0	b_1	b_2	b_3	Adj. R^2	N	F Ratio
Expected sign	+	+	+	+			
Dhaliwal's Model	0.891	0.160	0.241	0.227	0.24	55	N/A
	(4.13)	(1.77)	(1.86)	(1.91)			
Model (1)	0.208	0.422	0.268	0.471	0.57	63	28.40
t-ratio	(3.76)	(6.59)	(2.82)	(2.39)			
Prob >	(.0004)	(.0001)	(.0064)	(.0197)			(0.0001)
Model (2)	0.210	.413	0.233	0.496	0.59	63	30.91
t-ratio	(3.92)	(6.62)	(2.47)	(3.02)			
Prob >	(.0002)	(.0001)	(.0161)	(.0037)			(0.0001)
Model (3)	0.214	0.407	0.250	0.150	0.58	63	30.36
t-ratio	(3.98)	(6.49)	(2.68)	(2.89)			
Prob >	(.0002)	(.0001)	(.0093)	(.0053)			(0.0001)

Table 5. Debt Equivalency of Unfunded Pension Liabilities (Systematic Risk is the Dependent Variable and Accounting Beta is the Surrogate For Operating Risk)

Model	Null Hypothesis	F Ratio	$p > F$
(1)	Unfunded vested pension liability is similar to debt		
	$b_3 = b_2$	0.642	0.43
(2)	Unfunded accumulated pension liability is similar to debt		
	$b_3 = b_2$	1.368	0.25
(3)	Unfunded projected pension liability is similar to debt		
	$b_2 = b_2$	0.639	0.43

measures of unfunded pension liabilities (unfunded vested, unfunded accumulated and unfunded projected) as forms of debt in assessing the systematic risk of a firm.[9]

Table 5 presents the results of the second hypothesis which deals with the debt equivalency of the three measures of unfunded pension liabilities (i.e.,

Table 6. Correlation Matrix of Independent Variables in Models (1), (2), and (3)

Model (1)

	β_{ai}	$\beta_{ai}(1-t)\,(DEBT)$	$\beta_{ai}(1-t)\,(\Delta DEBTUVL)$
β_{ai}	1	0.243	0.081
$(\beta_{ai})\,(1-t)\,(DEBT)$		1	0.439
$(\beta_{ai})\,(1-t)\,(\Delta DEBTUVL)$			1

Model 2

	β_{ai}	$\beta_{ai}(1-t)\,(DEBT)$	$\beta_{ai}(1-t)\,(\Delta DEBTUAL)$
β_{ai}	1	0.243	0.138
$(\beta_{ai})\,(1-t)\,(DEBT)$		1	0.483
$(\beta_{ai})\,(1-t)\,(\Delta DEBTUAL)$			1

Model 3

	β_{ai}	$\beta_{ai}(1-t)\,(DEBT)$	$\beta_{ai}(1-t)\,(\Delta DEBTUPL)$
β_{ai}	1	0.243	0.157
$(\beta_{ai})\,(1-t)\,(DEBT)$		1	0.454
$(\beta_{ai})\,(1-t)\,(\Delta DEBTUPL)$			1

$b_3 = b_2$). The results indicate that the null hypothesis $b_3 = b_2$ could not be rejected at the 10% level for all three models. In other words, the market participants do regard unfunded vested, unfunded accumulated and unfunded project pension liabilities as similar to debt and other liabilities of a firm in assessing the systematic risk of a firm. Our findings are consistent with Dhaliwal [1986, p. 658] with reference to Model (1). Our findings have important implications for the accounting policy making on pensions. In other words, if the market participants regard unfunded projected pension liability as similar to debt, then this may justify the mandated disclosure of a firm's unfunded projected pension liability. However, our study does not resolve the issue of whether unfunded projected pension liability should be disclosed in the footnotes to the financial statements or within the balance sheet itself.

The problem of multicollinearity is unavoidable in this study due to the functional nature of the models examined. In all the three models, at least two independent variables are related. An examination of the correlation matrices presented in Table 6 reveals no serious problem of illconditioning.[10]

ADDITONAL ANALYSIS

In Models (1), (2), and (3), accounting beta was used as a surrogate for operating risk. Bowman [1979, p. 619] implies that if accounting earnings

Table 7. Results of Regression Analysis (Systematic Risk is the Dependent Variable and *PERSD* is the Surrogate For Operating Risk)

	b_0	b_1	b_2	b_3	Adj. R^2	N	F Ratio
Expected sign	+	+	+	+			
Model (4)	0.437	0.037	0.081	0.167	0.36	63	12.68
t-ratio	(9.11)	(1.87)	(2.16)	(1.88)			
Prob >	(.0001)	(.0659)	(.0349)	(.0644)			(0.0001)
Model (5)	0.434	0.042	0.073	0.179	0.31	63	10.61
t-ratio	(7.91)	(2.11)	(1.76)	(2.04)			
Prob >	(.0001)	(.0390)	(.0838)	(.0458)			(0.0001)
Model (6)	0.426	0.049	0.073	0.052	0.33	63	11.18
t-ratio	(7.70)	(2.52)	(1.80)	(1.94)			
Prob >	(.0001)	(.0145)	(.0770)	(.0577)			(0.0001)

captured economic income, then there is a direct theoretical relationship between systematic risk and accounting beta. In the event, accounting earnings fail to capture economic income, one may argue that there is no theoretical link between systematic risk and accounting beta.

Farrelly, Ferris, and Reichenstein [1985] investigated the issue of whether financial reports appear to convey, information on risk. They used earnings variability as a surrogate for operating risk. Earnings variability was the standard deviation of the price-earnings ratio, measured over a period of five years. We performed regression analysis on Models (1), (2), and (3) using standard deviation of the price-earnings ratio (*PERSD*) as a second surrogate for operating risk. The advantage of *PERSD* over accounting beta is that it is not entirely based on accounting data. Results of our analysis are presented in Table 7. Models (4), (5), and (6) correspond to Models (1), (2), and (3).

The coefficient b_3 is positive and significant in all the three models and these results support our earlier findings that the market participants regard unfunded vested, unfunded accumulated and unfunded projected pension liabilities as forms of debt. Results of the test on the second hypothesis $b_3 = b_3$ in Models (4), (5), and (6) are presented in Table 8. Once again, these results are consistent with the earlier findings that the market participants regard unfunded vested, unfunded accumulated and unfunded projected pension liabilities as similar to debt and other liabilities of a firm in assessing the systematic risk of a firm. An examination of the correlation matrices reported in Table 9 reveals no serious problem of multicollinearity.

Table 8. Debt Equivalency of Unfunded Pension Liabilities (Systematic Risk is the Dependent Variable and *PERSD* is the Surrogate For Operating Risk)

Model	*Null Hypothesis*	*F Ratio*	$p > F$
(4)	Unfunded vested pension liability is similar to debt		
	$b_3 = b_2$	0.548	0.46
(5)	Unfunded accumulated pension liability is similar to debt		
	$b_3 = b_2$	0.808	0.37
(6)	Unfunded projected pension liability is similar to debt		
	$b_3 = b_2$	0.125	0.73

Table 9. Correlation Matrix of Independent Variables in Models (4), (5), and (6)

Model (4)

	PERSD	*PERSD*(1−*t*) (*DEBT*)	*PERSD*(1−*t*) (Δ*DEBTUVL*)
PERSD	1	0.384	0.302
(*PERSD*)(1−*t*) (*DEBT*)		1	0.673
(*PERSD*) (1−*t*) (Δ*DEBTUVL*)			1

Model 5

	PERSD	*PERSD*(1−*t*) (*DEBT*)	*PERSD*(1−*t*) (Δ*DEBTUAL*)
PERSD	1	0.384	0.291
(*PERSD*) (1−*t*) (*DEBT*)		1	0.638
(*PERSD*) (1−*t*) (Δ*DEBTUAL*)			1

Model 6

	PERSD	*PERSD*(1−*t*) (*DEBT*)	*PERSD*(1−*t*) (Δ*DEBTUPL*)
PERSD	1	0.384	0.287
(*PERSD*) (1−*t*) (*DEBT*)		1	0.631
(*PERSD*) (1−*t*) (Δ*DEBTUPL*)			1

SUMMARY AND CONCLUSIONS

This study examined the debt equivalency of three measures of unfunded pension liabilities of a firm: (1) vested, (2) accumulated, and (3) projected. Evidence on the debt equivalency of these three measures of pension obligations can provide valuable input into the accounting policy making process on pensions. For example, if the market participants treat unfunded projected pension liability as similar to debt and other liabilities of a firm, then its disclosure in the balance sheet may be justified.

Based on a model proposed by Hamada [1972] and extended by Dhaliwal [1986] which relates the systematic risk of a firm to its operating risk, financial risk, and the tax rate, it was found that the market participants treat the above three measures of unfunded pension liabilities as forms of debt in assessing the systematic risk of a firm. The results also indicate that the market participants regard unfunded vested, unfunded accumulated and unfunded projected pension liabilities as similar to debt in assessing the systematic risk of a firm. Our results are consistent with the findings of Dhaliwal [1986].

However, two caveats are in order. First, is the use of accounting beta as a surrogate for operating risk. Bowman [1979] indicates that systematic risk is theoretically related to accounting beta under certain assumptions. For instance, Bowman assumes that accounting earnings capture economic income and firms can borrow and lend at the risk-free interest rate. The results of this study are subject to the validity of these assumptions. We also used a second surrogate for operating risk in our analysis. Farrelly, Ferris, and Reichenstein [1985] used the standard deviation of the price-earnings ratio (*PERSD*] as a surrogate for operating risk. The results obtained using *PERSD* are fully consistent with the findings based on accounting beta.

Second, there is possible measurement error associated with the estimation of projected benefit obligations. These obligations are estimated using the exponential procedure developed by Ippolito [1986b] and also used by Francis and Reiter [1987]. It is assumed that the ratio of active to total participants is 85% and there is homogeneity across firms in the expected growth of future wages. The adoption of these two assumptions may restrict the external validity of our findings. A follow-up study could use the actual (published) projected pension liability information over a period of four years to see how it compares with the study based on estimated projected pension liability.

ACKNOWLEDGMENTS

An earlier version of this paper was presented at the American Accounting Association's annual meeting held at Orlando in 1988. The authors thank all the participants for their helpful suggestions. The authors are grateful to two anonymous reviewers for their helpful comments and suggestions on an earlier draft of the paper. Helpful assistance from James Williams of Arthur Young (Washington, D.C.) is also appreciated.

NOTES

1. The terms "obligations" and "liabilities" are used interchangeably in this paper.

2. However, these studies did not examine the debt equivalency issue of unfunded vested pension liabilities nor the market valuation of unfunded projected pension liabilities.

3. For instance, the footnotes to the 1985 financial statements of Philadelphia Electric Company indicate that in the opinion of the company a comparison of the actuarial present value of accumulated plan benefits with the net assets available for benefits could be misleading. The firm emphasizes that its pension plan is of a long-term nature and is funded on a basis consistent with this concept. In other words, the firm implies that the concept of projected liability is more indicative of the firm's pension obligations than the accumulated liability.

4. Dhaliwal used the following three measures of tax rates: (1) income tax expense (excluding changes in deferred taxes) over pretax income; (2) total tax expense over pretax income; and (3) marginal tax rate equal to the maximum federal tax rate. Dhaliwal's estimates are reported for the model based on tax measure No. (2). The measure of the tax rate used in this study is identical to No. (2) above.

5. Consistent with the assumptions of Ippolito [1986b] and Francis and Reiter [1987], economic rates are 1% for actives and 1.5% plus 50% of inflation for retirees. For 1980, the Moody's average new bond issue rate was 12.46%. Assuming this reflects a real interest rate of 1.5%, the expected inflation component equals 10.96% (12.46% − 1.5%). Therefore, the economic rate used for retirees equals 6.98% (1.5% + 50% of inflation) for 1980. For 1981 through 1983 the Moody's average new bond issue rates are 14.17%, 14.23%, and 12.20% respectively. Therefore, the economic rates used for retirees are 7.835%, 7.865%, and 6.85% respectively.

6. The accumulated benefits are standardized by multiplying the reported benefits with the ratio of the actual interest rate assumption to a standardized rate. This procedure is consistent with Francis [1987]. The mean interest rate of the sample was used as the standardized rate. The mean interest rates were 7.02%, 7.45%, 7.72%, and 7.76% respectively for the years 1980 through 1983. We also performed regression analysis without adjusting for the cross-sectional differences in the interest rate assumptions. In all the six models, the coefficient b_3 was positive and significant and did not significantly differ from the estimates reported in Tables 4 and 7.

7. For the purposes of this study, the debt to equity ratio was calculated using the book value of debt and market value of equity (see table 1) as in the case of Dhaliwal [1986, p. 657]. Mulford [1985, p. 898] asserts that the above hybrid debt to equity ratio constitutes an empirical expedient to the market-based debt to equity ratio developed by Hamada [1972]. He reports a near perfect association (0.993) between debt to equity ratio based on book value of debt and market value of equity and debt to equity ratio based on market value of debt and market value of equity.

8. Dhaliwal's R^2 values range from 20% to 27%.

9. We also performed regression analysis using Dhaliwal's definition of t_1 for the tax rate (income tax expense excluding changes in deferred taxes over pretax income). The results obtained did not significantly differ from the results reported in Table 4. The estimated coefficients are presented as:

Model	b_0	b_1	b_2	b_3	*Adj. R^2*	*F-Ratio*
(1)	0.207 (3.74)	0.428 (6.59)	0.261 (2.74)	0.462 (2.35)	0.57	28.21 (0.0001)
(2)	0.210 (3.89)	0.418 (6.62)	0.227 (2.40)	0.488 (2.97)	0.59	30.68 (0.0001)
(3)	0.214 (3.96)	0.413 (6.49)	0.243 (2.60)	0.148 (2.86)	0.58	30.18 (0.0001)

10. Belsley, Kuh, and Welsch [1980] suggest that the impact of illconditioning is serious when the square of the condition index exceeds 50. The highest condition index for the models (1), (2), and (3) were respectively, 4.86, 4.91, and 4.89. The eigenvalues for the three models are given as:

Number	Model (1)	Model (2)	Model (3)
1	2.86	2.92	2.90
2	0.69	0.65	0.66
3	0.31	0.30	0.32
4	0.12	0.12	0.15

REFERENCES

Belsley, D.A., E. Kuh, and R.E. Welsch, *Regression Diagnostics: Identifying Influential Data and Sources of Collinearity* [Wiley, 1980].

Bowman, R.G., "The Theoretical Relationship Between Systematic Risk and Financial (Accounting) Variables," *Journal of Finance* [June 1979], p. 617-630.

Bulow, J.I., R. Morck, and L. Summers, "How Does the Market Value Unfunded Pension Liabilities?" in *Issues in Pension Economics,* edited by Z. Bodie, J.B. Shoven, and D.A. Wise [University of Chicago Press, 1987].

Dhaliwal, D., "Measurement of Financial Leverage in the Presence of Unfunded Pension Obligations," *The Accounting Review* [October 1986], pp. 651-661.

Farrelly, G.E., K.R. Ferris, and W.R. Reichenstein, "Perceived Risk, Market Risk, and Accounting-Determined Risk Measures," *The Accounting Review* [April 1985], pp. 278-288.

Financial Accounting Standards Board, *Preliminary Views on Major Issues Related to Employers' Accounting for Pensions and other Postemployment Benefits* [FASB, November 1982].

———, *Statement of Financial Accounting Standard No. 87,* "Employers' Accounting for Pensions" [FASB, 1985].

Feldstein, M. and R. Morck, "Pension Funding Decisions, Interest Rate Assumptions and Share Prices," in *Financial Aspects of the United States Pension System,* edited by Z. Bodie and J.B. Shoven [University of Chicago Press, 1983].

Feldstein, M. and S. Seligman, "Pension Funding, Share Prices and National Savings," *Journal of Finance* [September 1981], pp. 801-824.

Francis, J.R., "Lobbying Against Proposed Accounting Standards: The Case of Employers' Pension Accounting," *Journal of Accounting and Public Policy* [June 1987], pp. 35-57.

Francis, J.R. and S.A. Reiter, "Determinants of Corporate Pension Funding Strategy," *Journal of Accounting and Economics* [March 1987], pp. 35-59.

Hamada, R.S., "The Effect of the Firm's Capital Structure on the Systematic Risk of Common Stocks," *Journal of Finance* [May 1972], pp. 435-452.

Ippolito, R.A., "The Economic Burden of Corporate Pension Liabilities," *Financial Analysts Journal* [January-February 1986a], pp. 22-34.

________, *Pensions, Economics and Public Policy* [Dow Jones Irwin, 1986b].

Kotlifoff, L. and D. Smith (eds.), *Pensions and the American Economy* [University of Chicago Press, 1983].

Lorensen, L., and P. Rosenfield, "Vested Benefits—A Company's Only Pension Liability," *Journal of Accountancy* [October 1983], pp. 64-76.

Mulford, C.W., "The Importance of a Market Value Measurement of Debt in Leverage Ratios: A Replication and Extensions," *Journal of Accounting Research* [Autumn 1985], pp. 897-906.

Oldfield, G.S., "Financial Aspects of the Private Pension System," *Journal of Money, Credit and Banking* [February 1977], pp. 48-54.

Selling, T.I. and C.P. Stickney," Accounting Measures of Unfunded Pension Liabilities and the Expected Present Value of Future Pension Cash Flows," *Journal of Accounting and Public Policy* [Winter 1986], pp. 267-285.

PART II

EDUCATION

ADDITIONAL EMPIRICAL EVIDENCE ON THE RELATIONSHIP BETWEEN EXAM QUESTION SEQUENCING AND ACCOUNTING STUDENT PERFORMANCE

David E. Stout and Donald E. Wygal

ABSTRACT

This paper extends previous investigations that explored the relationship between accounting student examination scores and sequencing of questions. Three instructors from a medium-sized private college collected data from each of three semester (i.e., interim) exams in a "Principles of Financial Accounting" course. For each exam, two versions (differing only in the way multiple-choice questions were sequenced) were administered randomly to the classes: the first version ordered questions in the same sequence as material had been covered in class; the second version used a reverse sequencing order. After controlling for preexisting differences in general intelligence levels, the experimental treatment (test-item sequencing) was found to have had little impact on student exam

Advances in Accounting, Volume 8, pages 133-152.

ISBN: 1-55938-067-5

scores. Analysis of a second set of data from *comprehensive* final exams administered by three different instructors provided only slight evidence of a test-item sequencing effect on such exams. Implications of these findings to accounting educators in light of previously-published results are discussed.

Many accounting professors use multiple-choice questions for examination purposes. This is due partly to the relatively large number of students taught and the perceived grading efficiencies brought about by this testing strategy. To achieve control, some professors give different versions of the same exam to a class where the exams differ solely by how a common set of questions is sequenced.

Recent empirical evidence [Baldwin and Howard, 1983; Gruber, 1987], suggests that the intertopical sequencing of multiple-choice type questions may have an impact on examination (i.e., performance) scores. That is, student scores may be at least partially a function of the order in which questions appear on the exam. Questions can be arranged, for example, in the same order as topics are covered in class, in a reverse order compared to topical coverage in class, or in a random order. If, indeed, a sequencing effect exists, then an important implication arises: Should a student's grade be allowed to be affected by a noncontrollable factor such as how questions on examinations were sequenced?

The purpose of this paper is to provide additional experimental evidence on the relationship between multiple-choice exam question sequencing and accounting student performance scores.

PRIOR RESEARCH

Howe and Baldwin [1983], using a large sample of introductory accounting students ($N = 414$), investigated the impact of different sequencing arrangements based on test-item difficulty. On the basis of four in-class exams over the course of a semester, they found "no evidence to support the contention that question sequencing affected exam performance" [p. 135].

Attention has been focused also on the effect of test-item sequencing relative to topic presentation of material in class. Baldwin and Howard [1983] examined the impact of two sequencing strategies (ordered versus random) on student scores on a comprehensive multiple-choice final exam. Both introductory accounting students ($N = 83$) and students in a basic tax course ($N = 84$) were used in their study. They found that a sequencing effect occurred in both courses. Students who received questions that were arranged on the exam in the same order as topics were covered in class scored significantly better than students who received a version of the same exam in which questions were randomly-ordered. Additionally, the sequencing effect was not constant across "quality of student" subgroups: "better" students were found to be more adversely affected by the randomized version of the exam than either the "average" or "below average" student subgroups.

In contrast, Gruber [1987] used students ($N = 216$) in a managerial accounting course to determine whether sequencing pattern (ordered, reverse-ordered, or randomly-ordered) affected scores on a 50-item comprehensive (multiple-choice) final exam. All students were nonaccounting majors. Experimental results showed that test item sequencing pattern did affect student scores on the exam. Interestingly, students receiving the exam version where questions were reverse-ordered relative to in-class topic coverage performed the best out of the three groups. Gruber interprets this as supportive of a "recency effect." Students who received questions ordered in the same sequence as topics were covered in class did the worst while students who received a randomly-ordered version did, on average, somewhere in between. No differential effect of the experimental treatment across "high," "medium," and "low" student quality subgroups was uncovered.

These results have important implications for educators. From both an equity and a psychometric standpoint, an important characteristic of test instruments is that they be free from bias. Bias would exist, for example, if student exam scores are affected by version of exam received—something beyond the control of the student. The above studies are important, therefore, because they suggest the possibility of such test-instrument bias in multiple-choice exams where exam versions differ only in the way items making up the exams are sequenced.

THE PRESENT STUDY

The present study attempts to add to our knowledge in this area by providing additional empirical evidence of the relationship between test item sequencing and student exam scores. The importance of this type of research was underscored recently by the president of the American Accounting Association in his presidential address [Beaver, 1987, p. 4]:

> our knowledge of education research ... and its potential implications for accounting is embarrassingly limited. For example, it is painfully obvious that we know little about the effects of the form of testing on the teaching of accounting.

The present research adds to our knowledge on the one hand through replication of earlier studies. Its value in this regard has long been recognized by scholars. Katz [1953, p. 64], for example, states that "the history of social psychology literature illustrates the importance of the replication of findings in that many of its initial results have not been confirmed by later investigation." Replication, of course, provides evidence about the generalizability of previously reported results. As Runkel and McGrath [1972, p. 46] state:

> If, in an initial study, we obtain a substantial and interesting finding within an internally valid experiment, ...our finding cannot have any practical influences on the wider world until the first study is followed by other studies which explore the range of treatment, measurements, and actors over which the obtained results will hold.

Apart from the above, the research question under investigation is a timely one. Given the proliferation of microcomputer test banks that can easily generate multiple exam versions, the possibility exists that such devices will enjoy widespread use.[1] Virtually every major introductory accounting textbook has a microcomputer test bank. In addition, Fuglister and Murdock [1988] report on software they developed that allows instructors "to easily create multiple forms of an exam." This software is available at a nominal charge to accounting educators. To the extent that accounting educators use these test-generating facilities, the results of this line of research take on added importance to the profession.

Furthermore, the issue under investigation is an important one from an equity standpoint. Such a concern, in fact, was underscored recently by Benke and Hermanson [1988]. The existence of a sequencing effect implies bias. A student's exam score and, by extension, course grade should not be influenced by an extraneous factor such as the sequence in which exam questions are presented. If, in fact, initial evidence concerning the existence of this bias is confirmed upon replication and extension to other experimental settings, the continued use of a testing strategy based on intertopical sequencing of questions can be seriously questioned.

Finally, the need for additional research in this area would seem to be especially warranted given the somewhat contradictory results reported in previous studies and because of the types of exams employed in those studies. Previous studies dealing with test-item sequencing relative to topic presentation in class have used student scores on a comprehensive final exam as the dependent variable. While Baldwin and Howard [1983] concluded that students performed significantly better on ordered (as compared to randomly-sequenced) exams, Gruber [1987] found that students performed better on reverse-ordered exams in his study. Gruber suggested that his results relate to the "recency" of material covered. That is, students will gain confidence, and therefore, test-taking efficiencies, by answering questions pertaining to material covered most recently in class. Such material, it is posited, would be subejct to the most immediate and complete recall. Yet to be explored, however, is the effect of intertopical sequencing of questions on *interim* exams—those covering a shorter period rather than an entire semester. In such a case, it can be hypothesized that all material is "recent" so that no test item sequencing effect would exist. The present study, similar to Howe and Baldwin [1983], examines the impact of item sequencing on a set of shorter exams administered during the semester.

RESEARCH METHOD

Principal differences between the present study and previous studies are presented in Table 1. The null hypothesis tested in all these studies can be stated as follows:

> **H_0:** The sequencing of examination questions has no significant effect on accounting student scores on multiple-choice exams.

Three instructors, each teaching "Principles of Financial Accounting" (a sophomore-level course required of all business students), participated in the experiment. Class meeting times, number of sections and class sizes are given in Table 2.

Four class sections (100 students) were involved. Because the four sections met at different times of the day, generalizability of the research results is enhanced. These class meeting times are a representative sample of class times and days at the institution at which data were collected. Each of the three instructors taught from the same textbook (*Principles of Financial and Managerial Accounting* [Warren and Fess, 1986], covered the same material over the course of the semester, and taught in the normal manner.

Students took a total of three exams, two during the term and a noncumulative final exam. Each exam included a number of multiple-choice questions followed by a separate section of exercises and/or short problems. Thus, the present study differs from previous studies in that the exams do not consist wholly of multiple-choice questions. Such a testing strategy is reflective of what many accounting educators do in actual practice. That is, while instructors may be opposed to giving tests composed solely of multiple-choice questions, far fewer would likely be opposed to using a selection of multiple-choice questions in combination with exercises, short problems, and/or essay questions.[2]

For purposes of this study, then, the dependent variable was defined as student scores on the multiple-choice portion of the exam. Exam questions were drawn from the Computerized Test Bank that accompanies the text used in the course. For control purposes, each instructor generated a different version of the exam although each version covered the same amount of material—both in terms of number of chapters covered and with respect to the relative emphasis given to each chapter. (It was not possible to bring

Table 1. Research Design Summaries

	Howe and Baldwin [*1983*]	*Baldwin and Howard* [*1983*]	*Gruber* [*1987*]	*Stout and Wygal* (*Present Study*) [1990]
1. Sample	Introductory Accounting	Introductory Accounting & Taxation	Managerial Accounting	Principles of Financial Accounting
2. Sample Size	414	167	216	220
3. Design	One-Factor ANCOVA	Three-Factor ANOVA	Two-Factor ANOVA	Two-Factor ANCOVA
4. Dependent Variable	4 Separate Exam Scores	Comprehensive Final Exam Scores	Comprehensive Final Exam Scores	3 Separate Exam Scores and Comprehensive Final Exam Scores
5. Principal Finding	No Sequencing Effect Due to Item Difficulty	Effect Based on Intertopical Sequencing of Questions Found	Effect Based on Intertopical Sequencing of Questions Found	No Effect Based on Intertopical Sequencing of Questions Found

Table 2. Sample Size and Class Meeting Times by Instructor

Instructor	*Sample Size*	*Class Meeting Time*
A	27	9:10 a.m. - 10:10 a.m. M-W-F
B	24	11:30 a.m. - 12:30 p.m. M-W-F
	14	2:55 p.m. - 4:25 p.m. M-W
C	35	1:10 p.m. - 2:40 p.m. M-W

students together to administer common exams.) The multiple-choice section of the first exam consisted of 20 questions whereas 24 multiple-choice questions were on the second exam and 28 were on the final exam. This was done consciously for sensitivity analysis purposes. A basic hypothesis of this research is that the "recency effect" detected in previous empirical studies may be diminished, or nonexistent, when exams covering short periods of time, and consisting of fewer questions, are involved. Inclusion of varying numbers of questions permits an assessment of whether this is an important moderating variable in the model.

The experimental treatment consisted of two different test-item sequencing patterns. In Pattern 1, the multiple-choice questions were ordered in the same sequence as material was covered in the course.[3] In Pattern 2, the multiple-choice questions were reverse-ordered relative to the sequence in which material was covered in the course.[4] Each instructor administered the two versions randomly to students taking the exam. This procedure was thought to be reflective of what accounting instructors would actually do in practice.[5]

Obviously, variables other than the experimental treatment could possibly explain variance in student exam scores. Therefore, before the effect of the treatment is assessed, it is necessary to control, statistically, for the effect of these other explanatory variables. Eskew and Faley [1988], for example, found that aptitude, effort, and prior exposure to accounting (high school bookkeeping/accounting) were significant explanatory variables in a study of grade differences for introductory accounting students. Of the three variables, ability (as measured by SAT scores) was found to have the largest explanatory power. Evidence by Eckel and Johnson [1983] also points to the importance of SAT scores (and scores on other standardized instruments such as ACT) in explaining accounting student performance differences.

Other recent investigations [for example, Ingram and Petersen, 1987; Vruwink and Otto, 1987; Buehlmann and Techavichit, 1984] have used student cumulative grade point average (GPA) as a measure of aptitude in attempting to explain accounting grade differences. These studies all provide evidence in support of including GPA in a model predicting differences in student exam scores.

Thus, in order to reduce experimental error, both SAT scores and student GPAs were treated as covariates in the present research.[6] Because part of the present sample consisted of transfer students (who had little basis for establishing a GPA), the inclusion of SAT scores was thought to be particularly appropriate.

In addition to student ability variables, existing research has suggested the importance of prior exposure to accounting in explaining differences in introductory accounting test scores. Eskew and Faley [1988] and Smith [1968], for example, found that high school exposure to bookkeeping positively influences performance in college elementary accounting. Schroeder [1986], on the other hand, found that only students with more than one year of precollege study had a comparative advantage in the first college-level course. Jacoby [1975] and Baldwin and Howe [1982] found that the beneficial impact of a precollege course existed but only in the early stages of the first college course. Thus, there seems to be sufficient justification for including a "prior exposure to accounting" factor in the model.[7] The inclusion of this blocking factor in the model is intended to control for differences between treatment and control groups not otherwise captured and accounted for by the student ability variables.[8]

Thus, the initial design used to test the null hypothesis was a two-factor analysis of covariance (ANCOVA) with student GPAs and SAT scores serving as covariates in the model. The active (manipulated) factor in the model was the experimental treatment while prior exposure to accounting was the assigned (blocking) factor. A randomized blocks design was employed as students within each level of the blocking factor were assigned randomly to the experimental treatment.

RESULTS

Blocking Factor Effect

The blocking factor is included in the model in order to eliminate (i.e., "block out") the noise affecting the comparison of treatment groups because of student prior exposure to accounting. Significance tests of this factor were conducted; the results of such tests are reported in Table 3. As can be seen, the blocking factor was found to have no significant effect across all instructors and exams. Thus, it was eliminated from the model.[9] The final model used to test the research hypothesis, therefore, was a one-factor ANCOVA design.

Table 3. Covariate-Adjusted Mean Scores of Blocking Factor Categories (Prior Exposure to Accounting) and Significance Test Results of Blocking Factor by Instructor and Exam*

		Adjusted Mean Exam Scores		*Blocking Effect*	
Instructor	*Exam*	*Prior Exposure Group*	*No Prior Exposure*	*F*	*P*
A	1	14.71	14.71	0.01	.94
	2	15.07	16.07	0.10	.76
	3	19.05	21.45	0.01	.97
B	1	13.78	13.40	0.04	.84
	2	15.34	14.43	1.08	.31
	3	16.90	15.68	1.37	.25
C	1	16.11	14.73	2.51	.12
	2	17.04	16.11	0.90	.35
	3	18.41	18.10	0.02	.88

Note: * Results are derived using GPA as the covariate. However, similar results were obtained when the other covariate (SAT score) was used in the analysis—either alone or in conjunction with GPA. In all cases, the hierarchical variance decomposition method was used. That is, the effect of the covariate(s) was (were) assessed first to estalish statistical control. The effect of the blocking factor was then assessed.

Student Background Information

Background information relating to students who participated in the experiment is presented in Table 4. This information is provided to facilitate interpretation and generalizability of the primary test results. For example, in the present sample, approximately 56% of the students worked (mostly part-time); the average cumulative GPA (on a 4-point scale) was 2.54; the average total SAT score was 934; and, the average Quantitative SAT score was 501. It is not known, therefore, whether and to what extent the present findings can be generalized to other student populations.[10]

The data reported in Table 4 are also interesting in that they point to the importance of achieving statistical control through the use of covariates in the model. Even though random assignment of students to experimental groups was made, significant differences in the mean values of variables affecting exam scores can occur—especially given the sample sizes involved in the present experiment. It is necessary to control for these differences in the analysis before the effect of the experimental treatment is assessed.

Table 4. Student Background Data by Instructor and Section

	Background Data (Means)			
	GPA	*SAT-TOT*	*SAT-QUANT*	*Working (%)*
Instructor A				
Exam 1				
Ordered	2.40	984	542	58
Reverse-ordered	2.51	942	500	40
Exam 2				
Ordered	2.46	965	550	44
Reverse-ordered	2.44	966	497	56
Exam 3				
Ordered	2.64	998	549	44
Reverse-ordered	2.34	946	505	56
Overall Mean	2.45	965	524	50
Instructor B				
Exam 1				
Ordered	2.64	963	517	73
Reverse-ordered	2.64	908	488	47
Exam 2				
Ordered	2.66	977	516	64
Reverse-ordered	2.55	910	490	69
Exam 3				
Ordered	2.60	939	500	54
Reverse-ordered	2.63	947	505	62
Overall Mean	2.64	937	503	66
Instructor C				
Exam 1				
Ordered	2.42	875	461	41
Reverse-ordered	2.58	944	513	53
Exam 2				
Ordered	2.57	930	502	50
Reverse-ordered	2.47	872	460	42
Exam 3				
Ordered	2.58	899	479	38
Reverse-ordered	2.45	903	484	58
Overall Mean	2.50	908	486	47

Primary Statistical Tests

Table 5 presents unadjusted and covariate-adjusted mean exam scores by instructor and exam number. Such scores, and the resulting differences in scores between groups, should be interpreted on the basis of number of questions on each exam. Relative to the number of questions on each exam,

Table 5. Unadjusted and Covariate-Adjusted Mean Exam Scores by Instructor and Exam

		Ordered Group		*Reverse-Ordered Group*	
Instructor	*Exam*	*Unadjusted*	*Adjusted*	*Unadjusted*	*Adjusted*
A	1	14.50	14.40	15.02	15.05
	2	14.57	14.97	16.50	16.10
	3	19.50	19.20	20.71	20.95
B	1	12.61	12.62	14.74	14.73
	2	15.00	14.80	14.73	14.89
	3	15.96	16.02	16.59	16.52
C	1	15.15	15.11	14.89	14.94
	2	17.41	17.06	15.82	16.01
	3	18.24	18.17	17.82	17.89

Table 6. ANCOVA Results by Instructor and Exam (Dependent Variable = Exam Score)

	Exam 1		*Exam 2*		*Exam 3*	
Source of Variation	*F*	*P*	*F*	*P*	*F*	*P*
Instructor A						
Covariate(s)	6.58	.005	5.30	.030	2.71	.114
Ordering Effect	.73	.401	.80	.381	2.58	.122
Total Explained	17.12	.011	3.05	.065	2.64	.093
Instructor B						
Covariate(s)	15.61	.000	13.56	.001	13.86	.001
Ordering Effect	10.72	.002	.01	.920	.24	.624
Total Explained	13.21	.000	6.68	.003	7.05	.002
Instructor C						
Covariate(s)	4.95	.013	4.06	.048	5.38	.010
Ordering Effect	.05	.824	1.65	.208	.04	.838
Total Explained	3.32	.031	2.69	.093	3.60	.025

the mean percentage difference between the groups was 3.70% with a high of 10.6% (Instructor B, Exam 1) to a low of 0.4% (Instructor B, Exam 2).

Tests of significance on the data presented in Table 5 are shown in Table 6.[11] The results indicate a significant test item sequencing effect only in one out of the nine cases, namely, in Exam 1 for Instructor B. In this particular case, the reverse-ordered group scored significantly better than the ordered group. Overall, the data in Table 6 indicate a failure to reject the null hypothesis: after controlling for the effect of the covariate(s), the experimental treatment

Table 7. Experimental Results: Comprehensive Exams

A. Student Background Data

Instructor	Treatment	Class Means			
		GPA	*SAT-TOTAL*	*SAT-QUANT*	*Working (%)*
D	Ordered	2.54	895	474	60
	Reverse-Ordered	2.80	844	450	56
E	Ordered	2.44	873	476	50
	Reverse-Ordered	2.62	896	464	51
F	Ordered	2.59	959	515	50
	Reverse-Ordered	2.62	889	475	51

B. Blocking Factor Test Results

Instructor	Adjusted Mean Exam Scores		Blocking Effect*	
	Prior Exposure Group	*No Prior Exposure*	*F*	*P*
D	21.08	21.42	0.01	.98
E	19.28	20.45	1.71	.20
F	21.84	20.69	0.02	.92

C. Experimental Treatment Test Results

Instructor	Covariate-Adjusted Mean Scores		Treatment Effect	
	Ordered	*Reverse-Ordered*	*F*	*P*
D	22.21	20.30	3.81	.057
E	20.47	19.67	0.71	.408
F	21.86	21.70	0.02	.901

Note: * Prior exposure to accounting.

was found to have little effect on student exam scores. In addition, the explanatory power of the model predicting student exam scores was found to be high (as measured by *F*-tests on the total explained sums of squares).

Data from Comprehensive Exams

These results suggest the possibility that the sequencing effect observed in previous studies focused on introductory accounting students may be diminished when interim exams covering shorter periods of time (smaller amount of material) are involved. To provide more direct evidence concerning this issue, it was decided in a subsequent semester to collect a second set of data from *comprehensive* final exams administered by three different instructors. Each instructor included a selection of multiple-choice questions on the final exam (in addition to a section of exercises or short problems) arranged either in an ordered or reverse-ordered fashion. Instructors D and F included a total of 36 multiple-choice questions while instructor E included a total of 28. Sample size was 52 (two classes combined) for instructor D, 31 for instructor E, and 37 for instructor F. The percentage of correct responses to these questions served as the dependent variable in the analysis.

Results are presented in Table 7. Panel A presents student background information by instructor and type of treatment received. Panel B presents results of testing for the blocking factor effect while Panel C presents primary test results. After controlling for preexisting differences in student ability, there is little evidence ($p = .05$) that test-item sequencing affected exam scores.

DISCUSSION

Previous empirical investigations, using comprehensive multiple-choice exams, have pointed to a test-item sequencing effect—a bias that results as an unintended consequence of the testing process. Such results are extremely important to educators, particularly given the established practice of using multiple versions of exams and the rise in availability of computer-activated test banks.

The present study has exmained the effect of test-item sequencing for exams administered throughout the term and for comprehensive finals. In contrast to some earlier studies, no biasing effect is found. Importantly, the result of no sequencing effect in the present study is found to be independent of (1) the professor teaching the course, (2) the time of day in which the course was offered, (3) the particular set of questions constituting the exam for each instructor, and (4) the number of multiple-choice questions covered on each exam.

One implication of the findings pertains to interim exams. A "recency effect" has been posited as a reason why bias is associated with sequencing on comprehensive exams. However, when exams are administered during the course of the term, the recency effect is unnoticed, perhaps because all material on the exam is relatively recent. It is possible, therefore, that in order for a recency effect to be manifested, the amount of coverage in the exam would have to be sufficiently large.

The evidence shown herein is consistent with results reported by Howe and Baldwin [1983]. Their study found no sequencing effect on interim period exams based on test-item difficulty. The collective results suggest that a test-item sequencing strategy can be used in an unbiased fashion to achieve control over the testing process when only three or four weeks' worth of material is covered on the exam.

At the same time, the present findings call attention to previous studies of test-item sequencing. The comprehensive exam results presented here show no significant relationship between sequencing (ordered or reverse-ordered) and student exam scores. These findings, therefore, are contrary to the Baldwin and Howard [1983] and Gruber [1987] studies.

Before attempting to explain the current results, however, it is useful to examine more closely certain specific aspects of earlier research. Studies of sequencing have examined either the order of topical presentation (as does the present study) or test-item difficulty. Both types of sequencing study can provide useful insights for assessing present results and for identifying areas of future study.

In terms of topical presentation, Baldwin and Howard [1983] studied two types of sequencing: ordered (earliest to latest) and random ("scrambled"). Gruber [1987] studied three sequencing versions: ordered, reverse-ordered, and random. Baldwin and Howard found that students taking the ordered version of the exam scored significantly higher than did students taking the random version. Gruber, on the other hand, found that exam scores were significantly better for those students who received a reverse-ordered version; students who received the ordered version performed the poorest (compared to ordered and random versions). Despite the dramatic difference in the way ordered exams were characterized in the two studies, Gruber concluded that the "results of this study appear to be consistent with [earlier reported]results" [p. 82].

This observation is entirely appropriate with regard to an apparent sequencing effect. However, further inquiry is necessary concerning the underlying reasons for such sequencing effects. For example, one possible interpretation of the present findings regarding comprehensive exams pertains to the types of sequencing strategies. Both the present study and that of Baldwin and Howard examined two patterns. However, only one of the Baldwin and Howard versions truly reflected a "pattern," that being the ordered version. The alternative version ("scrambled") reflects a random, therefore, "unordered" sequence of questions.

The absence of a sequencing effect in the present study suggests that students performed equally well on each version. One possible reason for this result is the fact that, while the versions are different, each nonetheless reflects a discernible order or structure. The fact that neither version yielded significantly better results than the other suggests that students were able to accommodate each version about equally well.

It is possible, therefore, that students prefer some type of ordered structure in terms of item sequence and topical presentation. In this regard, both ordered and reverse-ordered versions provide a discernible sequencing structure. When compared, then, these versions may be more nearly the same because of their structured characteristic than they are different due to the exact sequence.

LIMITATIONS AND FUTURE EXTENSONS

Even though three different instructors participated in the experiment for both interim and comprehensive exam settings, it still must be recognized that results are based on the sampling of students at a single, medium-sized private institution. Therefore, the ability to generalize awaits replication of the study in other settings. In addition, it is unknown whether the specific test-bank used to generate exam questions is representative of any larger set of test-banks, although there is no reason to believe it is not. Furthermore, while students in the experiment were given different test-item sequencing patterns, the researchers could not control the sequence/order in which students answered the questions. Also, it should be noted that the exams did contain a section of short problems in addition to the multiple-choice questions.

The specific effect in the present study of including both multiple-choice and problem items in the exam cannot be assessed in a definitive sense. The inclusion of a section of problem exercises was a requirement of each of the six instructors who controlled data for the present experiment. It is possible that students taking the exams attempted the problems section before completing the multiple-choice questions. To the extent that the problems sensitized students to the various topics covered, then the effect of the order of multiple-choice question sequencing would be contaminated. There is no available evidence, however, as to whether this contaminating effect actually occurred.

It is also possible that previous experience in taking multiple-choice and/or problem-type exams could influence subsequent student test scores. In the present study, Instructor D included only problems in his exams prior to the comprehensive final. All other instructors, for interim and comprehensive results, used both problem sets and multiple-choice questions throughout the term. This may explain why a sequencing effect approaches statistical significance in the case of Instructor D. To the extent that students in this class became accustomed to solving problems, then the appearance of multiple-choice questions of a comprehensive nature represented a new and different test-taking environment.

It is useful to note here, as well, that similar questioning may be raised concerning earlier research efforts. Gruber [1987], for example, reported results from a comprehensive multiple-choice final exam. His subjects had previously taken interim exams consisting of both multiple-choice questions and problem sets. The extent to which this previous experience affected student results on the comprehensive final (which included only multiple-choice questions) is not addressed by Gruber. Furthermore, the types of ordering (if any) to which students were exposed in the interim exams is not reported. Given earlier reported findings [Howe and Baldwin, 1983] concerning the possibility of student adaptive behavior, it is possible that Gruber's results are at least partially influenced by the earlier exam experiences of the students.

While Gruber suggests that the reason for his students getting better scores on the reverse-ordered exams was due to recency of material covered, no attempt was made to explain why students taking ordered exams did the poorest—an important consideration given the Baldwin and Howard [1983] findings that ordered results were signficantly better than those obtained under random sequencing.

Taken as a whole, then, findings of the previous and present studies suggest that context is extremely important when considering the impact of test-item sequencing. The dynamics of the classroom environment and the potential diversity of instructional techniques underscore the need for continued research in this area.

The potential contribution of continued research, in fact, derives primarily from the contextual richness of the experimental setting. The classroom is not a sterile laboratory environment. Thus, if future studies are to seek to explain actual classroom dynamics, then completely identical replications of earlier studies may lead only to the ability to assert findings pertaining to a given, necessarily limited, set of circumstances. Stated differently, future research should focus primarily on issues not studied previously.

For example, it is not possible to speculate whether the results in this paper apply to upper-level accounting courses. Different material content and cognitive demands of these courses, as well as different motivation levels of students, may contribute to results different from those reported in this paper.

In addition, the importance of student type as a moderating variable in the model is yet to be explored. For example, a body of research [Baker, Simon, and Brazeli, 1986; Collins and Milliron, 1987] now suggests that the cognitive (including learning) styles of accounting majors (and practitioners) differ, on average, from those of other majors. That is, there may be significant differences among student groups in terms of the manner in which information is perceived and processed. Of related interest, therefore, is the finding of Howe and Baldwin [1983] that those students who received the random version of their exam showed significantly different (and more negative) attitudes regarding the course, instructor, and field of accounting than did students who received either the ordered or reverse-ordered version of the exam. Given that student preferences for structure and order have been linked also to learning styles, it is possible that sequencing effects and learning styles involve interrelated issues. A convergence of learning style research and test-item sequencing studies, therefore, would appear to be a fruitful extension to the present research.

To the extent that "type of student," "level of course," and other contextual items are important moderating variables in the model, future research can also benefit from a focus on the conditioning effects of different question types. For example, there is currently no available evidence concerning the interactive effects due to intertopical sequencing of questions and sequencing based on test-item difficulty. Similarly, there is currently no experimental evidence concerning the role of theory versus computational versus definitional question types. Given the evidence on differences in student cognitive styles, such research would seem to be particularly appropriate.

Further research is also needed concerning the relative effect of randomized presentation of questions. As noted earlier, both ordered and reverse-ordered presentations reflect a discernible order or structure. To the extent that sample size permits, future studies should incorporate all three sequencing strategies in the experimental design.

Finally, as noted in Table 1, prior studies have dealt with student intelligence levels differently in the experimental design. Some have treated student GPA as a factor with three levels in order to explore interaction effects between "student quality" and the experimental treatment. Other studies, including the present one, used student intelligence as a covariate in the design. The extent to which such design differences can lead to differences in results is left as a future exercise.

These considerations only serve to underscore the importance of Beaver's [1987] call for more research on the effects of the form of testing. Given the widespread use of computer-generated tests, continued research into item sequencing, for both comprehensive and interim exam settings, is indeed warranted.

NOTES

1. Lightner and Hartman [1985] provide a useful summary of computerized test banks available to accounting educators. More recently, Milano and Arens [1987] provide a review and evaluation of test-generating software that accompanies popular introductory accounting textbooks.

2. It is possible that these additional items could confound the results. As a control, such material was presented after the multiple-choice section of the exams. Further, items were sequenced in the same order as the multiple-choice questions. Ultimately, however, this issue will probably best be resolved empirically through experimentation.

3. The Test Bank used in the experiment includes page references to the text along with the solution to each multiple-choice question. Thus, it was possible in the experiment to sequence questions on the exams precisely in an order relative to text coverage of topics.

4. Random sequencing of questions was not used for several reasons. First, sample size in the experimental groups precluded the inclusion of too many factors in the design. Second, Baldwin and Howard [1983] have provided evidence that a randomized sequencing arrangement has both unintended negative effects as well as differential effects across categories of students. Thus, this sequencing arrangement is not very appealing from a pedagogical standpoint. Third, Gruber [1987] has shown that, across all categories of students in his sample, those taking a random exam version tended to score significantly above those who took an ordered exam but below those who took a reverse-ordered exam. Given the constraint imposed by the sample size in this study, it would seem appropriate to focus on the two extreme ends of the sequencing continuum suggested by the Gruber study.

5. Unlike Howe and Baldwin [1983], therefore, the present study was not interested in detecting student adaptive behavior over time. In their experiment, each student was intentionally given the same experimental treatment (exam type) over the course of the semester.

6. A recent empirical study by Stout and Bonfield [1986] found no difference in explanatory power when SAT scores were substituted for cumulative GPAs in a model predicting introductory accounting performance. Thus, one or the other of these two variables may be redundant.

7. To be sure, there is some contradictory evidence as to the importance of pre-college exposure to accounting on grades received in the first college course. Bergin [1983] and Baldwin, Wasson, and Howe [1978], for example, found this factor to be unimportant in the models they tested.

8. In statistical terms, the blocking factor is included in the hope it will increase the power (sensitivity) of the statistical analysis to a possible treatment effect. By separating out the blocking effect, a more precise estimate of experimental error (used as the denominator in the various *F*-tests) is sought—one which is not contaminated due to the blocking variable.

The courses in the present experiment were offered during the Fall semester. Normally, only a small percentage of students in these "Principles of Financial Accounting" courses are repeating the course. (This is more a problem in Spring semester offerings of the course.) Such was the case in the present experiment. For instructor A, no students were repeating the course. For instructor B, 1 student was repeating the course while 2 students for instructor C were so classified. Because of the insignificant numbers involved, it was not thought necessary to control statistically for this factor in the analysis.

9. There are sound statistical reasons for eliminating this factor. When the statistical test for the blocking factor proves to be nonsignificant, its inclusion in the model costs the researcher degrees of freedom for estimating σ^2 and, consequently, gives a less sensitive comparison of treatment effects [Kleinbaum and Kupper, 1978, pp. 300-301].

10. Generalizability of results may also be affected to the extent that the profile of students who withdrew from the course differed significantly from those students who completed the course. *T*-tests on GPA differences, total SAT score differences, and quantitative SAT score differences between the two groups were statistically significant ($p = .05$) for both instructor A and instructor B. (Scores of students who dropped the course were uniformly lower.) Thus, caution is advised in generalizing results obtained for these two instructors beyond the sample consisting of students who completed the course.

11. Statistical tests for each of the nine instructor-exam combinations were performed six different ways based on which covariate(s) was (were) included in the model. From among these results, the model exhibiting the greatest explanatory power (as measured by adjusted R^2 values) was chosen (and reported in Table 6) subject to meeting the following tests of underlying assumptions for the ANCOVA model [Wildt and Ahtola, 1978]: (1) the effect of the covariate(s) on the dependent variable was linear and statistically significant; (2) the effect of the covariate(s) was constant across the two experimental groups (regression slope homogeneity assumption); (3) the variance of the dependent variable was homogeneous between groups (so that the sample variances could be "pooled"). The first assumption was verified through examination of Ordinary Least Squares regression results and visual data plots. The second assumption was verified through partial *F*-tests on an interaction term (covariate by treatment) in a multiple regression model. The final assumption was verified through an *F*-test for significance applied to the ratio of the larger to smaller sample variance. Thus, the results reported in Table 6 relate to the "best" models explaining exam score differences after giving consideration to the underlying quality of the experimental data.

REFERENCES

Baker, R.E., J.R. Simon, and F.P. Bazeli, "An Assessment of the Learning Style Preferences of Accounting Majors," *Issues in Accounting Education* [Spring 1986], pp. 1-12.

Baldwin, B.A. and T.P. Howard, "Intertopical Sequencing of Examination Questions: An Empricial Evaluation," *Journal of Accounting Education* [Fall 1983], pp. 89-96.

Baldwin, B.A. and K.R. Howe, "Secondary-Level Study of Accounting and Subsequent Performance in the First College Course," *The Accounting Review* [July 1982], pp. 619-626.

Baldwin, B.A., D.D. Wasson, and K.R. Howe, "The Effect of Homework Requirements on Student Performance in an Introductory Accounting Course," Paper presented at the AAA Western Regional Meeting, Pasadena, CA [1978].

Beaver, W.H., "Accounting Education: Challenges and Opportunities" (Presidential Address), *Accounting Horizons* [December 1987], pp. 1-6.

Benke, R.L. and R.H. Hermanson, "Sequencing Questions: What is the Effect?," *Management Accounting* [April 1988], p. 60.

Bergin, J.L., "The Effect of Previous Accounting Study on Student Performance in the First College-Level Financial Accounting Course," *Issues in Accounting Education* [1983], pp. 19-28.

Buehlmann, D.M. and J.V. Techavichit, "Factors Influencing Final Examination Performance in Large versus Small Sections of Accounting Principles," *Journal of Accounting Education* [Spring 1984], pp. 127-136.

Collins, J.H. and V.C. Milliron, "A Measure of Professional Accountants' Learning Style," *Issues in Accounting Education* [Fall 1987], pp. 193-206.

Eckel, N. and W.A. Johnson, "A Model for Screening and Classifying Potential Accounting Majors," *Journal of Accounting Education* [Fall 1983], pp. 57-65.

Eskew, R.K. and R.H. Faley, "Some Determinants of Student Performance in the First College-Level Financial Accounting Course," *The Accounting Review* [January 1988], pp. 137-147.

Fuglister, J. and R.J. Murdock, "Use of the Computer in Preparation of Multiple Choice Examinations: A Multiple Form Generating Program," *Issues in Accounting Education* [Spring 1988], pp. 174-180.

Gruber, R.A., "Sequencing Exam Questions Relative to Topic Presentation," *Journal of Accounting Education* [Spring 1987], pp. 77-86.

Howe, K.R. and B.A. Baldwin, "The Effects of Evaluative Sequencing on Performance, Behavior and Attitudes," *The Accounting Review* [January 1983], pp. 135-142.

Ingram, R.W. and R.J. Petersen, "An Evaluation of AICPA Tests for Predicting the Performance of Accounting Majors," *The Accounting Review* [January 1987], pp. 215-223.

Jacoby, C.R., "The Effect of Teaching Methods and Experiences in Achievement of Business Students in the First College Level Accounting Course," Ph.D. dissertation [The Pennsylvania State University, 1975].

Katz, D., "Field Studies," in *Research Methods in the Behavioral Sciences,* edited by L. Festinger and D. Katz [The Dryden Press, 1953], pp. 56-97.

Kleinbaum, D.G. and L.L. Kupper, *Applied Regression Analysis and Other Multivariable Methods* [Duxbury Press, 1978].

Lightner, S. and M. Hartman, "Inventory of Computer Software Designed for Use in the Accounting Curriculum: Student Materials and Test Banks," *Journal of Accounting Education* [Spring 1985], pp. 15-35.

Milano, D.R. and J.R. Arens, "Microcomputer Test Banks for Accounting Principles: An Evaluation," *Journal of Accounting Education* [Spring 1987], pp. 85-93.

Runkel, P.J. and J.E. McGrath, *Research on Human Behavior* [Holt, Rinehart and Winston, 1972].

Schroeder, N.W., "Previous Accounting Education and College-Level Exam Performance," *Issues in Accounting Education* [Spring 1986], pp. 37-47.

Smith, J.W., "Articulation of High School Bookkeeping and College Elementary Accounting," Ph.D. dissertation [University of Oklahoma, 1968].

Stout, D.E. and E.H. Bonefield, "Experimental Evidence on the Relationship Between Class Meeting Time Compression and Accounting Student Performance, Evaluations and Drop-Out Experience," *Journal of Accounting Education* [Fall 1986], pp. 51-62.

Vruwink, D.R. and J.R. Otto, "Evaluation of Teaching Techniques for Introductory Accounting Courses," *The Accounting Review* [April 1987], pp. 402-408.

Warren, C.S. and P.E. Fess, *Principles of Financial and Managerial Accounting* [South-Western, 1986].

Wildt, A. and O. Ahtola, *Analysis of Covariance* (Sage University Series on Quantitative Applications in the Social Sciences, Series No. 07-022) [Sage, 1978].

USE OF MICROCOMPUTERS IN ACCOUNTING COURSES

Anwar Y. Salimi

ABSTRACT

This study presents the results of a survey of accounting instructors in the United States and Canada to determine the extent and type of microcomputer use in accounting curricula. The rise of microcomputer use within the accounting industry has created a demand for microcomputer literacy among graduates of accounting. In a response to industry, accounting instructors have incorporated microcomputer applications into their classes. This survey indicates that microcomputers are being used by a significant percentage of industructors in almost every type of accounting course. The applications taught and the software used vary from course to course; however, spreadsheets are by far the most popular kind of software used and are given the most importance by accounting instructors. Additionally, the survey shows that IBM and IBM compatible microcomputers are the brands most commonly used in schools.

Advances in Accounting, Volume 8, pages 153-177.

ISBN: 1-55938-067-5

INTRODUCTION

Microcomputer use in recent years has increased tremendously in the accounting industry as well as within business in general. Several studies have already documented the extensive use of microcomputers in the accounting industry. Connors [1983, p. 63] found in a survey of National Association of Accountants (NAA) members that 60% of his sample used microcomputers to perform daily business applications and, of those using microcomputers, 82% were using spreadsheets. Golden and Golden [1984, p. 38] reported that 50% of surveyed accounting firms were using spreadsheets in audit work. Fleenor and Danos [1985] reported that 82% of the CPAs they surveyed had a microcomputer in their office and used it for applications ranging from audit and tax to data-base management. A study in the *Journal of Accountancy* [1983, p. 24] reported that out of 2,800 U.S. companies, about 33% were using microcomputers.

These studies confirm a trend that ultimately translates into a demand from employers for accounting students to have familiarity not only with microcomputers but with their various applications as well. In fact, a number of studies have already detailed the impact of employer needs on educational institutions. Waller and Gallun [1985, p. 36], for example, have reported on microcomputer competency requirements for accounting graduates as defined by public accounting firms and industry. These researchers found that the firms surveyed wanted universities to provide curricular coverage of operating systems, electronic spreadsheets, and data base programs. Other applications, such as word processing, were also desired by most of the respondents. Similarly, Parmley and Parmley [1986a, p. 18], in a survey of public accounting firms, found that a high percentage of respondents wanted their beginning accountants to be capable of applying computer skills in practice areas such as tax, bookkeeping, auditing, and management advisory services (MAS). The percentages varied from 63% for bookkeeping to 21% for MAS. Eighty-six percent of those surveyed said they wanted additonal computer applications taught within existing accounting courses. Acknowledging the need for accounting graduates to have acquired computer operating skills, the American Assembly of Collegiate Schools of Business (AACSB) has revised its accreditation standards to now read: "1) students shall receive instruction in the design, use, control and audit of computerized accounting systems ... and 2) students are expected to use the computer in accounting courses" [AACSB, 1984, p. 44].

In response to industry demands and AACSB requirements, many schools and instructors have introduced the microcomputer into their accounting courses [Bialaszewski, Kocakulah, and Bialaszewski, 1986, p. 31]. Such innovation results in the need for instructors who have or can acquire computer skills, the necessity for new accounting textbooks containing computer applications, and a determination of the best software to be taught [Nash and England, 1986].

Several surveys have already been conducted on the usage of microcomputers in accounting curricula. Thomas [1984, p. 33] surveyed accounting departments and found that 31% of the sampled departments were using the microcomputer for teaching accounting at the time of the survey. Of those schools already using microcomputers, about three-fourths employ an electronic spreadsheet; about two-thirds use some form of computerized practice set or computerized accounting system. Cronan and Fries [1986, p. 24] surveyed accounting departments to determine the relative frequency (in percentages) of computer use in teaching various accounting courses. They found a range from a high of 76.5% for accounting information systems to a low of 4.5% for not-for-profit or governmental accounting. Their survey also determined specific computer use in upper division courses to discover whether students were required to program or to use preprogrammed packages, on-line accounting systems or existing databases.

Parmley and Parmley [1986b, p. 176] conducted a survey of the use frequency of computers and the percentages in various accounting courses at accredited institutions. The found that the first cost accounting course had the highest percentage of use with 40% and graduate managerial the lowest, with 2%. They also found that 71% of their responding institutions were using computer applications in accounting courses while 29% were not.

An American Accounting Association Report from the Committee on Integration of the Microcomputers into the Financial Accounting Curriculum [AAA, 1985a] delineates various pedagogical issues and system problems in using the microcomputer. The appendix of this report contains a list of microcomputer applications used in financial accounting. This list was developed from a survey of college professors and book publishers. Another AAA Report, this one from the Committee on Integrating the Microcomputer into the Managerial/Cost Curriculum [AAA, 1985b], addresses similar issues and provides a list of available microcomputer applications in cost/managerial accounting.

The present study offers the results of a survey of 1,696 accounting instructors in the United States and Canada conducted to determine the usage of microcomputers in accounting courses, but differs from the earlier surveys because it provides a more detailed investigation of computer integration into various accounting courses, the applications employed in each course, and the software used for each application. The survey also addresses other questions, such as accounting department policy toward computer education, the existence of computer facilities for student use, and accounting instructors' opinions about the relative importance of various computer applications. In addition to being more extensive, the present survey provides more recent data than earlier surveys.

METHODOLOGY

A questionnaire designed to elicit information about the use of microcomputers was sent to 1,696 accounting instructors in 135 different universities selected from the *Accounting Faculty Directory*.

The questionnaire asked for information about: (a) the respondent's accounting department and unviersity; (b) the existence of computer labs on campus and the kind of computers used; (c) the type of course taught most often by the respondent; (d) whether he or she used the microcomputer in the course named, and if so, how it was integrated into the course and what applications and software were used; and (e) the respondent's opinion about the relative importance of various software packages.

The questionnaire was sent out in April 1986. Four hundred and thirteen responses were received for a 24% response rate. This response rate is lower than that of some similar surveys mentioned above. Parmley and Parmley [1986b, p. 175] reported a 33% response rate while Cronan and Fries [1986, p. 238] had a 55% response rate.[1] The reason these studies had a higher response rate may be that respondents were chairpersons of accounting departments whereas ours were the accounting instructors who actually taught the courses. Earlier studies targeted their questionnaires to accounting chairpersons who may be, overall, a more responsive audience than a general cross-section of accounting instructors. Channeling the flow of information is one of the major functions of departmental chairpersons, whereas instructors, especially those who do not use computers, may have insufficient interest or knowledge of computer use to respond. However, it seemed advantageous to obtain first hand information by going directly to the accounting instructors themselves. Furthermore, the total number of questionnaires mailed out in earlier studies (200 in each) represented less than half the number of responses received in the present study. The large number of responses received (413), then, offsets the percentages of earlier studies and provides reasonable assurance that this study yields information about the state of microcomputer integration into accounting curricula.

RESULTS OF SURVEY

Table 1 presents descriptive information about the sizes of the universities, business schools, and accounting departments from which responses were received. Respondents to the survey came from universities, business schools and accounting departments of various sizes providing a good, representative cross section for the study. Neither large nor small schools were over-represented, thus size apparently did not cause a bias in the findings of the survey.

Table 1. Size of Respondents' Universities, Business Schools and Accounting Departments

	Frequency	*Percentage*
University Enrollment		
1 through 4000	36	8.7
4001 through 8000	60	16.5
8001 through 12000	62	15.0
12001 through 16000	92	22.3
16001 through 20000	51	12.3
20001 through Highest	34	8.3
No Response	78	18.9
Total	413	100.0
School of Business Enrollment		
1 through 1000	61	14.8
1001 through 2000	100	24.2
2001 through 3000	82	19.8
3001 through 4000	55	13.3
4001 through 5000	28	6.8
5001 through Highest	44	10.7
No Response	43	10.4
Total	413	100.0
Number of Accounting Majors: (Undergraduate)		
None	12	2.9
1 through 200	84	20.3
201 through 400	86	20.8
401 through 600	61	14.8
601 through 800	50	12.1
801 through 1000	34	8.2
1001 through Highest	40	9.7
No Response	46	11.2
Total	413	100.0
Number of Accounting Majors: (Graduate)		
None	79	19.1
1 through 20	75	18.2
21 through 40	46	11.1
41 through 60	37	9.0
61 through 80	7	1.7
81 through 100	27	6.5
101 through Highest	61	14.8
No Response	81	19.6
Total	413	100.0

Table 2. Type of Accounting Course Taught and Usage of Microcomputer in Course

Course	*Number of Responses*	*Percentage of Respondents Using Microcomputer*
Introductory	98	41.8
Cost/Managerial	98	58.1
Intermediate	87	42.5
Tax	52	48.0
Auditing	38	68.4
Advanced	35	42.9
A.I.S.	33	87.8
Other	26	34.6
Theory	12	25.0

Note: The data includes 54 responses with more than one course taught.

Table 2 presents the type of accounting course taught by the respondents as well as the percentage of computer use in their accounting courses. Here, the data offers a representational cross section of courses in accounting curricula, showing heavy concentration in introductory, cost/managerial and intermediate courses and lighter concentrations in other more specialized courses. This distribution is what should be expected from a representative sample given the mix of courses taught at most universities. The "Other" category in Table 2 is comprised mainly of international and governmental accounting courses.

Not surprisingly, Table 2 indicates that 88% of the respondents who taught accounting information systems used the microcomputer in their classes (the other 12% presumably used mainframe computers or did not use computers at all). Accounting information systems, which had the highest percentage, was followed by auditing with 68%, then cost/managerial with 58%. Forty-two percent of those who taught introductory accounting used the computer mainly for practice sets. The results reported in Table 2 are similar to the results obtained by Cronan and Fries [1986, p. 241] regarding the relative use frequence of microcomputers in different accounting courses. Cronan and Fries reported the following percentages:

AIS	76.5
Auditing	61.2
Cost/Managerial I	48.6
Cost/Managerial II	36.6
Tax	29.0

Other courses detailed in the Cronan and Fries study had a smaller percentage of use than those named above. The rank ordering of the courses listed above was the same in the Cronan and Fries survey as it is in Table 2, which suggests considerable validity for the present survey results. Although the percentage of use reported in this survey was higher for every course than in the Cronan and Fries survey, this may simply reflect an increasing trend toward the incorporation of microcomputers in accounting courses since the data of their study. This finding of increasing usage is also supported by the fact that Thomas [1984, p. 33] reported that only 31% of the responding institutions in his survey were using the computer in accounting courses, whereas Parmley and Parmley [1986b, p. 176], in a later survey reported 71% of the responding institutions using computer applications in accounting courses.

As evidenced in Table 2, significant differences in amount of microcomputer use in differing courses exists. These differences do not arise because of lack of computer facilities for some courses, since the same facilities are generally available for all courses. Neither do these differences arise because of lack of suitable software. The survey revealed that a tremendous amount of computer software is available for use in accounting courses, some of which has been listed in the tables below. Rather, the differences in computer use among the various courses relates primarily to the suitability of microcomputer use to the topics covered in specific courses. Suitability explains the high frequency in accounting information systems courses, which by their very nature are computer oriented, and low use in accounting theory, which is usually taught at a conceptual level.

The data indicate that, out of the 413 instructors who responded, there were 212 (51%) who incorporated the use of microcomputers, whereas 201 (49%) did not. The information on overall use, indicating that more than half of all instructors are making use of microcomputers, is an encouraging statistic considering the recent emergence of personal computers and the proability that most accounting instructors were not formally trained in their use. Such use will undoubtedly increase even more in the future, in large part because employers are already insisting that accounting graduates be computer literate. Parmley and Parmley [1986a, p. 19] report that 86% of the employers they surveyed felt that additional computer applications should be taught within existing accounting courses. In addition to employer demands, greater availability of computer hardware and software at most schools as well as increased expertise in microcomputer utilization among accounting faculty should also result in further incorporating computers into the curricula. However, even though usage is expected to increase, differences in the amount of microcomputer use in the various courses will still exist, because of the differing subject matter of the courses.

Table 3. Chi-Square Test of Use of Microcomputer Versus Enrollment

Use of Computer in Accounting Courses versus Enrollment of:	*Chi-Square Value*
1. University	.70 (NS)* df = 5
2. School of Business	4.65 (NS) df = 5
3. Undergraduate Accounting Students	3.44 (NS) df = 6
4. Graduate Accounting Students	8.96 (NS) df = 6

Note: * NS indicates not significant at the .05 level of significance.

Table 3 presents the results of Chi Square tests conducted in order to determine whether any difference in microcomputer use among schools with different enrollments at various levels—university, business school, undergraduate accounting students, and graduate accounting students—was demonstrable. The hypothesis was that schools with larger enrollments would have more funds available for computer facilities for their students, resulting in more microcomputer use, than smaller schools was not borne out by the tests. Results indicate no significant difference in computer use among schools with large or small enrollments. Thus, instructors at smaller schools are integrating the computer into their courses as frequently as instructors at larger schools. The Chi Square tests also indicate that smaller schools are able to provide sufficient funds for computer facilities for their smaller enrollments.

Various approaches to integration of microcomputers into accounting classes are indicated in Table 4. The data indicate that a wide variety of approaches as well as mix of approaches exist in the different courses. Other analysis of the data in Table 4, not shown here, indicates that in introductory and intermediate accounting, practice sets were the most popular approach to using the microcomputer. However, instructors of other courses, such as cost/managerial, auditing, tax and advanced accounting, relied most heavily on problem solving and cases. Overall, it appears that assigning specific exercises, problems, and cases to be solved using microcomputers is the most popular way of integrating the micro into accounting courses.

Table 5 presents information about both the applications taught in various accounting courses and the software used for these applications. It reveals that in introductory accounting, practice sets are the most popular use, accounting for 36% of the total applications. With 33%, the second most used application was the accounting cycle, consisting of parts of the cycle (e.g., making adjusting entries, preparing worksheets, and so forth). Financial statement analysis was

Table 4. Integration of Microcomputers into Coursework

	Frequency
Exercises, Problems and Cases[1]	168
Problems and Cases from Supplementary Text[2]	47
Major Assignment (including Practice Sets)[3]	60
Take Home Exam	1
Extra Credit	13
Other	9
Not Specified	180
No Response	3

Notes: Some questionnaires contained multiple responses.

[1] This category included specific exercises, problems, and cases that involved the use of microcomputers. All such assignments were included in this category unless it was specifically mentioned that the problems were from a supplementary text or were instructor developed applications (in which case they were included in the category of Problems and Cases from Supplementary text). This category consisted of bundled problem sets usually integrated with a specific text (e.g., templates for selected homework problems using an electronic spreadsheet, such as Lotus 1-2-3, to provide the computational framework). Most of these problems involved the use of software specifically programmed for these problems (e.g., prepared spreadsheet templates), but some required the students to use regular software to solve the problems (e.g., spreadsheets, accounting packages) and a few problems involved programming by students.

[2] This category included all problems and cases in which a supplementary text or instructor developed materials were mentioned. These assignments involved the use of software preprogrammed for the specific problem or case (e.g., spreadsheet templates, auditing case studies with prepackaged software, Harvard case studies, and so forth), use of regular software, and sometimes use of programming languages.

[3] This category included all assignments that required a significant part of the quarter or semester to complete (from a few weeks to the entire term). This category included practice sets and also applications that required the development or use of a financial model or data base to answer a more comprehensive question than the individual problems included in category 1 and 2 above.

third with 14%. The most used software for introductory accounting was practice sets (i.e., software created specifically for particular practice sets), which accounted for 36% of the total and was employed for teaching practice in accounting. The second most popular software was Lotus 1-2-3 templates (26%) used mostly for accounting cycle applications. Lotus 1-2-3 popularity was followed by other spreadsheets (10%). Generalizing, it seems that most instructors in introductory accounting used the microcomputer either for practice sheets, accounting cycle applications, or financial statement analysis (these three accounting for 83% of all applications) and employed either practice set software or spreadsheets for these purposes (these two packages accounting for 74% of all software used).

The fact that such a large percentage (41.8%) of introductory accounting instructors were using microcomputers is significant and indicates that instructors wish to expose students to a computerized accounting environment at an early stage of their studies. Furthermore, many introductory accounting instructors are not confining themselves to using practice sets but are also using

Table 5. Microcomputer Applications and Software Used in Accounting Courses

	Introductory Accounting										
	Lotus 1-2-3	*Other Spread-sheets*	*Commercial General Ledger Package*	*Practice Set*	*Textbook Tutorial*	*DBase Mgmt. System*	*Text/ Supplement Software*[1]	*Special Applica-tions*[2]	*Word Processing*	*Undefined*	*Row Total*
Practice Set	—	—	1	20	0	0	—	0	0	0	21 36.2%
Financial Statement Analysis	4	0	0	0	0	0	1	2	1	0	8 13.8%
Financial Statement/ Schedule Prep.[3]	0	1	1	0	0	0	0	0	0	0	2 3.4%
Tutorial	0	0	0	0	2	0	0	0	0	0	2 3.4%
Student Designed Project[13]	1	0	0	0	0	1	0	0	0	0	2 3.4%
Accounting Cycle[4]	10	2	1	1	0	0	2	1	0	2	19 32.8%
Special Topics I[5]	0	3	0	0	0	0	0	0	0	0	3 5.2%
Consolidation	0	1	0	0	0	0	0	0	0	0	1 1.7%
Column Total	15 25.9%	7 12.0%	3 5.2%	21 36.2%	2 3.4%	1 1.7%	3 5.2%	3 5.2%	1 1.7%	2 3.4%	58 100.0%

Intermediate Accounting

	Lotus 1-2-3	*Other Spread-sheet*	*Practice Set*	*DBase Mgmt. System*	*Text/ Supple-ment Software*	*Special Applica-tions*	*Acctg. Firm Audit Package*	*Undefined*	*Row Total*
Practice Set	2	1	8	1	1	0	0	4	17 37.8%
Financial Statement Analysis	1	0	0	0	0	0	1	0	2 4.4%
Financial Statement/ Schedule Prep.[3]	1	0	0	0	0	1	0	1	3 6.7%
Accounting Cycle[4]	1	0	0	0	0	0	1	2	4 8.9%
Special Topics I[5]	11	2	0	0	1	0	0	1	15 33.3%
Consolidation	1	0	0	0	0	0	0	0	1 2.2%
Not Stated	2	0	0	0	0	0	0	0	3 6.7%
Column Total	19 42.4%	3 6.6%	8 17.78%	1 2.2%	2 4.4%	1 2.2%	2 4.4%	9 20.0%	45 100.0%

(continued)

Table 5. (continued)

	Advanced Accounting						
	Lotus 1-2-3	*Other Spread-sheets*	*DBase Mgmt. System*	*Text/ Supple-ment Software*[1]	*Special Applica-tions*[2]	*Acctg. Firm Audit Package*	*Row Total*
Practice Set	1	0	0	0	0	0	1 4.5%
Consolidation	7	6	1	1	1	1	18 81.8%
Special Topics II[6]	2	0	0	0	0	0	2 9.1%
Not Stated	1	0	0	0	0	0	1 4.5%
Column Total	11 50.0%	6 27.2%	1 4.5%	1 4.5%	1 4.5%	1 4.5%	22 100.0%

	Auditing									
	Lotus 1-2-3	*Other Spread-sheets*	*Computer-ized Auditing Case*	*Text/ DBase Mgmt. System*	*Acctg. Supple-ment Software*[1]	*Special Applica-tions*[2]	*Firm Audit Package*	*Word Process-ing*	*Undefined*	*Row Total*
Practice Set	3	0		0	1	0	0	0	0	5 10.2%
Financial Statement/ Schedule Prep.[3]	0	0	0	0	0	0	2	1	0	3 6.1%
Accounting Cycle	1	0	0	0	1	0	0	0	0	2 4.1%
Analytical Review[7]	3	0	0	0	0	0	6	0	0	9 18.4%
Audit Sampling[8]	4	3	1	0	0	1	10	0	0	19 38.8%
Work Papers[9]	3	1	0	0	0	0	0	0	0	4 8.2%
Opinion Letter	0	0	0	0	0	0	0	1	0	1 2.0%
Not Stated	3	0	0	2	0	0	0	0	1	6 12.2%
Column Total	17 34.7%	4 8.1%	2 4.1%	2 4.1%	2 4.1%	1 2.0%	18 36.7%	2 4.1%	1 2.0%	49 100.0%

(continued)

Table 5. (continued)

	Tax Accounting											
	Lotus 1-2-3	*Other Spread-sheet*	*Commer-cial General Ledger Package*	*Practice Set*	*Tax Prep. Software*	*Tax Spread-sheets*	*Text/ Supple-ment Software*[1]	*Special Applica-tions*[2]	*Tax Planning Software*	*Communi-cations*	*Undefined*	*Row Total*
Financial Statement Analysis	1	1	0	0	1	0	1	0	0	0	0	4 8.5%
Financial Statement/ Schedule Prep.[3]	0	1	0	0	0	0	0	0	0	0	1	2 4.3%
Tax Computation	4	2	1	1	5	0	0	1	0	0	0	14 29.8%
Tax Research	6	3	1	0	5	1	0	1	6	1	1	25 53.2%
NPV Analysis[10]	1	1	0	0	0	0	0	0	0	0	0	2 4.3%
Column Total	12 25.5%	8 17.0%	2 4.3%	1 2.1%	11 23.4%	1 2.1%	1 2.1%	2 4.3%	6 12.8%	1 2.1%	2 4.3%	47 100.0%

Cost/Managerial Accounting

	Lotus 1-2-3	*Other Spread-sheet*	*Commercial General Ledger Package*	*Educational General Ledger Package*	*Practice Set*	*Computerized Case Study*	*DBase Mgmt. System*	*Text/Supplement Software*	*Special Applications*[2]	*Statistical Packages*	*Word Processing*	*Decision Support Software*	*Basic/Other Lang. Programs*	*Undefined*	*Row Total*
Product Costing	21	9	1	1	0	1	2	1	2	0	1	0	0	1	40 27.8%
Responsibility Accounting	6	4	0	0	0	0	0	0	0	0	0	0	0	0	10 6.9%
Decision Analysis[11]	22	12	1	1	1	0	1	3	2	5	2	2	0	0	52 36.1%
Stat. Technique[12]	8	2	0	2	0	0	0	2	2	6	0	2	0	0	24 16.7%
Not Stated	6	3	0	0	0	1	0	2	1	2	0	0	1	2	18 12.5%
Column Total	63 43.8%	30 20.8%	2 1.4%	4 2.8%	1 0.7%	2 1.4%	3 2.1%	8 5.6%	7 4.9%	13 9.0%	3 2.1%	4 2.8%	1 0.7%	3 2.1%	144 100.0%

(continued)

Table 5. (continued)

	Accounting Information Systems												
	Lotus 1-2-3	*Other Spread-sheet*	*Commer-cial General Ledger Package*	*Prac-tice Set*	*Text-book Tutor-ial*	*DBase Mgmt. System*	*Text/ Supple-ment Software*[1]	*Special Applica-tions*[2]	*Other*	*Word Process-ing*	*Basic/ Other Lang. Programs*	*Undefined*	*Row Total*
Practice Set	0	0	1	0	0	0	0	0	0	0	0	0	1 1.2%
Student Designed Project	12	9	5	1	1	5	0	2	1	4	1	4	45 55.6%
Opinion Letter	1	0	0	0	0	0	0	0	0	2	0	0	3 3.7%
Data Base Mgmt.	7	5	3	0	0	8	1	0	0	0	1	0	25 30.9%
Programming	1	0	1	0	0	0	0	0	0	0	0	0	2 2.5%
Not Stated	2	0	0	0	0	2	0	0	0	0	0	1	5 6.2%
Column Total	23 28.4%	14 17.3%	10 12.3%	1 1.2%	1 1.2%	15 18.5%	1 1.2%	2 2.5%	1 1.2%	6 7.4%	2 2.5%	5 6.2%	81 100.0%

	Other							
	Lotus 1-2-3	*Other Spread-sheets*	*Practice Set*	*Tax Prep. Software*	*DBase Mgmt. System*	*Special Applica-tions*[2]	*Word Processing*	*Row Total*
Accounting Cycle	0	0	0	0	0	1	0	1 3.7%
Special Topics II[6]	1	2	0	0	0	0	0	3 11.1%
Tax Computation	1	0	0	1	0	0	0	2 7.4%
Product Costing	1	0	0	0	0	1	0	2 7.4%
Responsibility Accounting	2	2	0	0	0	1	0	5 18.5%
Decision Analysis[11]	1	2	0	0	0	0	0	3 11.1%
Data Base Mgmt.	0	0	4	0	2	0	0	6 22.2%
Stat. Techniques[12]	1	0	0	0	0	1	0	2 7.4%
Not Stated	1	0	0	0	1	0	1	3 11.1%
Column Total	8 29.6%	6 22.2%	4 14.8%	1 3.7%	3 11.1%	4 14.8%	1 3.7%	27 100.0%

(*continued*)

Table 5. (continued)

Notes:
[1] Computer supplements published specifically to accompany textbook and also supplementary computer textbooks.
[2] Software for specific accounting applications such as Payroll or Accounts Receivable.
[3] Design and preparation of financial statements and various schedules (i.e., CGS).
[4] Parts of the Accounting Cycle such as Journal Entries, General Ledger Transactions, Accounting Worksheet Preparation, Adjusting Entries, and so forth.
[5] Specialized topics usually taught in Intermediate courses; specifically, Lease Calculations, Depreciation Schedules, EPS Calculations, and Bonds.
[6] Specialized topics usually taught in Advanced Accounting. Specifically Division of Partnership Income, Foreign Currency Transactions, and Price Level Adjustments.
[7] Analytical Review, Determination of Materiality, Audit Trial Balances, and so forth.
[8] Statistical Sampling, Compliance Tests, Data Gathering and Manipulation.
[9] Work Papers, Cash Audit, Work Sheet Preparation.
[10] PV, FV, calculations for single sums and annuities.
[11] Decision Analysis, Differential Costs, Capital Budgeting, Cash Flow Analysis.
[12] Regression, PERT, ANOVA, LINDO, and so forth.
[13] Design of Special Accounting Applications (i.e., Payroll), Design of Data Base Management Systems, Design of Accounting General Ledger Packages and Implementation of Commercial General Ledger Packages.

spreadsheet software to solve problems. The results in Table 5 indicate that many instructors feel the microcomputer can be a learning aid for the beginning student. This has implications for the controversy that suggests few benefits accrue to students in the understanding of accounting when computerized accounting methods are used for teaching accounting [AAA, 1985a]. Table 5 indicates that many instructors believe otherwise and also suggests that the microcomputer will continue to be used as a learning aid in introductory accounting.

For intermediate accounting, similarly to introductory courses, the most popular application was practice sets, followed closely by special topics including depreciation schedules, EPS calculations, and lease and bond calculations. The most popular software used was Lotus 1-2-3. For intermediate accounting, as in introductory, a significant number of instructors appear to feel that computer-aided-instruction is a valuable tool in teaching students certain topics.

For advanced accounting, the most used application related to preparing consolidation entries and consolidated financial statements (82% of all applications). The most employed software was Lotus 1-2-3 templates (50%), followed by other spreadsheets (14%) and other spreadsheet templates (14%). Thus, use of spreadsheets and spreadsheet templates accounted for about 78% of the total software used. On the basis of these figures, it may be said that most instructors in advanced accounting used microcomputers to perform consolidations using spreadsheets, illustrating the point that topic suitability will determine whether or not instructors will use microcomputers. Spreadsheet templates are highly suitable for performing consolidations, which explains the widespread use of the microcomputer for teaching them.

In auditing, the most employed application was audit sampling (39%), followed by analytical review (18%). The software most often used for audit sampling and analytical review (as well as overall use) was accounting firm auditing packages (37% of all software used) followed by Lotus 1-2-3 templates (33%). Audit sampling lends itself readily to microcomputer use; therefore, it is not surprising to find a large number of instructors using the computer for that application.

In tax accounting, the most popular applications were tax research (53%) and tax computation (30%). Together, the two accounted for 83% of all applications. Software packages most often used related to tax preparation (23%) and Lotus 1-2-3 templates (21%). Tax research and tax planning worksheets are ideal uses for the microcomputer.

In cost/managerial accounting, the most employed applications were found among those for decision analysis (36%), product costing (28%) and statistical techniques (17%). Together, the three applications accounted for 81% of the total applications. Lotus 1-2-3 templates were the most frequently used software (44%). Cost/managerial accounting had a high percentage use for the

Table 6. Ranking of Software Packages With Which Students Should be Familiar

	Rank	*Number of First Place Votes*	*Rank*	*Weighted Votes*
Spreadsheets	1	235	1	2321
Word Processing	3	22	2	1617
Data Base	4	6	3	1610
Accounting Packages	2	41	4	1585
Statistical Pacs	6	1	5	940
Graphics	7	0	6	881
Communications	8	0	7	662
Other	5	3	8	115

microcomputer and also had the largest variety of software employed, even more than accounting information systems, probably because cost/managerial accounting includes many topics that lend themselves readily to the microcomputer. Furthermore, since the topics in cost/managerial accounting are very diversified, a large variety of software is used, suggesting an increasing sophistication of cost/managerial instructors in finding software to suit the various topics they wish to teach.

In accounting information systems, student designed projects were the most popular application (56%). These projects ranged from design of special accounting applications (e.g., payroll) to design of the data base management systems and design of accounting general ledger packages. Projects also included implementation of commerical general ledger packages. The second most employed application related to data base management (31%). The most popular software used were Lotus 1-2-3 templates (28%), followed by data base management software (19%). The subject matter of AIS is ideal for microcomputer use; therefore, heavy use of the microcomputer was made by instructors responding to the survey.

In the other category, which consisted mostly of governmental/not for profit and international accounting, data base management was the most popular application, and Lotus 1-2-3 templates (30%), the most employed software. The use of computers for these courses was relatively low, however, perhaps because the topics taught in these courses do not lend themselves easily to computer applications.

Table 6 presents the rankings in order of importance for accounting students that accounting instructors gave to various software packages. Ranking was done in two ways. In one method, the number of first place choices received by each package was tabulated and the packages ranked according to the most first place choices received. In the other method, each ranking that a package

Table 7. Brand of Microcomputer Used

	Responses		*Total of Microcomputers of Respondents*	
	N	%	*N*	%
IBM	307	59.7	11,684	71.6
Apple	80	15.6	1,416	8.7
HP	19	3.7	471	2.9
Zenith	15	2.9	235	1.4
NCR	14	2.7	503	3.1
Tandy	12	2.3	238	1.5
ATT	11	2.1	135	9.8
Other	56	10.9	1,643	10.1
Total	514	100	16,325	100

Note: The data may be skewed due to multiple responses from some of the universities.

received was given a certain number of points. A first place ranking was worth 8 points, a second place ranking was worth 7 points and so on, with an eight place ranking worth 1 point. The points received by each software package were then added up and the packages ranked according to the total number of points they had received. In both methods of ranking, spreadsheet programs were ranked by far the highest, a finding consistent with the primary importance given to spreadsheet programs by the accounting industry [Waller and Gallun, 1985, p. 36]. Accounting packages received the second highest number of first place choices, which indicates that while they are considered important, they are not given as much importance as spreadsheet packages. The ease with which spreadsheets are used for numerous accounting purposes and the consequent high frequency of use both in industry and in academia probably account for the importance placed on them by accounting instructors.

The fact that spreadsheet programs were ranked highest and, as demonstrated in Table 6, were also employed the most consistently, indicates that, at least for spreadsheets, what instructors say is what they do.

The questionnaire elicited the following responses about the availability of computer labs:

Computer Laboratory available:	390	(94%)
Computer Laboratory not available:	23	(6%)
Total Responses:	413	(100%)

The data indicate that for most schools, the availability of computer labs is not a problem and most accounting instructors are not constrained when deciding to incorporate microcomputers into their coursework.

Table 7 presents information about the types of computers used. Most institutions surveyed have some sort of computer lab available. IBM is overwhelmingly the most popular: 59.7% of the respondents indicated use of IBMs; 15.6%, APPLE; 3.7%, HP; 21%, for all others (which individually constitute 3% or less of the total). According to the total of all computers available to respondents, IBM accounted for a great majority (72%) of the microcomputers reported. The responses tabulated in Table 7 correlate with the results reported by Parmley and Parmley [1986b, p. 175], regarding the predominance of IBM computers by those respondents who used microcomputers in their courses. Thomas [1984, p. 35], however, reports that Apple computers were used the most, even more than IBM.

An analysis of the findings reported by Parmley and Parmley and Thomas yields the following percentages:

	Parmley and Parmley [1986b]	Thomas[2] [1984]
IBM	54%	35%
Apple	19	54
Altos/Television/Micro Mag	8	—
TRS 80	5	25
Zenith	5	—
Sperry	3	—
Osbornes	3	9
Texas Instrument	3	—
Other Brands	—	40

The results reported by Parmley and Parmley accord with the results reported in Table 7 regarding the predominance of IBM whereas Thomas reports Apple computers being used more than IBM. These divergent findings are probably due to the fact that Thomas' survey is an early one, having been completed in 1983. Apple initially appears to have dominated the educational computer market but was later overtaken by IBM. In any case, IBM and Apple taken together account for the overwhelming majority of computers used by respondents in all three surveys. However, the ranking of the other computer brands does not correlate among the three surveys. This may be due to the fact that the percentages of use of the other brands are so small as to make a comparison of use across the studies meaningless. Another reason for the lack of correlation may be the volatile nature of the microcomputer industry in which market shares change dramatically in short periods of time and firms frequently go out of business.

The reason for the currently greater use of IBMs and IBM compatibles may not necessarily be greater availability of appropriate software. Lightner and Hartman [1985, p. 19] report in a survey of computer software designed for use in the accounting curricula that, out of the 33 products they identified, 31 products were designed for the Apple but 29 could be run on the IBM. The reason for IBM hardware being more popular than others may be due to the facts that there are more IBM and IBM compatible machines being used in business and industry and that IBM seems to have established itself as the standard product in the accounting industry [Hoffman, 1988, p. 148].

CONCLUSION

The survey results indicate that there is no difference in the extent of microcomputer use between large and small universities, schools of business and accounting departments among the sample. Instructors at smaller schools are integrating the computer into their courses as frequently as instructors at larger schools.

The use of microcomputers varies in different courses. It is highest in the courses such as AIS, auditing, and cost/managerial, because the topics included in those courses lend themselves easily to computer applications, perhaps relating to the "applied" rather than "conceptual" nature of these courses. The relatively infrequent use of computers, however, in some courses does not arise from lack of software availability; much software is already available and much of it can be adapted for almost any use.

There appears to be an upward trend in use of the microcomputer in accounting courses, and this trend will probably continue as more funds become available to schools for computer assisted instruction, more applications are designed that will be useful in accounting, and more accounting instructors become better trained in using the microcomputer for instructional purposes. Overall, it appears that accounting students will become computer literate, leading to a further increase in the use of computers in the accounting profession.

An analysis of microcomputer use in specific accounting courses revealed that in the various courses, micros were being used for a variety of applications with different software. The usage in different courses depended on the suitability of the topics taught in that particular course for microcomputer use as well as the availability and suitability of existing software for those topics.

IBM was the most consistently used brand of microcomputer. Its popularity could possibly stem from the fact that it is the standard for the accounting industry and accounting departments and schools are anxious to maintain computer hardware compatibility with the accounting profession as well as with other schools. Its popularity could also be derived from the fact that it is cheap.

The overall conclusion is that accounting instructors have already significantly adopted computers into their courses and the use of them is increasing, apparently an irreversible fact in accounting education. This fact suggests that, in the future, additional faculty with greater computer skills and more funds for laboratories and other facilities to support computer assisted instruction will be needed. In addition, publishers and software designers will have to develop more and better software in order to allow for more creative and useful integration of microcomputers into accounting curricula. These developments will be given added impetus by the fact that the accounting profession itself will favor students from those universities that teach their students to use the microcomputer and that produce computer literate graduates.

NOTES

1. Thomas [1984, p. 31] reports a 60% response rate. However, Thomas' response rate cannot be compared with the present study because of the informality of his sample selection procedure. He selected first "friends, then department heads (or equivalent), senior faculty, and individuals whose names were at the top of the alphabetized faculty list (in that order)."
2. This column does not add to 100% because many schools use more than one kind of microcomputer.

REFERENCES

American Accounting Association, Committee on Integrating the Microcomputer into the Financial Accounting Curriculum, *Report of the Committee on Integration of the Microcomputer into the Financial Accounting Curriculum* [AAA, 1985a].

________, Committee on Integrating the Microcomputer into the Managerial/Cost Curriculum, *Integrating the Microcomputer into the Managerial/Cost Curriculum* [AAA, 1985b].

American Assembly of Collegiate Schools of Business, Accreditation Council, *Accreditation Standards and Interpretations for Accounting Programs* [AACSB, 1984].

Bialaszewski, D., M. Kocakulah, and K. Bialaszewski, "Computer Usage in Accounting Curricula: The State of Integration," *Journal of Education for Business* [October 1986], pp. 31-34.

"Computers" (Newsbrief), *Journal of Accountancy* [October 1983], p. 24.

Connors, S., "NAA Research," *Management Accounting* [December 1983], pp. 62-63.

________, "NAA Research," *Management Accounting* [November 1984], pp. 16, 65.

Cronan, T.P. and C.E. Fries, "MIS and Computer Applications in Accounting Courses—Report of a Survey," *Journal of Accounting Education* [Spring 1986], pp. 237-244.

Fleenor, W.C. and J. Danos, "Usage of Microcomputers by Certified Public Accountants," Working Paper [Southeastern Louisiana University, 1985].

Golden, M.R. and C.W. Golden, "Electronic Worksheets: an Audit Tool," *Journal of Accountancy* [April 1984], p. 38.

Hoffman, R., "AICPA Computer Survey," *Journal of Accountancy* [September 1988], pp. 146-150.

Lightner, S. and M. Hartman, "Inventory of Computer Software Designed for Use in the Accounting Curriculum: Student Materials and Test Banks," *Journal of Accounting Education* [Spring 1985], pp. 15-35.

Nash, J.F. and T.G. England, "Computerizing the Accounting Curriculum," *T.H.E. Journal* [September 1986], pp. 89-91.

Parmley, J.E. and W.K. Parmley,"Required Computer Skills," *New Accountant* [November 1986a], pp. 16-19.

________, "Computerized Applications in the Accounting Discipline of Selected AACSB Member Institutions," *Journal of Education for Business* [January 1986b], pp. 174-177.

Thomas, A.L., "North American College and University Uses of Microcomputers in Teaching Accounting—1983 Survey," *Journal of Accounting Education* [Fall 1984], pp. 131-141.

Waller, T.C. and R.A. Gallun, "Microcomputer Competency Requirements in the Accounting Industry: A Pilot Study," *Journal of Accounting Education* [Fall 1985], pp. 131-140.

AN EMPIRICAL STUDY OF POST-INTERNSHIP ACADEMIC PERFORMANCE OF PUBLIC ACCOUNTING INTERNS

Don E. Giacomino

ABSTRACT

One of the many arguments for granting academic credit for accounting internships is increased academic performance of interns following their internship experiences. Previous studies by Koehler, at Penn State, and Knechel and Snowball, at the University of Florida, yield conflicting results. This study, at Marquette University, compared accounting interns (64) with a matched pairs group of noninterns (64) in terms of postinternship academic performance. Statistical testing (95% reliability level) found no significant differences between grades of interns and noninterns in accounting courses (except auditing grades at 90% level) completed after the internship. Overall, the results of this study are consistent with those of Knechel and Snowball at the University of Florida.

Advances in Accounting, Volume 8, pages 179-188.

ISBN: 1-55938-067-5

INTRODUCTION

At many universities, internship programs have become a formalized component of the accounting curriculum. Several studies have measured the frequency and popularity of these programs. As early as 1951, The American Accounting Association (AAA) appointed a Committee on Internship Programs. The committe's report [AAA, 1952] provided a state-of-the-art picture of the extent to which universities offered internships and how the programs were administered. Lowe [1965] reported the results of a similar study, which found that 102 of the 448 universities contacted sponsored an accounting internship program. A recent study by Schmutte [1986, p. 229] showed that 106 of 153 responding universities (of 350 institutions contacted) sponsor accounting internships. It also provides state-of-the-art information about the administration of the programs and provides information useful for evaluating the success of accounting internships. In addition, it evidenced a significant increase in the use of accounting internships since Lowe's 1965 study.

Schmutte [1986, p. 233] also reported that eighty percent of the institutions reporting existence of internships granted degree credit for the experience. One basis for granting degree credit is that "the student's education is enhanced by the internship experience" [Knechel and Snowball, 1987, p. 799]. One specific measure of such enhancement is improved academic performance of interns.

The Knechel and Snowball [1987] paper addressed this issue via an empirical study at the University of Florida. This paper describes a study at Marquette University that replicates certain features of the Knechel and Snowball study. The research issue is whether accounting internship experience significantly affects an intern's academic performance.

The issue deserves study because results of two internship studies—Koehler [1974] and Knechel and Snowball [1987]—are conflicting. Koehler's study, which was not tested statistically, found that interns' grades improved, while Knechel and Snowball found that interns' and noninterns' grades declined over the post-internship period (one semester). Based on these findings and the author's contact with interns and noninterns in his financial accounting and auditing courses, the following hypothesis is posed:

Hypothesis 1. The Grade Point Averages (GPA) at graduation for accounting interns will be higher than the interns' GPA immediately preceding the internship.

Subjects for this study were accounting graduates from Marquette University. Academic performance was measured in terms of the interns' and noninterns' overall change in GPA and their grades in selected accounting courses. Because student feedback in internships has been very positive, one might expect interns to perform even better academically than before the internship. Former interns in the author's classes in auditing clearly evidenced much greater interest in the course than did noninterns. This would be expected, since the internships were auditing positions. In turn, one might expect that the interns would earn higher grades in auditing and perhaps in other accounting courses. Thus, additional hypotheses are:

Hypothesis 2. Students with accounting internship experience will differ from those without such experience with respect to the change in GPA from preinternship to graduation.

Hypothesis 3. Students with accounting internship experience will differ from those without such experience with respect to the postinternship grades earned in each of these courses: Tax I, Tax II, Auditing, and the accounting electives average grade.

The expected difference for each hypothesis is that interns will outperform noninterns.

The next section describes prior studies on accounting internships and summarizes their findings. That section is followed by a description of the accounting internship program and discussion of the research procedure employed. Results of the study and a summary comprise the remaining sections.

PRIOR STUDIES OF ACCOUNTING INTERNSHIPS

Several studies have provided evidence as to the perceived value of accounting internships. Schmutte [1986] observed that "[t]he internship experience provides students with an opportunity to gain an education that cannot usually be obtained in the classroom" [p. 228]. He further stated that internship experiences allow students to consolidate classroom exposure with practical business aspects, to correct any perceived educational deficiency discovered during the internship, and, most importantly, to clarify career objectives before graduation and employment.

Lowe's [1965] study showed that of the 284 colleges not offering internships, 153 indicated that internships were potentially more valuable than an equivalent period of classroom instruction. The responding institutions that sponsor internships cited several other benefits: student placement (85%), increased cooperation and understanding between practitioners and members of the accounting faculty (83%), and attracting students to the accounting major (50+%).

Lowe also contacted 289 former accounting interns to obtain their opinions about the value of their internship experiences. Overall, the respondents were positive about their experience, with 99% stating that they would encourage other accounting majors to participate as interns. In addition, 90% considered the internship more valuable than additional courses in accounting would have been [Lowe, 1965, p. 843]. Other identified benefits were:

- Certain post-internship courses were more meaningful as a result of the internship (66%).
- The internship greatly increased understanding of business operations and procedures (65%).
- The internship improved ability to work with others (81%).
- Confidence in ability as accountants was increased materially (80%).
- Internships heightened or reduced interns' interest in public accounting as a career (90%).

When asked what they considered to be the two greatest advantages of the internships, interns in Lowe's study responded that they offer an opportunity for practical experience and that the internships allowed them to evaluate public accounting as a career field.

One might expect, then, that the benefits of internships identified by former interns would increase motivation and thereby improve the chances for better academic performance after the internship. For example, seeing courses as more meaningful, increased understanding of business operations, and increased confidence would be positive factors that might translate to better grades.

Some researchers have also argued that the internship experience improves subsequent academic performance. A study at Penn State University concluded: "My research findings emphasize the educational merit of these programs" [Koehler, 1974, p. 384]. In addition, Koehler concluded that accounting and general grades improve following an internship. His study measured the academic performance of interns before and after the internship but did not compare interns' performance with a control group (noninterns). Thus, one cannot conclude that the improved academic performance of interns after the internship was due to the internship experience. Perhaps noninterns outperformed interns, but no evidence was gathered.

Knechel and Snowball [1987] concluded a recent study on postinternship academic performance at the University of Florida. The authors state that granting of credit for accounting internships is based on the assumption that the student's education is enhanced by internship experience. Prior to the Knechel and Snowball study, little empirical evidence had been gathered to support that assumption.

Koehler's study found that interns improved academically after the internship experience. However, the Knechel and Snowball study used a control group of noninterns and found that the overall GPA of interns and noninterns both declined after the internship experience. With the exception of auditing, interns also did not outperform noninterns overall or in selected accounting courses. The Knechel and Snowball study improved on the Koehler research by comparing interns with a nonintern group in terms of postinternship academic performance. The control group was identified with a matched-pairs technique that selected noninterns who closely match the intern group before the internship period. Matching was done on the basis of grade-point average and seniority in the degree program. Knechel and Snowball found that interns and noninterns did not differ in overall GPA in courses taken after the internship, that the cumulative GPA of interns and noninterns declined after the internship period, and that auditing was the only course in which interns performed significantly better than noninterns. The fact that interns did outperform noninterns in the auditing course provides some evidence of the educational merits of the internship experience.

Although the Knechel and Snowball study improved upon the previous work by Koehler, a major limitation of the Knechel and Snowball study was the fact that most of the interns in their study graduated one semester after the internship. This period might be too short for measuring post-internship performance. In contrast, Marquette's interns worked during the second semester of the junior year, and the post-internship period consisted of three semesters. The length of the postinternship period is the major difference between the Knechel and Snowball study and this study, apart from the geographic location.

MARQUETTE'S INTERNSHIP PROGRAM

Competition for public accounting internship positions is intense at Marquette. Regular recruiters from the firms interview all qualified applicants on campus in the same manner as graduating seniors. The candidates are ranked on the basis of these interviews and the students' academic records. The coordinator of the internship program uses these rankings to assign students to firms. Eight to ten positions are available annually in Milwaukee and Chicago.

All interns employed by national public accounting firms work within a set of guidelines that specify a work period of three and one-half to four months, full-time audit staff assignments, and a set monthly salary. Interns are required to submit a 6-page paper on the internship, discussing the pros and cons of the program and relating the experience to their prior academic coursework. Employers also complete a form that assesses the internship experience and the program.

These standardized policies and procedures apply only to the public accounting internships. Internship arrangements with corporations and not-for-profit and government organizations vary considerably with respect to duties, work period, pay, and interviewing and selection procedures. Because of this variability, the nonpublic accounting interns were not included in this study.

RESEARCH PROCEDURE

The main objective of this study is to measure the effect of internship experience on subsequent academic performance. As described earlier, the study was designed to compare interns with noninterns in terms of their:

- change in overall GPA (preintern GPA vs. graduation GPA);
- grade in the tax 1 course;
- grade in the tax 2 course;
- grade in the auditing course; and
- grade average for accounting electives courses (two courses).

The intern group consisted of all public accounting interns who graduated from Marquette between 1982 and 1988. Nonintern accounting graduates for the same period were selected on a matched-pairs basis. The purpose was to obtain intern and nonintern groups with comparable academic records at the end of the semester immediately preceding the internship experience. Public accounting internships occur during the second semester of the intern's junior year. At that point, students have earned between 75 and 85 semester credit hours. By referring to official student records, each intern was matched with a nonintern who had a GPA within .10 grade point of the intern and who was within five credit hours of the total credits earned by the intern. This process yielded two groups of 64 subjects. Table 1 summarizes ACT and SAT scores and GPA before the internship for interns and noninterns.

RESULTS

Analysis of variance (ANOVA) was used to analyze the resutls. Each of the dependent variables related to grades earned in specific courses taken after the internship but before graduation. Testing for effects of internships, the independent variable was: INTERNS (Primary treatment, intern vs. nonintern). The dependent variables were: Final GPA, Auditing Grade, Tax 1 Grade, Tax 2 Grade, Accounting Electives (Average) Grade, and the difference in overall GPA (preinternship GPA vs. GPA at graduation).

Table 1. Preinternship Data

1. ACT and SAT Scores ($n = 128$)

	No. of Students	*No. of Students with ACT Comp.*	*No. of Students with SAT-Math SAT-Verbal*
Intern Group	64	49	47
Nonintern Group	64	36	49
Total	128	85	96

2. Preinternship GPA and Test Scores

	GPA Before Internships	*Preinternship Data (Mean Values)*		
		Composite ACT	*SAT-Math*	*SAT-Verbal*
Intern Group	3.1203	24.87	571	475
Nonintern Gruop	3.1013	25.20	566	484
Total (Interns + noninterns)	3.1108	25.04	568	484
F Prob (Interns (vs. Noninterns)	.7963	.7921	.7567	.2388

As Table 1 indicates, the interns were not significantly different from noninterns in terms of GPA before the internship period. Also, ANOVA results show that the groups did not differ significantly on the basis of ACT composite scores, SAT math scores, and SAT verbal scores. Thus, the control group selection process achieved a very close match between interns and noninterns immediately preceding the internship period. The next step was to follow the academic performance of all students included in the sample. A check of noninterns' records up to graduation was made to ensure that those students did not participate later in an internship role.

Table 2 summarizes the ANOVA results. As groups, interns and noninterns earned lower GPA's during the postinternship period than they had earned immediately before the internship period. The decrease in GPA was very slight, however, for each group (.0085 for interns and .0363 for noninterns). These results agree with the Knechel and Snowball [1987] study at the University of Florida; however, they conflict with Koehler's [1974] finding that interns' grades improved after the internship. Statistical testing showed that the change in GPA was not significant between interns and noninterns.

Student's grades in selected accounting courses were obtained from official records to compare interns with noninterns. For the Accounting Elective courses, interns' grades did not differ significantly from noninterns' grades. The Accounting Elective grade refers to the average GPA of the student for one or two accounting electives taken. In most instances, interns took only one

Table 2. Postinternship Data
(Mean Values for Grades)

	Final GPA	*Auditing Grade*	*Tax 1 Grade*	*Tax 2 Grade*	*Accounting Electives Average Grade*	*GPA Difference***
Intern Group	3.1118	3.00	2.95	2.80	3.32	-.0085
Nonintern Group	3.0803	2.82	2.99	2.73	3.26	-.0363
Total (Interns + Noninterns)	3.0918	2.91	2.97	2.76	3.29	-.0224
F Prob (Interns vs. Noninterns)	.6511	.0654	.7388	.5351	.5840	.2550

Note: ** Preinternship GPA vs. GPA at graduation.

elective, since the 3-credit internship counted as one of the two electives each student must complete. Because the internship grade is assigned on the pass/fail basis, it would not affect the interns' GPA or accounting electives grades. Conclusions about relative performance of interns versus noninterns are the same for each of the tax courses; there were no significant differences for Tax 1 and Tax 2 grades.

Although interns' post-internship grades exceeded those of noninterns in all post-internship accounting courses except Tax 1, the differences were not statistically significant. Like the Knechel Snowball study, which found that interns outperformed noninterns in the Auditing course, the auditing grades of interns in the Marquette study were higher than the grades of noninterns. However, the difference was not significant at the 95% reliability level used in the ANOVA. As evidenced by the "*F* Prob" value (.0654) for INT. vs. NONINT (Table 2), the difference bordered on being significant. Indeed, the auditing grade difference would be significant at a 90% reliability level.

SUMMARY AND CONCLUSION

This study was designed to measure the postinternship academic performance of public accounting interns compared with a matched-pairs set of noninterns. Grades in selected accounting courses and the changes in overall GPA (pre- and postinternship) were compared for each group. The hypothesized relationship between the postinternship academic performance of interns and noninterns was that interns would outperform noninterns. Interns and noninterns as groups showed declines (though not significant) in GPA from pre-internship to graduation, and there were no significant differences between interns and noninterns for change in GPA. Grades in each of the selected accounting courses did not differ significantly for the intern versus nonintern groups. With the exception of the grade in Auditing, this study supports the results of the Knechel and Snowball study. Thus, each of the three hypotheses must be rejected since the analysis of variance results show no differences between the interns' and noninterns' performance.

Results of this study and the Knechel and Snowball study cannot support the contention that internships should generate academic credit because they offer academic benefits. However, each study has shown the potential academic value of internships for improving the grade in the auditing course.

Considering the benefits of internships that interns, writers, and others have cited, some significant differences in academic performance overall, or in accounting courses, could have been expected. Grades of accounting interns at Florida [Knechel and Snowball, 1987] decreased after the internship. As the researchers suggested, "senioritis" probably was a factor. However, since the postinternship period for Marquette's interns is three semesters, one might expect that senioritis would not be a factor for them. One might also expect that the interns would be motivated to earn better grades as a result of the internship experience. Perhaps an explanation for the contrary results of this study relates to the fact that almost all public accounting interns in the study received offers of employment from the internship employer. Thus, having a job several months before graduation might have decreased the motivation of the interns. Many interns had admitted informally to this attitude.

A limitation of each of the internship studies to date is that it deals with a single and perhaps unique program. A regional or national study of interns' post graduation performance would provide better insight into the educational and professional merits of internships.

Marquette's internship program offers opportunities with government, not-for-profit organizations, corporations and public accounting firms. Because this study included only the public accounting interns, a study comparing results between types of interns might produce different results. A comparison between firms might prove interesting as well.

This study focused on only one hypothesized value of internships, academic improvement as measured by grades. Although the results call for rejecting the hypotheses, the values of internships should not be ignored. A recent study [Taylor, 1988] focused on the value of internships for improving employment opportunities, for reducing value conflicts and anxiety, and for helping interns to crystallize vocational abilities and interests. Results were mixed, but they showed support for the hypothesized positive effects of internships on employment evaluations and the proability of being hired.

Those who argue for granting credit for an internship experience may point to many benefits that could justify doing so. However, if the major or sole basis for granting of credit is improved academic performance, then the results of this study and of the Knechel and Snowball study should be considered.

ACKNOWLEDGMENT

The author wishes to acknowledge the assistance of Mr. Nikhil Gupta, MBA and V.P. of Gupta Industries, Dalehi, India, who obtained grades and GPA data for this study.

REFERENCES

American Accounting Association, Committee on Internship Programs, "Report of the Committee on Internship Programs," *The Accounting Review* [July 1952].

Knechel, R.W. and D. Snowball, "Accounting Internships and Subsequent Academic Performance: An Empirical Study," *The Accounting Review* (Educational Research Section) [October 1987], pp. 799-807.

Koehler, R.W., "The Effect of Internship Programs on Subsequent College Performance," *The Accounting Review* [April 1974], p. 384.

Lowe, R.E., "Public Accounting Internships," *The Accounting Review* [October 1965], pp. 839-846.

Schmutte, J., "Accounting Internships: The State of the Art," *Journal of Accounting Education* [Spring 1986], p. 229.

Taylor, M.S., "Effects of College Internships on Individual Participants," *Journal of Applied Psychology,* 73,3 [1988], pp. 393-401.

LEARNING STYLE:
A DETERMINANT OF STUDENT PERFORMANCE FOR THE INTRODUCTORY FINANCIAL ACCOUNTING COURSE

Dennis F. Togo and Bruce A. Baldwin

ABSTRACT

Prior studies have shown the convergent learning style to be predominant in accounting majors and professional accountants. This study tested the prediction that students possessing the convergent learning style would perform better than others in an introductory financial accounting course. Other established explanators of past academic performance (GPA), aptitude (composite ACT score), and motivation (declared major) were included as covariates in analyzing academic performance. The results showed that students with the convergent learning style performed at a higher level than other students. Descriptive data for the various majors and learning styles are presented as a basis for further educational research.

Advances in Accounting, Volume 8, pages 189-199.

ISBN: 1-55938-067-5

Studies in accounting education research have established past academic performance, academic aptitude, and motivation as significant determinants of student performance. The research has also suggested that the learning style of an individual may be another explanator of academic performance. This personality factor captures the subject's preferred mode of acquiring and using information when learning. In recent accounting studies, the convergent learning style has been found to be highly associated with students majoring in accounting and professional accountants. If the accounting discipline is indeed conducive to the convergent learning style, then the learning style a student possesses should impact academic performance for an accounting course. This study tested the inclusion of a student's learning style (classified as convergent versus nonconvergent) as another explanatory variable for academic performance in an introductory financial accounting course. The declared major of a student was categorized as accounting versus nonaccounting and included as a surrogate measure of motivation. To increase the reliability of the study, the student's GPA and composite ACT score were also included as established predictors of academic performance.

The next section reviews the Experiential Learning Model, its resultant Learning Style Inventory (LSI), and recent research in accounting utilizing the LSI. The literature review concludes with a discussion of established determinants of student performance in accounting courses. The testable hypothesis is presented and followed by a description of the study. Then the results of the hypothesis test and other descriptive statistics are examined. A summary of the study and its implications for further research utilizing the Learning Style Inventory are presented in the final section.

LITERATURE REVIEW

Learning Style

The Experiential Learning Model developed by Kolb [1976, 1984] postulates a circular process that shifts through a four-stage cycle depicted in Figure 1. Kolb modeled the circular learning process as moving from concrete experience (CE) to reflective observation (RO) to abstract conceptualization (AC) to active experimentation (AE) and back to concrete experience (CE). The learning process begins with an experience from which the individual draws reflections or observations. From these reflections, a concept is developed by the individual to rationalize the experience. The newly derived concept is utilized in subsequent decision making behavior. The result of these experiments becomes the beginning of another experiential learning cycle.

The Kolb model identified two dimensions of learning with each having opposing stages at ends of the continua. The concrete experience and abstract

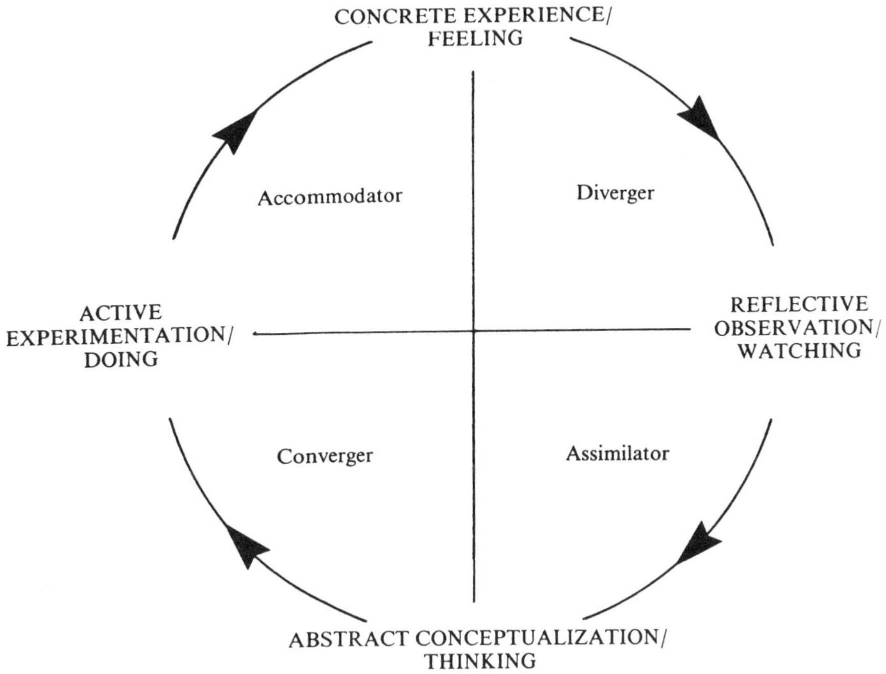

Source: Adapted from Kolb [1981].

Figure 1. Kolb's Learning Cycle and Learning Style Classifications

conceptualization (CE-AC) continuum represented a dimension of learning that contrasts feeling (CE) and thinking (AC). Another dimension of learning represented by the reflective observation and active experimentation (RO-AE) continuum contrasts watching (RO) and doing (AE). Kolb maintained that effective learning utilized each stage of the cycle but that an individual tended to develop over time a preferred combination of these four learning modes.

Kolb's *Learning Style Inventory* [1981] attempts to measure an individual's preferred combination of learning modes. The LSI asks respondents to rank order nine sets of four words that describe the four modes of learning. The total scores for each of the four modes of learning are paired with their difference plotted along the CE-AC continuum and the RO-AE continuum. Figure 1 displays the four quadrants into which the respondents' scores are mapped. Each quadrant represents a combination of two learning modes and is the basis for classifying an individual's learning style. Kolb named the four learning style types: Diverger, Assimiliator, Converger and Accommodator. Brief descriptions of the four learning style types follow:

1. *Diverger:* Their approach to a situation is to observe and gather information. They are imaginative, enjoy brainstorming, are sensitive to feelings, and tend to have broad cultural interests.
2. *Assimilator:* Their approach to a situation is centered around logical soundness. They excel at inductive reasoning, are concise, and are interested in abstract ideas more than people.
3. *Converger:* They are effective at solving problems using deductive reasoning and make decisions based on the practical applications of ideas or concepts. They prefer technical tasks rather than dealing with people.
4. *Accommodator:* They learn best from hands-on experiences, interacting with people, and often rely on intuition when making decisions. They enjoy challenges and new experiences, and are viewed as risk takers.

Kolb [1981] identified certain learning styles that tend to dominate specific professions. This finding was consistent with the research by Hudson [1966] that established cognitive style differences as explanators for career choices. Because learning style is one aspect of cognitive style, these findings explain why certain learning styles and career choices are highly correlated.

Baldwin and Reckers [1984] tested the LSI's ability to distinguish between groups having differing characteristics by surveying undergraduate business majors at a large public university. Their study not only provided additional support for the use of LSI but also determined that accounting majors have learning styles different from other business majors. Baker, Simon, and Bazeli [1984] assessed the learning style preferences of accounting majors and found 39% to be convergers with a strong preference for active experimentation (AE) and abstract conceptualization (AC) learning experiences. In a study of professional accountants' learning styles, Collins and Milliron [1987] classified 53% of their subjects into the convergent learning style. These prior studies identified a correlation between the accounting discipline and the convergent learning style. This study tested the hypothesis that students possessing the convergent learning style would perform better than other students for an introductory financial accounting course.

Established Determinants of Student Performance

The education literature has identified several factors that significantly affect student performance. Studies by Lavin [1965] and Astin [1971] determined that past academic performance is a consistent predictor of future performance. Common measures of past academic performance for college-level students have been high school or prior college grades. Eskew and Faley [1988] included both measures in modeling examination scores of students in their first college-level financial accounting course and found both to be significant explanators of student performance. Eckel and Johnson [1983] modeled student success or failure in an accounting program, rather than a specific course, and found the grade point average for the two accounting principles courses to be a significant factor. Dockweiler and Willis [1984] determined that the GPA earned prior to entering the introductory accounting courses was the best predictor of subsequent academic performance for students while enrolled in the undergraduate accounting curriculum.

Standardized measures of aptitude have also been accepted as reliable predictors of academic performance. Cattell and Butcher [1968] and Astin [1971] have documented the ability of college entrance examinations such as the SAT and ACT to predict academic performance. Eckel and Johnson [1983] utilized both the composite and mathematics ACT scores as predictors of success in an accounting program and found both to be significant. Schroeder [1986] included the student's composite ACT score in predicting college-level accounting exam performance and identified a strong positive association between them.

Although it is difficult to measure, motivation is an established predictor of student performance. Uguroglu and Walberg [1979] reported motivation to be associated with less variance in educational achievement on average than other factors in learning which are replicable correlates. Although motivation measures were weak correlates of learning, they suggested that multiple or multifactorial measures of motivation were likely to improve predictions. Eskew and Faley [1988] found the number of essentially voluntary quizzes to be a significant factor when modeling exam performance for an introductory accounting course. Lavin [1965] determined that students who were certain of their occupational choice and/or major field of study were likely to perform at a higher level than students who were unsure of their goals. Schroeder [1986] classified students as either accounting or nonaccounting majors in attempting to measure motivational differences and found it was a significant factor in predicting exam performance.

The literature review suggests that a personality factor representing an individual's preferred mode to acquire and use information may be another explanator of academic performance for college-level accounting courses. Kolb's convergent learning style has been highly associated with the accounting profession. A hypothesis is presented that tests the inclusion of the convergent learning stype with other established explanators of academic performance.

HYPOTHESIS

The hypothesis of interest tests the student's learning style, categorized as convergent versus nonconvergent, as another explanator of academic performance for an elementary financial accounting course. Established predictors of student performance such as GPA, ACT composite score, and declared major were included as covariates in the statistical analysis. This null form of the hypothesis is stated below:

H_0: For an elementary financial accounting course, there is no difference in exam performance between those students having a convergent learning style and those who have other learning styles.

METHOD

Description of the Study

The sample was obtained from randomly selected sections of elementary financial accounting at a large public university. The sections used a common textbook and were taught primarily by graduate teaching assistants. The elementary financial accounting course was usually the students' first college-level accounting course. It was a core requirement for business majors and it had a prerequisite of sophomore class standing. The final sample size of 218 students refleted deletions for withdrawals during the semester (135), unavailability of ACT scores (256), and other missing data points (77). A comparison of students withdrawing from the course to the final sample identified no significant differences for composite ACT score, GPA, and the composition of business majors and learning styles. ACT scores for some students were not available from the university's records file because transfer students were not required to submit them for admission purposes.

The final sample contained 26 students that received a grade in a prior semester for the same course but were repeating the course. A student repeating the introductory financial accounting course is not unusual but it possibly could confound the study's findings if not examined. The potential confounding was tested statistically by blocking on students that were repeaters. The analysis of covariance (ANCOVA) results found the blocking variable not significant ($p = .948$) after adjusting for the effects of learning style, GPA, ACT composite score, and declared major.

The dependent variable (*EXAMTOT*) used to measure academic performance for the course was the combined score for two mid-term examinations and a comprehensive final examination. Common examinations were administered to all sections of the course at the same time. The exams were in the multiple-choice response format and were comprised of narrative and computational questions. The comprehensive final examination was weighted about twice as much as a mid-term examination. The exam scores accounted for more than 75% of the student's final grade for the course.

The learning style inventory was administered to the students of the selected sections at the beginning of the semester. The students also reported their major, which was initially classified into seven categories: accounting, computer information systems, finance, management, marketing, general business, and other. The seven categories were later grouped into accounting versus nonaccounting majors for statistical analysis.

Past academic performance was measured by the student's grade point average for all courses completed at the subject university prior to enrollment in the introductory financial accounting course. The final sample had an average of 47.5 semester hours and a standard deviation of 23.5 semester hours earned at the subject university prior to entering the course. This study did not include the grade point average earned at another institution by a transfer student. This potential biasing of the study's results was examined with a blocking variable for transfer versus nontransfer students. Although 44% of the final sample had transfer hours accepted prior to entering the course, the ANCOVA results found the blocking variable not significant ($p = .253$) after adjusting for the effects of learning style, GPA, ACT composite score, and declared major.

RESULTS AND DISCUSSION

Hypothesis Test

Hypothesis $\mathbf{H_0}$ tested the inclusion of the student's learning style (*STYLE*), with its two categories of convergent (*CONVERG*) and nonconvergent (*NONCONV*), as a predictor of examination performance for an introductory financial accounting course. The hypothesis was tested using ANCOVA with the student's grade point average (*GPA*), ACT composite score (*ACT*), and declared major (*GROUP*) included as covariates to increase the reliability of the test. The concomitant variable *GROUP* had two categories for accounting (*ACC*) and nonaccounting (*NONACC*) majors.

Bartlett's test for homogeneity of variance of residuals among the four subgroups generated by the ANCOVA indicated that they were homogeneous in variance (chi-square $= 119.07, p = .834$). A test of the homogeneity of slopes assumption for an ANCOVA could not reject the null hypothesis of no difference among slopes.

Table 1 presents the ANCOVA results for hypothesis $\mathbf{H_0}$ utilizing partial sums of squares, sometimes referred to as type III sums of squares. In an

Table 1. ANCOVA for *STYLE, GROUP, GPA,* and *ACT*

Source	*Partial SS*	*DF*	*Mean Square*	*F-Ratio*	*P-Value*
STYLE	677.54	1	677.54	4.66	.0320
GROUP	591.49	1	591.49	4.07	.0450
GPA	5,588.01	1	5,588.01	38.41	.0001
ACT	2,843.38	1	2,843.38	19.54	.0001

Table 2. *EXAMTOT* Adjusted Means for *STYLE* and *GROUP*

Variable	*N*	*Adjusted Means*
STYLE		
CONVERG	46	70.41
NONCONV	172	66.05
GROUP		
ACC	22	71.00
NONACC	196	65.47

analysis of covariance, the partial sums of squares technique adjusts for the concomitant variables and is useful in assessing each predictor variable's marginal effect on the dependent variable. Hence, the results of this hypothesis test would be invariant to the ordering of effects in the model.

The categorical variable *STYLE* was significant with an *F*-ratio of 4.66 and a related *p*-value of .0320 using the partial sums of squares technique. The convergent versus nonconvergent categories for *STYLE* accounted for variance in exam scores beyond the concomitant variables for *GROUP, GPA,* and *ACT.* As expected, the three covariate measures were all significant at *p*-values less than .05. The adjusted means for the two categorical variables *STYLE* and *GROUP* are found in Table 2.

Students with the convergent learning style performed at a higher level than other students for an introductory financial accounting course. The classification scheme employed by the Learning Style Inventory was a significant determinant of the students' academic performance based on their convergent versus nonconvergent learning styles. The effectiveness of the *LSI* to explain examination performance further asserts that personality characteristics are relevant factors in predicting academic performance. Individuals possessing the convergent learning style are described as effective problem solvers who utilize deductive reasoning in decision making.

The statistical significance obtained for *GROUP* confirmed an expected difference in examination performance for accounting versus nonaccounting declared majors. Although this study found that students enrolled in a course of their declared major performed at a higher level than the other students, it did not attempt to determine the causal nature of this occurrence.

Table 3. ANCOVA for *LSI, MAJOR, GPA,* and *ACT*

Source	*Sums of Squares*	*DF*	*Mean Square*	*F-Ratio*	*P-Value*
LSI	1,278.39	3	426.13	2.90	.0363
MAJOR	2,157.70	6	359.62	2.44	.0265
GPA	8,523.66	1	8,523.66	57.91	.0001
ACT	2,786.03	1	2,786.03	18.93	.0001
Error	30,321.29	206	147.19		
Total	45,067.07	217			

Table 4. *EXAMTOT* Adjusted Means and Differences for *LSI*

LSI	*N*	*Adjusted Means*	*Differences Between Means*		
			ASSIMIL	*DIVERG*	*ACCOMMOD*
CONVERG	46	68.15	2.57	4.12	4.32*
ASSIMIL	59	65.58		1.55	1.75
DIVERG	70	64.03			0.20
ACCOMMOD	43	63.83			

Note: * Adjusted means were different at $p < .10$.

Descriptive Analyses

Further analyses were conducted for the original learning styles and classifications of major. The categorical variable for learning style (*LSI*) had four classifications: diverger (*DIVERG*), assimilator (*ASSIMIL*), converger (*CONVERG*), and accommodator (*ACCOMMOD*). The categorical variable for academic majors (*MAJOR*) had seven classifications: accounting (*ACC*), computer information systems (*CIS*), finance (*FIN*), management (*MGT*), marketing (*MKT*), general business (*GNB*), and other majors (*OTH*). An analysis of covariance found significant main effects for learning style (*LSI*) and major (*MAJOR*) as shown in Table 3.

The level of significance obtained for the predictor variables *LSI* and *MAJOR* suggests that certain classes within the categorical variables may have significantly impacted the dependent variable *EXAMTOT*. The adjusted means and paired comparisons for the various classes of *LSI* and *MAJOR* are shown in Tables 4 and 5. The comparisons among *LSI* classes found students possessing the *CONVERG* learning style scored higher than those with the *ACCOMMOD* learning style. The comparisons for *MAJOR* found students with *ACC* as their major scored higher than students with a *GNB* or *MKT* business major.

Table 5. *EXAMTOT* Adjusted Means and Differences by *MAJOR*

Major	*N*	*Adjusted Means*	*Differences Between Means*					
			FIN	*CIS*	*MGT*	*MKT*	*GNB*	*OTH*
ACC	22	69.87	3.16	3.75	3.91	6.48*	7.97*	6.06*
FIN	27	66.71		0.59	0.75	3.32	4.81	2.90
CIS	24	66.12			0.16	2.73	4.22	2.31
MGT	30	65.96				2.57	4.06	2.15
MKT	37	63.39					1.49	-0.42
GNB	43	61.90						-1.91
OTH	35	63.81						

Notes: *ACC* = Accounting
FIN = Finance
CIS = Computer Information Systems
MGT = Management
MKT = Marketing
GNB = General Business
OTH = Other majors
* Adjusted means were different at $p < .10$.

SUMMARY

The research findings strongly supported learning style as another determinant of academic performance for an introductory financial accounting course. The cognitive strengths of students possessing the convergent learning style are conducive to the present college-level accounting curriculum and instruction. A related study could examine the complementary relationship between the convergent learning style and an accounting curriculum. While this study did identify another explanator of academic performance for an introductory financial accounting course, the findings do not imply that a convergent learning style is a prerequisite to successful completion of an accounting program or success in professional accountancy.

The study also identified the students' declared major as another determinant of academic performance in the accounting course. The declared major of a student probably captured individual differences in motivation, aptitude, and the need to achieve. Students often choose to major in accounting because of its job opportunities upon graduation. Some students will select accounting as their major because "it comes naturally" while others may change from being an accounting major because they "just don't think like an accountant." The latter comments support the causal effects on academic performance for the major students selected and their learning style.

Another potential explanator of academic performance that was not included in the analysis is the learning style of the instructors. If the teaching methods of instructors are a reflection of their underlying learning style, then a compatible matching of the instructor and student learning styles should impact academic performance. This may explain why accounting instructors usually can recognize students that "think like accountants." It would not be surprising to find a predominance of the convergent learning style among accounting instructors because they are very often subsets of both accounting professionals and students who majored in accounting.

The findings of this study are limited in its generalizability because the examination was conducted (a) at only one educational institution, (b) for only the introductory financial accounting course, and (c) with tests containing only multiple choice questions.

REFERENCES

Astin, A.W., *Predicting Academic Performance in College* [Free Press, 1971].

Baker, R.E., J.R. Simon, and F.P. Bazeli, "An Assessment of the Learning Style Preferences of Accounting Majors," *Issues in Accounting Education* [Spring 1986], pp. 1-12.

Baldwin, B.A. and P.M. Reckers, "Exploring the Role of Learning Style Research In Accounting Education Policy," *Journal of Accounting Education* [Fall 1984], pp. 63-76.

Cattell, R.B. and H.J. Butcher, *The Prediction of Achievement and Creativity* [Bobbs-Merrill, 1968].

Collins, J.H. and V.C. Milliron, "A Measure of Professional Accountants' Learning Style," *Issues in Accounting Education* [Fall 1987], pp. 193-206.

Dockweiler, R.C. and C.G. Willis, "On the Use of Entry Requirements for Undergraduate Accounting Programs," *Accounting Review* [July 1984], pp. 496-504.

Eckel, N. and W.A. Johnson, "A Model for Screening and Classifying Potential Accounting Majors," *Journal of Accounting Education* [Fall 1983], pp. 57-65.

Eskew, R.K. and R.H. Faley, "Some Determinants of Student Performance in the First College-Level Financial Accounting Course," *Accounting Review* [January 1988], pp. 137-147.

Hudson, L., *Contrary Imaginations* [Penquin, 1966].

Kolb, D.A., "Management and the Learning Process," *California Management Review* [Spring 1976], pp. 21-31.

________, *Learning Style Inventory: Technical Manual* [McBer and Company, 1981].

________, *Experiential Learning* [Prentice-Hall, 1984].

Lavin, D.E., *The Prediction of Academic Performance* [Russell Sage Foundation, 1965].

Schroeder, N.W., "Previous Accounting Education and College-Level Accounting Exam Performance," *Issues in Accounting Education* [Spring 1986], pp. 37-47.

Uguroglu, M.E. and H.J. Walberg, "Motivation and Achievement: A Quantitative Synthesis," *American Educational Research Journal* [Fall 1979], pp. 375-389.

THE IMPACT OF CHANGES IN THE UNIFORM CPA EXAMINATION ON ACCOUNTING EDUCATION

Ali M. Sedaghat and Charles L. Martin Jr.

ABSTRACT

The Board of Examiners of the American Institute of Certified Public Accountants (AICPA) issued an Exposure Draft (ED)—"Proposed Changes in the Uniform CPA Examination"—on March 16, 1987. The ED contained several major suggestions regarding changes in the form and content of the Uniform CPA Examination. This study was stimulated by that ED. It presents the results and analysis of a survey of academic and practicing accountants undertaken during the summer of 1987 regarding the impact of the examination's changes on accounting education. In general, the results of this study indicate that accounting faculty and practitioners believe changes in the Uniform CPA Examination will affect accounting education. This effect may directly or indirectly influence accounting education as it is implemented through accounting texts and academic instruction. Accounting practitioners, however, differentiate the degree by which various accounting programs are influenced by changes in the CPA examination.

Advances in Accounting, Volume 8, pages 201-218.

ISBN: 1-55938-067-5

INTRODUCTION

The CPA certificate is well established as a highly respected designation in the accounting profession. Holders of the certificate are the only ones granted the legal right and responsibility to perform the external financial audit function, attesting to the fairness of the financial statements.

In order to obtain the designation of CPA, one must meet specific state requirements. These requirements typically include two academic components and one practical component. The two academic components include attainment of a college degree and passing a national examination. The practical component requires the CPA candidate to have relevant work experience.

The attainment of a college degree and passing a national examination assure that CPAs have obtained the initial minimum competencies to conduct their professional activities. Furthermore, neither of these components stand alone; they are interrelated. Due to this interrelationship, it is useful to study the association between accounting education and the Uniform CPA Examination.

Accounting faculty and practitioners, as members of the accounting profession, have an expertise and a clear and direct interest in influencing the form and content of the CPA examination. Their opinion is particularly important when considering the apparent influence the certification process has on accounting education. It is the purpose of this study to investigate the perception of accounting educators and practitioners regarding the CPA examination's impact on accounting education.

BACKGROUND OF THE EXAM

The Uniform CPA Examination has undergone numerous changes since it was first administered in 1917, particularly after it became nationally uniform in 1962. Early changes are documented in an article, "The Changing Content of the CPA Examination" by H.S. Hendrickson, in the July 1971 issue of the *Journal of Accountancy.*

In early 1980, the AICPA Board of Directors authorized the Board of Examiners to study the feasibility of changes in the form and content of the Uniform CPA Examination in order to ensure its validity and reliability. The Board of Examiners charged a Task Force with making suggestions regarding the study. The principal objectives of this assignment were:

1. To correlate the Content Specification Outlines for the Uniform CPA Examination with the knowledge, skills, and abilities identified by the practice analysis study.
2. To modify, as appropriate, the Content Specification Outlines in accordance with the practice analysis data and other information acquired.

3. After taking into account the proposed modifications to the Content Specification Outlines, to study the format and structure of the entire Uniform CPA Examination from the viewpoint of appropriateness for covering the content domain [Board of Examiners, 1987, p. 1].

In September 1984, the Board received and accepted *Report Number 1* focusing on the first two objectives. This report resulted in revision of the *1983 Uniform CPA Examination Content Specification Outline* effective with the May 1986 administration of the CPA examination. In October 1986, the Board received and accepted *Report Number 2* focusing on the third objective [Board of Examiners, 1987, p. 1]. This report served as the foundation for the March 16, 1987, AICPA Board of Examiners' Exposure Draft, "Proposed Changes in the Uniform CPA Examination." Major changes suggested in the Exposure Draft were as follows:

1. Combining the contents of the current Accounting Theory and Accounting Practice sections into a single (but two part) section.
2. Condensing the examination to consist of the following four separately scored sections:

    a. Accounting and Reporting—A (4 1/2 hrs.)
    (Business Enterprises)
    b. Accounting and Reporting—B (4 hrs.)
    (Taxation; Managerial; Governmental and Not for Profit Organizations)
    c. Auditing (4 hrs.)
    d. Business Law (2 1/2 hrs.)

3. Modifying the Examination to comprise only objective items, including objective formats other than multiple choice.
4. Shortening the exam period from two-and-one-half to two days.

An open meeting of the Board of Examiners was held on September 15, 1987 to consider the proposed changes. After comments on the Exposure Draft, the Board decided to continue discussion of the proposed changes with the 1987-88 Board of Directors of the National Association of State Boards of Accountancy (NASBA) through a joint coordinating committee (JCC). Based on the August 29, 1988 JCC Report, February 1, 1989 report of NASBA's Committee on the CPA Examination and Professional Writing Skills, and the response and comments from 35 state boards of accountancy, NASBA proposed changes in the CPA Examination's structure and format [NASBA, 1989]. This proposal is set forth in greater deal in the "Present Status of the Exposure Draft" section of this paper.

METHODOLOGY

In order to obtain the views of accounting educators and practitioners, we surveyed 1,170 faculty members and 1,670 practitioners. Faculty members' names were selected from the *1987 Accounting Faculty Directory* [Hasselback, 1987]. At least one faculty member holding a CPA certificate was selected from each school. Practitioners' names were randomly selected from a roster of 5,000 AICPA members provided by the Institute's public relations office. The survey instrument was mailed during the summer of 1987, prior to the AAA Annual Meeting. Four hundred usable responses were received from accounting faculty while 520 usable responses were received from the practitioner group. This represents a 34% and 31% response rate, respectively. In order to respond to the Board of Examiners in a timely manner, a test for nonresponse bias was not planned or performed.

The survey instrument was a 5-choice questionnaire. It requested the accounting faculty member or practitioner to indicate his/her level of agreement/disagreement with each question focusing on the CPA examination's influence on accounting education. The questionnaire also requested information regarding the respondent's background as well as encouraging him/her to provide pertinent comments. The respondents' profile appears in the Appendix.

FINDINGS

In general, the results of this study indicate that accounting faculty and accounting practitioners believe that changes in the Uniform CPA Examination will affect accounting education. This effect may directly or indirectly influence accounting education as it is implemented through accounting texts and academic instruction [Zeff, 1986]. Both accounting communities repeatedly mentioned that the purpose of accounting education has to be broader than just preparing candidates for the CPA examination.

The Objective and Scope of Accounting Education

As the complexity of government and business operations has increased, the role of accounting in society has expanded. No longer are accountants required to have just knowledge of financial accounting and reporting. Accountants are called upon to perform accounting, auditing, tax, and consulting services. These services must be performed within the context of complex pronouncements, changes in information technology, and ethical requirements. In order to accomplish this and more, accountants are required to obtain knowledge, skills, and abilities that go far beyond those that were once

Table 1. The Objective and Scope of Accounting Education (in percent)

Question 1: Should the purpose of accounting education be much broader than preparing candidates for the CPA examination?

	Academicians	*Practitioners*
Strongly Agree	64.3	36.7
Agree	31.5	57.5
Total Agree	95.8	94.2
Disagree	0.0	1.2
Strongly Disagree	0.8	0.8
Total Disagree	0.8	2.0
Not Sure	1.0	2.1
No Response	2.4	1.7
Total	100.0	100.0

required. Accounting education requires a proper balance of technical skills and conceptual understanding in order to meet the broader and more complicated needs of society [AICPA, 1983]. It is incumbent on accounting educators to provide the proper foundation.

As set forth in Table 1, 96% of the accounting educators and 94% of the practitioners responding to this survey agreed that the purpose of accounting education should be much broader than preparing students for the CPA examination (Question 1). The uniformity of this response was aptly summarized by an accounting practitioner: "I believe that it's important for education to concentrate more on teaching students to think rather than pointing students toward the questions and content of a specific examination. Anyone can learn to pass an examination through force feeding of information and immediate regurgitation—but I believe that someone who has been taught to investigate and think through problems will ultimately be a more valuable human being. The objective of accounting education and the CPA exam are not the same and the two should be separated."

Technical Versus Analytical Skills

In order to function successfully as a professional accountant, CPAs need to acquire not only technical and factual knowledge, but higher level cognitive and analytical skills [Board of Examiners, 1987, p. C18]. Support for this assertion is found in the first volume of *Taxonomy of Educational Objectives*

Table 2. Technical Versus Analytical Skills (in percent)

Question 2: Is there a necessary balance in accounting education today concerning the teaching of technical skills as well as analytical skills?

	Academicians	*Practitioners*
Strongly Agree	8.3	3.7
Agree	44.3	39.4
Total Agree	52.5	43.1
Disagree	25.5	20.2
Strongly Disagree	3.8	1.9
Total Disagree	29.3	22.1
Not Sure	14.0	32.5
No Response	3.9	2.3
Total	100.0	100.0

where academic objectives were identified ranging from lower-level skills, such as the ability to recall and understand facts, to higher-level skills, such as the ability to synthesize and evaluate facts [Chance, 1987]. However, it has been argued that problems requiring higher level cognitive skills have rarely been presented on the Uniform CPA Examination [Shute, 1979]. Further, when Shute's methodology was applied to objective questions appearing on the November 1982 and May 1983 exams, it was found that a very high percentage of these questions tested lower-level cognitive skills, such as memorization and the use of algorithms [Baker and Simon, 1985].

According to the response to Question 2 found in Table 2, there is not overwhelming agreement or disagreement by either accounting community regarding a necessary balance in accounting education concerning the teaching of technical skills and analytical skills. Fifty-three percent of the academic participants and 43% of the practitioner participants responded that there is such a balance while 25% and 22%, respectively, did not agree. Nonetheless, any change in the exam that results in more emphasis on one skill over another may also change the balance in accounting education. One academician noted: "Some schools are driven to a great degree by the CPA exam, others are not. On average, changes in the exam will affect how accounting is taught and, in the long run, affect the analytic and conceptual skills of accountants. Objective questions are abysmal, however, in measuring analytic and conceptual skills." Although multiple choice questions asked on past exams may not have adequately tested a candidate's analytic and conceptual skills, objective questions on future exams are to be psychometrically designed to better test those skills [Board of Examiners, 1987, p. 12].

Others believe that college and university programs should emphasize a conceptual and theoretical foundation with practical skills being learned through work experience. One practitioner noted: "Up to a point, university and college accounting courses emphasize conceptual knowledge; given that, the staff accountant or graduate needs to master the techniques of accounting; that is, whether he or she can perform quality work within economic time constraints. The medical profession solved this problem years ago through their rigorous intern and extern programs."

Differences in respondent views regarding a balance between the teaching of technical and higher level cognitive skils were expressed. On one hand, according to one practitioner, "most new accountants coming out of college know very little about bookkeeping. It seems like you need to know this to be able to account for any financial information." On the other hand, another practitioner replied: "So many times I've seen recent graduates leave public accounting (Big 8) because they had no idea of what auditing really was. Accounting education should be a mixture of theory and practical application." If that is the case and if accounting education is influenced by the skill testing level of questions appearing on the Uniform CPA Examination, an entirely objective exam may well influence the balance between higher and lower cognitive skills emphasized in accounting education.

College Education and CPA Examination Qualification

Certified public accountants hold one of the most demanding and responsible professional positions in society. Accounting education plays a major role in preparing students for entrance into the accounting profession [Zeff, 1986]. Yet, the goals of the CPA examination and accounting education are vastly different. The primary purpose of the exam is to test a candidate's technical competence in the discipline of accounting [Board of Examiners, 1987, p. 1]. The primary goal of accounting education is much broader than the development of the student's technical competencies in accounting. Accounting education includes, but is not limited to, the development of critical thinking skills calling upon students to identify problems, exhibit sound judgment, grasp fundamentals in developing solutions, and analyze the consequences of taking alternative actions [Zeff, 1986].

As presented in Table 3, over 94% of each accounting community agreed that preparation for the CPA examination should not be seen as a substitute for extensive college education (Question 3). As noted by a practitioner: "The first line of defense is the professional training process, a process controlled by academia. Nonetheless, due to the variations in size, structure, and direction

Table 3. College Education and CPA Examination Qualification (in percent)

Question 3: Should prepartion for the CPA examination not be seen as a substitute for extensive college education?

	Academicians	*Practitioners*
Strongly Agree	65.0	43.8
Agree	29.8	51.0
Total Agree	94.8	94.8
Disagree	1.0	1.5
Strongly Disagree	1.0	0.2
Total Disagree	2.0	1.7
Not Sure	0.8	1.7
No Response	2.4	1.8
Total	100.0	100.0

of the many accounting programs throughout the country, there are tremendous difficulties inherent in such a screening process. Therefore, unless uniformity is demanded of all programs, the exam along with appropriate public accounting experience is the only means by which one may enter the profession."

The Impact of the CPA Examination on Accounting Education

According to American Accounting Association past President Stephen Zeff: "The examination [has a] profound impact on the texture and quality of accounting education in the United States. Changes in the coverage of the CPA Examination are promptly reflected in major accounting and auditing textbooks, and the questions and problems appearing on the Examination are faithfully reproduced in the textbooks and in their accompanying packages of teaching and learning materials. As the Examination is seen to concentrate more on technical details, a responsive chord is sounded in textbooks and course syllabi. We cannot ignore the effect the CPA Examination has on the way in which accounting, auditing, taxation, and business law are taught in colleges and universities. Indeed, if it were one's wishes to see more emphasis placed in accounting education on developing students' diagnostic, analytical, and judgmental skills, the quickest and surest way would be for the organized profession to devote more attention to testing these qualities on the CPA Examination" [Zeff, 1986].

Table 4. The Impact of the CPA Examination on Accounting Education (in percent)

Question 4: Are accounting educators generally influenced by the form and content of the CPA examination?

	Academicians	*Practitioners*
Strongly Agree	29.0	18.5
Agree	53.0	57.3
Total Agree	82.0	75.8
Disagree	6.5	5.0
Strongly Disagree	0.8	1.0
Total Disagree	7.3	6.0
Not Sure	8.5	16.3
No Response	2.2	1.9
Total	100.0	100.0

Question 5: Is accounting education influenced by the form (i.e., objective versus essay) of the CPA examination?

	Academicians	*Practitioners*
Strongly Agree	18.8	10.6
Agree	44.5	40.6
Total Agree	62.3	51.2
Disagree	15.5	17.9
Strongly Disagree	3.0	1.9
Total Disagree	18.5	19.8
Not Sure	16.0	27.1
No Response	2.2	1.9
Total	100.0	100.0

Question 6: Would changing the CPA examination form eventually influence accounting education as well?

	Academicians	*Practitioners*
Strongly Agree	28.3	16.0
Agree	41.0	49.8
Total Agree	69.3	65.8
Disagree	10.3	6.9
Strongly Disagree	2.0	0.8
Total Disagree	12.3	7.7
Not Sure	16.0	24.6
No Response	2.4	1.9
Total	100.0	100.0

Further support of this view is acknowledged by the Board of Examiners where they warn that "some accounting programs appear to be structuring their curricula narrowly around Examination content, rather than broadly to encompass the entire field of accountancy." The academic community should be cautious in using the Examination as the primary guide for curriculum development. "To the extent this practice exists, the Examination is being misused" [Board of Examiners, 1987, p. 19]. It would therefore appear that changing the form and content of the Uniform CPA Examination may influence more than just the selection process of future CPAs. It may also significantly influence accounting education by providing an incentive for the development of higher level cognitive skills.

Those responding to this survey are in agreement with both Zeff and the Board of Examiners (Table 4). They do not separate academic training from CPA exam preparation when preparing students for entry into the public accounting profession. One faculty member noted: "I'm extremely concerned about the ultimate effects on the accounting education process in most universities. Many professors pattern mid-term and final exams after the CPA exam (60% multiple choice, 40% essay or problems). If the exam changes to 100% objective, so will many accounting course mid-term and final exams in these universities." However, some institutions of higher education do differentiate between accounting education and CPA exam preparation. As one practitioner stated: "Although my undergraduate institution placed a heavy emphasis on preparation for a career in public accounting, the University did not offer a program aimed at only passing the CPA exam. A well rounded accounting and general education were stressed." According to the survey, accounting faculty (82%) and practitioners (76%) agreed that accounting educators are generally influenced by the form and content of the CPA examination (Question 4).

One faculty member said: "Whether we admit it or not, the accounting program here is aimed at the CPA exam. We do not structure the courses as CPA preparation, but the content is largely determined by chances of appearing on the CPA exam." A practitioner tempered this view by stating: "Accounting education cannot avoid being influenced by the Exam. Furthermore, it shouldn't avoid this influence assuming both education and exam are concentrating on teaching/testing important, current, and relevant accounting topics crucial for the understanding of accounting." When asked if accounting education will be influenced by the form of the examination, less than 20% of all respondents disagreed. However, many indicated they were "not sure" (Question 5 and 6). This result represents a significant difference from that which was reported by the *Public Accounting Report* (PAR). According to the December 1, 1987 issue, 64% of the responding professors indicated that the AICPA's tentative plan to eliminate essay questions from the Uniform CPA Examination would have little or no effect of their teaching method. It was

Table 5. The Impact of Other Professional Examinations on Accounting Education (in percent)

Question 7: Are accounting educators more sensitive to questions appearing on CPA examinations than to questions appearing on CMA examinations?

	Academicians	*Practitioners*
Strongly Agree	34.5	18.3
Agree	46.8	41.2
Total Agree	81.3	59.5
Disagree	5.3	0.8
Strongly Disagree	0.3	0.0
Total Disagree	5.6	0.8
Not Sure	11.0	37.6
No Response	2.1	2.1
Total	100.0	100.0

Question 8: Are accounting educators more sensitive to questions appearing on CPA examinations than to questions appearing on CIA examinations?

	Academicians	*Practitioners*
Strongly Agree	41.8	21.3
Agree	45.0	39.8
Total Agree	86.8	61.1
Disagree	2.0	0.6
Strongly Disagree	0.3	0.3
Total Disagree	2.3	0.9
Not Sure	8.8	35.3
No Response	2.1	2.7
Total	100.0	100.0

not stated why the adoption of an all objective exam would have little or no effect on their teaching method. It is possible that accounting educators responding to PAR's survey presently emphasize objective questions.

The Impact of Other Professional Examinations on Accounting Education

Three professional certifications are based upon accounting education—Certified Public Accountant (CPA), Certified Management Accountant (CMA), and Certified Internal Auditor (CIA). Each certification has an associated professional organization. Each professional organization and accompanying certification reflects a different focus for the professional accountant. The CPA is primarily associated with protecting the interests of users of financial statements by attesting to the fairness of those statements. The authority to perform such a function is granted by the state in which the individual is licensed. The CMA and CIA designations are intended to signify a level of professional attainment. A license to practice is not bestowed upon the recipient.

The Uniform CPA Examination is by far the oldest certification exam for professional accountants. It was first administered in 1917. At present, over 135,000 candidates sit for the exam each year. In comparison, the CMA and CIA examinations were first administered in 1972 and 1974, respectively. Typically, the yearly draw for the CMA exam and CIA exam are 4,500 and 2,000 candiates, respectively. Based upon the long and successful history of the CPA examination relative to the other two examinations, one would expect it to have a greater effect on accounting education. This speculation is supported by positive responses from 83% of the academicians and 77% of the practitioners responding to the questionnaire (see Table 5). According to both groups, accounting educators are more sensitive to questions appearing on CPA examinations than to questions appearing on either the CMA of CIA examinations; however, over 35% of the responding practitioners indicated they were "not sure" (Questions 7 and 8). This "not sure" position may, in part, be explained by the large number of practicing respondents (45%) who are not presently working in public accounting (see Table A.1). Due to their employment, they may exhibit a greater sensitivity towards CMA and CIA questions. According to one practicing accountant, "I think accounting educators are more sensitive to questions appearing on CPA examinations than to questions appearing on CMA or CIA examinations, but I don't think educators necessarily should be more influenced by the CPA examination than the CMA or CIA. This sensitivity may be observed by a review of accounting textbooks. Many end of chapter review questions and problems are adopted from professional examinations with the greatest number coming from past CPA examinations."

The extent to which professional examination questions are incorporated in accounting textbooks was not addressed in this survey; however, it is questionable whether the adoption of professional examination questions into accounting textbooks is desirable or not. By incorporating these questions, textbook authors are reinforcing the direction of accounting education towards the technical proficiencies tested on the professional exams.

Desirability of Publishing CPA Examination Questions and Unofficial Answers

The AICPA has a long history of publishing the questions and solutions to the CPA examination. Since 1917, CPA candidates have been permitted to retain their examination booklets for comparison with the AICPA's unofficial solutions. The Board of Examiners' reasons for continued publication of the *Questions and Unofficial Answers* are:

1. The unofficial answers provide feedback to candidates permitting them to check their answers against those provided.
2. The above process provides an element of quality control because the candidates also check their answers against other available sources referenced in the publication.
3. The boards of accountancy and the educational community can provide constructive feedback upon reviewing the examination.
4. The Board's openness to the public and other interested parties is evidenced by publication.
5. Reviewing this publication will help candidates to be more efficient and effective in their study and preparation for the examination [Board of Examiners, 1987, p. 18].

The Board of Examiners also present disadvantages of publishing the *Questions and Unofficial Answers* of the examination; some of their reasons are:

1. Pretesting of the questions is desirable since it would enhance the examination's pyschometric qualities. However, publication of the *Questions and Unofficial Answers* would mitigate the security of these questions thereby eliminating their reuse.
2. Inability to use technological innovations in psychometric methodology that would permit the testing to be more accurate and efficient with questions being tailored to the candidate's ability.
3. Some accountancy programs misuse the exam by structuring their curricula around the CPA examination's content.
4. A high development cost is being incurred since the Examination must be entirely rewritten each time [Board of Examiners, 1987, p. 19].

Approximately 84% of the participating faculty members and 66% of the responding practitioners believe that publication of the *Questions and Unofficial Answers* influence accounting education (Table 6, Question 9), and more than 88% of all respondents indicated that the AICPA should continue publication of the CPA examination as well as the *Questions and Unofficial Answers* (Questions 10 and 11). Published or unpublished, the form and content of the Uniform CPA Examination will continue to influence accounting education.

By publishing the *Questions and Unofficial Answers,* the AICPA helps provide the basis for CPA exam-emphasized material to be incorporated into the classroom through textbook questions and course examinations. Eliminating the AICPA's *Questions and Unofficial Answers* and prohibiting the candidates from taking their exam booklet may be the most efficient and effective means to reducing CPA exam targeted instruction in the classroom. However, it is quite possible that a new emphasis will now be placed on the CMA and CIA professional examinations assuming continued publication of their *Questions and Unofficial Answers.*

Table 6. Desirability of Publishing the CPA Examination Questions and Unofficial Solutions (in percent)

Question 9: Does the publication of CPA Examination, *Questions and Unofficial Answers,* influence accounting education?

	Academicians	*Practitioners*
Strongly Agree	23.3	12.9
Agree	51.3	53.1
Total Agree	74.6	66.0
Disagree	7.0	8.3
Strongly Disagree	1.5	0.4
Total Disagree	8.5	8.7
Not Sure	14.8	23.8
No Response	2.1	1.5
Total	100.0	100.0

Question 10: Should the Board continue the publication of the exmaination questions?

	Academicians	*Practitioners*
Strongly Agree	49.5	26.5
Agree	42.0	63.7
Total Agree	91.5	90.2
Disagree	1.0	1.9
Strongly Disagree	1.3	0.2
Total Disagree	2.3	2.1
Not Sure	4.0	6.0
No Response	2.2	1.7
Total	100.0	100.0

Question 11: Should the Board continue the publication of the examination, *Questions and Unofficial Answers*?

	Academicians	*Practitioners*
Strongly Agree	51.3	27.1
Agree	39.3	61.7
Total Agree	91.6	88.8
Disagree	1.8	2.7
Strongly Disagree	1.0	0.4
Total Disagree	2.8	3.1
Not Sure	4.5	6.5
No Response	1.1	1.6
Total	100.0	100.0

PRESENT STATUS OF THE EXPOSURE DRAFT

As of this writing, the Board of Examiners is considering six changes approved by the National Association of State Boards of Accountancy (NASBA) at their April 28, 1989 meeting. These changes are consistent with the concerns of accounting educators and accounting practitioners regarding the effect of the examination's form and content on accounting education. In its proposal, NASBA recommended:

1. Increasing the length of the examination by 1 hour from the proposed 15 hours to 16 hours.
2. Increasing the number of essay/problem questions to at least 20% on three sections of the exam.
3. Grading selected essay questions for writing skills.
4. Adding Professional Responsibility to the Business Law Section of the exam. This section will include questions focusing on professional conduct, audit controls, and other responsibilities which normally appear on the exam's audit section.
5. The percentage of 4-option multiple choice questions will not exceed its present composition of 60%. Exclusive of essay/problem questions, other objective answer formats will be used for the remaining questions in each section.
6. Hand-held calculators will be provided to candidates for use in the Accounting and Reporting Sections A and B [NASBA, 1989].

CONCLUSIONS

Based on the views of the respondents, the scope and objective of accounting education should continue to be much broader than preparing students for the successful completion of the CPA examination. Nevertheless, the form and content of professional accounting examinations, especially the CPA examination, have a significant impact on accounting education. This impact influences accounting education directly and indirectly. Some ways in which it influences are:

1. Accounting faculty at some schools have stated that they are driven either explicitly (by the mission of the school) or implicitly (by the need to maintain their reputation in the local professional community) to prepare their students for passing the CPA examination. Many of the faculty members responding to this questionnaire have stated that CPA examination questions are incorporated into their accounting courses.
2. Accounting practitioners are concerned that the educational philosophy of these schools is heavily influenced by professional examinations. They have expressed their concern about the use of CPA examination questions as a teaching and examination tool.

3. Accounting practitioners expect more from accounting programs than the preparation of CPA candidates. A majority of the responding practitioners commented that they are dissatisfied with the emphasis many accounting programs place on a career in public accounting and passing the CPA exam. They believe that accounting programs should enlighten students as to the various career opportunities available in the field of accounting.

Changes in the Uniform CPA Examination proposed by the Board of Examiners will have an impact on accounting education and influence on the accounting practice. The competence of future CPAs is an important issue for accounting faculty and accounting practitioners as well as society as a whole. Accounting faculty and practitioners have the right and obligation to actively participate in shaping the form and content of future CPA examinations. If that obligation is ignored, or if that opinion is not strongly voiced, then there is an abrogation of educational and professional responsibility.

APPENDIX: PROFILE OF RESPONDENTS

Both groups were requested to provide data regarding their age, sex, year of certification, years of experience in public accounting, and highest position held in public accounting. Accounting faculty were also asked to provide data regarding years of teaching. Accounting practitioners were requested to indicate their present position in the work force.

As presented in Table A.1, approximately 83% of the responding accounting faculty were male, with most being at least 40 years old and having at least 11 years of experience teaching accounting. In comparison, over 81% of the responding practitioners were male with most being at least 30-years-old and having a minimum of 10 years of accounting experience. At the time of this survey 54% work in public accounting, 30% work in industry, and the remaining 16% are employed in government, nonprofit organizations, and other business sectors.

All of the faculty members replying to this survey have attained professional certification and have had substantial experience practicing public accounting. Over 62% have been certified for at least 11 years and 74% have held a position with a public accounting firm. Much of their experience in public accounting has been with larger firms at entry level positions; however, almost 20% have held senior level positions of manager or partner. Similarly, the majority of practitioners replying to this survey indicated that they have held positions in public accounting firms ranging from 4 to 20 years. Approximately

Table A.1. Profile of Respondents

Description	*Academicians (n = 400)*	*Practitioners (n = 520)*
Age (%)		
20-29	2.0	20.0
30-39	24.4	45.0
40-49	36.8	20.4
50 and over	35.8	14.4
No Response	1.0	0.2
Sex (%)		
Male	82.5	81.2
Female	16.8	18.7
No Response	0.7	0.1
Years of Certification (%)		
1-10 years	38.8	60.0
11-20 years	36.5	24.0
More than 20 years	24.7	11.0
No Response	0.0	5.0
Held Position in Public Accounting Firm (%)		
Yes	74.0	92.7
No	25.5	6.9
No Response	0.5	0.4
Experience in Public Accounting (%)		
1-3 years	39.8	18.7
4-6 years	21.5	27.7
7-10 years	6.0	19.6
11-20 years	3.8	18.8
More than 20 years	3.5	8.3
No Response	25.4	8.9
Highest Position Held in Public Accounting Firm (%)		
Partner	10.7	29.4
Manager	8.3	25.0
Senior	26.5	29.4
Staff Member	28.5	8.7
No Response	26.0	7.5
Size of Public Accounting Firms Worked For* (Frequency)		
Multi-National/National	204	282
Regional	51	73
Local	110	240
Teaching Experience: Academicians Only (%)		
1-10 years	38.8	
11-20 years	36.5	
21-30 years	19.2	
More than 30 years	5.5	
Present Position: Practitioners Only (%)		
Public Accounting		54.2
Industry		36.2
Government		3.5
Nonprofit Organization		1.2
Other		4.6
No Response		0.3

Note: * Some individuals worked for more than one type.

half of the practitioners acquired their public accounting experience through employment with multinational/national firms as opposed to regional or local firms. Further, 54% of the practitioner respondents have held senior level positions as managers or partners.

ACKNOWLEDGMENTS

The authors wish to acknowledge the administrative support of Loyola College and also the helpful comments made by Paul B.W. Miller and two anonymous reviewers.

REFERENCES

American Institute of Certified Public Accountants, Commission on Professional Accounting Education, *Implementation of a Postbaccalaureate Educational Requirement for the CPA Profession* [AICPA, 1983].

American Institute of Certified Public Accountants, "Examiners Defer Action on Changes," *Journal of Accountancy* [November 1987], p. 31.

Baker, R.E. and J.R. Simon, "An Assessment of the Cognitive Demands of the Uniform CPA Examination and Implications for CPA Review/Preparation Courses," *Journal of Accounting Education* [Fall 1985], pp. 15-29.

Board of Examiners of the American Institute of Certified Public Accountants, Exposure Draft, "Proposed Changes in the Uniform CPA Examination," [AICPA, March 16, 1987].

Chance, P., "Master of Mastery," *Psychology Today* [April 1987], pp. 43-46.

Hasselback, J.R., *Accounting Faculty Directory 1987* [Prentice-Hall, 1987].

Henderickson, H.S., "The Changing Content of the CPA Examination," *Journal of Accountancy* [July 1971], pp. 60-67.

National Association of State Boards of Accountancy, "Action of NASBA Board of Directors on Proposed Changes in the Uniform CPA Examination," *Memorandum* [April 28, 1989].

Professional Publication, "Professors Divided on Exam Changes," *Public Accounting Report* [December 1, 1987], p. 2.

Shute, G.E., *Accounting Students and Abstract Reasoning: An Exploratory Study* [AAA, 1979].

Zeff, S.A., "President's Message," *Accounting Education News* [AAA, June 1986].

PART III

AUDITING

COMPETITION IN AUDITING AND THE PRODUCT DIFFERENTIATION HYPOTHESIS:

AN OVERVIEW AND ANALYSIS OF POLICY IMPLICATIONS

Michael C. Knapp

ABSTRACT

In recent years, increasing concern has been expressed by several parties, both critics and supporters of the auditing profession, that excessive price competition among audit firms is damaging the overall quality of professional audit service. Such concern has led to suggestions that regulatory intervention may be required to restrain price competition in the audit market to ensure that economically constrained time budgets do not impose undue restrictions on the scope of independent audits. However, the results of numerous studies into the nature of competition in the audit market question the need for such intervention. The purpose of this paper is to provide an integrative overview and discussion of the policy implications of this body of research. Most important, the results of recent studies which have investigated the nature of competition in the audit market tend to refute the contention of the Cohen Commission, as well as other parties, that price is the principal or sole basis for competition among audit firms.

Advances in Accounting, Volume 8, pages 221-232.

ISBN: 1-55938-067-5

During the 1970s, the AICPA-sponsored Cohen Commission [AICPA, 1978] concluded that price was the principal basis for competition in the audit market and warned that aggressive pricing strategies by audit firms might eventually threaten the economic viability of the independent audit function. More recently, the repeal of such ethical rules as the prohibitions against advertising and client solicitation have led to mounting concern that excessive price competition is having a pervasive and adverse impact on the auditing profession [Keefe, 1985; "Audit Fees Fall," 1985]. Audit firms are allegedly downgrading the importance of auditing as a revenue function and treating the audit as a 'loss leader' used principally to gain access to more profitable consulting opportunities with audit clients ["CPA Firms Diversify," 1985]. Hermanson, Dykes, and Turner [1987] suggest that unless regulatory authorities adopt measures to reverse this trend, economically constrained time budgets could impose unreasonable limits on the scope of independent audits resulting in potentially serious consequences for the profession, the most severe being an increase in the number of audit failures.

Over the past ten years, several researchers have investigated the degree of price competition in the audit market. This research documents that audit firms do, in fact, compete on a price basis and confirms that aggressive pricing strategies are being employed by certain audit firms [Simunic, 1980; Simon and Francis, 1988]. However, this research fails to corroborate the contention of several parties that 'cutthroat' pricing is widespread and strongly refutes the contention that price is the sole basis for competition in the audit market [Palmrose, 1986; Simunic and Stein, 1986]. Given these results, there is a need to obtain a more thorough understanding of the nature of competition in the audit market prior to considering recent recommendations for regulatory intervention to curb supposedly excessive price competition among audit firms. Toward this end, this paper provides an integrative overview of a body of theoretical and empirical research which suggests that factors other than price serve as the primary basis for competition among suppliers of audit services.

ALTERNATIVE EXPLANATIONS FOR THE TWO-TIER STRUCTURE OF THE AUDIT MARKET

Because competitive forces over the past several decades are responsible for the present structure of the audit market, most research investigating the nature of competition in the auditing profession has focused on explaining the audit market's definite two-tier structure. Palmrose [1986] identified three hypotheses developed in recent years to account for the structure of the audit market:

H1. The suggestion by the Cohen Commission that lower audit fees, resulting from economies of scale, are responsible for Big Eight firms' domination of the audit market.

H2. The contention by the Metcalf Committee [U.S. Senate, 1977] that Big Eight firms operate as a cartel and in doing so employ anti-competitive practices to expand their market shares and sustain their fees at an artifically high level.

H3. The product differentiation hypothesis developed by DeAngelo [1981], Dopuch and Simunic [1982], and Simunic and Stein [1986] maintains that Big Eight audits are perceived to be value-differentiated from non-Big Eight audits and that this perceived differential accounts for the market dominance of the Big Eight firms and justifies the generally higher cost of a Big Eight audit.

The first issue raised by these competing hypotheses is clearly of an empirical nature: Are Big Eight fees higher or lower than non-Big Eight fees? Since the Congressional hearings and Cohen Commission study of the past decade, at least ten empirical studies have investigated the level of audit fees charged by public accounting firms.[1] Although the results of this research have not been totally consistent, the more recent of these studies suggest that Big Eight fees are higher than non-Big Eight fees [Francis and Simon, 1987]. This is especially true for small to moderately sized public companies which is the segment of the audit market in which Big Eight and non-Big Eight firms are most likely to compete for the same audit clients. This finding tends to refute the 'economies of scale' hypothesis but is consistent with both the product differentiation and cartel hypotheses.

The intuitive appeal of the cartel hypothesis has been diminished in recent years by the repeal of many of the ethical rules that, according to the Metcalf Committee, inhibited competition in the audit market. The expanding market shares of Big Eight firms in recent years [McConnell, 1984], in spite of the existence of competitive bidding on a wide scale and the elimination of the prohibitions against client solicitation and advertising, suggest that audit clients prefer Big Eight auditors even though Big Eight audits are generally more costly than non-Big Eight audits. This conclusion leaves the product differentiation hypothesis as the most viable explanation, of the three theories identified by Palmrose, for the two-tier structure of the audit market. Because it is viewed by many parties as having pejorative connotations for small audit firms, the product differentiation hypothesis has spurred considerable debate within the profession. The following section summarizes the key focus on this debate, the allegation that product differentiation, if it does exist in the audit market, is a function of illusory rather than actual differences in the quality of audit service provided by different sized audit firms. Additionally, the following section discusses the most widely accepted version of the product differentiation hypothesis which is predicated on the assumption that purchasers of audit services have collectively induced audit firms to provide distinctly different levels of audit quality.

OVERVIEW OF THE PRODUCT DIFFERENTIATION HYPOTHESIS

Illusory Versus De Facto Product Differentiation

In the late 1970s, representatives of non-Big Eight firms asserted that the preference for Big Eight auditors by public companies stemmed from an illusory, rather than *de facto*, differential in the quality of audit service provided by the two size classes of auditors [AICPA, 1980]. This conclusion served as the basis for the allegation that non-Big Eight firms were being subjected to unfair discrimination, not by the Big Eight firms, as the Metcalf Committee contended, but rather by corporate executives, loan officers, and other parties influential in auditor selection decisions [Arnett and Danos, 1979]. According to the Derieux Committee [AICPA, 1980], a group formed by the AICPA to study the unique problems of small and medium sized CPA firms, audit clients often base their auditor selection decisions on the 'size factor' alone, while ignoring the fact that the quality of audit service, as maintained by the Cohen Commission, is independent of firm size. The Derieux Committee urged the profession to take affirmative measures to eliminate such discrimination. One of its principal recommendations was for the AICPA to undertake a campaign to educate parties involved in the selection of independent auditors that the obligation of all audit firms to comply with GAAS serves to ensure that audit quality is independent of audit firm size.

The Derieux Committee's conclusions and prescription for 'educating' consumers of audit services were almost immediately contested by academic researchers. Generally, these researchers contended that Big Eight firms possessed superior audit technologies which made their services more desirable than those of smaller firms.[2] DeAngelo [1981], however, reached the same conclusion in an argument that was independent of the technological capabilities of the two size classes of auditors. According to her analysis, the perceived likelihood that an auditor will report a discovered material error determines the degree of credibility that financial statement users impute to an audit opinion. Given the larger clienteles of Big Eight firms compared to non-Big Eight firms, the former are subject to a much higher opportunity cost for failure to report known client errors. This higher opportunity cost supposedly increases the perceived likelihood that Big Eight auditors will report discovered material errors, and thus serves to enhance the credibility and intrinsic economic value of a Big Eight audit opinion vis-à-vis the opinion of a non-Big Eight auditor.[3]

Market-Induced Product Differentiation

DeAngelo's theory provides an explanation for the two-tier structure of the audit market which assumes de facto product differentiation. A more developed and widely discussed version of the product differentiation hypothesis, also based upon an underlying assumption of de facto product differentiation, was presented by Dopuch and Simunic [1982] and extended subsequently by Simunic and Stein [1986]. One of the more appealing aspects of the Simunic and Stein view of product differentiation is that it does not have pejorative connotations for non-Big Eight firms. Contrary to DeAngelo's model of audit quality, these researchers assume that the likelihood auditors will choose to ignore discovered material errors is essentially nil for all size classes of audit firms, given the servere sanctions imposed for such malfeasance by professional and regulatory bodies.

Simunic and Stein posit that audit clients demand varying levels of assurance that their financial statements are free of material errors and that for competitive purposes audit firms, like most commercial enterprises, specialize in providing a quality of service or product demanded by a specific and limited class of consumers. Implicit in this argument is the assumption that generally accepted auditing standards (GAAS) establish a minimum threshold for audit quality but do not preclude audit firms from providing a higher level of audit assurance to their clients.[4] Big Eight firms, according to Simunic and Stein, have defined their market segment as consisting primarily of fairly large, publicly-owned companies which, because of their size and capital resource requirements, demand an extremely high level of credibility for their financial statements and, consequently, an independent audit that provides a comparably high level of audit assurance. Alternatively, smaller audit firms have defined their market segment as consisting of small to moderately-sized public and privately owned companies, audit clients that do not demand as high a level of audit assurance as large public companies. Since Simunic and Stein assume that these smaller audit firms are providing quality audits—in fact, high quality audits as dictated by GAAS—their argument does not have pejorative connotations for these firms.

The high cost of developing and maintaining an audit technology geared to provide a specific level of audit assurance, according to Simunic and Stein, generally precludes audit firms, particularly smaller firms, from providing the levels of audit service demanded by both classes of audit clients. Consequently, as the clients of non-Big Eight auditors grow larger and come to demand greater access to the capital markets and a higher overall degree of financial statement credibility, their non-Big Eight auditors cannot readily supply the higher level of audit assurance demanded. As a result, such companies are forced to switch to larger auditors.

EMPIRICAL EVIDENCE REFLECTING ON THE VALIDITY OF THE PRODUCT DIFFERENTIATION HYPOTHESIS

The theoretical research leading to the development of the product differentiation hypothesis (PDH) has spurred considerable empirical research in recent years. Most of this research focuses on two key issues at the center of the product differentiation controversy: (1) whether there is evidence that Big Eight audits are, in any sense, of higher quality than non-Big Eight audits; (2) whether financial statement users perceive that Big Eight audits are superior to non-Big Eight audits or, at least, impute a greater degree of credibility to financial statements audited by Big Eight firms as compared to financial statements audited by non-Big Eight firms.

Empirical Evidence of De Facto Product Differentiation

DeAngelo [1981] and Dopuch and Simunic [1982] maintain that de facto audit quality is generally unobservable. Nevertheless, certain fairly objective surrogates are readily observable and can be measured. Two such surrogates are the relative frequency of sanctions imposed against audit firms by regulatory authorities and the rate of meritorious lawsuits filed against audit firms. Regarding the frequency of regulatory sanctions, for a 5-year period, 1981-1986, the Treadway Commission [National Commission on Fraudulent Financial Reporting, 1987] reported that 74% of all enforcement actions imposed on auditors by the Securities and Exchange Commission involved non-Big Eight auditors even though 84% of SEC registrants are audited by Big Eight firms. Likewise, in a recent longitudinal study of the litigation activity of audit firms, Palmrose [1988] documented that Big Eight firms, as a group, are sued less frequently than smaller firms and experience comparatively fewer unsuccessful outcomes of the lawsuits filed against them.

A third surrogate for de facto audit quality which is more difficult to observe and measure than regulatory sanctions or meritorious lawsuits is the number of hours expended on audit engagements. In a survey study, Palmrose [1986] found evidence that, ceteris paribus, Big Eight audits are more time-intensive than non-Big Eight audits, a finding supportive of Simunic and Stein's [1986] contention that Big Eight clients demand more rigorous audits than non-Big Eight clients.

Each of these surrogates for audit quality is subject to certain criticisms. For instance, regarding litigation activity, a number of variables other than audit quality influence the litigation risk to which audit firms are exposed, and these risk factors likely vary across the different size classes of audit firms. Similarly, the Treadway Commission's findings regarding the disparate rate of enforcement actions imposed on audit firms of different size classes may be more a function of latent characteristics of the clienteles of Big Eight and non-Big Eight firms than being indicative of differences in the quality or rigor of Big Eight versus non-Big Eight audits.[5] Nevertheless, when considered together, these data, at the very least, suggest a need for further research examining the issue of de facto product differentiation in the audit market.

Empirical Evidence of Perceived Product Differentiation

The bulk of the empirical research intended to test the PDH has focused on perceived rather than de facto differences in the quality of audit service provided by large and small audit firms. Typically, researchers addressing this issue have attempted to determine whether financial statement users impute varying degrees of credibility to the financial statements of companies audited by audit firms of different size classes. To accomplish this objective, researchers generally have used either a capital markets events methodology to measure user reactions to inter-tier auditor changes or have attempted to gauge experimentally whether the size class of a given company's auditor influences financial statement users' decisions.

Capital Market Studies

Capital market researchers have tested the PDH by monitoring stock market reactions to two types of auditor changes, Big Eight to non-Big Eight (BE-NBE) and non-Big Eight to Big Eight (NBE-BE). If the PDH is valid, that is, if users impute a higher degree of credibility to Big Eight-audited financial statements, a NBE-BE switch should result in a positive, post-switch movement in the firm's stock price. Conversely, a BE-NBE change should have an adverse impact on a firm's stock price. In the earliest of these studies, Fried and Schiff [1981] found that the capital markets generally react negatively to all auditor changes regardless of the size class of the predecessor and successor auditors. However, in a subsequent, larger scale study, Nichols and Smith's [1983] results suggested that NBE-BE changes have a positive impact on stock prices while BE-NBE changes have a negative impact, although neither case showed these post-switch stock movements to be statistically significant.[6] Finally, two more recent, even larger scale market studies demonstrated that NBE-BE changes have essentially no impact on switching firms' stock prices while BE-NBE changes have a statistically significant negative effect [Mangold, 1984; Eichenseher, Hagigi, and Shields, 1987].

Overall, capital market research has provided empirical evidence fairly consistent with the prediction of the PDH that financial statement users react negatively to a BE-NBE auditor change. However, the prediction that NBE-BE changes are viewed favorably by users has not been supported because these switches tend to have at most a nominal impact on stock prices. Mangold [1984] maintains that this latter finding is not inconsistent with the PDH but rather is an artifact of the capital market events methodology when applied to auditor changes. The announcement of NBE-BE changes have little or no impact on stock prices, Mangold contends, because the capital markets anticipate such changes and react to them long before they are announced. NBE-BE switchers tend to be prosperous, growth-oriented companies, firms that historically tend to retain a NBE auditor in their early years of existence before moving to a BE auditor after becoming better established. Since the markets are aware of this tendency, the positive stock market reaction to a NBE-BE auditor switch by such firms should occur prior to the time that the actual auditor change is announced, a conclusion supported by empirical data collected by Mangold.[7]

Behavioral Studies

Nichols and Smith [1983], among others [Shaw and Francis, 1987], have noted that the capital market events methodology is not particularly well suited to test the PDH. When employing that methodology in this context, researchers are forced to use post-switch stock price movements to infer changes in investors' assessments of the level of audit assurance associated with the switching firm's financial statements. However, as Nichols and Smith observe, uncontrolled variables in these studies likely confound the impact of a change in users' imputed level of audit assurance on a switching firm's stock price. For example, a NBE-BE switch is likely accompanied by an increase in the audit fee which would have a negative effect on the switching firm's stock price and thus mitigate, to some degree, the positive impact of the higher level of imputed audit assurance. Notwithstanding Mangold's argument outlined above, this methodological problem may account for the fairly weak support that prior capital market studies have provided for the PDH.

Two recent behavioral studies avoided the methodological problem noted by Nichols and Smith by directly investigating, in an experimental context, the impact of auditor size class on users' assessments of financial statement credibility. McKinley, Pany, and Reckers [1985] found that loan officers imputed a higher degree of credibility to financial statements audited by Big Eight auditors compared to non-Big Eight auditors, although this difference in imputed credibility was not sufficiently strong to influence the loan officers' lending decisions. In a related study, Knapp [1988] investigated whether companies could strengthen the credibility of their financial statements by changing auditors. His results demonstrate that an auditor change generally diminshes the credibility of a firm's financial statements; however, the financially distressed firms in his study that switched from a NBE to a BE auditor did realize a statistically significant increase in financial statement credibility.

CONCLUDING REMARKS

Recent proposals calling for consideration of measures to restrain price competition in the audit market are predicated on two key assumptions: (1) that audit firms provide an undifferentiated product, and (2) that in any market characterized by a fungible product, price will eventually become the principal basis for competition among suppliers. Extant empirical research questions the validity of each of these assumptions. Empirical tests of the product differentiation hypothesis demonstrate that the services of audit firms are perceived as differentiated, to some degree, by financial statement users. Additionally, limited empirical evidence points to the existence of de facto product differentiation in the audit market. Regarding the second assumption, a large number of empirical studies have investigated price competition among audit firms. This body of research has yielded largely inconclusive findings but, overall, has clearly failed to establish that price is the principal basis for competition among audit firms. Collectively, these findings suggest that measures intended to curb allegedly excessive price competition among audit firms should be considered with great caution.

Recent empirical research into the nature of competition in the audit market has yielded important insights on this phenomenon that were not available in the past decade when the Cohen Commission and Metcalf Committee reports were issued. Although this research tends to refute many of the conclusions reached by those bodies, the establisment of a coherent framework to guide policy development in this area will require a considerable amount of additional research. Most importantly, there is a need for replication and extension of several key studies to eliminate or at least account for seemingly contradictory research results. This need is particularly evident with regard to two critical research questions: To what extent are aggressive pricing strategies, such as lowballing on initial engagements, employed by audit firms? Does de facto product differentiation exist within the audit market?

Additionally, there is a need for research focusing on a number of important questions in this area that have yet to be addressed. Recent technological changes in the provision of audit services, for instance, have likely affected the competitive balance in the audit market. Research exploring the impact of new audit technologies on the overall level of audit fees and on the cost-competitiveness of individual firms would provide important insight on the future structure of the audit market. There is also a need to investigate how the dramatic increase in the rate of auditor changes by audit clients over the past decade has affected both the de facto and perceived quality of audit services. Competition on either a price or product quality basis that induces a high rate of auditor switching by audit clients may be detrimental to the integrity of the audit function if a significant learning curve effect is present in auditing or is perceived to be present by financial statement users.[8] Finally, recent evidence that some degree of product differentiation exists in the audit market suggests the need for a better understanding of how firms effectively differentiate their audit services from those of competitors and then effectively market those services to a target class of audit consumers. Audit firms that choose to ignore one or both of these tasks will likely find themselves at a significant competitive disadvantage in the near future.

In summary, recent criticism of the auditing profession stemming from a series of alleged 'audit failures' has spurred regulatory authorities to re-examine the societal role of the independent auditor. Much of this criticism has focused on the nature of competition in the audit market and its impact on the quality of professional service provided by audit firms. Additional research investigating the competitive nature of the audit market should yield important insights on the problems facing the auditing profession as well as recommendations to ensure that the integrity of the independent audit function is maintained.

NOTES

1. For a discussion of these studies, see Francis and Simon [1985] and Simon and Francis [1988].

2. For one such argument, see Watts and Zimmerman [1981]. For expediency purposes, the product differentiation literature tends to focus on Big Eight versus non-Big Eight firms. However, it is widely recognized that the largest of the non-Big Eight firms are more similar, and perceived to be more similar, to Big Eight firms than smaller non-Big Eight firms.

3. A different explanation for the greater utility of Big Eight audits is provided by Bar-Yosef and Livnat [1984]. These researchers, like DeAngelo, contend that the incremental utility of Big Eight audits, compared to non-Big Eight audits, is independent of any technological capabilities that may exist between the two size classes of audit firms. According to their insurance hypothesis, Big Eight firms are perceived as being more capable of 'sharing' expected litigation losses than smaller audit firms. This greater ability of Big Eight firms to indemnify their clients' officers and stockholders from such losses provides an economic incentive for corporate managers and audit committees to choose Big Eight rather than non-Big Eight auditors.

4. Underlying any unqualified audit opinion is some degree of risk that the opinion is inappropriate, that is, that the financial statements are not materially accurate [see AICPA, 1983]. GAAS do not specify to what level this risk should be reduced, leaving that decision to the professional judgment of the auditor (for illlustrative purposes, *SAS 39* uses a 5% audit risk level; see AICPA [1981]). Simunic and Stein are not suggesting that audits performed in accordance with the 'minimum' standards established by GAAS are low quality audits. (In fact, given the rigorous nature of GAAS, audits performed in accordance with them, by definition, will be high quality audits.) Instead, these researchers suggest that an audit client may demand a higher level

of audit assurance than that provided by a GAAS audit. For instance, an auditor might decide that an audit risk of 5% would be appropriate for a given engagement and design his/her audit accordingly. However, the client might request a higher level of audit assurance, for instance, an audit that reduces audit risk to 3%.

5. Additionally, one recent study provided data inconsistent with DeAngelo's assertion that large audit firms are less likely to capitulate to client demands than small audit firms [see Wyer, White and Janson, 1988]. DeAngelo's model of audit quality implies that large audit forms should be more likely to issue qualified opinions than small firms; however, Wyer et al. found no relationship between auditor size and the type of audit opionion issued.

6. Results very similar to these were achieved in a related study that examined the correlation between earnings forecast errors and abnormal returns for Big Eight and non-Big Eight auditees [see Ettredge, Shane, and Smith, 1988].

7. Another explanation for the insignificant market impact of NBE-BE switches is that users may perceive that a 'learning curve' effect in the first year of the BE auditor's tenure will counteract, to some degree, the generally high quality of audit service provided by that firm compared to the NBE predecessor.

8. See St. Pierre and Anderson [1984]. St. Pierre and Anderson's research confirms that audit failures occur more frequently in the first few years following an auditor change which suggests that a learning curve effect may influence the quality of audit service provided.

REFERENCES

American Institute of Certified Public Accountants, *Commission on Auditors' Responsibilities: Report, Conclusions, and Recommendations* [AICPA, 1978].

________, *Report of the Special Committee on Small and Medium Sized Firms* [AICPA, 1980].

________, *Statement of Auditing Standards No. 39* (*SAS 39*), "Audit Sampling" [AICPA, 1981].

________, *Statement of Auditing Standards No. 47* (*SAS 47*), "Audit Risk and Materiality in Conducting an Audit" [AICPA, 1983].

Arnett, H.E. and P. Danos, *CPA Firm Viability* [University of Michigan, 1979].

"Audit Fees Fall as CPA Firms Jockey for Bids," *Wall Street Journal* [January 28, 1985], p. 33.

Bar-Yosef, S. and J. Livnat, "Auditor Selection: An Incentive-Signalling Approach," *Accounting and Business Research* [Autumn 1984], pp. 301-309.

"CPA Firms Diversify, Cut Fees, Steal Clients in Battle for Business," *Wall Street Journal* [September 10, 1985], pp. 1, 24.

DeAngelo, L.E., "Auditor Size and Auditor Quality," *Journal of Accounting and Economics* [December 1981], pp. 182-199.

Dopuch, N. and D. Simunic, "Competition in Auditing: An Assessment," *Fourth Symposium on Auditing Research* [University of Illinois, 1982].

Eichenseher, J., M. Hagigi, and D. Shields, "Market Reaction to Auditor Changes by OTC Companies," Working paper [University of Wisconsin, Madison, 1987].

Ettredge, M., P.B. Shane, and D.B. Smith, "Audit Firm Size and the Association Between Reported Earnings and Security Returns," *Auditing: A Journal of Practice and Theory* [Spring 1988], pp. 29-42.

Francis, J.R. and D.T. Simon, "A Test of Audit Pricing in the Small-Client Segment of the U.S. Audit Market," *Accounting Review* [January 1987], pp. 145-157.

Fried, D. and A. Schiff, "CPA Switches and Associated Market Reactions," *Accounting Review* [April 1981], pp. 326-341.

Hermanson, R.H., L.M. Dykes, and D.H. Turner, "Enforced Competition in the Accounting Profession—Does It Make Sense?" *Accounting Horizons* [December 1987], pp. 13-19.

Keefe, P.W., "Arthur Young's Unrewarded Virtue," *Dun's Business Month* [January 1985], pp. 58-62.

Knapp, M.C., "Toward A More Coherent Regulatory Policy for Auditor Changes: An Empirical Study of Their Impact on Financial Statement Credibility," *Research in Accounting Regulation* [1988], pp. 41-59.

Mangold, N., "The Effect of Auditor Changes on Earnings, Opinions and Stock Prices," Ph.D. dissertation [University of California, Berkeley, 1984].

McConnell, D.K., "Are the Big 8 Increasing Their Share of the NYSE, AMEX, and OTC Audit Markets?" *Journal of Accounting, Auditing and Finance* [Winter 1984], pp. 178-181.

McKinley, S., K. Pany, and P.M.J. Reckers, "An Examination of the Influence of CPA Firm Type, Size and MAS Provision on Loan Officer Decisions and Perceptions," *Journal of Accounting Research* [Autumn 1985], pp. 887-896.

National Commission on Fraudulent Financial Reporting, *Report of the National Commission on Fraudulent Financial Reporting* [NCFFR, 1987].

Nichols, D.R. and D.B. Smith, "Auditor Credibility and Auditor Changes," *Journal of Accounting Research* [Autumn 1983], pp. 534-544.

Palmrose, Z.V., "Audit Fees and Auditor Size: Further Evidence," *Journal of Accounting Research* [Spring 1986], pp. 97-110.

————, "An Analysis of Auditor Litigation and Audit Service Quality," *Accounting Review* [January 1988], pp. 55-73.

St. Pierre, K. and J.A. Anderson, "An Analysis of the Factors Associated with Lawsuits Against Public Accountants," *Accounting Review* [April 1984], pp. 242-263.

Shaw, W. and J. Francis, "The Market Reaction to A Media Disclosure of A Change in Auditors," Unpublished working paper [Cornell University, 1987].

Simon, D.T. and J.R. Francis, "The Effects of Auditor Change on Audit Fees: Tests of Price Cutting and Price Recovery," *Accounting Review* [April 1988], pp. 255-269.

Simunic, D.A., "The Pricing of Audit Services: Theory and Evidence," *Journal of Accounting Research* [Spring 1980], pp. 161-190.

Simunic, D.A. and M. Stein, "On the Economics of Product Differentiation in Auditing," *Auditing Symposium VIII: Proceedings of the 1986 Touche Ross/University of Kansas Symposium on Auditing Problems* [University of Kansas, 1986].

U.S. Senate, Subcommittee on Reports, Accounting and Management of the Committee on Government Operations, *The Accounting Establishment* [U.S. Government Printing Office, 1977].

Watts, R. and J. Zimmerman, "The Markets for Independence and Independent Auditors," Unpublished manuscript [University of Rochester, 1981].

Wyer, J.C., G.T. White, and E.C. Janson, "Audits of Public Companies by Smaller CPA Firms: Clients, Reports, and Quality," *Auditing: A Journal of Practice and Theory* [Spring 1988], pp. 164-173.

A LONGITUDINAL EXAMINATION OF LARGE CPA FIRM AUDITORS' PERSONNEL TURNOVER

Adrian Harrell

ABSTRACT

Data from a 4-year longitudinal study are used to examine proposed relationships between junior-level auditors' personnel turnover, long-term career intentions, organizational commitment and job satisfaction. The Mobley, Griffeth, Hand, and Meglino conceptual model of personnel turnover, modified to incorporate subsequent research, was the basis of the proposed relationships. The results imply personnel turnover is directly determined by auditors' long-term career intentions, which are directly determined by both organizational commitment and job satisfaction. Organizational commitment and job satisfaction interact to directly determine auditors' long-term career intentions, indicating a reciprocal relationship between these two constructs. Theoretical and practical implications of the results are discussed.

Advances in Accounting, Volume 8, pages 233-246.

ISBN: 1-55938-067-5

Few research areas have received as much attention as personnel turnover [Cotton and Tuttle, 1986; Ferris and Dillard, 1988]. Turnover research is performed in several disciplines such as psychology, sociology, economics, and accounting [Williams and Hazer, 1986]. Within accounting, such research has emphasized the turnover of accounting professionals employed by large public accounting firms, which has been described as a migration from the large public accounting firm work environment to other work environments [Rhode, Sorensen, and Lawler, 1977]. The large body of turnover research has prompted some researchers [e.g., Locke, 1976; Mobley, 1982] to argue that the primary factors which explain personnel turnover (job satisfaction, organizational commitment, and future employee intentions) are well known. As a result, they propose that future turnover research should focus on determining how the major constructs in conceptual models of the turnover process relate to each other.

Curry, Wakefield, Price, and Mueller [1986] note that knowledge of the correct causal relationships between these constructs has both theoretical and practical implications. If the actual relationships differ from those proposed, personnel turnover studies may employ incorrect theoretical models and reach erroneous inferences. In a practical vein, the loss of valued professionals through undesirable levels of personnel turnover can result in substantial costs to a firm. Managers must understand the correct causal relationships between these constructs if they are to provide incentives which positively influence turnover. Accordingly, this paper employs data from a 4-year longitudinal study of junior-level auditors to examine the proposed relationships between the constructs of the Mobley, Griffeth, Hand, and Meglino (MGHM) [1979] turnover model.[1]

THEORETICAL ISSUES

Several models of the turnover process have been proposed [e.g., March and Simon, 1958; Price, 1977; Mobley, Horner, and Hollingsworth, 1978; Mobley et al. 1979; Steers and Mowday, 1981]. The MGHM Model was selected because it is a reasonable conceptual model of the turnover process. It is a diagramatic model which incorporates the contributions of present-oriented constructs such as job satisfaction and organizational commitment and future-oriented constructs such as long-term career intentions. The model implies that personnel turnover is directly determined by future employment intentions, which are directly determined by organizational commitment, which in turn is directly determined by job satisfaction. Mobley et al. [1979] specifically indicate that longitudinal research and multivariate analysis techniques are appropriate for examining the model's proposed relationships.

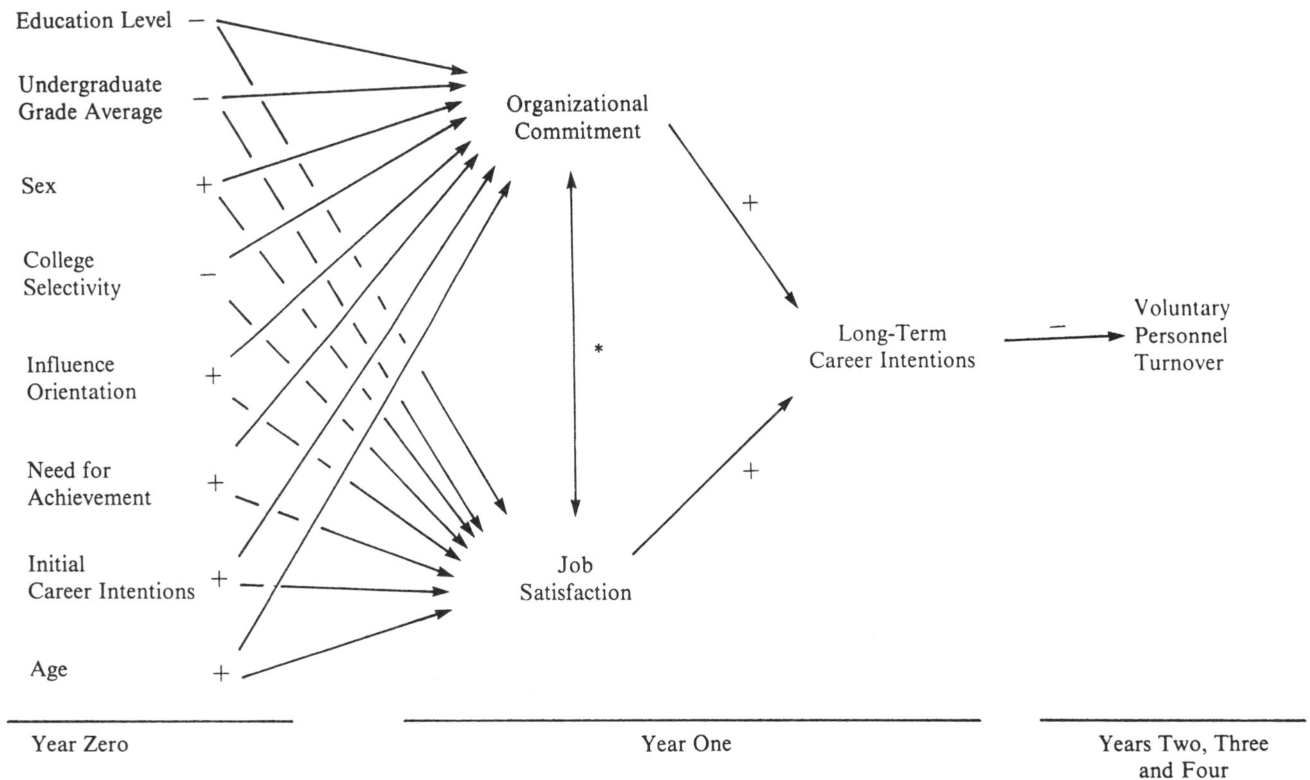

Notes: The direction of the expected relationships is indicated as − or + in each instance.
* An interaction between these two variables is expected.

Exhibit 1. Expected Direct Relationships Between the Variables

A large number of empirical studies indicate personnel turnover is directly determined by future employment intentions, as proposed by the MGHM model [Cotton and Tuttle, 1986]. The results of empirical studies have, however, disagreed about the relationship between organizational commitment and job satisfaction. Michaels and Spector [1982] and Arnold and Feldman [1982] conclude that future employment intentions are directly determined by both job satisfaction and organizational commitment. Bateman and Strasser [1984] conclude that future employment intentions are directly determined by job satisfaction, which in turn is directly determined by organizational commitment. Supporting the MGHM model, Williams and Hazer [1986] conclude that their evidence indicates "less support for a causal link from commitment to satisfaction than for a path in the reverse direction." Their results, however, also "suggest the possibility of a reciprocal relation between satisfaction and commitment" [1986, p. 229].

This study examines the relationships presented in Exhibit 1, which are based on the MGHM model, modified to incorporate subsequent research. In this model, turnover is directly determined by long-term career intentions, which are directly determined by both organizational commitment and job satisfaction [Michaels and Spector, 1982; Arnold and Feldman, 1982]. As suggested by Williams and Hazer [1986, p. 229], organizational commitment and job satisfaction interact reciprocally to directly determine long-term career intentions. A number of factors—for example, education level, undergraduate grade average, male status, collge selectivity, influence-orientation, achievement motivation, initial career intentions, and age—are proposed in the literature to have a direct impact on organizational commitment and job satisfaction [Cotton and Tuttle, 1986; Harrell and Stahl, 1984; McClelland and Boyatzis, 1982; Cornellius and Lane, 1984]. These factors are presented in this study as presented in Exhibit 1.

METHOD

Data gathered from a 4-year longitudinal study of junior-level auditors' turnover[2] in one large public accounting firm were used to examine the proposed relationships presented in Exhibit 1. This population group is particularly appropriate for the examination of these relationships, since most of the migration of accounting professionals takes place during their initial few years of employment. The longitudinal study was performed with the cooperation of the firm which employed the participants.

The data collection procedures are summarized in Exhibit 2. The initial data were gathered from individuals with approximately six months of work experience who attended one of the firm's training programs for newly-hired auditors (Year Zero in Exhibit 2). Participation was voluntary, but the

Questionnaire Data Collected at Audit Training Courses

	Year Zero
Individuals attending training courses	520
Less	
Individuals who were not auditors	9
Individuals who provided random responses in initial questionnaires	21
Individuals who refused to participate in the longitudinal study	64
Volunteer longitudinal study participants	426

Questionnaire Data Collected by Mail

	Year One	
Participants surveyed	426	(100%)
Respondents providing completed questionnaires	175	(41%)
Nonrespondents (includes 54 separated in Year One)	251	(59%)

Turnover Data Provided by the Firm

	Year Two		Year Three		Year Four		Cumulative	
Inquiries	426	(100%)	242	(57%)	91	(21%)	426	(100%)
Still employed	242	(57%)	91	(21%)	35	(8%)	35	(8%)
Separated	169	(40%)*	84	(20%)	15	(3%)	268	(63%)
No response	15	(3%)	67	(16%)	41	(10%)	123	(29%)

Notes: The Year Zero data were collected from the study participants during their attendance at the firm's training course for newly-hired auditors. The Year One data were collected by mailed questionnaire directly from the study participants. The turnover data (Year Two through Year Four) were provided by the firm (the Director of Audit at each participating office).
* (Includes 54 [13%] separated during Year One and 115 [27%] separated during Year Two.)

Exhibit 2. Summary of Data Collection Procedures

participants were asked to provide the initial data even if they wree unwilling to participate in the longitudinal study. Each participant sealed the completed questionnaire in an envelope to preserve confidentiality and the responses were mailed to the researcher.

As shown in Exhibit 2, 520 individuals completed the initial data gathering instruments. Nine were not junior-level auditors and 21 provided random responses; these individuals were eliminated from the study, leaving 490 participants. Sixty-four were unwilling to participate in a longitudinal study and refused to provide their identities. Accordingly, 426 volunteers agreed to participate in the study. The average participant was age 22, had completed a bachelors' degree with an undergraduate grade average of about 3.5, and had worked as an auditor for less than six months. About 55% were males.

The initial participants provided demographic information relating to the factors in Exhibit 1. The index of selectivity of colleges and universities provided by Cass and Birnbaum [1979] was used to judge the selectivity of the university each participant attended as an undergraduate. The participants also indicated their initial long-term career intentions in the large public accounting firm work environment. The Job Choice Exercise, which measures an individual's affiliation, power, and achievement needs, was also completed. Measurements using the job choice exercise are free from social desirability problems and are sexually and racially neutral. Its test-retest reliability of 0.82 is considered high [Harrell and Stahl, 1981; Stahl and Harrell, 1983; Stahl, 1986]. Using the split-halves approach to determine internal reliability, coefficient alpha [Cronbach, 1951] was estimated to be 0.86 for this study. To operationalize the influence-orientation construct, each individual's need for affiliation was subtracted from the person's need for power in the manner described by McClelland [1981], McClelland and Boyatzis [1982], and Cornelius and Lane [1984].

About one year after the initial data were gathered (Year One in Exhibit 2), the participants were contacted by mail and asked to provide additonal information. Of the 426 volunteer participants, 175 (41%) provided responses and 251 (59%) did not respond. Markings on returned questionnaires indicated that 54 nonrespondents were no longer employed by the firm. The participants provided responses to a single question about their long-term career intentions. They also completed Hoppock's [1935] measure of job satisfaction. Hoppock's instrument was validated by McNichols, Stahl, and Manley [1978] who demonstrated it performed well in terms of distribution, construct, covergent and concurrent validity across four sample populations totaling over 29,000 subjects. Reliability was high, with coefficient alpha values ranging from 0.76 to 0.89 being reported. A coefficient alpha of 0.88 was determined for this study. In addition, the participants completed the organizational commitment scales developed by Porter, Steers, Mowday, and Boulian [1974]. These scales have been shown to be highly reliable when used with accounting professionals by Ferris and Arranya [1983], who reported a coefficient alpha of 0.92 for these scales. In this study, a coefficient alpha of 0.91 was computed for this instrument.

About two years after the collection of the initial data (Year Two in Exhibit 2), the firm which employed the participants indicated which participants were still employed. Of the 426 volunteer participants, 242 (57%) were still employed and 169 (40%) were separated with 54 (13%) separating in the first year and 115 (27%) separating in the second year. No response was provided for 15 (3%) individuals.

About three years after the collection of the initial data (Year Three in Exhibit 2), the firm again indicated which individuals were still employed. Of the remaining 242 participants (57% of the original 426), 91 (21% of the original

426) were still employed and 84 (20% of the original 426) had separated during the third year. No response was provided for 67 (16% of the original 426).

About four years after the collection of the initial data (Year Four in Exhibit 2), the firm again indicated which individualsl were still employed. Of the remaining 91 individuals (21% of the original 426), 35 (8% of the original 426) were still employed and 15 (3% of the original 426) had separated during the fourth year. No response was provided for 42 (10% of the original 426) indiviudals. In summary, at the end of the 4-year study, 35 (8%) of the original 426 participants were known to be still emplyed by the firm, 268 (63%) were known to have separated, and the status of 123 (27%) was unknown due to a lack of response information.

RESULTS

Tests were performed to determine if nonresponse bias affected the results of the study. Initially, tests were performed to determine whether the 64 individuals who refused to participate in the longitudinal study differed from the 426 who expressed their willingness to participate (see Exhibit 2). The quantitative variables of interest (selectivity of undergraduate college; undergraduate grade average, initial career intentions, age, influence-orientation, and achievement movitation) were compared using *t*-tests. The categorical variables (education level and sex) were compared using contingency tables and Chi-square tests. No significant differences were observed between the individuals who refused to participate in the longitudinal study and the voluntary participants.

Next, the 175 first-year respondents were compared with the remaining 315 (251 nonrespondents + 64 who declined to participate; see Exhibit 2) for the variables of interest. No significant differences were observed between the respondents and the others for seven of the eight variables. The respondents were found to differ somewhat from the others as to education level (Chi-square = 4.2; $p = 0.045$). Twenty-three of the 175 respondents (13%) possessed the masters' degree, whereas only 25 of the other 315 subjects (8%) possessed the masters' degree.[3] In order to examine this issue further, analysis of variance was used to compare the job satisfaction, organizational commitment and long-term career intentions of the initial 30 individuals and the last 30 individuals to respond (Year One in Exhibit 2). No significant differences were observed. Accordingly, it was concluded that nonresponse bias was unlikely to have affected the results of the study.

Path analysis (Duncan, 1966; Heise, 1969; Asher, 1976) was used to examine the expected direct relationships proposed in Exhibit 1. Two multivariate techniques—stepwise discriminant analysis and multiple regression analysis—were used to determine where direct relationships existed between variables.

	1	2	3	4	5	6	7	8	9	10
1. Long-Term Career Intent										
2. Organizational Commitment	.63**									
3. Job Satisfaction	.71**	.74**								
4. Educational Level	-.08	-.21**	-.08							
5. Undergraduate Grade Average	-.10	-.17*	-.15	-.05						
6. Sex	.00	-.06	.00	.01	-.10					
7. College Selectivity	-.16*	-.15	-.15*	.06	-.05	-.02				
8. Influence Orientation	.28**	.10	.17*	.09	.07	.07	-.04			
9. Need for Achievement	.00	.04	.01	.12*	.00	-.07	-.05	.06		
10. Initial Career Intent	.28**	.20**	.22**	.01	-.10*	.13*	-.03	.03	.05	
11. Age	.08	-.03	.04	.31*	.01	.07	-.14*	.11*	.09	-.04

Notes: * Significant at .05 level.
** Significant at .01 level.
For correlations between variables 4 through 11 ($n = 426$); for correlations between all other variables ($n = 175$).

Exhibit 3. Correlations Between Variables

Because an individual's employment status is a categorical variable, stepwise discriminant analysis was employed to examine the existence of direct relationships between personnel turnover and the remaining variables. Only one variable—long-term career intentions—was statistically significant in the model ($F = 4.9$, $p = 0.015$). The same direct relationship between personnel turnover and long-term career intentions was obtained when the several years of turnover were considered together and when each individual year of turnover was considered separately. This implies that, although some may leave sooner than others, an individual's migration from public accounting is determined by the person's long-term career intentions.

A series of multiple regression analyses were performed to examine the remaining proposed relationships. As shown in Exhibit 3, some of the variables of interest are highly correlated, indicating the need to consider the potential effects of multicollinearity upon the analysis [Mansfield and Helms, 1982; Berry and Feldman, 1985, p. 41]. The size of the variance inflation factors (VIFs) associated with an examination of latent roots and latent vectors of the correlation matrix indicate whether multicollinearity is a threat [Mansfield and Helms, 1982]. If any VIF exceeds 10, there is reason for some concern. Because VIFs ranged from a low value of 1.05 to a high value of 2.3, in this study, so multicollinearity was not considered to present a significant problem [Myers, 1986, p. 219].

In performing the regression analyses, the auditors' long-term career intentions were initially considered as the regression equation dependent variable, with the variables to the left of this variable in Exhibit 1 being considered the regression equation independent variables. A premise of path analysis is that the association of a statistically significant (using an alpha level of 0.05) standardized beta weight value with one of the independent variables implies that, when the effects due to the other independent variables have been controlled for, a direct relationship exists between that independent variable and the dependent variable. Subsequently, organizational commitment and job satisfaction were each in turn considered the regression equation dependent variable, with the variables to the left of these two variables in Exhibit 1 being considered as the regression equation independent variables. Each of these multiple regression models was statistically significant at the 5% level. The direct relationships between the variables indicated by the path analysis procedures are presented in Exhibit 4. Where multiple regression analysis was employed, R^2 and standardized beta weight values are indicated to provide an indication of the strength of the relationships involved.

Hierarchical regression analysis was used to examine the proposal that an auditor's organizational commitment and job satisfaction interact reciprocally to directly influence the individual's long-term career intentions. Cohen [1978] and Cohen and Cohen [1975, Chapt. 8] provide detailed descriptions of the hierarchical regression analysis procedures. The results indicate job satisfaction

Exhibit 4. Actual Direct Relationships Between the Variables

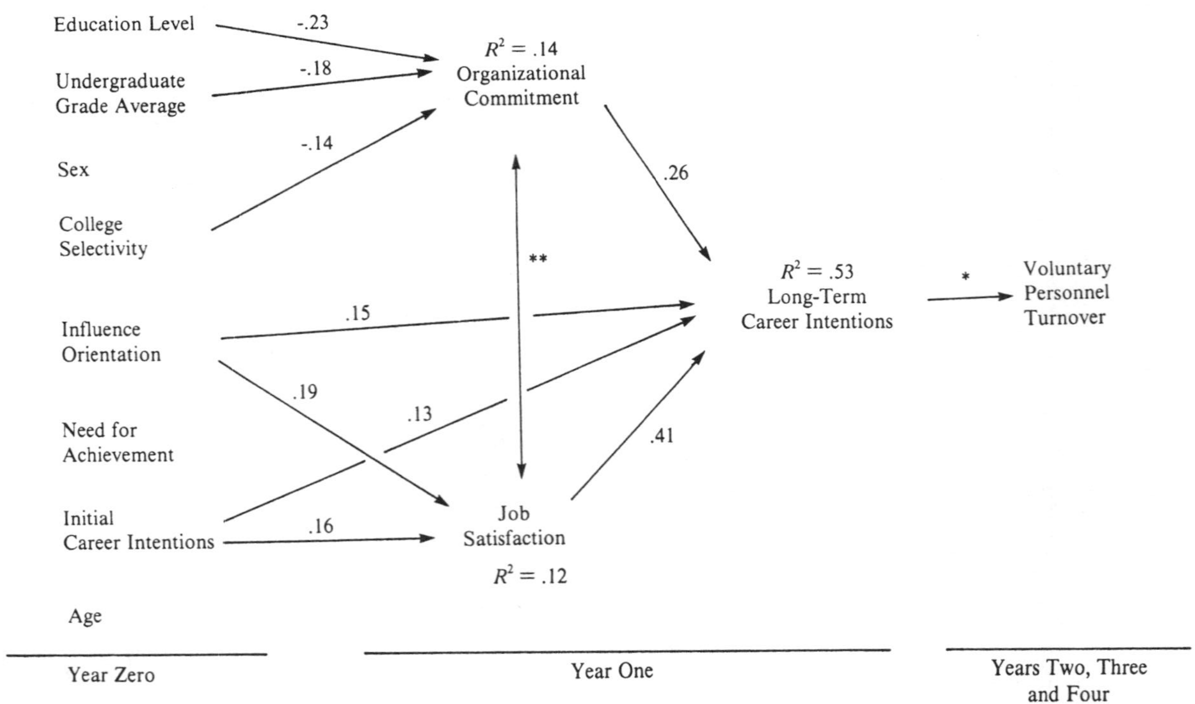

Notes: Multiple regression analysis was used to examine the remaining relationships. An alpha value of .05 was used to determine when standardized regression weights indicate direct relationships.

* Stepwise discriminant analysis was used to examine this relationship ($F = 4.9$; $p = 0.015$).

** Hierarchical regression analysis was used to examine the interaction of these two variables ($F = 10.6$; $p < .01$).

and organizational commitment interact reciprocally with each other, indicating that each of these constructs may be considered a direct determinant of the other ($F = 10.7$; $p < 0.001$).

DISCUSSION

Initially, some limitations and strengths of this study should be mentioned. As noted earlier, the participants were all employees of one large public accounting firm. They were selected because of their availability, so caution is recommended in making generalizations to other firms and groups.[4] However, some strengths of this research include the use of a national sample of subjects, since each major United States' office of the participating firm was represented by individuals in the original sample and no significant response bias was evident. In addition, the demographic and other variables associated with the subjects are similar to those reported in previous studies and no evidence was found to suggest the participants differ from the junior-level auditors employed by other large accounting firms. Further, the longitudinal study approach and the use of multivariate analysis techniques meet Mobley et al.'s (MGHM) [1979] recommendations for examining the MGHM model.

The results presented in Exhibit 4 support the relationships between the major constructs proposed in Exhibit 1. An auditor's personnel turnover is directly determined by the person's long-term career intentions. An auditor's long-term career intentions are directly determined by both the individual's job satisfaction and organizational commitment. The latter two variables interact reciprocally with each other, implying that each of these constructs is a direct determinant of the other.

These findings have both theoretical and practical implications. The finding that job satisfaction and organizational commitment interact reciprocally offers a logical explanation for the conflicting evidence presented in prior research as to which of these constructs is a determinant of the other [Bateman and Strasser, 1984; Williams and Hazer, 1986]. The conceptual models implied by these prior studies may be misspecified, which could lead researchers to make incorrect inferences about these constructs.

The finding that job satisfaction and organizational commitment reciprocally influence each other also has practical implications for managers who wish to positively influence junior-level auditors' long-term career intentions. A strategy which aims at simultaneously increasing job satisfaction and organizational commitment should have a synergetic effect on long-term career intentions. Such an strategy logically should produce the maximum positive effect. A manager seeking to implement such a strategy would, however, discover that although a large number of factors have been identified as determinants of organizational commitment and job satisfaction [Cotton and Tuttle, 1986], the conceptual relationships are not well-defined. For example, the determinants of organizational commitment and job satisfaction considered in this study (see Exhibit 4) leave much of the variation in these constructs unexplained ($R^2 = 0.14$ and 0.12, respectively).

The best explanators, influence-orientation and initial career intentions, are factors over which managers currently have little control.[5] Better determinants of job satisfaction and organizational commitment which are under the control of a firm's management may, however, exist in the current work environment (e.g., challenging assignments, a clearly-defined career path, leadership opportunities, and so forth) [Williams and Hazer, 1986]. Accordingly, future research in this area should be aimed at gaining an increased conceptual understanding of the determinants of auditors' job satisfaction and organizational commitment.

ACKNOWLEDGMENT

Appreciation is expressed to Touche Ross & Co. for the financial and other assistance provided in this research.

NOTES

1. The longitudinal study was guided by the original MGHM turnover model, modified to reflect the empirical findings of Michaels and Spector [1982] and Arnold and Feldman [1982]. When the results reported by Williams and Hazer [1986] suggested a reciprocal relationship between job satisfaction and organizational commitment, the model was modified further to facilitate the examination of this issue. The proposed relationships examined in this paper are presented in Exhibit 1.

2. The junior-level auditors who participated in the longitudinal study were identified and data were initially collected when they attended their firm's training sessions during November and December 1982 (Year Zero in Exhibit 2). The job satisfaction, organizational commitment, and long-term career intentions information were collected by mailed questionnaires during November and December 1983 (Year One in Exhibit 2). The turnover data were collected during November and December of subsequent years (Years Two, Three, and Four in Exhibit 2), with the final data being received in late 1986.

3. The same path relationships were determined to exist when the participants who had earned masters' degrees were deleted from the sample as when these individuals were included into the sample. This implies education level differences did not significantly affect the results of the study.

In a few instances, significant differences were observed between the job satisfaction, organizational commitment and long-term career intentions of junior-level auditors of offices in different geographical regions. No obvious explanation for these regional differences was apparent.

4. Swieringa and Weick [1982] argue that the generalizability of studies which examine a conceptual model or theory should be determined by the generalizability of the model or theory. Those who accept this rationale may argue the results of this study are generalizable to all those circumstances for which the MGHM model is appropriate. Many readers may, however, prefer a more conservative viewpoint.

5. Waller [1985] suggests that large public accounting firms could control turnover by offering employment contracts designed to attract a greater percentage of individuals who have positive initial career intentions. Similarly, Pulaskos and Schmidt [1983] suggest hiring preference be given to individuals who are likely to experience high job satisfaction in a particular work environment. A firm might, therefore, influence turnover by designing employment contracts which attract a greater percentage of individuals with a strong influence-orientation (e.g., an employment contract which offers the opportunity for supervisory responsibilities relatively early in the person's career).

REFERENCES

Arnold, H. and D. Feldman, "A Multivariate Analysis of the Determinants of Turnover," *Journal of Applied Psychology* [1982], pp. 350-360.

Asher, B., *Causal Modeling* [Sage, 1976].

Bateman, T. and S. Strasser, "A Longitudinal Analysis of the Antecedents of Organizational Commitment," *Academy of Management Journal,* 27 [1984], pp. 95-112.

Berry, W. and S. Feldman, *Multiple Regression in Practice* [Sage, 1985].

Cass, J. and M. Birnbaum, *Comparative Guide to American Colleges* [Harper & Row, 1979].

Cohen, J., "Partialed Products are Interactions; Partialed Powers are Curve Components," *Psychological Bulletin,* 85 [1978], pp. 858-866.

Cohen, J. and P. Cohen, *Applied Multiple Regression/Correlation Analysis for the Behavioral Sciences* [Wiley, 1975].

Cotton, J. and J. Tuttle, "Employee Turnover: A Meta-Analysis and Review with Implications for Research," *Academy of Management Review,* 11 [1986], pp. 55-70.

Cornelius, E. and F. Lane, "The Power Motive and Managerial Success in a Professionally Oriented Service Industry Organization," *Journal of Applied Psychology,* 69[1984], pp. 32-39.

Cronbach, L., "Coefficient Alpha and the Internal Structure of Tests," *Psychometrika,* 16 [1951], pp. 297-334.

Curry, J., D. Wakefield, J. Price, and C. Mueller, "ON the Causal Ordering of Job Satisfaction and Organizational Commitment," *Academy of Management Journal,* 29 [1986], pp. 847-858.

Duncan, O., "Path Analysis: A Sociological Example," *American Journal of Sociology* [July 1966], pp. 1-16.

Ferris, K. and N. Aranya, "A Comparison of two Organizational Commitment Scales," *Personnel Psychology* [1983], pp. 87-98.

Ferris, K. and J. Dillard, "Individual Behavior: Evidence From the Accounting Environment," in *Behavioral Accounting Research: A Critical Analysis,* edited by K. Ferris [Century VII Publishing, 1988], pp. 281-304.

Harrell, A. and M. Stahl, "A Behavioral Decision Theory Approach for Measuring McClelland's Trichotomy of Needs," *Journal of Applied Psychology,* 66 [1981], pp. 242-247.

________, "Need for Achievement, Need for Affiliation and the Academic Performance and Career Intentions of Accounting Students," *Journal of Accounting Education* [Fall 1983], pp. 149-153.

________, "McClelland's Trichotomy of needs Theory and the Job Satisfaction and Work Performance of CPA Firm Professionals," *Accounting Organizations and Society* [1984], pp. 241-252.

Heise, D., "Problems in Path Analysis and Causal Influence," in *Sociological Methodology,* edited by E. Borgatta and G. Bohmedt [Jossey-Bass, 1969].

Hoppock, R., *Job Satisfaction* [Harper & Row, 1935].

Locke, E., "The Nature and Consequences of Job Satisfaction," in *Handbook of Industrial and Organizational Psychology,* edited by M. Dunnette [Rand-McNally, 1976].

Mansfield, E. and B. Helms, "Detecting Multicollinearity," *The American Statistician,* 36 [1982], pp. 158-160.

March, J. and H. Simon, *Organization* [Wiley, 1958].

McClelland, D., "Is Personality Consistent?" in *Further Explorations in Personality,* edited by A. Rubin, J. Aronoff, A. Barclay, and R. Zucker [Wiley, 1981].

McClelland, D. and R. Boyatzis, "Leadership Motive and Long-Term Success in Management," *Journal of Applied Psychology* [1982], pp. 737-743.

McNichols, C., M. Stahl, and T. Manley, "A Validation of Hoppick's Job Satisfaction Measure," *Academy of Management Journal* [December 1978], pp. 737-742.

Michaels, C. and P. Spector, "Causes of Employee Turnover: A Test of the Mobley, Griffeth, Hand and Meglino Model," *Journal of Applied Psychology,* 67 [1982], pp. 53-59.

Mobley, W., *Employee Turnover: Causes, Consequences and Control* [Addison-Wesley, 1982].

Mobley, W., R. Griffeth, H. Hand, and B. Meglino, "Review and Conceptual Analysis of the Employee Turnover Process," *Psychological Bulletin* [1979], pp. 493-522.

Mobley, W., S. Horner, and A. Hollingsworth, "An Evaluation of Precursors of Hospital Employee Turnover," *Journal of Applied Psychology,* 63 [1978], pp. 408-414.

Myers, R., *Classical and Modern Regression With Applications* [Duxbury Press, 1986].

Porter, L., R. Steers, R. Mowday, and P. Boulian, "Organizational Commitment, Job Satisfaction, and Turnover Among Psychiatric Technicians," *Journal of Applied Psychology,* 59 [1974], pp. 603-609.

Price, J., *The Study of Turnover* [Iowa State University Press, 1977].

Pulakos, E. and N. Schmitt, "A Longitudinal Study of a Valence Model Approach for the Prediction of Job Satisfaction of New Employees," *Journal of Applied Psychology,* 68 [1983], pp. 307-312.

Rhode, K., J. Sorensen, and E. Lawler, "Sources of Professional Staff Turnover in Public Accounting Firms Revealed by the Exit Interview," *Accounting Organizations and Society* [1977], pp. 165-176.

Stahl, M., *Managerial and Technical Motivation* [Praeger, 1986].

Stahl, M. and A. Harrell, A., "The Evolution and Validation of a Behavioral Decision Theory Measurement Approach to Achievement, Power and Affiliation," *Journal of Applied Psychology,* 67 [1982], pp. 744-751.

Steers, R. and R. Mowday, "Employee Turnover and Post-Decision Accomodation Processes," in *Research in Organizational Behavior,* vol. 3, edited by L. Cummings and B. Staw [JAI Press, 1981].

Swieringa, R. and K. Weick, "An Assessment of Laboratory Research in Accounting," *Journal of Accounting Research* [1982], pp. 56-101.

Waller, W., "Self-Selection and the Probability of Quitting: A Contracting Approach to Employee Turnover in Public Accounting," *Journal of Accounting Research* [Autumn 1985], pp. 817-828.

Williams, L. and J. Hazer, "Antecedents and Consequences of Satisfaction and Commitment in Turnover Models: A Reanalysis Using Latent Variable Structural Equation Methods," *Journal of Applied Psychology,* 71 [1986], pp. 219-231.

OPTIMAL HIRING DECISIONS FOR ENTRY-LEVEL AUDITORS IN A CPA FIRM:

A COMPUTERIZED MODEL FOR IMPROVING HIRING PRACTICES

Abraham K. Charnes, William W. Cooper,
James W. Deitrick, William Hank Moody,
and Hong-Chul Shin

ABSTRACT

Each public accounting office faces the annual problem of determining the number of new staff auditors to hire. This decision has become more difficult in recent years because of the increasingly cost-competitive environment facing CPA firms, and the growing reliance on paraprofessionals and part-time employees. This paper presents a model that has been developed for microcomputers and tested in the office of a Big Eight firm in the Southwest.

Advances in Accounting, Volume 8, pages 247-270.

ISBN: 1-55938-067-5

The model's output shows a decision maker the number of new staff accountants to hire given the office's expected demand for services and its revenue and cost functions. The model, which is menu driven, allows for expected profit maximization and sensitivity analysis of several variables. The output includes a summary of expected profits at various hiring sizes, the probability of achieving the expected profits, and the probability of having losses at each hiring size. The model is subsequently expanded to accommodate chance constraints.

INTRODUCTION

Accounting firms often have difficulty determining the number of new people to hire each year. This problem has become increasingly difficult in recent years because of the tendency of some firms to hire paraprofessionals and part-time staff as well as new, full-time college graduates. It is a complex task for many firms to balance the mix of all employee groups while also providing quality services at reasonable prices. Some problems and solutions associated with the mix issue are addressed by Cooper, Mitchell, Welsch, and Shin [1986]. The purpose of this paper, however, is to present a systematic approach that can be used to help determine the number of new full-time auditors to hire in a given year.[1] This approach recognizes that the hiring problem is influenced by such factors as (1) the expected demand for audit services, (2) the turnover, attrition and promotion rates of audit personnel, and (3) several cost and revenue components. More specifically, this paper introduces a probabilistic model designed for implementation with a microcomputer that considers possible forecast errors of expected demand for auditing services, and that also allows for a variety of sensitivity analyses.

Forecast errors result from hiring too many or too few new staff auditors for the demand level that actually occurs. Ideally, all possible demand levels should be taken into account when formulating hiring strategies intended to maximize an office's expected profits or to minimize its expected costs. Further, in an uncertain environment, hiring strategies should be based on analyses that explicitly consider the probabilities associated with each possible demand level. It is conceivable that some plans which yield expected profits may also have loss probabilities that are unacceptable to management. For example, losses from overstaffing could occur if the actual demand for audit services falls short of forecasted levels. Alternatively, potential revenues and profits may be sacrificed if an office is not prepared to handle service demands that exceed forecasted amounts. These possibilities should be evaluated when hiring plans are being formulated. When this happens, an office may want to examine trade-offs between such things as increases in expected profits and increases in the probability of incurring losses at varying levels of demand. The approach or model presented in this paper makes it possible for an office to develop a rational basis for planning its hiring activities that can balance risk (e.g., the probability of loss) against expected increments in profit from hiring additional staff.

We have developed a mathematical model that enables an office to consider several variables when planning its hiring strategy. The model is based on an assumption of expected profit maximization. Given certain input data provided by an accounting office, the model proceeds to identify the number of new auditors needed to provide a level of service that will maximize expected profits. The model is subsequently expanded to incorporate two constraints which an office might want to impose: (1) a minimum probability that the break-even point for additional hiring is reached or exceeded (called α_1) and (2) a probability that the actual demand for audit service does not surpass planned service capacity (called α_2). Both α_1 and α_2 are set by each office and may be varied in subsequent iterations as a form of sensitivity analysis.

To simplify the discussion, only one class of personnel, called staff auditors (SAs), will be considered for hiring. The SAs are traditionally new to public accounting and are recruited from colleges and universities. The hiring models and examples presented in this paper have been developed from information obtained during interviews with audit partners and other personnel of several Big Eight offices in Texas. Following their development, the models were successfully tested in the office of a Big Eight firm. The models have been prepared for utilization on a microcomputer, such as an IBM PC, Apple,[2] or Macintosh. Specific details about the mathematical models are presented in the Appendix. This paper is confined to discussions about model formulation, presentations of examples, and interpretations of the results.

The second section identifies some key variables that are relevant to the hiring decision, and describes or illustrates how they may be determined. The basic model for maximizing expected profits is described in the next section. The fourth section explores the sensitivity of the profit maximization results to changes in selected variables. The next section expands the model by introducing two chance constraints. These chance constraints are included in order to evaluate trade-offs between increases in expected profits and associated increases in the risk of losses. Finally, the last section summarizes the paper.

VARIABLES AND DATA FOR A HYPOTHETICAL CASE

The hiring decision for new staff auditors requires some basic information about expected revenues and costs for the coming year. It also requires information about the expected demand for audit services, the standard billable hours per year provided by both a new SA and an experienced SA, and the turnover-attrition rate of SAs. It is assumed that accounting firms are profit maximizers and that new staff auditors will be hired only if currently employed SAs are not capable of providing enough billable hours to meet expected demand.

The model's primary variables are:

q = The level of billable hours provided next year by newly hired SAs when profits are maximized.
p = Billing rate per billable hour for a SA (it is assumed that the billing rate equals the collection rate).
c = Variable cost per billable hour for a SA.
H = Total fixed costs committed to recruiting and hiring new SAs.

The remaining variables are introduced as they appear in the model's subsequent development and modification.

The individual costs and revenues should be estimated or measured as accurately as possible. For example, the fixed costs for recruiting and hiring new staff auditors (H) might include the estimated costs of having firm personnel travel to college campuses, office vists by recruits, training, and the value of the time committed by partners and employees to the various recruiting and training activities. The variable cost per billable hour for a new SA (c) may be estimated by dividing the annual costs associated with employing a SA (e.g., salary, fringe benefits, overtime, and a share of office overhead) by the estimated annual billable hours of a new SA. The billing rate per billable hour for new SA (p) is set by the office in its usual way. With this and other information, the firm's objective is to determine the optimum level of service that will maximize expected profits. According to our model, this level of service is obtained at demand level q. The probability model simultaneously considers several alternative levels of demand and their probabilities of occurring, as well as the revenue and cost data provided by the firm in order to arrive at level q.

To illustrate these features, assume that $p = \$40$, $c = \$18$, and $H = \$240{,}000$. Further assume that a new SA historically provides about 1,700 billable hours of service in his or her first year and that an experienced SA with over one year of experience typically provides 1,900 billable hours. The 200-hour difference reflects the additional training and other allowances needed by new SAs. Exhibit 1 presents these and other key variables and their assumed values.

A critical input for the hiring decision is the estimated number of audit service hours expected next year. This estimate should be obtained from the audit partners. To assist in the testing of our model, 22 audit partners of a Big Eight office provided estimates of the expected billable hours under their responsibility for the coming year. These estimates included the possibility of obtaining new clients as well as losing current ones. Because of the recognized

Exhibit 1. Hypothetical Input Data

Staff auditor's billing rate per billable hour	$p = \$40$
Staff auditor's variable cost per billable hour	$c = \$18$
Fixed recruiting cost per year for staff auditors	$H = \$240{,}000$
New staff auditor's standard billable hours per year	1,700 hours
Experienced staff auditor's standard billable hours per year	1,900 hours
Staff auditor's rate of turnover, attrition, promotion, etc.	50%
Percentage of total audit hours performed by SAs	30%
Number of staff auditors currently employed	40

uncertainty in these estimates, the partners were asked to allocate their time estimates across the following four risk categories: (1) "secure," (2) "very likely," (3) "probable," and (4) "unlikely."[3] The researchers assigned probability levels to these categories in the following order: 100%, 95%, 50%, and 5%. While these percentage values were reviewed with the partners for reasonableness, it is important to note that they are essentially starting points. The model's results should be examined to determine their sensitivity to changes in the percentage values, as will be demonstrated later. The overall time estimates are summarized in Exhibit 2.

As Exhibit 2 shows, the estimates from partners with similar allocation patterns are aggregated within risk categories. For example, Group 1 (partners 1, 6, 7, 8, and 15) believe that their 75,600 estimated billable hours for next year are quite certain. Thus, 75,600 hours are reported under the "secure" column. Similarly, the members of Group 2 (partners 3, 4, 5, 12, and 16) believe that most of their expected audit work is "secure" (20,700 billable hours) while the remainder is "probable" (11,500 billable hours).

By aggregating the partner's estimated billable hours within each risk category, the number of possible combinations to evaluate is reduced. But even after this reduction, the number of remaining combinations can be extremely high. Nevertheless, the model retains the original information provided by each partner, thereby making it possible for the user to establish finer groupings in subsequent analyses.

Once these estimates are obtained, the model requires an assignment of probabilities to each of the established risk categories. These assignments can be made, for example, by the firm's office manager or by consensus of the audit partners. In the hypothetical case, recall that the probabilities set for the four risk categories were 100%, 95%, 50%, and 5%.

After these input values are determined, the model proceeds to calculate the expected levels of incremental demand for service at each possible combination of billable hours. The incremental demand for expected billable hours is then translated into the number of new SAs needed to meet this demand. The model

Exhibit 2. Estimated Billable Hours for Next Year From 22 Audit Partners

	Probabilities					
Audit Partners	*100% Case: "Secure"*	*95% Case: "Very Likely"*	*50% Case: "Probable"*	*5% Case: "Unlikely"*	*Total Hours*	*Remarks (Basis of grouping)*
Group 1: Partners 1,6,7,8,15	75,600	√	√	√	75,600	All audits are secure
Group 2: Partners 3,4,5,12,16	20,700	√	11,500	√	32,200	Audits are secure or probable
Group 3: Partners 11,13,14	34,800	√	7,700	6,500	49,000	Audits are secure, probable or unlikely
Group 4: Partners 10,18	√	21,000	1,200	√	22,200	Audits are very likely or probable
Group 5 Partners 2,9,17,19 20,21,22	23,100	9,600	15,600	18,700	67,000	Audits in all categories
Total	154,200	30,600	36,000	25,200	246,000	

Note: √ = the partners in this group did not assign auits to this category.

also computes and reports additional information as described in a subsequent section.

Calculating Incremental Demand

All combinations of estimated demand must be evaluated to determine the optimal hiring size for new SAs. This includes a careful assessment of the audits regarded as "secure" as well as each uncertain audit: those that are "very likely," "probable," and "unlikely." At each estimated demand level, the portion that is expected to be provided by SAs must be determined. In addition, it is necessary to know the number of billable hours of service expected from existing SAs, recognizing that some will be lost to normal attrition and promotion (i.e., turnover). At each level of estimated demand, the difference between the total billable hours expected from SAs and the expected number of hours provided by existing SAs equals the incremental demand for new SA hours. This result, which is expressed in billable hours, can be easily converted

Exhibit 3. Steps for Computing the Incremental Demand for New Staff Auditors (SAs)

Step 1. Develop office-wide estimates of the demand for auditing services in the next year. The estimates should be expressed in billable hours. Arrange the estimates in the form of a frequency distribution as demonstrated in Exhibit 2.

Step 2. For each level of expected demand, compute the portion of total estimated billable hours expected to be performed by new and experienced SAs.

This portion equals the product of the total estimated billable hours under evaluation and the fraction of this work expected to be performed by SAs.

Step 3. Compute the estimated billable hours of auditing service to be performed by existing SAs.

This is determined by multiplying the standard hours of billable service expected from an experienced SA by (a) the number of existing SAs and by (b) one minus the SA turnover rate.

Step 4. Compute the estimated billable hours of service needed from *new* SAs.

This result is obtained by subtracting the estimated billable hours of audit service to be provided by existing SAs (Step 3) from the estimated demand for total billable hours to be provided by all SAs (Step 2).

Step 5. Compute the number of new SAs needed to provide the level of service determined in Step 4.

The number of new SAs needed is found by dividing the estimated billable hours of audit service to be provided by new SAs by 1,700 hours.

to the number of new SAs needed. This is accomplished by dividing the incremental demand by the standard number of billable hours expected from a new SA (i.e., 1,700 hours in our hypothetical case). This general process is summarized in Exhibit 3.

To illustrate these points, once again consider the input data presented in Exhibits 1 and 2. The smallest level of expected demand for next year is represented by the "secure" audits in Exhibit 2. These audits are expected to require 154,200 total hours of service. At the other extreme, the maximum level of expected demand is 246,000 hours of service. These end-points and each combination in between is systematically evaluated by the computer model. For just the "secure" audits, the number of new SAs needed is determined in the following fashion:

Estimated billable audit hours provided by SAs:	$154{,}200 \times 0.3$	= 46,260
Estimated hours provided by existing SAs:	$40 \times 1{,}900 \times (1-.50)$	= 38,000
Estimated hours needed from new SAs:		= 8,260
Number of new SAs needed:	8,260 / 1,700	= 4.86

Exhibit 4. Hypothetical Probability Tables (Frequency Distribution)*

Combination Number	*Hiring Size (new SA hrs)*	*Probability*	*Cumulative Probability*	*1−Cumulative Probability*
1	8,260	0.000141	0.000141	0.999859
2	8,620	0.000141	0.000282	0.999718
3	10,210	0.000007	0.000289	0.999711
.	.	.	.	.
.	.	.	.	.
.	.	.	.	.
24	14,890	0.000007	0.017834	0.982166
25	14,920	0.002679	0.020514	0.979486
.	.	.	.	.
.	.	.	.	.
.	.	.	.	.
31	15,820	0.002679	0.026444	0.973556
32	15,970	0.000007	0.026452	0.973548
33	16,180	0.002687	0.029139	0.970861
.	.	.	.	.
.	.	.	.	.
.	.	.	.	.
112	23,170	0.000001	0.511608	0.488392
113	23,200	0.053586	0.565194	0.434861
114	23,380	0.000007	0.565201	0.434799
.	.	.	.	.
.	.	.	.	.
.	.	.	.	.
165	28,090	0.002679	0.919976	0.080024
166	28,240	0.050914	0.970889	0.029111
167	28,300	0.000141	0.971031	0.028969
.	.	.	.	.
.	.	.	.	.
.	.	.	.	.
190	32,920	0.000007	0.994075	0.005925
191	33,130	0.000141	0.994216	0.005784
192	33,490	0.002820	0.997036	0.002964
193	33,850	0.002679	0.999716	0.000284
194	35,440	0.000141	0.999857	0.000143
195	35,800	0.000141	0.999998	0.000002

Note: * Dots between numerical values indicate that these parts of the complete probability table are omitted.

This result is reported in Exhibit 4 opposite combination number one. The second column of this exhibit shows that the smallest expected demand level (i.e., "secure" audits only) requires 8,260 additional new staff hours. The model repeats this process for each successive level of incremental demand, which includes the possible addition of all uncertain (less than 100%) audits.

Determining the Number of Possible Combinations

There are eight occupied cells in Exhibit 2 reporting expected demand levels which are less than "secure" (i.e., those in the "very likely," "probable," and "unlikely" columns). Because each demand level may or may not occur, it is binary in nature. With eight separate binary situations in our example, the total number of possible combinations is 2^8 or 256. The 256 possible combinations include the extreme cases of no uncertain demands occurring (i.e., only "secure" audits are realized for 154,200 billable hours) and of all uncertain demands occurring (i.e., an expected total of 246,000 billable hours).

The computer model calculates the expected number of billable hours for each of the 256 possible combinations and ranks the results from lowest to highest. This array is examined by the model and any duplicate values are combined. It is reasonable to expect some duplicates to occur by chance alone. For example, there are two combinations of possible demand reported in Exhibit 2 that have a combined total of 161,900 billable hours: (1) 154,200 "secure" hours plus 7,700 "probable" hours from Group 3, and (2) 154,200 "secure" hours plus 6,500 "unlikely" hours from Group 3 plus 1,200 "probable" hours from Group 4. There are 61 duplicates, in our example. The net result is 195 different combinations (256 − 61 = 195) that require further analyses. These combinations involve varying demands for new SA hours. A representative sample of them is presented in Exhibit 4.

Calculating the Probabilities

Our model of the optimal hiring problem explicitly considers uncertainty. For example, each of the four risk categories of Exhibit 2 has a different probability level ranging from 100% to 5%. Similarly, the 195 different hiring sizes expressed in billable hours also have probabilities of occurring. Our hypothetical example is used again to demonstrate how these probabilities are calculated.

Consider the situation in which only "secure" audits are realized (i.e., a demand of 154,200 billable hours). The probability of this occurring equals the probability of "secure" audits (1.00) multiplied by the probabilities that the demands in the other categories of Exhibit 2 will *not* occur. This can be expressed as:

$$(1.00)\,(1-.95)^2\,(1-.5)^4\,(1-.5)^2 = \underline{\underline{.00141}}$$

Each term in this expression represents a risk category. The probability assigned to the "very likely" category in Exhibit 2 is .95; thus, the probability that an audit in this category does not happen is (1 − .95). Because there are two groups of partners reporting estimates in this category, the probability that neither of their demands will materialize is found by multiplying their probabilities together: $(1 - .95) \times (1 - .95)$ or $(1 - .95)^2$. This is the second term in the above calculation. The third and fourth terms are similarly derived from the data in Exhibit 2. Note that the exponents equal the number of occupied cells within their respective probability categories. The overall probability of realizing only "secure" audits (.000141) is reported in column 3 of Exhibit 4 opposite the incremental hiring size of 8,260 new staff hours. The computer model computes the probabilities for the other 194 possible demand levels following these same procedures.

Exhibit 4 also summarizes the cumulative probabilities at each of the 195 hiring sizes. These values may be interpreted as the probability that the demand for new SA hours is *equal to or less* than hiring size X_i. On the other hand, the probability that demand is *equal to or greater* than X_i is one minus the cumulative probability at the *previous* demand size: X_{i-1}.

A MAXIMUM EXPECTED PROFIT MODEL (MODEL 1)

An expected profit optimization model like the one used by Levy and Thompson [1984] provides an appropriate foundation for our model and a basis for comparison with any subsequent extensions. As previously mentioned, the number of new SAs to hire in a given year is influenced by several factors, including uncertainty in the expected demand for service, the specific revenue and cost parameters presented in Exhibit 1, and the estimated turnover rates of existing SAs. These factors have been incorporated into our model of the hiring decision (for details, see the Appendix). The remaining sections of this paper emphasize the type of results produced by the models and their interpretation. To enhance simplicity and clairty, the results are presented in Exhibits 5 through 8.

The model provides several statistics for each level of expected demand for new SA billable hours (see Exhibit 5). They include the equivalent number of new SAs needed, the expected incremental profit from hiring this number of new SAs, the probability of achieving this level of incremental profit, the probability of incurring an incremental loss at this level of new hires (e.g., incremental revenues from the new SAs will not cover the related costs), the maximum incremental profit at this hiring level, and the probability of achieving maximum profits.

Given the various assumptions and input data from the hypothetical case, Exhibit 5 shows that expected profits are maximized when enough new SAs are hired to provide 23,200 incremental billing hours of audit service.[4] This is equivalent to hiring 13.6 new SAs (23,200 hours ÷ 1,700 hours). At this level, the expected profit increment is $201,756 (this amount is calculated in detail

Exhibit 5. Summary of Initial Results

Hiring Size		*Expected Profit (\$) = E(Π)*	*Probability of*		*Maximum Possible Profit (\$) = Max Π*	*Probability of Achieving Max Π*
Billable Hours (New SA)	*Number of SAs*		*Achieving E(Π)*	*Making a Loss*		
13,090	7.7	47,506	0.994	0.006	47,980	0.994
16,180	9.5	113,411	0.974	0.007	115,960	0.974
18,340	10.8	154,798	0.854	0.012	163,480	0.852
20,080	11.8	181,282	0.837	0.023	201,760	0.778
21,580	12.7	195,592	0.723	0.024	234,760	0.615
23,200	13.6	201,756	0.618	0.029	270,400	0.488
25,930	15.3	184,960	0.538	0.107	306,040	0.273
26,800	15.8	177,618	0.500	0.146	349,600	0.145
29,170	17.2	143,259	0.497	0.155	401,740	0.026
33,490	19.7	67,477	0.497	0.330	496,780	0.006

in Part 1 of the Appendix). The maximum possible profit at demand level X_i is based on the assumption that this level of demand occurs with certainty ($p = 1.00$). Thus, with a certain incremental demand of 23,200 hours and a billing rate of \$40 per hour, the expected revenue increment is \$928,000. The variable cost of service at this level is \$417,600 (23,200 hours x \$18), and the fixed hiring cost is \$240,000. As a consequence, the incremental profit is \$270,400 (\$928,000 − \$417,600 − \$240,000). The probability of reaching maximum profit at this level is the probability that the demand for service equals or exceeds 23,200 incremental hours. This probability is .488, which is found in the one minus the cumulative probability column of Exhibit 4 opposite the previous value of X_i (i.e., 23,170 hours).

Exhibit 5 also shows that an office can hire fewer than 13.6 new SAs and increase its probability of earning incremental profits. However, these incremental profits are below their optimum. In contrast, the office can hire more than 13.6 new SAs and increase its maximum possible profits. But these increases are accompanied by reductions in the probabilities of achieving them. This information can be extremely valuable to management as trade-offs between expected profits and their risks are considered. Other information of this type is presented in the next two sections.

SENSITIVITY ANALYSES

It is reasonable for management to be interested in knowing how the initial results produced by the expected profit maximization model vary with changes in the input values. In our hypothetical example, the results presented in Exhibit 4 are dependent on the input values of Exhibits 1 and 2. Some of these values will now be changed in order to evaluate their impact on the hiring decision.

Exhibit 6. Summary of Initial Results and Price Sensitivity Analysis

Hiring Size		Initial Results					Price Sensitivity: Change Unit Billing Rate From \$40/hour to \$43/hour			
			Probability of					Probability of		
Billable Hours	Equivalent Number of SAs	Expected Profit (\$) = E(Π)	Achieving E(Π)	Making a Loss	Maximum Possible Profit = Π	Probability of Achieving Π*	Expected Profit (\$) = E(Π)	Acheving E(Π)	Making a Loss	Maximum Possible Profit = Π*
13,090	7.7	47,506	0.994	.006	47,980	0.994	87,250	0.994	0	98,960
16,180	9.5	113,411	0.974	.007	115,960	0.974	154,338	0.974	.0001	164,500
18,340	10.8	154,798	0.854	.012	163,480	0.852	205,216	0.854	.0003	218,500
20,080	11.8	181,282	0.837	.023	201,760	0.778	235,049	0.837	.0004	262,000
21,580	12.7	195,592	0.723	.024	234,760	0.615	256,890	0.723	.0006	299,500
23,200	13.6	201,756	0.618	.029	270,400	0.488	264,756	0.618	.0060	349,000
23,560	13.9	198,028	0.613	.031	306,040	0.432	266,440	0.613	.0230	430,000
29,170	17.2	143,259	0.497	.155	401,740	0.026	210,161	0.497	.1120	489,250
33,490	19.7	67,477	0.497	.330	496,780	0.006	87,960	0.497	.2500	597,250

Changes in Billing Rates

A likely issue for management to consider is the change in optimal hiring size and expected profits resulting from an increase in the billing rate (p) (e.g., from \$40 to \$43 per hour for a SA). The results of this \$3 increase are reported in Exhibit 6 under the caption "Price Sensitivity." For brevity, only a subset of critical hiring sizes is presented. The underlined values indicate that the revised optimum hiring size is 13.9 new SAs who should provide 23,560 billable hours. The expected incremental profit at this level is \$266,440. These results take into account the incremental opportunity cost of not having one additional unit of SA capacity when the billing rate is increased.

A few important differences and similarities between the initial results and the price sensitivity results of Exhibit 6 should be noted. First, with only a billing rate change, the probabilities associated with the expected profits and the probabilities of achieving maximum profits remain the same; therefore, they are not repeated among the price sensitivity results. However, adjustments in the billing rate produce changes in expected profits, maximum possible profits, and the probability of making a loss for each hiring size. These differences are readily apparent by comparing both panels of Exhibit 6.

Changes in Probabilities

Management may wish to consider the effects of changes in the probabilities assigned to the estimated demands for audit services reported in Exhibit 2. To illustrate, assume that the Group 5 partners now believe that the 9,600 hours originally termed "very likely" (95%) are "unlikely" (5%), and the 18,700 "unlikely" (5%) hours are now "very likely" (95%). By reversing the probabilities for these two groups of hours, the optimal hiring size is increased to 25,930 hours of service, or 15.3 new SAs. The optimum expected profit is now \$255,960. The sensitivity results and their related probability changes are reported in Exhibit 7 under the caption "Probability Sensitivity." Because of changes in the probabilities of estimated demand, the probabilities presented in Exhibit 4 are no longer applicable and new probabilities are needed for each level of demand. These calculations are made by the computer model.

These two examples involve independent changes in prices and probabilities. Similar analyses can be performed separately or jointly on changes in other input variables.[5] For example, management might ask about the range of possible price changes for which the optimal hiring size is not increased or decreased by one new SA. Sensivity analysis shows that the decision to hire 13.6 SAs remains optimal over a billing range of \$68 to \$29 per hour; however, the amounts of expected profit and maximum possible profit vary within this price range.

Exhibit 7. Summary of Initial Results and Probability Sensitivity Analysis

		Initial Results (Before Sensitivity Analaysis)					*Price Probability Sensitivity: Change Probabilities of Group 5; Uncertain Clients As Follows: 9,600 hours: 0.95 to 0.05; 18,700 hours: 0.05 to 0.95*			
Hiring Size			*Probability of*					*Probability of*		
Billable Hours	*Equivalent Number of SAs*	*Expected Profit ($) = E(Π)*	*Achieving E(Π)*	*Making a Loss*	*Maximum Possible Profit = Π*	*Probability of Achieving Π**	*Expected Profit ($) = E(Π)*	*Achieving E(Π)*	*Making a Loss*	*Probability of Achieving Max Π*
13,090	7.7	47,506	0.994	.006	47,980	0.994	67,857	0.995	.0001	0.997
16,180	9.5	113,411	0.974	.007	115,960	0.974	110,338	0.987	.0001	0.986
18,340	10.8	154,798	0.854	.012	163,480	0.852	159,216	0.895	.0003	0.874
20,080	11.8	181,282	0.837	.023	201,760	0.778	190,049	0.872	.0040	0.830
21,580	12.7	195,592	0.723	.024	234,760	0.615	225,229	0.760	.0120	0.670
23,200	13.6	201,756	0.618	.029	270,400	0.488	243,556	0.650	.0160	0.494
25,930	15.3	184,960	0.538	.107	306,040	0.273	255,960	0.600	.0270	0.472
26,800	15.8	177,618	0.500	.146	349,600	0.145	248,047	0.540	.0320	.0247
29,170	17.2	143,259	0.497	.155	401,740	0.026	227,161	0.520	.0420	0.096
33,490	19.7	67,477	0.497	.330	496,780	0.006	185,550	0.515	.0750	0.014

A CHANCE CONSTRAINED MODEL TO ASSURE BREAK-EVEN (MODEL 2)

The previous examples determined optional hiring policies using expected profit maximization. These models have other applications in manpower planning as demonstrated by Brockett, Charnes, Cooper, and Shin [1984], who developed a chance constrained model to control and evaluate the probability of incurring losses as a result of a firm's personnel decisions. The output from a chance constrained model can help management select the best course of action from among several alternatives.

For example, the expected profit maximization model can be modified so that the optimum hiring size not only maximizes expected profits but also satisfies one or more constraints imposed by management. A possible constraint might involve placing a limit on the probability of losses from a particular hiring decision. That is, management may not want to adopt a particular hiring strategy if it has a probability greater than α of creating losses. (See the Appendix for the derivation and discussion of this chance constrained model). An attempt to control the risk of losses from failure to break-even[6] will be illustrated with our hypothetical data.

The break-even condition presented by the second constraint in model (A.7) of the Appendix implies that there is a floor to the number of billable hours from new SAs if losses are to be avoided, as shown below:

$$q \geq \frac{H}{p-c} \quad \text{or} \quad \frac{\$240{,}000}{\$40 - \$18} = \underline{\underline{10{,}909}} \text{ hours}$$

Because any hiring size less than 10,909 billable hours of incremental service will produce losses, the preferred hiring size in our hypothetical case should equal or exceed 10,909 billable hours. This is equivalent to hiring at least 6.4 new SAs (10,909 hours ÷ 1,700 hours). The profit contribution from this minimum number of new SAs is needed to recover the fixed costs of hiring (H). While this constraint can help a firm avoid losses from hiring too few SAs, the firm is still vulnerable to losses if too many new SAs are hired relative to expected demand. Such losses occur when the realized revenues from actual demand fail to cover the fixed costs of hiring plus the variable costs associated with SAs. The probability of incurring these losses may be determined in a manner analogous to the way in which the probability of achieving maximum profit was determined.

The *unconstrained* optimum hiring size is 23,200 billable hours for new SAs (see Exhibit 4). At this level of service and with an \$18 per hour variable cost for SAs, the total variable cost is \$417,600. Once the fixed hiring costs of \$240,000 are included, the aggregate cost is \$657,600. By dividing this amount by the \$40 billing rate per billable hour for a SA, the result is a required minimum of 16.440 billable hours. Any realized demand below this level will result in losses if 13.6 new SAs are hired, which is the equivalent of 23,200

Exhibit 8. Sensitivity Analysis (Constrained Risk of Loss)

	Without Chance Constraint (Unconstrained Case)				*With Chance Constraint (Break-even Constrant)* $\alpha = 0.02$[a]					
			Probability of		*Risk Controls*				*Probability of*	
	Optimal Size of Hiring (in new SA hrs)	*Expected Profit (\$) = E(Π)*	*Achieving E(Π)*	*Making a Loss*	*Lower Bound* $(= q_l)$	*Upper Bound* $(= q_u)$	*Optimal Size of Hiring*	*Expected Profit (\$) = E(Π) (in new SA hrs)*	*Achieving E(Π)*	*Making a Loss*
Case 1	23,200 (13.6)[b]	201,756	0.618	.029	10,909	19,750	19,750 (11.6)	176,953	0.84	.018
Case 2	23,560 (13.9)	266,440	0.613	.023	9,600	22,270	22,270 (13.1)	262,651	0.67	.018
Case 3	25,930 (15.3)	255,960	0.600	.027	10,909	23,890	23,890 (14.1)	248,167	0.71	.019

Notes: Case 1 corresponds to the initial results presented in Exhibit 5.
Case 2 corresponds to the price sensitivity case of Exhibit 6.
Case 3 corresponds to the probability sensitivity case of Exhibit 7.
[a] The maximum probability of loss acceptable to management.
[b] Equivalent number of new staff auditors (SA).

billable hours. The probability of demand being below 16,440 hours is found in the cumulative probability column of Exhibit 4 opposite the previous hiring size of 16,180 billable hours. This probability is .029, as reported in Exhibit 5 as the probability of making a loss at the optimum hiring size. It is conceivable that this probability is too high for management to accept. A chance constrained programming model can be used to address unacceptable risks from over-hiring. To do this, a level of acceptable risk—α—of not breaking even must be specified.

The choice of $\alpha = .02$ in the Appendix reduces the risk of loss by over 30 percent relative to the unconstrained risk level of .029. The derivation of maximum expected profits subject to this constraint is also shown in the Appendix. The optimum constrained results for our hypothetical firm (Case 1) are reported in the right side of Exhibit 8. The unconstrained results are reported in the left side of this exhibit for comparative purposes. It can be seen that this constraint reduces expected profits from $201,756 to $176,953 and that the optimal hiring size has been lowered from 23,200 billable hours (13.6 new SAs) to 19,750 hours (11.6 new SAs). The risk of loss is now .018. Management can now assess the 12% drop in *expected* profit (from $201,756 to $176,953) relative to the 38 percent drop in the risk of making a loss (from .029 to .018) when evaluating these two options.

In addition, Exhibit 8 also shows the results from introducing the break-even constraint to the sensitivity analyses involving changes in billing rates (Exhibit 6) and changes in the probabilities of demand (Exhibit 7). These are identified as Cases 2 and 3, respectively. As in the first case, the break-even constrant has lowered the level of expected profits and the optimal hiring size. However, as intended, the probability of making a loss is less than .02 in all cases. In the "Risk Controls" section of Exhibit 8, the lower and upper bounds on hiring sizes, after considering all specified constraints, are presented. Hiring sizes that fall outside these ranges will have probabilties of making a loss that are greater than .02.

Objectives other than maximizing expected profit can be used in our model. For instance, management might wish to maximize the probability of attaining a specific level of profit. Charnes and Cooper [1963] discuss this objective as it relates to the "satisficing models" of H.A. Simon.

A CHANCE CONSTRAINED MODEL TO ASSURE BREAK-EVEN AND TO CONTROL DEMAND OVERLOAD (MODEL 3)

While controlling for the probability of losses from the hiring decision, management might also want to include in its employment policy a minimum staffing level which will ensure that the probability of experiencing demand overload (e.g., where available capacity is below demand) is less than some predetermined value. To distinguish this risk from the probability of not breaking-even, model (A.9) in the Appendix identifies the break-even constraint as α_1, and the allowable probability of experiencing demand overload as α_2.

Model (A.9) illustrates how a constraint on demand overload may enter into the optimal hiring decision. For this model, α_1 is set at .02 and α_2 is set at .08. The other input data remain the same as in previous examples. Management also has determined that k percent of its annual total demand falls during a peak time period (e.g., $k = .50$); the details show that the minimum service level constraint is 14,045 new SA hours. The upper bound of the break-even constraint is 19,750 hours, and its lower bound is 10,909 hours. Consequently, the new optimum hiring size for maximizing expected profits subject to these two constraints lies between 14,045 and 19,750 new SA hours.

SUMMARY AND CONCLUSIONS

This paper presents a probabilistic model that CPA firms can use with a microcomputer to generate valuable quantitative information about the number of new staff accountants to hire in a given year. This model was developed with the assistance of several Big Eight accounting firms in Texas, and it was tested in a Big Eight office in the southwest. While the focus was on auditors, the model is equally applicable to other areas of a firm's practice. The model incorporates input about the expected demand for services in the next period, measures of their likelihood of occurring, and certain revenue and cost data. The output includes information about expected profit at each combination of hiring sizes, the corresponding probability of achieving that level of profit, as well as the probability of experiencing losses at each hiring size. The model was expanded in later sections of the article to include chance constraints on breaking even from the hiring decision and to control the possibility of having excess demand. The model can be modified by individual users to meet their particular needs.

Although the models discussed in this paper may help CPA firms reduce their employment costs through a more calculated approach to hiring, its results are not necessarily the final answer. Firms may have legitimate reasons for overhiring (e.g., to develop talent for future growth or to give partners an incentive to generate new business) or underhiring (e.g., to encourage increases in productivity) at any particular point in time. However, the approach presented here may help management assess in monetary terms its various alternatives. The model also enables management to evaluate the effects of trade-offs between increased expected profits from additional hiring against increased probabilities of not breaking even (i.e., having losses). In other words, the model allows management to better assess the potential risks and benefits of an inherently risky process. This is especially important given the increasing cost-competitive environment facing accounting firms today.

It was demonstrated that chance constrained programming models permit various types of "sensitivity analyses" for studying changes in cost/benefit parameters and for evaluating changes in the estimates of client demand probablities. Such models can also be used to examine alternative assumptions about staff turnover in a "turnover rate sensitivity" analysis that is analogous to what was done in Exhibit 7 [for more details, see Shin, 1985]. Because these models are designed for microcomputers, the entire process can be performed easily.

Another possible use for the models includes an evaluation of alternative hiring sizes to assist a firm that desires to achieve specific future growth objectives. In addition, the effect of a firm's policy toward establishing a certain mix of professionals (such as seniors, managers, and partners) can be assessed in a chance constrained programming context. This expansion requires a considerable amount of data in the form of a so-called transition matrix. For that reason, it was not undertaken in this paper; however, Shin [1985, Chapter 5] discusses how it can be done. Another perspective may be obtained from Charnes, Cooper and Niehaus [1972] and from Niehaus [1979], who extended this type of analysis to a firm's entire hierarchy of positions in a multiperiod context.

APPENDIX

The Expected Profit Maximization Model

An optimal hiring model that maximizes expected profits can be expressed mathematically as:

$$\max_{q} E\Pi\ (X,q) \tag{A.1}$$

where the notation $\Pi\ (X,q)$ represents the profit realization function. This function implies that profit depends jointly on the chocie of q and the demand for services that actually occurs, i.e., the random variable X. The term $\max_{q}\ E\Pi\ (X,q)$ means that the objective is to find the demand level q that will maximize expected profits. Hereafter, $E\Pi\ (X,q)$ will be expressed as $E(\Pi)$.

The equation that defines expected profit at demand level X_j is:

$$E(\Pi) = p \sum_{i=1}^{i} x_i\, P(x_i) + pq \sum_{i=j+1}^{m} P(x_i) - cq - H \tag{A.2}$$

where $P(X_i)$ is the probability of demand for billable hours at level x_i, j identifies the demand level being evaluated, m equals the total number of demand combinations and H equals the fixed costs of recuriting and hiring new staff auditors. In the hypothetical situation described in Exhibits 1 and 2, $m = 195$. This is reflected in Exhibit 4, which also reports the probabilities of occrrence for serveral values of x_i, where i ranges from 1 to 195.

Equation (A.2) has two separate parts which are added together to yield expected revenues at demand level j. If $q = X_j$, the first term shows that expected demand at level X_j is calculated as

$$\sum_{i=1}^{j} x_i P(x_i).$$

This result is then multiplied by the billing rate to produce the expected revenue at this level of service. The second term, which is

$$\sum_{i=j+1}^{m} P(x_i),$$

gives the probability that demand greater than x_j (i.e., $x_i > q$) will happen. For all cases in which $x_i > q$, only revenue in the amount of pq will be obtained and

$$pq \sum_{i=j+1}^{m} P(x_i)$$

will give its expected value. By substracting the total variable cost, cq, and the fixed recruiting cost, H, from the sum of the expected revenue terms, the expected profit amount is produced.

For any level of demand q we can write:

$$\text{Prob}\,(X \leq q) = \sum_{i=1}^{j} P(x_i). \tag{A.3}$$

This equation shows that the probability of having demand equal to or less than q, which is the level being examined, is the sum of all demand probabilities up to and including x_j. The objective is to choose the optimal q, or q^*, so that $E(\Pi)$ is maximized. As shown in Shin [1985] and in Levy and Thompson [1984], this maximum is achieved at the following probability level:

$$\text{Prob}\,(X \leq q^*) = \frac{p - c}{p} \tag{A.4}$$

For our hypothetical case, this is: $\dfrac{\$40 - \$18}{\$40} = \underline{\underline{0.55}}.$

By finding the value closest to 0.55 in the cumulative probability column of Exhibit 4, the hiring size of 23,200 billable hours is identified as q^*. The expected profit from hiring 23,200 incremental billable hours is calculated as:

$$E(\Pi) = p \sum_{i=1}^{j} x_i \, P(x_i) + pq \sum_{i=j+1}^{m} P(x_i) - cq - H \qquad \text{(A.5)}$$

$= (\$40 \times 11{,}396) + (\$40 \times 23{,}200 \times 0.43486) - (\$18 \times 23{,}200) - \$240{,}000$
$= \underline{\underline{\$201{,}756}}.$

Therefore, the optimum expected incremental profit from hiring enough new SAs to provide 23,200 billable hours is $201,756. This result is reported in Exhibit 5, along with the equivalent number of new hires: 13.6.

A Chance Constrained Programming Model (Break-even Constraint)

Part 1 shows that model (A.1) is designed to evaluate expected profits at various levels of possible demand. The computer model evaluates each demand level and identifies the one with the largest expected profits. This model is not subject to any constraints; however, management may want to restrict its hiring alternatives to only those that satisfy some desirable condition. For example, management may wish to impose a probability level α on the risk of not breaking-even with its new hires. This adjustment is made by replacing (A.1) with the following:

$$\max_{q} E\,\Pi(X,q)$$

subject to (A.6)

$$\text{Prob}\,[\Pi\,(X,q) \geq 0] \geq 1-\alpha.$$

The "subject to" constraint in (A.6) restricts the choice of q to those values that will produce an incremental profit level of zero or greater with a probability of at least (1- α). Thus, if $\alpha = 0.02$, then $(1 - \alpha) = 0.98$. With this constraint, the model will only consider q values that have at least a 98% probability of breaking even or, alternatively, less than a 2% chance of loss.

As shown in Brockett et al. [1984], this chance constrained model may be replaced by the following deterministic expression:

$$\max_{q} E\Pi(X,q)$$

subject to

$$q \leq \frac{p\,F^{-1}(\alpha) - H}{c} \tag{A.7}$$

$$q \geq \frac{H}{p - c}$$

This expression is deterministic because it does not contain any random variables. Note for instance that the values of p, c, and H are all known in advance of the choice of q. The symbol $F^{-1}(\alpha)$ is a standard expression for locating the maximum value of x_i which has a probability of loss (i.e., not breaking even) less than α. For instance, with $\alpha = 0.02$ in the hypothetical case, Exhibit 4 shows that the largest demand level with a cumulative proability less than .02 is 14,890 hours. Its substitution in the first expression in (A.7), coupled with other input values from Exhibit 1, yields:

$$q \leq \frac{p\,F^{-1}(\alpha) - H}{c} = \frac{p \times 14{,}890 - H}{c} \tag{A.8}$$

$$= \frac{\$40 \times 14{,}890 - \$240{,}000}{\$18} = \underline{\underline{19{,}750}}$$

This value is the upper limit of the billable hours for the first case reported in Exhibit 8.

The second constraint in (A.7) does not contain a random variable. In our example, its solution is 10,909 new SA hours as shown in the discussion of Model 2 in the text. Because no randomness is present in model (A.7), it is the deterministic equivalent of model (A.6).

Chance Constrained Programming Model
(Break-even and Service-level Constraints)

If a service level constraint is also desired, the problem can be extended into:

$$\max_{q} E\Pi(X,q)$$

subject to (A.9)

Prob $[\Pi\,(X,q) \geq 0] \geq 1 - \alpha_1$: Break-even constraint

Prob $[q \geq k\,X] \geq 1 - \alpha_2$: Service level constraint

$0 \leq \alpha_1, \alpha_2 \leq 1 \qquad 0 < k < 1$

where α_1 represents the risk level chosen by the firm for not breaking even and the second constraint reflects the firm's requirement of having a staffing level q^* such that the probability of demand overload is less than α_2.

Based on the same data utilized in the previous example and with values of $\alpha_2 = 0.08$ and $k = 0.5$, where k is an adjustment factor to allow for peak demands, the deterministic equivalent of (A.9) becomes:

$$\max_{q} E\Pi(X,q)$$

subject to

$$q \leq \frac{p\,F^{-1}(\alpha_1) - H}{c} \quad = \quad \underline{\underline{19{,}750}} \qquad \text{(A.10)}$$

$$q \geq \frac{H}{p - c} \quad = \quad \underline{\underline{10{,}909}}$$

With a maximum probability of .080 assigned to the chance of having excess demand, Exhibit 4 shows that the highest acceptable demand level is 28,090 new SA hours (one minus the cumulative probability at this level is .08). However, the break-even constraint limits the result to 19,750 hours and the service level constraint imposes a minimum of 10,909 hours. The second constraint can be modified to allow for peak demands. Applying an adjustment factor k (e.g., $k = .50$) to the 18,090 hour limit determined from Exhibit 4 yields an adjusted result of 14,045 hours, shown as:

$$q \geq k\,F^{-1}(1 - \alpha_2) = 0.5 \times 28{,}090 \quad = \quad \underline{\underline{14{,}045.}}$$

This result satisfies both the first and second constraints (i.e., it is between 19,750 and 10,900 hours).

The optimal solutions shown in Exhibit 8 for Cases 1, 2, and 3 all exceed 14,045 billable hours. However, this is not always the case. Consequently, care must be exercised when interpreting the results generated by Model 3.

NOTES

1. The approach presented in this paper is quite general in nature and may easily be applied to other areas of an accounting firm, such as taxation, consulting and litigation support. The auditing area simply has been chosen as a vehicle for demonstration.

2. The software for implementing these models on an Apple computer is available from: Dr. James W. Deitrick, Department of Accounting, Graduate School of Business, CBA 4M.202, University of Texas at Austin, Austin, Texas 78712-1170. A nominal charge is assessed to cover the cost of the diskette and mailing.

3. The computerized model is flexible enough to accommodate several risk categories. The user specifies the number of categories and the associated probabilities. Again, these variable may be changed in subsequent iterations as part of a sensitivity analysis.

4. For simplicity, the optimal demand size will be expressed or measured in billable hours. Occasionally these hours will be converted to the required number of new SAs by dividing them by the 1,700 hours expected from each new SA.

5. It is often the case that reductions (increases) in the billing rate increase (decrease) the probability of obtaining new clients and of retaining existing clients. This is an example of joint sensitivity between price and probability. A sensitivity analysis involving joint changes can be conveniently performed with our model.

6. See Cooper and Ijiri [1983, pp. 74-75] for a definition and discussion of break-even points.

REFERENCES

Brockett, P., A. Charnes, W.W. Cooper, and H.C. Shin, "A Chance-Constrained Programming Approach to Cost-Volume-Profit Analysis," *The Accounting Review* [July 1984], pp. 474-487.

Charnes, A. and W.W. Cooper, "Deterministic Equivalents for Optimizing and Satisficing under Chance Constraints," *Operations Research* [1963].

Charnes, A., W.W. Cooper, and R.J. Niehaus, *Studies in Manpower Planning* [Office of Civilian Manpower Management, Washington, DC, July 1972].

Cooper, W.W., L. Mitchell, G.A. Welsch, and H.C. Shin, "A Model for Planning Staff Mix Recruitment in Public Accounting Firms," Working paper [The University of Texas at Austin, 1986].

Cooper, W.W. and Y. Ijiri, eds., *Kohler's Dictionary for Accountants,* 6th ed. [Prentice-Hall, 1983].

Levy, F.K. and G.L. Thompson, "The Optimal Size of Law Firms and the Contingency Fee Decision," Working paper [The University of Georgia, 1984].

Niehaus, R.J., *Computer-Assisted Human Resources Planning* [Wiley-Interscience, 1979].

Shin, H.C., "Optimal Hiring Decisions For Entry-Level Auditors in Public Accounting Firms," Working paper [The University of Texas at Austin, December 1985].

THE CHANGING ENVIRONMENT OF AUDITORS' BUSINESS RISK:

UNDERSTANDING AND ANTICIPATING ITS IMPACT ON ACCOUNTING FIRMS AND ASSESSING THE EFFICACY OF RESEARCH

Christine V. Zavgren and Michael T. Dugan

ABSTRACT

The purpose of this paper is to discuss recent trends in auditors' business risk in relation to litigation trends in the economy as a whole, describe how this risk relates to audit risk, and assess the current status of research that bears on this topic. In addition, potentially fruitful areas for research that effectively addresses the issues of the auditor's business risk are explored. In the process, the professional literature on audit risk is analyzed, and academic research that has been conducted on the topic of audit risk is surveyed.

Advances in Accounting, Volume 8, pages 271-292.

ISBN: 1-55938-067-5

INTRODUCTION

The purpose of this paper is to discuss recent trends in auditors' business risk in relation to litigation trends in the economy as a whole, describe how this risk relates to audit risk, and assess the current status of research that bears on this topic.

Contractual, common law, and statutory obligations require honest and responsible work from auditors. But auditors are professionals who typically hold themselves to even higher levels of moral responsibility. "[The auditor's] responsibility is ... the moral obligation assumed by a public accountant, as a member of a profession, in certifying to a financial statement from which information may be sought by management, creditors, and investors" [Kohler, 1983].

The assurances resulting from an audit involve the greatest legal liability and hence the greatest business risk for auditors. "An auditor may be sued (business risk) whether or not the audit and the financial statements comply with professional standards (audit risk)" [Brumfield, Elliott, and Jacobson, 1983, p. 60]. Of course the problem of business risk involves many factors outside the control of auditors. Business risk is defined in *SAS 47* [AICPA, 1983] as:

> In addition to audit risk, the auditor is also exposed to loss or injury to his professional practice from litigation, adverse publicity, or other events arising in connection with financial statements that he has examined and reported on. This exposure is present even though the auditor has performed his examination in accordance with generally accepted auditing standards and has reported appropriately on those financial statements. Even if an auditor assesses this exposure as low, he should not perform less extensive procedures than would otherwise be appropriate under generally accepted auditing standards [312.03, fn. 1].

Business risk and audit risk have been addressed by both practitioners and academics. This paper suggests that future research on those topics (especially audit risk) be more consistent with the profession's need for a precise analysis of the issues and their ramifications.

Potentially frutiful areas for research that effectively addresses the issues of the auditor's business risk are explored. The professional literature on audit risk is also analyzed for insights about the issues, as well as cues as to important variables, or descriptions of techniques in practice that attempt to address concerns related to the auditor's business risk. The implications for effective research in this area are developed.

Academic research that has been conducted on the topic of audit risk is surveyed. Various concepts of risk are examined from the finance and economics literatures that have been used in some of these studies to proxy audit risk. This paper then addresses whether the use of such proxies in those studies was appropriate and whether insights as to the nature of auditors' business risk provide operational guidelines for practice and for additional research.

THE PROFESSIONAL VIEWPOINT

The profession has tried to manage its liability problems by exploring several methods of refining auditing techniques; attempting to better understand society's perceptions about the auditor's role and the effect of these perceptions on the law; modifying the objectives of the audit to match more closely the standards to which auditors are being held; and enhancing public understanding of the audit and the reports that it produces. These methods are new, have their attendant difficulties, and have had mixed results. However, they serve to highlight several areas worthy of further serious study.

The Expectations Gap

The public's perceptions place burdens on the audit that the profession has had difficulty addressing. Injuried parties, and quite often juries and judges, have a broad interpretation of auditors' role in the dissemination of financial information and of their role in its reliability. On the other hand, auditors have attempted to keep the standards to which they are held as narrow as possible. The voluminous hearings record from the Dingell Commitee reveals that the members of the committee expect that:

1. The audit mission, no excuses excepted, is to prevent the publication of misleading financial statements from whatever source.
2. Warning the public of impending business failure is an inherent part of the auditor's responsibility.
3. Devices within the system will prevent substandard audit performance and will mete out swift punishment if it occurs [*CPA Journal,* 1986, p. 5].

This description is clearly different from the profession's view of its responsibilities. A recent sociological study concluded, similar to the findings of the Cohen Commission, that the "burden for narrowing expectations gaps rests primarily with the accounting profession" [Arrington, Hillison, and Williams, 1983, p. 249]. The same study found that non-CPAs are more likely than other CPAs to attribute cuplability to CPAs, and non-CPAs deem CPAs' opinions about accounting issues much less important than do CPAs [p. 249].

An alternative argument is that the expectations gap does not exist, and that the greater inclinations of injured parties to sue auditors merely result from their perceptions of auditors as having "deep pockets." If an expectations gap does exist, the difficulty is attributable to the lack of public understanding of the division between management's role in record keeping and reporting, and the auditor's role.

Auditing for Fraud

Fortunately, the erosion of the privity doctrine has not been so complete as to lead the courts to hold auditors to the standard of strict liability, although some courts and law review articles have suggested that it is a trend to watch [Goldwasser, 1985, p. 42]. If courts were to do so, auditors would be responsible in a manner similar to manufacturers of football helmets, folding chairs, and hairdryers for injury caused by their product in any foreseeable use by any party, regardless of their remoteness along the chain of production and sale. Thus, contractual relationships between manufacturer and user are not required. The burden is on the manufacturer to make the product safe under all foreseeable circumstances, and warning labels and restrictive warranties do not obviate this responsibility. As Goldwasser [1985] quite succinctly notes, the application of this standard to auditors would require assuming auditors have strict control over financial statements. Such a standard obviously would require a need for stronger assurances that the financial statements are correct, which in turn would necessitate an audit for fraud.

In testimony during the Dingell Committee hearings, SEC Chairman Shad indicated that since only 1% of audits result in audit failures, an audit for fraud would impose substantial costs on all companies for increased audit procedures and liability insurance "which is likely to result in a benefit in less than one out of 100 cases" [Goldwasser, 1985, p. 44]. Goldwasser believes that these costs would be passed on to the client and then to the purchasers of the client's product, thereby resulting in the wrong group (consumers) bearing the cost of protection of the shareholders [p. 43]. Whether he is correct depends on one's assumptions about the structure of the market at two critical points of juncture: the market for audit services and the market for the final product. The market for audit services is certainly becoming more competitive. Recently the AICPA and Federal Trade Commission entered into an agreement under which the AICPA may no longer prohibit its members from taking commissions or contingent fees from clients for which the member does not perform audits, reviews, compilations, or examinations of prospective financial statements [*The CPA Letter,* 1988]. These pressures will certainly result in increasing price competition among accounting firms, which will find it more difficult to pass on the costs of additional services, and in the firms bearing those costs themselves. To the extent that auditors can pass on the costs of these services, they will be borne by either consumers or shareholders depending on the nature of the market for the final product. If the market for the final product is not price competitive, those costs can be passed on to consumers.

If auditors were able to pass on those costs, it would be purely an insurance scheme. If the burden is borne by auditors, this result would still shelter investors, but at the cost of parties usually not at fault. Usually shareholder losses result from managment fraud, and the auditor is as much a victim as the public. If fraud audits were imposed on auditors and clients, several difficulties would arise. Attempting to detect and eliminate the effects of even all materially fraudulent transactions is difficult because of the auditor's lack of control over the accounting records. This lack of control obviously impedes the auditor's examination.

> 1. The examination embodies a well-recognized and accepted concept of selective testing of recorded transactions, accounts, locations, etc., and the judgments involved in that selection process.
> 2. Management has the ability to override internal accounting controls on which the auditor might have placed reliance.
> 3. There are difficulties in detecting fraud committed through collusion, forgery, falsification of documents, and failure to record transactions [Serlin, 1985, p. 139].

Further difficulties the auditor would encounter while trying to detect fraud would be: (1) investigating an allegation of fraud while maintaining confidentiality, to avoid defamation of character or infringement of civil rights; (2) changing the focus of the audit from sampling representative transactions to searching for exceptions to standard procedures, regardless of their materiality; (3) extensive reliance on comparison between accounting records and physical evidence; and (4) recognition of the importance of non-accounting data, such as unusual behavior or unusual responses to questions. These represent difficulties beyond those for which most auditors are trained. An article noted frauds detected by non-auditors who had first observed small irregularities, using "a common-sense approach to observing a problem and questioning the reason for its existence" and surmised that "a non-auditor may be in a better position to discover a problem, since the auditor's training and experience in judging events by their materiality from an audit perspective may be counter to uncovering the problem" [Armstrong, 1985, p. 79]. Another article concludes that an audit designed to circumvent this myopia would be:

> concerned with what lies behind transactions, without regard to materiality, and is not concerned with the application of generally accepted accounting principles unless misapplication has led to fraudulent statements. In its purest form, therefore, it is a hybrid of auditing and management advisory services [Levy, 1985, p. 79].

What the several indicia of fraud that Levy enumerates (such as failure to use serially numbered documents, excessive use of cash transactions, failure to reconcile check accounts, excessive number of checking accounts, and so forth) have in common is their inconsistency with the profit motive. Thus, to notice these signs, the auditor must be evaluating the prudence of many business decisions. If these observations are correct, they highlight flaws in the training of auditors and in the focus of the standards to which they attempt to adhere. Detecting and following up on these types of signs require the astute use of data beyond the scope of internal accounting controls, thus requiring intensified use of analytical procedures.

Analytical procedures are an attempt to inject common sense into the audit process, and as such have deserved the increased attention recently devoted to them. The many facets of analytical procedures and their integral role in the audit are beyond the scope of this survey, but Wallace [1983a, 1983b; Arrington et al., 1983] provide excellent surveys of this topic. *SAS 23* [AICPA, 1978] describes analytical procedures as "substantive tests of financial information made by a study and comparison of relationships among data." *SAS 56* [AICPA, 1988b] requires auditors to use analytical procedures at the planning and final review stages of all audits and provides guidelines for their effective use. By comprehensively examinig trends in account balances, ratios, comparison of budgets to actual performance, patterns of payments, and so forth, the auditor can try to develop a broader perspective about the company's performance and attempt to highlight problem areas. The role of analytical procedures in providing valuable clues, similar to those noted by Serlin [1985] and Armstrong [1985], cannot be overstated. For example,

> in the 'Salad Oil King' discovery, an important question arose of why wasn't the client's inventory compared with the reported world's supply of salad oil? Similarly, in Equity Funding, the public questioned why someone did not notice the implied growth rate in reinsurance would have shortly led to 100 percent of the market being controlled by a single company? Surely such techinques would have been preferable to many of the detailed tests which were performed on bogus documentation to evaluate the fairness of financial statements [Wallace, 1983b, p. 18].

These cases are particularly troublesome for the profession because they show that sophisticated methods are not very effective when they override basic common sense.

Quantifying Audit Risk

The professional literature is replete with discussions of the business risk problem, ranging from tolling the death knell of the profession to more calculated responses such as increasing the scope of the audit. An example of such a calculated response is a Coopers and Lybrand monograph which attempts to define audit risk exactly to help auditors enhance their performance and limit business risk. Their approach to considering audit risk consists of several factors: (1) risk resulting from breakdowns in the client's internal control process, or, (2) from environmental factors outside the scope of the client's internal control system, and (3) audit detection risk, or the risk that neither the auditor's analytical procedures nor tests of substantive details will reveal the existence of errors or misstatements [Coopers and Lybrand, 1983, pp. 4-10]. This model differs slightly from another audit risk model explicated in *SAS 39,* "Audit Sampling" [AICPA, 1981] but both are intended to serve as guides for the auditor in strategically assessing risks in the audit process and responding appropriately to them.

Such an approach to audit risk is closely related to approaches to risk measurement appearing in professional standards (e.g., *SAS 47* [AICPA, 1983]; *SAS 55* [AICPA, 1988a]). In its more practical form, this approach attempts to use quantifications of audit risk to assess rationally the types and extent of tests required in the audit and document thoroughly the process.

Summary: What Can be Done?

Constructive approaches to controlling auditors' business risk that have been examined so far include extending analytical procedures, quantifying audit risk and its relation to audit tests, assessing the potential of auditing for fraud and its attendant benefits and problems, attempting to understand and narrow the expectations gap, and undertaking efforts to codify more clearly the auditor's professional role through uniform standards. These approaches all have in common their goal of defending the profession through improving the quality of auditing services. They are relatively new and need much extension in both theoretical development and implementation before they can produce a noticeable effect on the liability problems of auditors. Implementation of some of these ideas requires political activity as well as analytical development.

These political problems originate in the expectations gap, which in turn results in public demands for audits for fraud, evaluation of the prospects of businesses, and stronger assurances. Any reasonable person hardly objects to undertaking a duty that is well defined and that he or she has the competency to perform. This requires that the responsibilities of all parties and penalties for failure to perform adequately be understood by all. The greatest pressures on auditors arise because of the current transitory nature of the law and certain public perceptions of auditors' responsibilities that it reflects. The rules are changing, and this situation leaves those who ridigly reply on past standards of conduct exposed to the vagaries of this change, and hence to greater business risk.

A more positive response requires a constructive brand of pragmatism. Although the defense of traditional rights is often essential and worthwhile, the exploration of new professional roles and the attendant rights and responsibilities is a more worthwhile undertaking in the long run. Wisdom is essential to know what is the most appropriate response to any specific issue. The public's and Congress's broadened demands for auditors' services and assurances based upon them imply opportunities for enhanced professional responsibilities and the improved status that should result from those enhanced responsibilities. Rigid adherence to the profession's limited view of the focus of the audit and the type of assurances auditors are willing to give in light of this political sentiment would appear to be unwise. This position would continue to invite public scorn and the lawsuits that attend it. The current political environment prods the profession to assess its role, but also creates the opportunity to redefine the rules.

This perspective makes the discussion surveyed above concerning auditing for fraud and its problems especially critical. It makes little sense for auditors to refuse to audit for fraud it they are in grave danger if they do not. It also does not make sense for auditors to undertake an audit objective they cannot adequately perform. Thus, an astute analysis of the technical problems associated with a fraud audit is immediately necessary. To the extent that these problems are insurmountable, auditors must participate in writing the rules of the audit so they are not left in the breach. Everyone's responsibility must be clearly articulated, not just to the participants, but also to the public. As the Cohen Commission recognized, this probably necessitates rewriting the audit report (the new "Expectations Gap" standards already take steps in this direction) to require genuine communication with the investing public. The expectations gap must be narrowed from both sides. Auditors must face up to the legal standards to which they are being measured.

In the subsequent section of this paper, research conducted on audit risk is surveyed and critiqued. Most of the studies reviewed use various risk concepts and proxies developed in the economics and finance literatures. These studies also vary in their definitions of audit risk, some of which do not exactly correspond with the definition of the term appearing in professional pronouncements (e.g., *SAS 47* [AICPA, 1983]). In critiquing the studies, their suitability for providing insights about the issues addressed in the first part of the paper concerning the auditor's business risk is considered. Suggestions for increasing the likelihood that future academic research in the area will have a more substantial impact on practice also are offered.

THE ACADEMIC VIEWPOINT

Introduction

Most academic research in accounting and auditing can be classified into two broad categories—analytical research and empirical research. Analytical research attempts to develop theory through the use of logical arguments to be able to provide insights about interrelationships that should exist among the phenomena of interest to the researcher.

For example, a researcher wishing to devise a theory about how the tradeoff among various types of audit tests should affect audit risk would need to undertake analyses of the components of audit risk and determine how those components should be related to each other (as was attempted in *SAS 39* [AICPA, 1981] and *SAS 47* [AICPA, 1983]). Logical linkages would need to be formed among the components of audit risk and the various audit tests. In the process, assumptions about the relative effectiveness and efficiency of the various audit tests may be required.

The set of linkages developed among the components of audit risk and types of audit tests would then constitute a theory about those phenomena and their interrelationships. Whether the interrelationships posited in the theory are completely consistent with what is actually occurring in audit practice would not necessarily be of concern to the analytical researcher.

On the other hand, empirical research attempts to test theory through actual observation of phenomena related to some conjectural hypothesis. For example, if a researcher hypothesizes an association between the type of audit opinion received by a client firm and certain financial ratios of that firm, both the audit opinion and financial ratios are observable phenomena and may be obtained from the client firm's annual report. Statistical procedures provide measures of the strength and significance of the association.

It is important that either the phenomena of interest are directly observable or substitute measures of the phenomena (referred to as surrogates or proxies) are available. Even if surrogate measures are available, researchers do not always agree about what surrogates are the most appropriate for a given phenomenon. For instance, if a researcher wanted to determine whether an association exists between the audit risk of a client firm and certain of its financial ratios, that researcher would need to select a proxy for the client's audit risk because it is not directly observable (as compared with the directly observable type of audit opinion). A theory of audit risk and its underlying components might suggest a proxy for which greater consensus would be achieved, or that would allow for an unambiguous test of such a hypothesis. As yet, no consensus exists about the appropriate empirical proxy for audit risk.

Theory of Risk Measurement

Thus, theories play a critical role in the process of empirical investigations. Developing a comprehensive theory of audit risk and using it to guide the choice of audit risk proxy for empirical testing purposes involve considering several issues related to the measurement of risk and its applications in an audit context.

Hirshleifer and Shapiro [1970] clarify the problem by noting that two very different senses of the work "risk" are often confused. Risk refers to "a situation in which, whether for objective or subjective reasons, analysis requires us to take into account the possibility of a number of alternative outcomes or consequences of actions" [p. 292]. In one sense, risk is "the danger that reality might somehow fall short of over-optimistic beliefs or promises" [p. 292]. In a decision-making context, reality refers to new information received by the decision maker, and beliefs or promises may be found overly optimistic in light of this new information.

The second sense of the word "risk" is a more neutral one, where risk refers to variability of outcome, whether favorable or unfavorable" [Hirshleifer and Shapiro, 1970 p. 292]. When speaking of risk in the first sense, one might say that a certain bond may default, a certain asset may be impaired, or an additional liability may exist. When speaking of risk in the second sense, one might say that a utility blue chip stock is less risky than a "high flyer," which means that the investor holding the high flying stock has a chance of earning significantly more and also significantly less than if s/he holds the blue chip stock.

When an investor adjusts for the first type of risk, a mathematical adjustment is made to which Hirshleifer and Shapiro refer as an "adjustment for optimistic bias." The adjustment involves the calculation of a probability-weighed expected value. Adjustments for this type of risk have been a part of accounting theory and practice for many years. For example, assets are not to be valued above net realizable value (NRV) whenever NRV is below their existing book values based on historical cost. In other words, existing book values are overly optimistic, given new information about net realizable value. Determining net realizable value involves an estimation that is actually an "adjustment for optimistic bias."

The second type of risk—variability risk—cannot be reflected in a mathematical adjustment. The degree of variability risk that an investor will accept depends on his/her degree of risk aversion. The degree of variability risk associated with a firm is the type of risk that is captured in beta. Beta is a measure of variability of returns of the market as a whole. The measure of beta allows the investor to choose the degree of variability risk that he or she will accept and to pool investments to minimize the variability of returns, while still attempting to achieve an acceptable rate of return.

If circumstances call for an uncertainty qualification, such a situation indicates that the firm's financial condition has a danger of falling short of the amounts currently reported, which clearly calls for an adjustment for optimistic bias. Accordingly, the use of a measure of variability risk in these circumstances is inappropriate. The existence of those types of uncertainties facing a firm can be evaluated only by the estimation of the expected values of the assets or liabilities involved, and cannot be identified by past trends in variability of returns or earnings.

Empirical Approaches to Audit Risk Measurement

Several empirical studies have appeared in the literature that have attempted to determine whether a variability risk measure and certain accounting-based variables are appropriate proxies for audit risk.

Warren

Two studies by Warren [1975, 1980] examined uniformity in the application of auditing standards. Warren assumed that audit risk was distributed randomly across audit firms and developed two uniformity surrogates that he employed as dependent variables in his research design. The first uniformity surrogate was the percentage of qualififed opinions (i.e., both consistency exceptions and uncertainty qualifications) to the total number of audit opinions issued by the firm in the year(s) under study.[1] Warren obtained cross-sectional data on audit opinions from firms' 1972 10-K filings contained in Volume 1 of the *Disclosure Journal* for his 1975 paper, and used data on firms' audit opinions for 1973 and 1974 from Volumes 2 and 3 for his replication.

His ANOVA model in both studies included size (proxied in two different ways), industry category, existence of extraordinary items (in the 1975 study only), direction of the firm's earnings, the firm's fiscal year, and observation year (in the 1980 study only) as various main effects in the different ANOVA runs. In addition, both uniformity surrogates were coded as dichotomous dependent variables.

The results of the 1975 study were consistent with the hypothesis that "the likelihood of receiving a qualified opinion (the first uniformity surrogate) is independent of the auditor" [1975, p. 175]. Additionally, the probability of a firm's receiving an uncertainty qualification (as opposed to a consistency exception) was independent of the auditor. Warren attributed such findings either to the random distribution of "audit conditions" across auditing firms or to the existence of market competitiveness within the profession.

The results of the 1980 replication were partially inconsistent with those of the 1975 study. Specifically, the auditor main effect was significant in three of the six ANOVA tests in which the first uniformity surrogate was used as the dependent variable. Warren offered two explanations for the inconsistencies between the studies:

> First, auditing standards may or may not, in fact, be uniformly applied among auditors. These differences may become more pronounced as economic conditions fluctuate. Specifically, in 1973 and 1974, some auditing firms may have adjusted their standards more than others as economic conditions deteriorated. Second, auditing conditions may not be randomly distributed among firms. This nonrandomness may become more pronounced during recessionary periods [1980, p. 234].

Shank and Murdock

Shank and Murdock [1978] questioned the validity of Warren's assumption that audit risk is distributed uniformly among auditing firms. Specifically, they studied over 1,100 uncertainty qualifications that were rendered during a 4-year period (1972-1975) and found that a majority (79%) of those qualifications related to uncertainties of asset realization or future financing. They argued that for those types of uncertainty qualifications:

> the firm's financial results are tied more closely than normal to economy-wide movements. Financial results are heavily dependent on what happens to the industry and/or the economy. For these kinds of qualifications, audit risk may be directly related to those factors impounded in the concept of 'return to systematic risk' in the capital asset pricing literature [p. 826].

In essence, the authors argued that beta (systematic security risk) may be a surrogate for *audit risk* as "those aspects of the audit environment for a client company which relate to the likelihood that the auditor will have to qualify the audit opinion" [p. 825].[2]

Shank and Murdock selected 2,716 companies that had received audit opinions (both uncertainty qualifications and unqualified opinions) during the 1972-1975 period and formed 10 portfolios of those companies based on the ranges of the magnitudes of their beta coefficients. The authors ran a one-way analysis of variance (ANOVA), using beta as the "treatment" effect and type of audit opinion (coded 1 if the company received an uncertainty qualification, and 0 if the company received an unqualified opinion) as the dependent variable.

The *F*-statistic from the ANOVA was significant at an alpha level of .10, providing some evidence of a significant direct association betwen beta and the operationalized measure of audit risk (i.e., likelihood of uncertainty qualifications), although the authors did not disclose the actual value of the computed *F*-statistic. They also ran additional tests to determine the association between the likelihood of qualifications and SIC industry classification, the debt-to-equity ratio, and the cumulative abnormal return metric to verify that beta was not acting as "a proxy for some other factor" [p. 828]. Finding no statistically significant associations in these additional tests, they conclude that "underlying variables which lead the auditor to qualify the audit opinion are positively related to the variables impounded in beta" [p. 829].

The conceptual foundations of beta as an audit risk proxy need to be critically examined. If the auditor decides that the client should receive an uncertainty qualification, such circumstances indicate that the firm's financial condition has a potential for falling short of the amounts reported, which appear to require the need for an adjustment for optimistic bias. Thus, the use of a variability risk measure such as systematic risk in those circumstances appears to be inappropriate.

Further, it may be argued that audit risk should be an ex ante concept, while beta is computed ex post from the market model. Thus, a problem of expectations versus realizations may exist with regard to information about the client available to the auditor prior to the issuance of the audit opinion. Such information available to the auditor would include operating budgets, forecasts, capital budgets, and analyses of operating variances.

Finally, economy-wide effects are reflected in the return on the market portfolio. Although macroeconomic and industry effects may be contributory factors, an argument can be made that uncertainty qualifications normally arise more from firm-specific issues such as the lack of ability to obtain financing or impairment of the value of certain assets. Based on our discussion of theories of risk measurement, the relationship posited between systematic risk (beta) and audit risk in the Shank and Murdock study is conceptually problematic. Without appropriate theoretical foundation, these statistical results are difficult to interpret. The existence of a statistical correlation between beta and the operationalized measure of audit risk is not sufficient to be able to infer a sound predictive relationship.

Chow

Chow [1983] called to question the approach used by both Warren [1975, 1980] and Shank and Murdock [1978] in their studies on the uniformity of auditing standards. He found both conceptual and methodological problems with their use of the percentage of qualified opinions issued as the dependent variable in their studies. His methodological criticism relates to the use of the ANOVA technique with a dichotomous dependent variable, which violates the homoscedasticity assumption of the technique.[3]

Chow's conceptual criticism was that even if audit standards affect the propensity to issue qualified opinions, observed percentages of qualified opinions may not reflect this difference. Chow's logic centered around an agency theory-based argument that an audit is a monitoring mechanism that helps to keep the conflicts of interests that exist among the managers, shareholders, and bondholders of the firm under control. Chow argued that different firms hire different levels of monitoring as a function of the serverity of those conflicts, and that auditors specialize by level of monitoring to enhance the value of the service they provide. Because of this auditor specialization, Chow stated that "client firms will self-select when they choose an external auditor" [p. 24]. Thus:

> even if auditing standards directly affect the *propensity* to issue qualified opinions given identical circumstances, differences in these standards may not be reflected in the *observed*

> percentages of qualified opinions because auditors will not face the same circumstances due to client self-selection [p. 24, emphasis in original].

If this is the case, the differences in circumstances that are attributable to the client self-selection process ensure that audit risk will not be distributed uniformly across the Big Eight and other auditing firms. This calls into question Warren's [1975, 1980] use of percentage of qualified opinions as the basis for the uniformity surrogates and his assumption that audit risk is distributed randomly across auditing firms. Further, Shank and Murdock's [1978] finding that beta is significantly associated with the percentage of uncertainty qualifications is not necessarily surprising since a systematic relationship might well exist between a client firm's beta and the level of monitoring that it desires from its auditor. However, the existence of such an association does not indicate that beta is an appropriate proxy for audit risk if the percentage of qualified opinions is not a valid measure of the uniformity in application of auditing standards.

Simunic and Stein

Simunic and Stein [1985] derive an analytical model in a mean-variance asset pricing context to explain the linkage between audit risk and systematic security risk (beta). They define audit risk as "the change in the standard deviation of return of a particular portfolio caused by adding a particular audit to an existing set of investments" [p. 2]. They showed that audit risk (as defined) is a function of: (1) the variance of the auditor's rate of return from the additional audit, and (2) the covariance between the auditor's rate of return from the additional audit and the return on the audits in his/her existing portfolio. In turn, Simunic and Stein argued that the auditor's rate of return from the additional audit client is (in part) a function of the client's systematic risk. Accordingly, a dependency exists between audit risk and beta. Simunic and Stein note:

> this dependency arises through the uncertainty surrounding ... economy wide risk. The more sensitive are the client's cash flows to movements in the economy (the higher the beta), then *ceteris paribus,* the greater the uncertainty surrounding the auditor's own return [p. 19].

Simunic and Stein argued that increases in beta will result in increased audit fees through the bidding function, in which audit risk is a component of the minimum fee bid. They tested empirically the relationship between beta and audit risk, using a subset of the data set from the Simunic [1980] study, and computed betas for those firms that satistifed their other selection criteria. The betas were included as an additional independent variable in the multiple regression models originally developed in the Simunic [1980] study for explaining audit fees.

Simunic and Stein could not reject the hypothesis of an association between beta and audit fees. They failed to find support for a relationship between beta and type of audit opinion [p. 27]. These results appear to undermine the use of measures of security risk as measures of audit risk. Although they are inconsistent with those of Shank and Murdock [1978], they may be attributable to the relatively small number of uncertainty qualifications in the Simunic and Stein sample—only 9 out of a total of 133 observations.

Of more general concern, however, is the nature of the analytical model developed by Simunic and Stein. The model attempted to explain the linkage between systematic risk and audit risk, with the same attendant weaknesses we discuss above.

Bell and Tabor, and Dopuch, Holthausen, and Leftwich

Bell and Tabor [1987] and Dopuch, Holthausen, and Leftwich [1987] developed models to explain/predict uncertainty qualifications based on accounting and market variables.[4] These studies used either the logit or probit analysis procedure. Logit and probit procedures are qualitative choice techniques in which the distributional assumptions underlying the independent variables are not as stringent as those of multiple discriminant analysis, and the predicted value of the dependent variable may be interpreted as a probability (in this case, the likelihood that the firm in question would receive an uncertainty qualification conditioned on the independent variables included in the model). Although no explicit statement to the effect is made in either paper, both appear to consider the likelihood that a client firm will receive an uncertainty qualification as a dimension of its audit risk, consistent with Shank and Murdock's definition. To the extent that selected accounting and market variables possess significant explanatory power in the logit models, they would be said to represent proxies for that dimension of audit risk.

Dopuch et al. partitioned their sample of uncertainty qualifications between litigation-related uncertainty qualifications and all other uncertainty qualifications, and developed separate models for the partitioned samples as well as the overall sample. On the other hand, Bell and Tabor excluded litigation-related uncertainty qualifications.

Bell and Tabor included as independent variables seven ratios that had the highest average factor loading on the seven factors identified by Pinches, Mingo, and Caruthers [1973] in their descriptive study of firms' underlying financial dimensions. The ratios were used in the form of change from previous year and deviation from industry mean. The estimation and holdout sample models developed by Bell and Tabor yielded statistically significant measures of overall significance and classificatory accuracy.

Dopuch et al. included several financial statement variables, market variables, and two dummy variables as independent variables in their probit models. One dummy variable indicated whether the firm's income available for common shareholders was negative for the current year, and the other indicated whether the firm had been listed on the New York or American Stock Exchange for more than five years. Most of the financial and market variables were in one year change form. The estimation and holdout sample models developed by Dopuch et al. also yielded statistically significant measures of overall significance and classificatory accuracy.

The major limitation of the Bell and Tabor and Dopuch et al. papers centers around the ad hoc nature of the models developed by both sets of authors. Even though no attempt was made in either study to model the auditor's decision process, no underlying theory or rationale was used to guide the choice of independent variables included in the models. Additionally, until more is known about the nature of the auditor's loss function relative to Type 1 vs. Type 11 errors, the selection of the appropriate value for a probability cutoff for classification purposes is problematic. Such a situation would pose difficulties for auditors trying to use the Bell and Tabor or Dopuch et al. model as a type of analytical procedure.

Dugan and Shriver

Dugan and Shriver [1987] used the same definition of audit risk but extended the Shank and Murdock study to examine the association between two of a firm's real-asset determinants of systematic risk—its degree of operating leverage (DOL) and its degree of financial leverage (DFL)—and its likelihood of receipt of an uncertainty qualification. The authors hypothesized that DOL and DFL should "capture more fully the firm-specific aspects of the audit environment that motivate the auditor to render an uncertainty qualification" [p. 3], and, therefore, should be directly associated with a firm's likelihood of receiving an uncertainty qualification.

Dugan and Shriver used Mandelker and Rhee's [1984] time-series regression procedures to calculate the degree of operating leverage and degree of financial leverage coefficients for their samples of uncertainty qualifications and unqualified opinions drawn from the same period (1972-1975) and source (*The Disclosure Journal*) as the Shank and Murdock data set. The authors then ran probit analyses to test their association hypotheses and found that those real-asset risk measures (i.e., DOL and DF) were "not significantly associated with the incidence of receipt of uncertainty qualifications" [p. 14]. They attributed the conflicting findings betweeen their study and the Shank and Murdock [1978] study to differences in methodology, potential model misspecification, and potential error in the measurement of the DOL and DFL coefficients at the individual firm level.

These results are consistent with the empirical finding of no significant association between beta and percentage of qualified opinions reported by

Simunic and Stein [1985], if one assumes that a firm's degrees of operating and financial leverage capture a significant dimension of its systematic risk. However, they are inconsistent with those of Shank and Murdock [1978], who found a weakly significant association between beta and incidence of uncertainty qualifications.

Summary

Several points become apparent from the above analysis. First, the ex post percentage of qualified opinions does not appear to be an appropriate proxy for audit risk.[5] Warren [1975, 1980] used the percentage of qualified opinions as the dependent variable in his studies on the uniformity in the application of auditing standards and tested whether the measure varied significantlyl across auditing firms. Warren *assumed* that audit risk was distributed randomly across auditing firms and attributed any significant variation in the dependent variable to lack of uniformity in application of auditing standards or other factors.

However, Chow [1983] argues convincingly that client firms are not homogeneous with respect to the severity of the agency conflicts that they face and thus require different levels of monitoring. If he is correct, audit risk will *not* be distributed randomly across auditing firms. A client firm will select an auditor to achieve congruence between the level of monitoring that it requires as a function of the severity of its agency conflicts and the level of monitoring its auditor wishes to provide. Because of this phenomenon, the portion of any observed variation in the percentage of qualified opinions across auditing firms attributable to lack of uniformity in the application of auditing standards is virtually impossible to extricate empirically. This indicates that future research should move away from the use of percentage of qualified opinions as a measure of audit risk and attempt to develop a measure that does not contain as much noise attributable to the auditor self-selection process.

Second, even if one accepts the argument that percentage of qualified opinions is an appropriate measure of audit risk, a client firm's systematic risk does not appear to be capturing empirically those factors related to the likelihood that it would receive a qualified opinion. The findings reported by Simunic and Stein [1985] and Dugan and Shriver [1987] provide support for this contention. Shank and Murdock [1978] only provide weak evidence to the contrary.

On both theoretical and empirical grounds, a variability risk construct such as systematic risk is not an appealing proxy for audit risk. Such a measure captures all information available to the auditor about the client prior to issuing the audit opinion. Thus, such a proxy should possibly include information not ultimately reflected in published financial statement and related disclosures and therefore not available to capital market agents. Also, if circumstances of the client are such that the auditor deems an uncertainty qualification appropriate, such circumstances normally indicate that the firm's financial condition may fall short of the amounts reported in the financial statements. The existence of such uncertainties facing the client may be evaluated only by the estimation of the expected values of the assets and/or liabilities involved, which may require private information. The existence of such uncertainties will not be revealed by past trends in the variability of returns and earnings. In summary, its appears that future research should move away from the use of systematic risk variables as proxies for audit risk and work on developing an operationalizable proxy for adjustment for optimistic bias.

Finally, Bell and Tabor [1987] and Dopuch et al. [1987] have developed multivariate models for explaining/predicting the receipt of a qualified opinion which may posses potential value as attention-directing analytical procedures. Nevertheless, the likelihood of qualified opinions does not seem to be a good measure of audit risk. Audit risk is failure to qualify when underlying economic events require it. It appears that future research should develop a better understanding of the auditor's decision process, determine what circumstances of the client call for an uncertainty qualification, and offer better insights as to how auditors trade off Type I and Type II errors in their audit risk loss function.

DIRECTIONS FOR THE FUTURE

As already implied, the academic research in the auditors' business risk area deals principally with a narrow but important part of the technical aspect of the problem: theoretical analyses of risk measurement and the pragmatic extension of these theories to the audit risk situation. Successful research in this area would potentially have vast import for practicing auditors. However, these studies have made little impact on practice to date, as the risk measures chosen have been unrealistic, and the empirical studies designed around those measures have been inconclusive. Consequently, the preceding analysis of the audit risk environment isolates two critical areas for further research: technical issues and social issues. The second has been particularly neglected, undoubtedly because of the strong technical bias of most researchers themselves. Nevertheless, there are even technical areas that need shoring up. Those areas are considered first.

Important technical issues that remain to be adequately explored include studying the role of analytical procedures in fraud detection. In general, there is a need to define characteristics of and standards for an audit for fraud. Not enough is yet understood about the theory of risk measurement, let alone how to extend these measurement concepts to the audit risk situation. Also, more needs to be understood about how to make an analysis of audit risk and its relation to audit tests. When these issues are understood, it will be possible to develop improved tests.

Specifically, several alternative research questions dealing with technical matters suggest themselves:

1. Researchers could attempt to estimate inherent risk (as defined in *SAS 39* [AICPA, 1981] and *SAS 47* [AICPA, 1983]). Critical questions which arise would then be: How should researchers attempt this? Would it be appropriate to use accounting and/or market variables as proxies for inherent risk? Should proxies for inherent risk be linked with those factors related to likelihood of occurrence of financial fraud within the firm?
2. A proxy for audit risk could be based on an adjustment for optimistic bias. A difficulty with this approach might be: Since adjustment for optimistic bias is inherently an ex ante concept without a direct empirical referent, what proxy, based on adjustment for optimistic bias, could be employed in ex post facto empirical studies?
3. Researchers could attempt to develop a better measure of audit risk than percentage of qualified opinions. Since percentage of qualified opinions is contaminated because of the self-selection of auditors by clients, a better understanding of the market for auditing services and contracting arrangements might provide researchers insights about a more appropriate proxy. Further, such understanding also might enable researchers to extricate the self-selection effect from the percentage of qualified opinions measure.

New developments in professional standards suggest many other more specific and potentially productive research topics. For example, no distinction is now made between accounting controls and administrative controls, but the implications of this are unclear. Further, auditors may need to be concerned about evaluating aspects of the firm's administrative (management) control system. Research questions also are suggested by these developments:

1. How should components of audit risk from *SAS 39* [AICPA, 1981] and *SAS 47* [AICPA, 1983] be affected by risks associated with the client firm's management control system?
2. Would inherent risk be affected? If so, how?
3. Would control risk be affected? If so, how?
4. How would administrative controls and accounting controls be differentially weighed in arriving at a judgment about a client firm's control risk?
5. How could an auditor limit his/her audit risk with respect to a client's management control system?

6. Is it possible to link those attributes associated with fraudulent financial reporting to aspects of the client's management control system? (For example, might the type of budgeting system used in the client firm [authoritative versus participative] impact the likelihood that its middle managers will be motivated to engage in "book cooking"?)

Second, and perhaps more urgently, there needs to be some constructive thinking about the broad social implications of the auditor's role and the economic nature of the market for audit services. This requires an assessment of the adequacy of professional standards. The standards should rely on a thorough study of the sociology of the auditor's professional role and the auditor's responsibility for affecting its change. The standards also should rely on a determination of the nature of the markets for clients' securities and the types of assurances and degree of reliance on them that should be reasonably expected. This should provide a basis for assessing the economics of the insurance situation. In general, clarifying the characteristics of the social contract might help greatly in providing reasonable and legitimate assurances to all parties.

Answering such questions requires research tools beyond those traditionally applied to this area. Empirical modeling based on financial statement data certainly has its place, as do knowledge of the nature of our efficient stock market and its use of information, the economic theory of contracting for services when imperfect information exists, insights concerning the sociology of auditors' relationships with client firms and the public, and historical analysis of the regulatory environment and its impact on professional standards and public expectations. This broad-based research effort must, to be useful, produce improved understanding of the public's interest in auditors' work and their economic role. This broad understanding may provde the theoretical basis necessary to guide further research and provide a solid foundation for normative approaches to auditors' problems.

The knowledge obtained from this theoretical base and its related technical investigations could pave the way for improved audit quality along with greater self and public esteem for those in the profession. It would also provide our schools with sophisticated guidelines for broadening and humanizing the increasingly technical training they provide their accounting students.

ACKNOWLEDGMENTS

The authors appreciate the financial support for this research provided by Clarkson University School of Management and University of Alabama College of Commerce and Business Administration Summer Research Grants. The authors acknowledge the helpful comments of an anonymous reviewer and the Associate Editor.

NOTES

1. Although *SAS 58* [AICPA, 1988c] eliminated the "subject to" qualification, the auditor is now required to discuss material uncertainties in an explanatory paragraph following the opinion paragraph of his/her report. Accordingly, research on those factors related to the likelihood of receipt of an uncertainty qualification (i.e., an explanatory paragraph in the audit report describing the uncertainty) continues to be important since the auditor must still describe what gave rise to the uncertainty.

2. Note that this definition of audit risk is not entirely consistent with descriptions and definitions of the term that have subsequently been developed in the professional literature, such as those in *SAS 39* [AICPA, 1981] and *SAS 47* [AICPA, 1983].

3. The application of ANOVA to dichotomous data violates the homoscedasticity assumption because the variance of a binomial distribution equals $np\,(1-p)$, where

n = cell sample size
p = probability of a qualified opinion
$1-p$ = probability of an unqualified opinion

It may be observed from this relationship that the variance will differ as the likelihood of qualification varies across the cells of the research design. The interested reader is referred to the educational measurement literature [Lunney, 1970; D'Agostino, 1971] for guidance about the circumstances under which the homoscedasticity assumption violation is apparently not as serious.

4. It is important to remember that the primary objective of these studies was *not* to explain/predict bankruptcy. While both papers included going concern qualifications as a subset of the uncertainty qualifications in their experimental samples, none of the observations in their samples was a bankrupt firm. In addition, the primary objective of the Bell and Tabor as well as Dopuch, Holthausen and Leflwich papers was *not* to model the auditor's decision process for determining what circumstances dictate issuing an uncertainty qualification. While an accurate predictive model of uncertainty qualifications might have potential value as an attention-directing analytical procedure, neither study actively attempted to use as independent variables those specifically identified by auditors as relevant to the uncertainty qualification decision. Hence, neither study should be criticized for failing to include all variables germane to the qualification decision since this was not the stated objective.

5. From an ex ante perspective, of course, audit risk is necessarily related to the propensity to issue qualified opinions and the likelihood of the auditor's giving an incorrect opinion on the financial statements.

REFERENCES

American Institute of Certified Public Accountants, *Statement of Auditing Standards No. 23,* "Analytical Review and Procedures" [AICPA, 1978].

________, *Statement of Auditing Standards No. 39,* "Audit Sampling" [AICPA, 1981].

________, *Statement of Auditing Standards No. 47,* "Audit Risk and Materiality in Conducting an Audit" [AICPA, 1983].

________, *Statement of Auditing Standards No. 55,* "Consideration of the Internal Control Structure in a Financial Statement Audit" [AICPA, 1988a].

________, *Statement of Auditing Standards No. 56,* "Analytical Procedures" [AICPA, 1988b].

________, *Statement of Auditing Standards No. 58,* "Reports on Audited Financial Statements" [AICPA, 1988c].

Arrington, C.E., W.A. Hillison, and R. Icerman, "Research in Analytical Review: The State of the Art," *Journal of Accounting Literature* [Spring 1983], pp. 151-186.

Arrington, C.E., W.A. Hillison, and P.F. Williams, "The Psychololgy of Expectations Gaps: Why Is There So Much Dispute About Auditor Responsibility?," *Accounting and Business Research* [Autumn 1983], pp. 243-250.

Armstrong, J.E., "Auditing to Detect Fraud," *CPA Journal* [September 1985], pp. 78-80.

Bell, T.B. and R.H. Tabor, "Empirical Analysis of Audit Uncertainty Qualifications," Working paper [University of Texas-Austin, January 1987].

Brumfield, C.A., R.K. Elliott, and P.D. Jacobson, "Business Risk and the Audit Process," *Journal of Accountancy* [April 1983], pp. 60-68.

Chow, C.W., "On the Measurement of Auditing Standards," *Journal of Business Finance and Accounting* [Spring 1983], pp. 21-35.

Coopers & Lybrand, *Audit Risk: A Framework for Assessment and Control* [Coopers & Lybrand, 1983].

CPA Journal, "News & Views" [February 1986], pp. 4-5.

The CPA Letter [September 1, 1988], p. 1.

D'Agostino, R., "A Second Look at Analysis of Variance on Dichotomous Data," *Journal of Educational Measurement* [Winter 1971], pp. 327-333.

Dopuch, N., R. Holthausen, and R. Leftwich, "Predicting Audit Qualifications with Financial and Market Variables," *Accounting Review* [July 1987], pp. 431-454.

Dugan, M. and K. Shriver, "Real-Asset Determinants of Systematic Risk and the Incidence of Receipt of Uncertainty Qualifications," Working paper [The University of Alabama, October 1987].

Goldwasser, D.L., "The Accountant as Middleman," *CPA Journal* [September 1985], pp. 42-46.

Hirshleifer, J. and D.L. Shapiro, "The Treatment of Risk and Uncertainty," in *Analytical Problems in Policy Analysis,* edited by R. Haveman and J. Margolis [Markhave, 1970], pp. 291-313.

Kohler, E., *A Dictionary for Accountants,* 6th ed. [Prentice-Hall, 1983].

Levy, M.M., "Financial Fraud: Schemes and Indicia," *Journal of Accountancy* [August 1985], pp. 78-87.

Lunney, G., "Using Analysis of Variance with A Dichotomous Dependent Variable: An Empirical Study," *Journal of Educational Measurement* [Winter 1970], pp. 263-269.

Mandelker, G. and S.G. Rhee, "The Impact of the Degrees of Operating and Financial Leverage on Systematic Risk of Common Stock," *Journal of Financial and Quantitative Analysis* [March 1984], pp. 45-57.

Pinches, G., K. Mingo, and J.K. Caruthers, "The Hierarchical Classification of Financial Ratios," *Journal of Business Research* [October 1975], pp. 295-310.

Serlin, J.E., "Auditing Developments: Fraud and the Auditor," *Journal of Accounting, Auditing and Finance* [Winter 1985], pp. 136-143.

Shank, J.K. and R.J. Murdock, "Comparability in the Application of Reporting Standards: Some Further Evidence," *The Accounting Review* [October 1978], pp. 824-835.

Simunic, D.A., "The Pricing of Audit Services: Theory and Evidence," *Journal of Accounting Research* [Spring 1980], pp. 161-190.

Simunic, D.A. and M. Stein, "Audit Risk in a Cliemt Portfolio Context," Working paper [The University of British Columbia, May 1985].

Wallace, W.A., "Analytical Review: Misconceptions, Applications and Experience—Part I," *CPA Journal* [January 1983], pp. 24-37.

———, "Analytical Review: Misconceptions, Applications and Experience—Part II," *CPA Journal* [February 1983], pp. 18-27.

Warren, C.S., "Uniformity of Auditing Standards," *Journal of Accounting Research* [Spring 1975], pp. 162-176.

———, Uniformity of Auditing Standards: A Replication," *Journal of Accounting Research* [Spring 1980], pp. 312-324.

EXTERNAL AUDITOR RELIANCE ON INTERNAL AUDITORS WHEN AUDIT RISK IS HIGH: SOME EMPIRICAL FINDINGS

Loren Margheim and Wayne Label

ABSTRACT

This study examines external auditor reliance on internal auditors when audit risk is high. Specifically, a between-subjects case study was used that focused on the effects of three factors on the external auditors' reliance decisions: management integrity, internal auditor objectivity, and a special internal auditor investigation. Results of the study indicate that the external auditors reacted to low management integrity by budgeting more substantive audit hours, however, internal auditor objectivity was not found to affect budgeted audit hours. The external auditors did respond to the special internal auditor investigation by budgeting less substantive audit hours. Finally, the external auditors' decisions regarding direct usage of internal auditors were generally unaffected by any of the above factors. Policies that auditing firms should have in place to help ensure that their auditors consider reliability related factors when making reliance decisions are discussed.

Advances in Accounting, Volume 8, pages 293-311.

ISBN: 1-55938-067-5

SAS 9 [AICPA, 1975] indicates that external auditors may rely on internal auditor work when determining the nature, timing and extent of their audit procedures or may use internal auditors to provide direct assistance during the external audit. While such reliance may increase the efficiency of an audit, there is a danger that due to high audit risk, cost-cutting pressures and the lack of specific policies and procedures external auditors may overrely on internal auditors. This possibility should be of important concern to the profession, especially in light of an FDIC lawsuit that alleges a major public accounting firm overrelied on internal audit for confirmation of four failed banks' commercial loans [see "News Briefs," 1987].

Prior research has primarily examined external auditor reliance on work already performed by internal auditors in case studies describing low audit risk situations or through the use of general surveys [Ward and Robertson, 1980; Clark, Gibbs, and Schroeder, 1980; Brown 1983; Schneider, 1984, 1985; Margheim, 1986]. The present study extends this research by examining whether the following three factors affect external auditors' reliance decisions when the audit risk is high: internal auditor objectivity, management integrity and a special internal auditor investigation.

The study utilized a between-subjects design that examined the main effects of the three factors as well as the interaction between internal auditor objectivity and management integrity. Specifically, external auditors were given a case describing an up-coming audit of accounts receivable where the risk of material misstatement was very high (i.e., there had been a major computer software breakdown) and were asked to budget external audit hours. The respondents also indicated on 9-point Likert scales the extent to which they would use internal auditors to provide direct assistance during the field audit.

The results indicated that the external auditors reacted to low management integrity by budgeting more substantive audit hours, however, management integrity had little effect on the usage of direct internal auditor assistance. Internal auditor objectivity and the interaction between internal auditor objectivity and management integrity were not found to affect the external auditors' audit time budgets or their decisions to use direct internal auditor assistance.

The results also indicated that when a highly reliable internal audit staff (high competence, objectivity, and work performance) performed a special investigation over the risk situation and concluded the situation was being handled properly, the external auditors reduced the planned amount of their substantive test audit hours. The special investigation by the internal auditors, however, did not significantly affect the external auditors decisions to use direct internal auditor assistance during the field audit.

The next section discusses the background of the study. The following sections include the research method, the results, limitations, and a discussion of the results.

BACKGROUND

Surveys

Several studies have examined external auditor reliance on internal auditors. Surveys by Ward and Robertson [1980] and Clark et al. [1980] examined auditor perceptions of the extent external auditors were relying on internal auditors and attempted to determine the specific criteria used when evaluating internal auditor competence, objectivity and work performance as required by *SAS 9* [AICPA, 1975]. The results generally indicated that external auditors rely on internal auditors as an important part of the internal control structure and often use internal auditors to perform a variety of substantive audit procedures.

Case Studies

Studies by Brown [1983], Schneider [1984, 1985], and Margheim [1986] furthered this area of research by examining the relative importance of internal auditor competence, objectivity and work performance to external auditor reliability decisions. Further, the studies by Schneider [1985] and Margheim [1986] examined how the assessment of internal auditor reliability impacted on the external auditors' planned audit hour budgets. These case studies concentrated on work already performed by internal auditors and did not examine the use of direct internal auditor assistance. In a related study, Abdel-khalik, Snowball, and Wragge [1983] examined the effects of four internal auditor EDP related procedures and internal auditor independence[1] on planned external audit man-hours and the use of direct internal auditor assistance during the external audit.

Competence and Work Performance Results

Overall, the results of the above research has consistently shown that external auditors consider internal auditor competence and work performance to be important reliability factors affecting their evaluation of overall internal auditor reliability. In addition, Schneider [1985] and Margheim [1986] found external auditors would rely on the internal auditors and reduce planned audit hours when the internal auditors had high competence and work performance.

Objectivity Results

Research results relating to internal auditor objectivity, however, have been mixed. Abdel-khalik et al. [1983] and Brown [1983] found objectivity to have a major impact on external auditor reliance decisions. Schneider [1985], however, found objectivity to have a lesser effect while Margheim [1986] found objectivity to have no effect on reliance decisions.

The difference in results suggest that external auditor sensitivity to internal auditor objectivity may depend on whether the auditor explicitly considers only one or serveral potential levels of the variable. Abdel-khalik et al. [1983], Brown [1983], and Schneider [1984, 1985] used within-subjects designs (i.e., subjects were able to consider all levels of internal auditor objectivity) to gather data while Margheim [1986] used a between-subjects design (i.e., subjects considered only one level of objectivity). Research by Joyce and Biddle [1981] and Pany and Reckers [1987] has shown that auditors may not attend to some reliability factors unless they are exposed to several levels of the factor. This is of considerable importance because external auditors are usually exposed to only one level of a reliability factor on a given audit. For example, external auditors only examine one internal audit department on each audit. Therefore, they may not be sensitive to internal audit's reliability unless they explicitly contrast their reliability to other client's internal audit departments.

RESEARCH METHOD

Case Development

Auditors were asked to reply to cases describing an up-coming audit of accounts receivable for a hypothetical client. Six two-page cases were designed for use in the study. A between-subjects design was used where each auditor received only one of the six cases (see Table 1). Therefore, subjects were explicitly exposed to only one level of each of the independent variables. This should have helped to eliminate any "demand characteristics" where subjects exposed to all levels of the independent variables (i.e., within-subjects designs) respond in a manner which they believe the experimenter desires [see Pany and Reckers, 1987].

The first part of the cases included a description of the client and the appropriate levels of the independent variables. The client was described as a medium-sized manufacturer who had been an audit client for several years. The description provided basic financial data and indicated that the prior year's audit of accounts receivable involved no high risk situations. The case also indicated that the prior year's workpapers noted that the company had competent internal auditors with very good previous work performance. During the middle of the current year, the internal auditors examined the accounts receivable internal control structure and tested an adequate sample of account balances and found no problems. Based on their normal rotation system, the internal auditors had not examined the accounts receivable system during the previous year. This information was held constant in all cases.

Table 1. Independent Variable Manipulations

Independent Variable	*Case 1*	*Case 2*	*Case 3*	*Case 4*	*Case 5*	*Case 6*
Mgt. integrity	low	low	high	high	high	high
I.A. objectivity	low	high	low	high	high	high
High audit risk	yes	yes	yes	yes	yes	no
I.A. investigation	yes	yes	yes	yes	no	no

Cases 1-4 were used to examine the effects of the two reliability factors examined (i.e., internal auditor objectivity and management integrity) on the external auditors' planning decisions. Due to the use of the between-subjects design and the number of available subjects, only two levels of each variable (i.e., low and high) were examined. These levels were fully crossed in Cases 1-4 in order to examine their main effects and interaction (i.e., each level of internal auditor objectivity was paired with each level of management integrity—see Table 1). The levels are described in the independent variable section.

The four cases indicated that a major unexplainable computer software breakdown occurred near year-end resulting in much of the accounts receivable recording duties being performed by temporary workers. The purpose of this situation was to redflag the subjects that there was a high potential of material misstatements in accounts receivable. In addition, the cases indicated that the internal auditors had performed additional work dealing with the breakdown (i.e., a special internal audit investigation) and concluded that the internal controls in place during the computer breakdown were adequate.

Case 5 was identical to the above cases except internal auditor objectivity and management integrity were controlled at their high levels and the internal auditors had not performed the special investigation. Responses to this case were compared to the appropriate case containing the high levels of internal auditor objectivity and management integrity where a special investigation was conducted (i.e., Case 4) to determine how the external auditors reacted to the additional work performed by the internal auditors. Objectivity and management integrity were controlled at their high levels because reliance on the internal auditor special investigation is most likely to occur in this situation.

Case 6 was included as a control case in order to evaluate whether the subjects had interpreted the computer breakdown as being a high audit risk situation. The case was identical to Case 5 except that it indicated there were no major unexplainable problems in the accounts receivable system during the year. A summary of the independent variable manipulations in the cases is shown in Table 1.

The second part of the cases asked subjects to budget audit hours for the current year's external audit of accounts receivable. The subjects were also asked to indicate on 9-point Likert scales the extent to which they would use and test direct internal auditor assistance. These responses served as the dependent variables which will be discussed below.

In the final section of the cases, the subjects were asked to respond to manipulation check questions relating to the internal auditor's objectivity, management integrity and whether a special internal auditor investigation was conducted in the particular case they had received. In addition, the subjects were asked to provide demographic data.

Independent Variables

Internal auditor objectivity, management integrity and a special internal auditor investigation served as the independent variables in the study. As noted in the background, the impact of internal auditor objectivity on external auditors' reliance decisions has been examined in the prior research with mixed results. Internal auditor objectivity is reexamined in the present study where subjects have not been exposed to all levels of the variable (i.e., a between-subjects design is used) and where the high audit risk involved should have caused internal auditor objectivity to be of much more importance to the external auditors' reliance decisions than it would have been in prior research containing low audit risk situations.

Low and high levels of objectivity were used in the study. The low level described the internal auditors as reporting to the controller. In addition, the scenario indicated that during the current year department heads were getting more power to deter internal auditor investigations and the internal auditors were finding it more difficult to have their recommendations implemented. The high level of objectivity described the internal auditors as reporting to the audit committee. They had no trouble conducting investigations and management was receptive to their recommendations.

External auditors should evaluate internal auditor and management reliability related variables before making reliance decisions. Therefore, management integrity was used as a second independent variable and was fully crossed with internal auditor objectivity in order to examine the interaction between these two reliability related variables.

Low and high levels of management integrity were also used in the study. All of the cases indicated that a new management had taken over at the beginning of the current year following the retirement of the old executives. The low management integrity level indicated that the new executives had been forced out of a similar company because of allegations of security fraud and accusations they had attempted to circumvent internal controls. The high level indicated the new executives had managed a similar company and were well-known and respected in the industry.

While this is an extremely strong management integrity manipulation, it is very similar to the manipulation used by Kaplan and Reckers [1984]. Their study found that management integrity was not a significant factor in auditors' planning process for accounts receivable. Therefore, the present study attempts to reexamine management integrity using a similar manipulation and the same account (accounts receivable) to determine if external auditors' budgeted audit hours and direct usage of internal auditors is affected by management integrity when a high level of audit risk is present.

A special internal auditor investigation of the computer breakdown served as the third independent variable. This variable was examined in order to examine whether additional, special work by internal auditors would result in increased reliance by external auditors on internal auditors. Only the main effect of this independent variable was examined because of resource constraints and the use of the between-subjects design. Two levels of the variable were used. Cases 1-4 indicated that the internal auditors had performed a special investigation and found internal controls to be adequate during the computer breakdown while Case 5 indicated that they had not performed the special investigation.

Dependent Variables

Based on the information in the case received, subjects were asked to budget external audit hours to accounts receivable internal control structure tests (i.e., control tests) and substantive tests.[2] Using 9-point Likert scales the subjects were also asked (1) the extent to which they would use internal auditors to perform external audit work that they could adequately supervise and test (2) the extent to which they would test such work, and (3) the extent to which they would use internal auditors to perform work that they would be unable to adequately supervise or test.

Subjects

A total of 13 offices of six Big-8 firms from three large western citites participated in the study by having the personnel partner distribute the case materials to their audit seniors and managers.[3] While the engagement partner would normally be responsible for any final decisions regarding reliance on internal auditors, individuals at the senior and manager levels will normally make the initial evaluation and reliance decision. Therefore, these individuals appeared to be the most appropriate subjects to respond to the cases used in this study.

A total of 75 of each of the six cases were distributed for a total sample size of 450. A return envelope was provided to allow the auditors to return their responses directly to the researchers. Second requests were not distributed because it would not have been possible to ensure that the auditors received the same case originally distributed to them.

RESULTS

Response Rate

A total of 125 (28%) usable responses were received with responses for each case varying from 19 to 23.[4] This response rate is similar to other studies that utilized responses returned my mail [e.g., Margheim, 1986; Pany and Reckers, 1987].

Demographic Data

Demographic responses indicated an average age of 29.4, 6.1 years of audit experience, and 4.4 years of college. Of those responding, 78% were male, 87% had CPA certificates and 92% specialized in auditing. In addition, 93% were at the senior or manager level which suggests that the cases were appropriately distributed by the firms.[5]

Hypotheses and Statistical Analyses

Audit Risk Effect

Prior to examining the independent variables, the following two alternative hypotheses were tested to determine the impact of the computer software breakdown on the auditors' planning decisions.

Hypothesis 1. Mean audit hours assigned to control tests and substantive tests will vary depending upon the existence of the high audit risk (computer breakdown) situation.

Hypothesis 2. Usage and testing of direct internal auditor assistance will vary depending upon the existence of the high audit risk (computer breakdown) situation.

Hypotheses 1 and 2 were tested using the responses from Cases 5 and 6. As shown in Table 1, these cases were identical except for the existence of the computer software breakdown. It was expected that the external auditors would view the computer breakdown as creating a high audit risk situation and would assign more control test and substantive test hours and use less direct internal auditor assistance when the breakdown situation was present.

Table 2. Audit Risk Means (Standard Deviations)

	High Audit Risk Situation: Yes (Case 5 only) (n = 19)		High Audit Risk Situation: No (Case 6) (n = 19)
Mean Budgeted Hours			
Mean Control Testing Hours	24.6 (12.5)	*	17.9 (10.8)
Mean Substantive Hours	75.0 (16.6)	**	33.8 (12.2)
Mean Responses to the Usage of Internal Auditor			
1. Usage of internal auditors to perform work that could be supervised and tested[a]	7.26 (1.49)		7.94 (1.08)
2. Amount of internal auditor work that would be tested[b]	6.26 (2.66)		6.36 (2.87)
3. Usage of internal auditors to perform work that could not be tested[a]	2.05 (1.18)		2.74 (1.76)

Notes: * Significant at the .10 level.
** Significant at the .01 level.
[a] Measured on a 9-point Likert scale going from (1) not at all to (9) to a great extent.
[b] Measured on a 9-point Likert scale going from (1) a small sample to (9) all work.

Due to the interrelationship of the audit hour assignments, a one-way Multivariate Analysis of Variance (MANOVA) was used to test Hypothesis 1.[6] The existence of the computer breakdown served as the independent variable and the budgeted audit hours to control tests and substantive tests served as the dependent variables. The MANOVA indicated that the mean hours were significantly different (p = .0001). Analysis of Variance tests (ANOVAs) on the individual test hours indicated there was a marginally significant difference in the budgeted control test hours (p = .089) as well as a significant difference in the budgeted substantive test hours (p = .0001). Examination of the mean hours in Table 2 indicates the auditors would perform approximately 37% (6.7 hours) more control testing and 122% (41.2 hours) more substantive testing when the computer breakdown was present.

To further evaluate the strength of the relationship between the variables, omega-squared percentages [Hayes, 1963, p. 382] were calculated that showed the breakdown accounted for 5.3% of the variation in the control testing hours and 66.5% of the variation in the substantive testing hours among the cases.[7] Therefore, the computer breakdown appears to have been viewed as creating a high audit risk situation requiring more work on the part of the external auditors.

A similar one-way MANOVA was used to test Hypothesis 2. The test indicated that the usage of direct internal auditor assistance would not be affected by the higher audit risk present in the breakdown case ($p = .334$). The means in Table 2 indicate that the subjects would make substantial use of direct internal auditor assistance to perform testable work and they would test a majority of that work regardless of whether the high audit risk was present. However, the internal auditors would be used to perform only a small amount of untestable work whether or not the audit risk was high.

Objectivity and Management Integrity Effects

The following alternative hypotheses were tested to examine the effects of the two reliability related variables and their interaction on budgeted audit hours.

Hypothesis 3. Mean audit hours assigned to control tests and substantive tests will vary depending upon internal auditor objectivity in a high audit risk situation.

Hypothesis 4. Mean audit hours assigned to control tests and substantive tests will vary depending upon the integrity of management in a high audit risk situation.

Hypothesis 5. Mean audit hours assigned to control tests and substantive tests will vary depending upon the interaction between internal auditor objectivity and management integrity in a high audit risk situation.

Hypotheses 3, 4, and 5 were tested using a two-way MANOVA on the audit hour responses to Cases 1-4. Internal auditor objectivity and management integrity served as the independent variables while the budgeted audit hours served as the dependent variables. Given the high audit risk situation, it was expected that low levels of the variables would result in a substantial reduction in the amount of reliance placed on internal auditors and higher budgeted external audit hours. In addition, it was expected the auditors would spend most of the additional time performing substantive tests rather than performing control tests over the internal control structure which was disrupted by the computer breakdown. Further, the actual impact of internal auditor objectivity was expected to depend on the level of management integrity (i.e., budgeted audit hours would be at their highest when both internal auditor objectivity and management integrity were at their low levels). Therefore, an interaction effect was also expected.

The results of the MANOVA indicate that objectivity ($p = .508$) and the interaction ($p = .650$) had no significant effect on the budgeted audit hours. Management integrity, however, significantly affected the budgeted hours

($p = .018$). Individual ANOVAs were performed to examine the impact of management integrity on control testing hours and substantive testing hours. The results of the two ANOVAs indicate that management integrity affected substantive test hours ($p = .005$; omega-square = 7.8%) but did not affect control test hours ($p = .341$). The means in Table 3 indicate there was approximately a 21% (12 hours) increase in substantive test hours when management integrity was at the low level.

The following three alternative hypotheses were tested to examine the effects of the same independent variables on the direct usage of internal auditor assistance:

Hypothesis 6. Usage and testing of direct internal auditor assistance will vary depending upon internal auditor objectivity in a high audit risk situation.

Hypothesis 7. Usage and testing of direct internal auditor assistance will vary depending upon the integrity of management in a high audit risk situation.

Hypothesis 8. Usage and testing of direct internal auditor assistance will vary depending upon the interaction between internal auditor objectivity and management integrity in a high audit risk situation.

Hypotheses 6, 7, and 8 were tested using a two-way MANOVA on the three Likert scale responses relating to direct internal auditor assistance. It was expected that the auditors would use less direct internal auditor assistance and would test more of their work when the two reliability related factors were at their low levels. As with budgeted audit hours, an interaction between the variables was expected.

The MANOVA results were similar to the MANOVA on the budget audit hours. Internal auditor objectivity ($p = .402$) and the interaction ($p = .829$) did not significantly effect the subjects' planned usage and testing of direct internal auditor assistance while management integrity was marginally significant at the $p = .100$ level.

Individual ANOVAs were performed on each usage response to determine the specific effects of management integrity. The results of the ANOVAs indicate management integrity did not effect the usage of internal auditors to perform testable work ($p = .294$) or the amount of such work that would be tested ($p = .550$), however, it did significantly effect the subjects' usage of internal auditors to perform untestable work ($p = .015$; omega-square = 5.8%). The means in Table 3 indicate the subjects were less willing to use internal auditors to perform untestable work when management integrity was low. Overall usage of the internal auditors to perform such work was, however, very low in all cases.

Table 3. Internal Auditor Objectivity and Management Integrity Means (Standard Deviations)

Mean Budgeted Hours					
	I.A. Objectivity		*Mgt. Integrity*		
	Low ($n = 46$)	*High* ($n = 41$)	*Low* ($n = 44$)		*High* ($n = 43$)
Mean Control Testing Hours	25.69	28.61	28.41		25.89
	(12.92)	(11.40)	(12.31)		(11.97)
Mean Substantive Hours	64.12	63.12	69.61	**	57.63
	(19.35)	(18.75)	(17.06)		(21.05)
Mean Responses to the Usage of Internal Auditors					
1. Usage of internal auditors to perform work that could be supervised and tested[a]	5.98	6.11	5.80		6.30
	(2.13)	(2.19)	(2.04)		(2.28)
2. Amount of internal auditor work that would be tested[b]	7.11	7.14	7.28		6.97
	(2.40)	(2.42)	(2.36)		(2.45)
3. Usage of internal auditors to perform work that could not be tested[a]	1.81	2.28	1.70	*	2.40
	(1.29)	(1.34)	(1.31)		(1.33)

Notes: * Significant at the .05 level.
** Significant at the .01 level.
[a] Measured on a 9-point Likert scale going from (1) not at all to (9) to a great extent.
[b] Measured on a 9-point Likert scale going from (1) a small sample to (9) all work.

Special Internal Auditor Investigation Effect

The following two alternative hypotheses were tested in order to examine the effect of the special internal auditor investigation on the auditors' planning decisions.

> **Hypothesis 9.** Mean audit hours assigned to control tests and substantive tests will vary depending upon whether a special internal auditor investigation had been performed.

> **Hypothesis 10.** Usage and testing of direct internal auditor assistance will vary depending upon whether a special internal auditor investigation had been performed.

As described in the research method section, only the main effects of the special internal auditor investigation were examined when internal auditor objectivity and management integrity were controlled at their high levels and the results of the special investigation revealed adequate internal controls

Table 4. Special Internal Auditor Investigation Means (Standard Deviations)

Mean Budgeted Hours

	Special Internal Auditor Investigation Yes (*Case 4 only*) ($n = 20$)		No (*Case 5*) ($n = 19$)
Mean Control Testing Hours	28.4 (10.4)		24.6 (12.5)
Mean Substantive Hours	56.4 (25.3)	*	75.0 (16.7)

Mean Responses to the Usage of Internal Auditor

	Yes (*Case 4 only*)	No (*Case 5*)
1. Usage of internal auditors to perform work that could be supervised and tested[a]	6.50 (2.06)	7.26 (1.49)
2. Amount of internal auditor work that would be tested[b]	6.85 (2.56)	6.26 (2.66)
3. Usage of internal auditors to perform work that could not be tested[a]	2.75 (1.41)	2.05 (1.18)

Notes: * Significant at the .05 level.
[a] Measured on a 9-point Likert scale going from (1) not at all to (9) to a great extent.
[b] Measured on a 9-point Likert scale going from (1) a small sample to (9) all work.

during the computer breakdown. It was expected the special internal auditor investigation would result in lower budgeted audit hours and higher usage of direct internal auditor assistance than when no special investigation was conducted.

A one-way MANOVA was used to test Hypothesis 9. The existence of the special investigation served as the independent variable while the budgeted audit hours served as the dependent variables. The results of the MANOVA indicate that the special investigation significantly affected budgeted audit hours ($p = .016$). Individual ANOVAs on the control test and substantive test hours indicate control test hours were not affected ($p = .308$) while substantive test hours were affected ($p = .012$; omega-square = 13.6%). Examination of the mean hours in Table 4 indicate the auditors reduced substantive tests by approximately 25% (18.6 hours) in reliance on the internal auditor special investigation. A similar one-way MANOVA was used to test Hypothesis 10. The results indicated that the special investigation did not impact on the usage or testing of direct internal auditor assistance ($p = .117$).

Supplemental Analyses

Four supplemental analyses were performed to assess the validity of the results. First, several MANOVAs were performed that indicated that differences in respondents' demographics among the cases (e.g., sex, age, and years of college) did not statistically affect the study's results.

Second, two MANOVAs were performed to assess the impact of the respondent's location on the audit planning decisions. Results indicate location had no effect on budgeted audit hours ($p = .770$) or direct usage of internal auditors ($p = .300$).

Third, the statistical tests of the study's hypotheses were performed using only those subjects who responded correctly to the independent variable manipulation check questions. The retested independent variables were found to be significant at approximately the same levels as those reported above that utilized all respondents. Overall, 13 respondents responded incorrectly to one or more of the manipulation check questions and 6 respondents failed to respond to one or more of the questions.[8]

Fourth, two MANOVAs were performed to test for a nonresponse bias. These MANOVAs compared early responses to late responses (over four weeks after distribution) and indicated that time of response did not affect budgeted audit hours ($p = .437$) or usage of direct internal auditor assistance ($p = .461$). Overall, the results of these supplemental tests tend to support the validity of the study's results.

LIMITATIONS

Several limitations of the study should be noted. First, the study examined only one audit area and risk situation, therefore, the results should not be generalized to other areas or situations. Future research may wish to examine reliance on internal auditors in areas where little external evidence can be gathered and, hence, are more vulnerable to management manipulation. Examination of such areas will provide better evidence of possible overreliance on internal auditors since reliance on internal auditors should be fairly low. Second, the study used very strong independent variable manipulations, however, these manipulations provided the best scenarios for evaluating whether the external auditors would react to all to the independent variables. Finally, the results are dependent on the normal MANOVA and ANOVA statistical assumptions.[9]

DISCUSSION OF THE RESULTS

This study provided preliminary evidence as to whether external auditors react to management integrity, internal auditor objectivity (i.e., reliability related factors) and the amount of work performed by the internal auditors (i.e., whether a special investigation was performed) when making reliance decisions in high audit risk areas. The results may be summarized as follows:

1. the external auditors responded to low management integrity by budgeting more substantive test audit hours;
2. the external auditors did not respond to internal auditor objectivity or the internal auditor objectivity/management integrity interaction when budgeting audit hours;
3. the external auditors responded to the special investigation performed by the internal auditors over the risk situation by budgeting less substantive test audit hours; and
4. the two reliability related factors (management integrity and internal auditor objectivity) and the additional special investigation work performed by the internal auditors within the risk area had very little effect on the external auditors' decisions on usage of direct internal auditor assistance.

First, the auditors' reaction to management integrity appear to be consistent with the research of Albrecht and Romney [1986] (which found integrity related characteristics tended to redflag auditors to management fraud), and the research of Haskins [1987] (which found that auditors were very concerned with attributes that may indicate the possibility of management override of financial reporting controls). However, the results differ from those found by Kaplan and Reckers [1984]. Their study found management integrity did not affect auditors' assessments of the likelihood of a material error occurring in the accounts receivable system while the present study found that the auditors would increase the amount of substantive testing if the integrity of management was low.

The result of the present study should be of interest to the profession because it suggests auditors are evaluating and reacting to some aspects of management reliability when examining high audit risk areas in a manner consistent with the requirements of *SAS 53,* "The Auditor's Responsibility to Detect and Report Errors and Irregularities."[10] Given the potential negative consequences (e.g., circumvented internal controls and misstated financial statements) of low management integrity, audit firms should:

1. have an established checklist of redflags to be used by their auditors in evaluating the *personal* integrity of management (e.g., the extent of exhibited greed);
2. have an established checklist of redflags to be used by their auditors in evaluating *company circumstances* that may predispose management to misstate financial information (e.g., management bonuses tied to company net income);[11]

3. encourage their auditors to always approach an engagement with an attitude of professional skepticism [see Report of the *National Commission on Fraudulent Financial Reporting,* 1987]) since checklists will never be foolproof methods of assessing management integrity;[12]
4. define what audit areas or audit decisions are most affected by questionable management intergrity—the related audit risk and materiality would be important considerations;
5. have established guidelines as to how the nature, timing and extent of substantive audit procedures should be altered if there is any concerns about management integrity (e.g., assessing the actual existence of credit customers in addition to sending receivable confirmations); and
6. have an established policy that requires higher level individuals in the firm to be informed and to evaluate potential management integrity problems to determine the risk to the firm in retaining the client.

Second, the results indicate that the auditors did not focus on the objectivity of the internal auditors even though they were budgeting audit hours to a high audit risk area. This is a disturbing result in that it indicates that the auditors either did not feel internal auditor objectivity was an important reliability factor or the auditors did not focus on the factor in the absence of other potential levels of the variable being presented to them.[13] Because prior opinion surveys [e.g., Ward and Robertson, 1980] and case studies that presented subject with all levels of internal auditor objectivity (i.e., within-subjects designs) have consistently found objectivity to be an important reliability factor [see Abdel-khalik et al., 1983; Brown, 1983], it is likely that the responding auditors were not focusing on internal auditor objectivity.

From a practical viewpoint, this finding suggests that auditing standards relating to reliance on internal auditors should provide more operational clarity [see Brown and Karan, 1986]. Currently, *SAS 9* [AICPA, 1975] provides only general guidance as to what specific criteria should be used when evaluating internal auditors or what work performed by internal auditors it would be most appropriate to rely on. In the absence of a more operational audit standard, audit firms should have established policies that:

1. define what specific criteria should be used to evaluate internal auditor reliability related factors;[14]
2. require the evaluation of the internal auditor's reliability to be documented in the work papers;
3. require that the audit risk and the materiality of the audit area be considered before relying on work previously performed by the internal auditors within the area; and
4. encourages their auditors to compare the internal auditor's reliability with other client's internal auditors. This would create a situation where

the external auditor would have explicitly considered other, differentially reliable internal auditors before making any reliance decisions.

Third, the external auditors were willing to rely more extensively on internal auditors if they performerd additional special investigation work over the risk situation. Therefore, the external auditors did react to the amount of evidence gathered by the internal auditors when making reliance decisions. In order to most effectively rely on this additional work, audit firms should have established policies that:

1. require the firm's auditors to discuss the potential benefits of special internal audit investigations with the client (e.g., reduction of external audit time and fees, improved internal controls, and a potential increase in fraud detection capabilities) and to indicate the firm's desire to be notified of unusual situations and to be involved in the planning of any related special investigations;
2. define the types of special internal auditor work that it would be most appropriate (and inappropriate) to rely on; and
3. require auditors to evaluate and document any reliance on internal audit special investigations in the workpapers.

Finally, the external auditors indicated they would make substantial use of direct internal auditor assistance, but they generally did not react to the variables in the study when determining the amount of usage. This appears to be in contradiction to the requirements of *SAS 9* which indicate that the objectivity of the internal auditors must be considered when making decisions on direct usage of internal auditors. Therefore, in addition to the policies noted above, audit firms should have established policies that:

1. indicate what audit procedures it is most appropriate (and inappropriate) to ask internal auditors to perform—this would make it less likely that internal auditors would be assigned inappropriate work in order to allow the external auditor to meet the audit time budget; and
2. indicate the minimum levels of external auditor supervision and testing of internal auditor work that is necessary in audit areas where the firm is most likely to use direct internal auditor assistance.

To help firms establish such policies, furture research should examine what external audit procedures are currently most likely to be assigned to internal auditors and how external auditors' evaluations of the audit area's risk and materiality as well as the specific audit procedure's importance and difficulty affect the reliance decisions.

NOTES

1. Independence has generally been found to be one of the most important criteria external auditors use to define overall internal auditor objectivity which is consistent with *SAS 9* requirements [see Clark et al., 1980].

2. The prior year's budgeted and actual control test and substantive test audit hours for accounts receivable are provided to the subjects to serve as a common anchor. The budgeted and actual audit hours were identical in the prior year which helped to reinforce the case description of a routine prior year audit. In addition, the prior year's hours provided a common base for the auditors which probably reduced the variability in responses.

3. The firms were also allowed to distribute the cases to supervisors, if that level existed in their firm. A total of five large offices received approximately 60 cases for distribution while the remaining eight smaller offices received approximately 18 cases for distribution.

4. Usable responses per case were: Case 1 = 23 (18.5% of the usable responses); Case 2 = 21 (17%); Case 3 = 23 (18.5%); Case 4 = 20 (16%), Case 5 = 19 (15%); and Case 6 = 19 (15%).

5. Responses per level were: staff = 1 (1% of the usable responses); senior/supervisor = 67 (54%); manager = 49 (39%); partner = 4 (3%); and other or not responding = 4 (3%). The statistical analyses were rerun excluding those who were not at the senior/manager level and those not specializing in auditing. The results were not significantly different from those presented in the paper which includes all usable responses.

6. While the audit hour assignments and the use of direct internal auditor assistance are also interrelated decisions, they were analyzed separately because of the different ways they were measured in the study (i.e., hours versus Likert scale responses).

7. In general, omega-squares indicate the percentage of variation in the dependent variable accounted for by the independent variable.

8. The number of responses per case where one or more manipulation check questions were answered incorrectly were: Case 1 = 4; Case 2 = 3; Case 3 = 2; Case 4 = 3; Case 5 = 0; and Case 6 = 1.

9. The assumption that responses are from normal distributions was violated when noncontinuous Likert scale responses were used as dependent variables. However, Glass and Stanley [1970] indicate that this assumption violation has only a slight impact on the levels of significance.

10. This study did not attempt to determine if the external auditors assessment and reaction to the low management integrity was adequate under the circumstances. Research by St. Pierre and Anderson [1982] suggests that auditors tend to inadequately assess management integrity.

11. For additional personal and company related checklist items see Albrecht and Romney [1986], *Report of the National Commission on Fraudulent Financial Reporting* [1987], and AICPA [1988].

12. *SAS 53* [AICPA, 1988] provides a detailed discussion of how professional skepticism might be applied when planning and performing an audit.

13. It is also possible that the external auditors preferred to test the internal auditor work at a very high level regardless of the level of internal auditor objectivity. If so, the external auditors could have performed too much audit work when internal auditor objectivity was high.

14. See Clark et al. [1980] for additional criteria used to evaluate internal auditor reliability.

REFERENCES

Abdel-khalik, A.R., D.A. Snowball, and J.H. Wragge, "The Effects of Certain Internal Audit Variables on the Planning of External Audit Programs," *The Accounting Review* [April 1983], pp. 215-227.

Albrecht, W.S. and M.B. Romney, "Red Flagging Management Fraud—A Validation," in *Advances in Accounting,* vol. 3, edited by B.N. Schwartz [JAI Press, 1986], pp. 323-333.

American Institute of Certified Public Accountants, *Statement on Auditing Standards No. 9,* "The Effect of an Internal Audit Function on the Scope of the Independent Auditor's Examination" [AICPA, 1975].

________, *Statement on Auditing Standards No. 53,* "The Auditor's Responsibility to Detect and Report Errors and Irregularities" [AICPA, 1988].

Brown, P.R., "Independent Auditor Judgment in the Evaluation of Internal Audit Functions," *Journal of Accounting Research* [Autumn 1983], pp. 444-455.

Brown, P.R. and V. Karan, "One Approach for Assessing the Operational Nature of Auditing Standards: An Analysis of SAS 9," *Auditing: A Journal of Practice and Theory* [Fall 1986], pp. 134-147.

Clark, M., T.E. Gibbs, and R.B. Schroeder, "Evaluating Internal Audit Departments Under SAS 9," *The Woman CPA* [July 1980], pp. 8-11 and 22.

Commission on Auditors' Responsibilities, *Report, Conclusions and Recommendations* [AICPA, 1978].

Glass, G.V. and J.C. Stanley, *Statistical Methods in Education and Psychology* [Prentice-Hall, 1970].

Haskins, M.E., "Client Control Environments: An Examination of Auditors' Perceptions," *The Accounting Review* [July 1987], pp. 542-563.

Hays, W.L., *Statistics for Psychologists* [Holt, Rinehart and Winston, 1963].

Joyce, E.J. and G.C. Biddle, "Are Auditors' Judgments Sufficiently Regressive?" *Journal of Accounting Research* [Autumn 1981], pp. 323-349.

Kaplan, S.E. and P.M.J. Reckers, "An Empirical Examination of Auditors' Initial Planning Processes," *Auditing: A Journal of Practice and Theory* [Fall 1984], pp. 1-19.

Margheim, L.L., "Further Evidence on External Auditors' Reliance on Internal Auditors," *Journal of Accounting Research* [Spring 1986], pp. 194-205.

"News Briefs," *Journal of Accountancy* [July 1987], p. 48.

Pany, K. and P.M.J. Reckers, "Within- vs. Between-Subjects Experimental Designs: A Study of Demand Effects," *Auditing: A Journal of Practice and Theory* [Fall 1987], pp. 39-53.

Report of the National Commission on Fraudulent Financial Reporting. James C.Treadway, Chairman [National Commission on Fraudulent Financial Reporting, 1987].

Schneider, A., "Modeling External Auditors' Evaluations of Internal Auditing," *Journal of Accounting Research* [Autumn 1984], pp. 657-678.

________, "The Reliance of External Auditors on the Internal Audit Function," *Journal of Accounting Research* [Autumn 1985], pp. 911-919.

St. Pierre, K. and J. Anderson, "An Analysis of Audit Failures Based on Documented Legal Cases," *Journal of Accounting, Auditing and Finance* [Spring 1982], pp. 229-247.

Ward, D.D. and J.C. Robertson, "Reliance on Internal Auditors," *Journal of Accountancy* [October 1980], pp. 62-73.

A CRITICAL EVALUATION OF THE AICPA RECOMMENDED SAMPLE SIZES FOR COMPLIANCE TESTING

David W. Wright

ABSTRACT

This paper analyzes the recommended compliance test sample sizes published in the AICPA *Audit and Accounting Guide: Audit Sampling,* with emphasis on their implied risks of underreliance. The distinguishing feature about these sample sizes is that the accept/reject critical value equals the *expected* number of deviations in the sample. The results show that this produces risks of underreliance which vary widely and converge toward 50% as the sample size and expected error rate increase. *SAS 60* establishes the auditor's responsibility to report to the audit committee deficiencies in the operation of the control structure. Furthermore, a recent SEC release proposes that management *publicly* report on auditor-identified "reportable conditions" under *SAS 60.* Thus, the combination of *SAS 60* and the SEC proposal (if enacted) potentially elevates the auditor's decision about the control system based on a compliance test from purely a matter of audit efficiency to a potential de facto public opinion. The results of this study indicate that auditors should reassess the use of the AICPA recommended sample sizes with respect to their implicit risks of underreliance and the resulting "weight" which should be placed on sample results when forming a judgment about the existence of an *SAS 60* "reportable condition."

Advances in Accounting, Volume 8, pages 313-330.

ISBN: 1-55938-067-5

Statement on Auditing Standards No. 39 (*SAS 39*), "Audit Sampling" [AICPA, 1981], distinguishes between two aspects of sampling risk in the auditor's compliance tests of the client's internal control system. *SAS 39* and the accompanying *Audit and Accounting Guide: Audit Sampling* [AICPA, 1983], emphasize measuring and controlling the risk of overreliance. This is because overreliance on controls results in a potentially ineffective audit while underreliance on controls was asserted to imply an inefficient, but no less effective audit. As a result, little to no attention is paid in *SAS 39* or the Audit Guide to the accurate measure or control of the risk of underreliance. Indeed, the tables of recommended sample sizes given in the Audit Guide do not report the implicit expected risk of underreliance inherent in their use.

However, the recently issued *Statement on Auditing Standards No. 60* (*SAS 60*), "Communication of Internal Control Structure: Related Matters Noted in an Audit," establishes the responsibility of the auditor to report to the audit committee "deficiencies in the design *or operation* of the control structure" [AICPA, 1988, par. 2, emphasis added]. Further, a recent Securities and Exchange Commission release, "Report of Management's Responsibilities," proposes a requirement that management state in their Form 10-K and annual reports to shareholders how it has "responded to any significant recommendations concering the system of internal control made by its ... independent accountants." The release indicates that these "significant recommendations" would include "those matters considered by the auditor to be 'reportable conditions' pursuant to SAS No. 60" [SEC, 1988].[1] Thus, the combination of *SAS 60* and the SEC proposal (if enacted) has the potential to elevate the auditor's decision to reject the control system based on a compliance test from a matter purely concerned with audit efficiency to one with the potential of an inaccurate de facto public report about the failure in the operation of the control structure. This increases the attention that should be paid to risk of underreliance inherent in the auditor's compliance test and in the determination of whether the results from the compliance test together with additional information from alternative collateral assessments of the operation of the control system are sufficient to communicate a reportable condition under *SAS 60*.[2]

While the recommended tables in the AICPA Audit Guide adequately control for a constant risk of overreliance, this paper demonstrates that the risk of underreliance varies dramatically within the tables. Further, the algorithm used to derive the sample size produces a risk of underreliance which converges to 50% as the sample size and population deviation rate increase. Finally, neither the authoritative literature nor any of nine leading auditing and audit sampling textbooks reviewed by this author specify a general technique for measuring the expected risks of over- and underreliance in a given sampling plan, nor do they report the underreliance risks embodied in the sample sizes they recommend.[3]

This paper specifies the formulas for determining the expected sampling risks in a contemplated compliance test. These are used to evaluate the inherent risks of underreliance in published sets of recommended sample sizes.

The paper is organized as follows. The first section formalizes the definitions of the two aspects of sampling risk identified in the authoritative literature. The second section examines the algorithm used to produce the sample sizes contained in the tables published in the AICPA Audit Guide and analyzes the implicit risks of underreliance embodied in those sample sizes. The final section summarizes the conclusions and implications of the results.

AUTHORITATIVE INTERPRETATIONS OF SAMPLING RISK

SAS 39 models the auditor's compliance sampling procedures as a hypothesis test about the reliability of the client's internal control system. The auditor's "tolerable rate" (p_t) represents "the maximum rate of deviations from a prescribed control procedure that (the auditor) would be willing to accept without altering his planned reliance on the control" [AICPA, 1981, par. 33]. Denote the true rate of noncompliance with the control procedure as p. The auditor wishes to accept the control procedure as reliable if $p \leq p_t$ and reject it if $p > p_t$.

If the auditor were to examine the entire population of transactions subject to the control, there would be no sampling risks of under- or overreliance. However, the auditor's action choice is, of course, based on the results of a compliance test sample of size n. If the number of deviations observed in the sample (e) is sufficiently low, the auditor will accept the control as reliable. If the observed number of deviations in the sample is "too high," the auditor may reduce reliance upon the control system in the conduct of subsequent substantive tests.[4] The risk of overreliance is the probability the attributes sample will support the auditor's planned degree of reliance when, in fact, the true deviation rate, if known, would be judged intolerable. The statistical decision rule is chosen so that the erroneous decision to accept as reliable a control with an intolerable noncompliance rate occurs with probability less than or equal to the auditor's desired risk of overreliance (β^*):

$$\text{Prob}\{\text{Accept } H_0\text{: } p \leq p_t \mid H_a\text{: } p > p_t\} \leq \beta^*$$

The criteria for whether to accept or reject the control as reliable can be stated in the form of any one of the following three equivalent decision rules.[5]

Decision Rule 1. Accept the control as reliable if the sample results yield a $1-\beta^*$ computed upper (precision) limit for the true error rate which is less than or equal to the tolerable rate:[6]

$p_{cul(n,e,\beta^*)} \leq p_t$, where

$$\sum_{x=0}^{e} \binom{n}{x} p^{x}_{cul(n,e,\beta^*)} (1 - p_{cul(n,e,\beta^*)})^{n-x} = \beta^*$$

e = observed number of deviations in the sample of size n

Decision Rule 2. Accept the control as reliable if the sample results yield an ex post risk of overreliance ($\hat{\beta}$) which is less than or equal to the ex ante desired risk:[7]

$$\hat{\beta} = \sum_{x=0}^{e} \binom{n}{x} p_t^x (1 - p_t)^{n-x} \leq \beta^*$$

Decision Rule 3. Accept the control as reliable if the observed number of errors is less than or equal to the preestablished critical value ($e^*_{(n,\beta^*)}$) which, if observed, would yield an ex post risk of overreliance no greater than β^*:

$e \leq e^*_{(n,\beta^*)}$ where $e^*_{(n,\beta^*)}$ is the largest integer such that

$$\sum_{x=0}^{e^*_{(n,\beta^*)}} \binom{n}{x} p_t^x (1 - p_t)^{n-x} \leq \beta^*$$

Decision Rule 1 is based on the relationship between the tolerable rate, p_t, and the "computed upper limit," $p_{cul(n,e,\beta^*)}$. This is the decision rule for fixed sample size compliance tests specified by the AICPA Audit Guide which publishes tables of computed upper limits for a variety of sample results and desired risks of overreliance [AICPA, 1983, pp. 104, 108-109]. Most auditing and audit sampling textbooks follow this approach by expressing the decision rule in this manner and reproducing the AICPA prepared tables of computed upper limits.

The Audit Guide also describes the use of Decision Rule 3 when it correctly recognizes that the parenthetical expected number of deviations in the tables of "statistical sample sizes" it provides can serve as critical values [$e^*_{(n,\beta^*)}$] in evaluating the sample. Meigs et al. [1989, p. 277] follow this approach in describing the evaluation of an attributes sample.

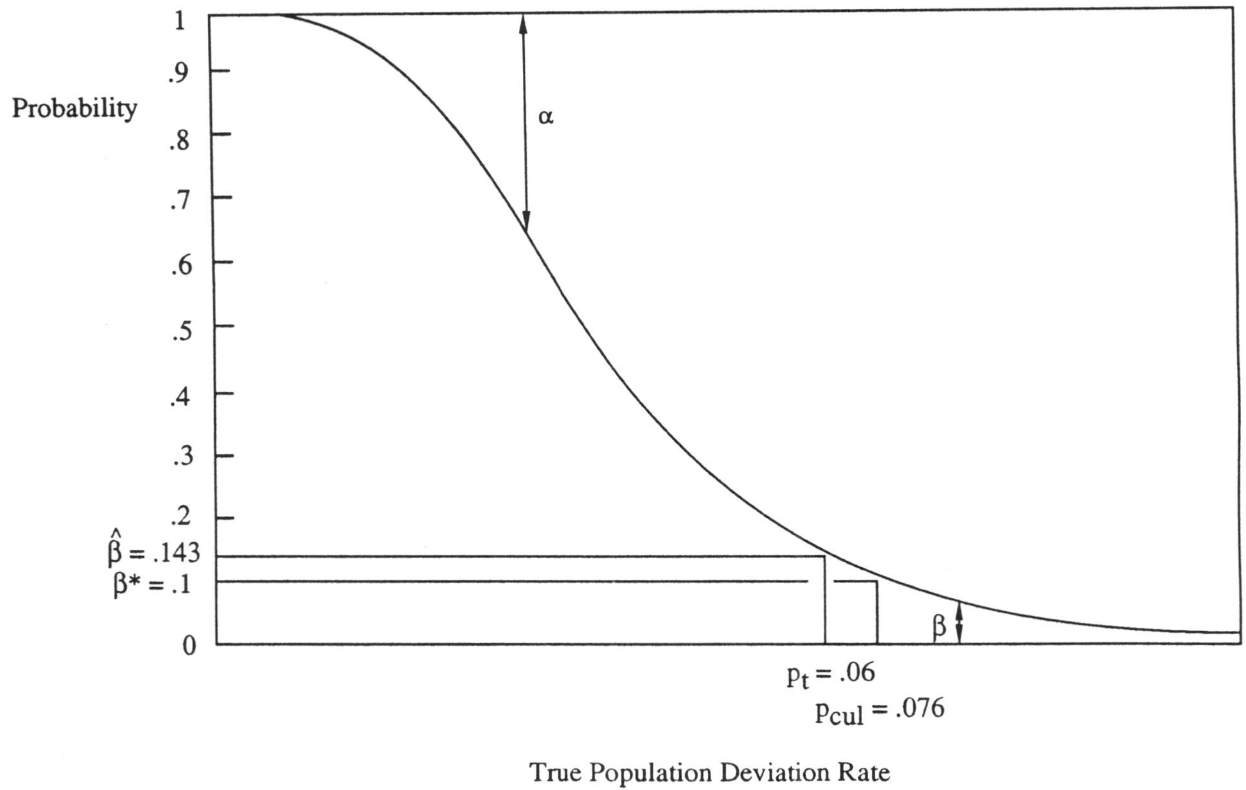

Figure 1. Operating Characteristics Curve ($n = 100$, $e = 3$)

Decision Rules 1 and 3 are, undoubtedly, more amenable to manual evaluation in the field since the respective critical decision values ($p_{cul(n,e,\beta^*)}$ and $e^*_{(n,\beta^*)}$, respectively) are easily tabled while tables of the cumulative binomial probability distribution required for Decision Rule 2 can be voluminous for a large variety of n and p_t. However, pedagogically Decision Rule 2 has some virtue since it is most closely allied to the definition of risk of overreliance. Finally, in the era of high computer accessibility, field evaluation of a given sample result can be made simultaneously under both Decision Rules 1 and 2. The auditor would interpret the output of $p_{cul(n,e,\beta^*)}$ as the lowest noncompliance rate on which substantive tests could be structured at the ex ante desired risk of overreliance, β^*. Similarly, the output of $\hat{\beta}$ would be interpreted as the risk of overreliance if the auditor structured tests assuming the noncompliance rate was p_t.

Graphically, this simultaneous evaluation of the results can be made using the operating characteristic (*oc*) curve [Bamber and Bylinski, 1984]. Given the sample size (n) and observed number of errors (e) the *oc* curve graphs the cumulative sampling distribution evaluated at e against various population error rates (i.e., Prob $\{x \leq e \mid n,p\}$).

Figure 1 shows an example of the *oc* curve for $n = 100$, $e = 3$. In this example let the auditor's tolerable rate be $p_t = .06$ at a desired risk of overreliance of $\beta^* = .1$. Decision Rule 1 implies an achieved computed upper precision limit of .076 based on the results of 3 deviations in a sample of 100. Thus, the control system is rejected since $p_{cul} > p_t$. Decision Rule 2 indicates an achieved risk of overreliance of $\hat{\beta} = .143$ based on the sample results. Thus, the control system is rejected since $\hat{\beta} > \beta^*$.

Because the three decision rules are equivalent,[8] for mathematical convenience the remainder of the paper utilizes Decision Rule 3 without loss of generality.

The risk of underreliance (α) is the probability the attributes sample will not support the planned degree of reliance when, in fact, the true compliance rate, if known, would be judged to be tolerable. Thus, it is the probability of accepting the alternative hypothesis when the null is true:

$$\alpha = \text{Prob}\,\{\text{Accept } H_a\text{: } p > p_t \mid H_0\text{: } p \leq p_t\}$$

$$= \sum_{x=e^*_{(n,\beta^*)}+1}^{n} \binom{n}{x} p^x\,(-p)^{n-x}$$

Given n and β^* the auditor's Decision Rule is fixed. That is to say, the critical value e^* is a function of n and β^* only. Thus, the *evaluation* of sample results controls exclusively for the risk of overreliance. Given a statistical decision rule which controls β^*, the only method for controlling α is the manipulation of the sample size itself.

ANALYSIS OF THE AICPA RECOMMENDED SAMPLE SIZES

The AICPA Audit Guide, *Audit Sampling,* published a set of "Statistical Sample Sizes for Compliance Testing" [AICPA, 1983, pp. 106-107]. These are used as a prototype for the presentation of sample size tables in every auditing and audit sampling text reviewed by this author. Tables 1 and 2 reproduce the AICPA recommended sample sizes for 5% and 10% risks of overreliance, respectively.

Before analyzing the implicit risks of underreliance represented by these sample sizes, it is instructive to note that the use of the adjective "statistical" in describing the sample sizes can be misleading. As the three decision rules reveal, any sample size (selected appropriately under a simple random sampling scheme) can be evaluated to measure or control the risk of overreliance based on the sample results. Thus, it is the method by which the sample is obtained, that is, according to a known probability scheme— simple random sampling, and not the magnitude of the sample size itself which will allow the results of the auditing procedures to be statistically quantified. In practical terms, the evaluation tables [AICPA, 1983, Tables 3 and 4, pp. 108-109] can be utilized without regard to the source of determination of the sample size. In point of fact, the purpose of the sample size table is to guide the auditor in the selection of a sample size which, when evaluated to control the risk of *over*reliance, is adequate (given the auditor's expectation of the true deviation rate) to control the risk of *under*reliance. Nonetheless, the tables do *not* publish the risk of underreliance embodied in the recommended sample sizes. This paper examines the algorithm used to calculate the AICPA recommended sample sizes and the resulting implicit risks of underreliance.

As noted earlier, the parenthetical amounts in Tables 1 and 2 represent the expected number of errors in the sample (rounded up to the next highest integer) given the auditor's expected population deviation rate (p_0). The AICPA Audit Guide sample sizes are set at the smallest size possible so that if the observed number of errors is as expected (or less), then the population can be accepted at the β^* risk of overreliance. Thus, the parenthetical expected number of errors serves as the critical value (e^*) for Decision Rule 3. Indeed, it is often noted that these tables can be used for both ex ante sample size determination and ex post evaluation of the results [e.g., AICPA, 1983, pp. 103-104; Meigs et al., 1989, p. 277].

Table 1. AICPA Recommended Sample Sizes for Compliance Testing—5% Risk of Overreliance

Expected Population Deviation Rate	*Tolerable Rate*										
	2%	*3%*	*4%*	*5%*	*6%*	*7%*	*8%*	*9%*	*10%*	*15%*	*20%*
.25%	236(1) [.118]	157(1) [.059]	117(1) [.035]	93(1) [.023]	78(1) [.017]	66(1) [.012]	58(1) [.009]	51(1) [.007]	46(1) [.006]	30(1) [.003]	22(1) [.001]
.50	*	157(1) [.186]	117(1) [.117]	93(1) [.079]	78(1) [.058]	66(1) [.043]	58(1) [.034]	51(1) [.027]	46(1) [.022]	30(1) [.010]	22(1) [.005]
.75	*	208(2) [.206]	117(1) [.219]	93(1) [.155]	78(1) [.116]	66(1) [.088]	58(1) [.071]	51(1) [.056]	46(1) [.047]	30(1) [.021]	22(1) [.012]
1.00	*	*	156(2) [.206]	93(1) [.238]	78(1) [.184]	66(1) [.141]	58(1) [.115]	51(1) [.092]	46(1) [.078]	30(1) [.036]	22(1) [.020]
1.25	*	*	156(2) [.310]	124(2) [.203]	78(1) [.255]	66(1) [.200]	58(1) [.164]	51(1) [.134]	46(1) [.113]	30(1) [.054]	22(1) [.031]
1.50	*	*	192(3) [.326]	124(2) [.285]	103(2) [.202]	66(1) [.261]	58(1) [.216]	51(1) [.178]	46(1) [.152]	30(1) [.074]	22(1) [.043]
1.75	*	*	227(4) [.366]	153(3) [.280]	103(2) [.270]	88(2) [.200]	77(2) [.153]	51(1) [.224]	46(1) [.192]	30(1) [.097]	22(1) [.056]
2.00	*	*	*	181(4) [.297]	127(3) [.250]	88(2) [.258]	77(2) [.200]	68(2) [.155]	46(1) [.235]	30(1) [.121]	22(1) [.071]
2.25	*	*	*	208(5) [.327]	127(3) [.321]	88(2) [.318]	77(2) [.251]	68(2) [.197]	61(2) [.158]	30(1) [.146]	22(1) [.087]
2.50	*	*	*	*	150(4) [.322]	109(3) [.291]	77(2) [.303]	68(2) [.242]	61(2) [.196]	30(1) [.172]	22(1) [.104]

2.75	*	*	*	*	173(5) [.341]	109(3) [.352]	95(3) [.266]	68(2) [.288]	61(2) [.236]	30(1) [.199]	22(1) [.122]
3.00	*	*	*	*	195(6) [.369]	129(4) [.345]	95(3) [.319]	84(3) [.245]	61(2) [.277]	30(1) [.227]	22(1) [.140]
3.25	*	*	*	*	*	148(5) [.350]	112(4) [.300]	84(3) [.292]	61(2) [.318]	30(1) [.255]	22(1) [.159]
3.50	*	*	*	*	*	167(6) [.368]	112(4) [.355]	84(3) [.339]	76(3) [.276]	40(2) [.164]	22(1) [.179]
3.75	*	*	*	*	*	185(7) [.392]	129(5) [.355]	100(4) [.321]	76(3) [.319]	40(2) [.189]	22(1) [.199]
4.00	*	*	*	*	*	*	146(6) [.367]	100(4) [.371]	89(4) [.284]	40(2) [.214]	22(1) [.219]
5.00	*	*	*	*	*	*	*	158(8) [.393]	116(6) [.361]	40(2) [.323]	30(2) [.188]
6.00	*	*	*	*	*	*	*	*	179(11) [.389]	50(3) [.353]	30(2) [.268]
7.00	*	*	*	*	*	*	*	*	*	68(5) [.340]	37(3) [.258]

Notes: Number of expected errors in parenthesis.
Implicit risk of underreliance in brackets.
* Sample size is too large to be cost-effective for most audit applications.

Table 2. AICPA Recommended Sample Sizes for Compliance Testing—10% Risk of Overreliance

Expected Population Deviation Rate	Tolerable Rate										
	2%	3%	4%	5%	6%	7%	8%	9%	10%	15%	20%
.25%	194(1) [.086]	129(1) [.042]	96(1) [.005]	77(1) [.016]	64(1) [.011]	55(1) [.009]	48(1) [.007]	42(1) [.005]	38(1) [.004]	25(1) [.002]	18(1) [.001]
.50	194(1) [.253]	129(1) [.137]	96(1) [.084]	77(1) [.057]	64(1) [.041]	55(1) [.031]	48(1) [.024]	42(1) [.019]	38(1) [.016]	25(1) [.007]	18(1) [.004]
.75	265(2) [.320]	129(1) [.252]	96(1) [.162]	77(1) [.114]	64(1) [.084]	55(1) [.064]	48(1) [.051]	42(1) [.040]	38(1) [.033]	25(1) [.015]	18(1) [.008]
1.00	*	176(2) [.258]	96(1) [.249]	77(1) [.180]	64(1) [.135]	55(1) [.105]	48(1) [.083]	42(1) [.066]	38(1) [.055]	25(1) [.026]	18(1) [.014]
1.25	*	221(3) [.299]	132(2) [.229]	77(1) [.250]	64(1) [.191]	55(1) [.151]	48(1) [.121]	42(1) [.097]	38(1) [.082]	25(1) [.039]	18(1) [.021]
1.50	*	*	132(2) [.318]	105(2) [.209]	64(1) [.249]	55(1) [.200]	48(1) [.162]	42(1) [.131]	38(1) [.111]	25(1) [.054]	18(1) [.029]
1.75	*	*	166(3) [.331]	105(2) [.279]	88(2) [.200]	55(1) [.250]	48(1) [.205]	42(1) [.167]	38(1) [.143]	25(1) [.070]	18(1) [.039]
2.00	*	*	198(4) [.363]	132(3) [.272]	88(2) [.258]	75(2) [.190]	48(1) [.249]	42(1) [.205]	38(1) [.176]	25(1) [.089]	18(1) [.050]
2.25	*	*	*	132(3) [.346]	88(2) [.318]	75(2) [.239]	65(2) [.180]	42(1) [.244]	38(1) [.210]	25(1) [.108]	18(1) [.061]
2.50	*	*	*	158(4) [.361]	110(3) [.296]	75(2) [.289]	65(2) [.222]	58(2) [.177]	38(1) [.246]	25(1) [.129]	18(1) [.073]

2.75	*	*	*	209(6) [.353]	132(4) [.298]	94(3) [.259]	65(2) [.265]	58(2) [.214]	52(2) [.172]	25(1) [.150]	18(1) [.087]
3.00	*	*	*	*	132(4) [.363]	94(3) [.312]	65(2) [.310]	58(2) [.252]	52(2) [.205]	25(1) [.172]	18(1) [.100]
3.25	*	*	*	*	153(5) [.379]	113(4) [.304]	82(3) [.277]	58(2) [.292]	52(2) [.239]	25(1) [.195]	18(1) [.115]
3.50	*	*	*	*	194(7) [.369]	113(4) [.362]	82(3) [.323]	73(3) [.252]	52(2) [.274]	25(1) [.218]	18(1) [.130]
3.75	*	*	*	*	*	131(5) [.368]	98(4) [.307]	73(3) [.293]	52(2) [.309]	25(1) [.241]	18(1) [.145]
4.00	*	*	*	*	*	149(6) [.387]	98(4) [.355]	73(3) [.334]	65(3) [.262]	25(1) [.264]	18(1) [.161]
5.00	*	*	*	*	*	*	160(8) [.407]	115(6) [.353]	78(4) [.351]	34(2) [.241]	18(1) [.226]
6.00	*	*	*	*	*	*	*	182(11) [.411]	116(7) [.395]	43(3) [.251]	25(2) [.187]
7.00	*	*	*	*	*	*	*	*	199(14) [.422]	52(4) [.299]	25(2) [.253]

Notes: Number of expected errors in parentheses.
Implicit risk of underreliance in brackets.
* Sample size is too large to be cost-effective for most audit applications.

Table 3. Examples of Sample Size/Critical Value Combinations

Tolerable deviation rate:	$p_t = .05$		
Risk of overreliance:	$\beta^* = .10$		
Expected deviation rate:	$p_0 = .015$		

*Critical Value e**	*Sample Size*	*Expected*[a] *Deviations*	*Risk of Underreliance*
0	45	1	.493
1	77	2	.321
2	105[b]	2	.209
3	132	2	.138
4	158	3	.091
5	184	3	.060

Notes: [a] Rounded up if np_0 is not an integer.
[b] Sample size of $n = 105$ and critical value of $e^* = 2$ is the recommended combination in the AICPA *Audit and Accounting Guide* [1983, Table 2, p. 107].

Formally, the algorithm used to derive these sample sizes is:

$$\min n \in \textit{Integers}$$

$$\text{subject to: } \sum_{x=0}^{e^*} \binom{n}{x} p_t^x (1 - p_t)^{n-x} \leq \beta^*$$

$$e^* = \text{smallest integer greater than or equal to } np_0$$

For example, consider:

$$p_0 = .015$$
$$p_t = .05$$
$$\beta^* = .10$$

The recommended sample size is 105 and the expected number of errors in the sample is 2. Thus,

$$\sum_{x=0}^{2} \binom{105}{x} (.05)^x (.95)^{105-x} = .099 \qquad \text{and}$$

$$\sum_{x=0}^{2} \binom{104}{x} (.05)^x (.95)^{104-x} = .103$$

imply 105 is the minimum sample size for which the population can be accepted with 2 or fewer deviations in the sample at a risk of overreliance less than 10%.

The expected number of errors in the sample is 105 x .015 = 1.575, which is rounded up to 2.[9]

The above verifies that 105 is the minumum sample size which can be used in testing a tolerable error rate of 5% at the 10% risk of overreliance, *when the decision rule is to accept with two or fewer errors in the sample.* Other decision rules would, of course, imply different sample sizes. Table 3 provides several examples of sample size/critical value combinations each of which tests against a tolerable error rate of 5% at the 10% risk of overreliance.

Table 3 illustrates that numerous sample sizes can be used to control the risk of overreliance at 10%. Thus, given the population rate is 5% (or just intolerable), the probability is 10% (β^*) of observing 0 deviations in a sample of 45, or 1 or fewer deviations in 77, or 2 or fewer deviations in 105, and so forth.

However, only one sample size has a critical value $e^*_{(n,\beta^*)}$ (purely a function of n and β^*) which equals the *expected* number of errors in the sample (rounded up) given the expected deviation rate, p_0. This is the distinguishing feature of the "Statistical Sample Size" published in the Audit Guide—it is constructed so that the accept/reject critical value equals the *expected* number of errors in the sample, given the auditor's expected rate. This produces relatively high α risks of underreliance. Indeed, if the auditor's expectation is accurate and if the sampling distribution was continuous and symmetric, then the distribution's mean and median are the same and this technique would imply a risk of underreliance of 50%! The binomial sampling distribution is, in fact, discrete and positively skewed—resulting in risks of underreliance somewhat below 50%. However, as the population error rate and the sample size increase, the binomial distribution approaches the symmetric continuous normal distribution—driving the risk of underreliance toward 50%.

The bracketed amounts in Tables 1 and 2 give the implied risks of underreliance associated with the AICPA recommended sample sizes. They are obtained from the above formula for the risk of underreliance (α) with $p = p_0$.[10] Three observations can be made about these implicit underreliance risks embodied in the AICPA sample sizes but not reported in the Audit Guide.

First, there is a wide disparity of α risks between the various cells in the tables. With a 5% risk of overreliance (Table 1) the AICPA sample sizes produce risks of underreliance from a low of .1% (p_0 = .25%, p_t = 20%, $n = 22$, $e^* = 1$) to a high of 39.3% (p_0 = 5%, p_t = 9%, $n = 158$, $e^* = 8$). With a 10% risk of overreliance (Table 2) the risks of underreliance range from .1% to 42.2%.

Second, as noted earlier, the risk of underreliance increases, converging toward 50%, as the sample size and the expected error rate increase, since the binomial distribution is converging to the normal distribution. This results in the somewhat counterintuitive notion of higher risks of underreliance tending to be associated with the larger sample sizes in the table. It is, of course, true that increasing the sample size while holding the population deviation rate and the risk of overreliance constant will decrease the risk of underreliance. An example of this relationship is provided in Table 3. Thus, given a fixed expectation for the population deviation rate, the auditor wishing to decrease (increase) the expected risk of underreliance from the level associated with the AICPA recommended sample size as reported in Tables 1 and 2 should increase (decrease) the sample size in the manner of Table 3.

However, in the AICPA sample size table, the expected deviation rate is not, of course, held constant across the various cells. In fact, if the binomial sampling distribution were continuous and symmetric, the AICPA sample size algorithm would produce a constant risk of underreliance of 50% throughout the tables. For the higher expected deviation rates and sample sizes the binomial distribution approaches the symmetric normal distribution—producing relatively high risks of underreliance. For the lower expected deviation rates and sample sizes, the binomial distribution is much more positively skewed (mean, and hence e^*, greater than the median) which produces lower risks of underreliance. This explains the apparent paradox of lower (higher) risks of underreliance being associated with the smaller (larger) AICPA recommended sample sizes as reported in Tables 1 and 2.

Third, the decision about the communication of a reportable condition under *SAS 60* should include consideration of the implicit risk of underreliance in the sampling plan. For example, consider the case of an auditor selecting a sample of size 181—expecting a 2% noncompliance rate with a desired risk of overreliance of 5% and a 5% tolerable rate. If the auditor's expectation is accurate and the true population rate is indeed only 2%, then as shown in Table 1, the results from this relatively large sample will incorrectly signal the control to be unreliable 29.7% of the time. If the auditor bases the decision to communicate a reportable condition under *SAS 60 solely* on the sample results, then the risk of an incorrect communication of a reportable condition is equal to the 29.7% risk of underreliance. The sample size/evaluation tables do consistently control the risk of overreliance (risk of failure to communicate an existing reportable condition) to the relatively low prespecified levels (i.e., 5% or 10%). However, as Tables 1 and 2 document, the risks of underreliance (risk of incorrect communication of a nonexistent reportable condition) vary dramatically and range up to relatively high levels. Thus, it may be the case that accepting the controls as reliable based on the sample evidence also adequately controls the risk of failing to communicate an existing reportable condition. However, basing the decision to communicate a reportable condition *strictly* on the sample evidence may expose the auditor to widely divergent and excessively high risks of incorrect communications of perceived failures in the operation of the control system.

Clearly, *SAS 60* does not imply that the decision to communicate a reportable condition concerning the operation of the control system should be based entirely on the results of the compliance tests. Indeed, the decision would be based not only on the compliance tests but also on the continuing evaluation of the system including information from inquiries, observations and the results of subsequent substantive tests. Presumably, the auditor will judgmentally combine the information from each of these sources in reaching the decision on the existence of a reportable condition. However, in making this judgmental combination of sample data and collateral information, the inherent sampling risk of underreliance should be considered when "weighting" the sample information in forming the overall conclusion. Conversely, if the auditor wishes a priori to "weight" the sample evidence heavily relative to the collateral information, then ex ante the sample should be planned to produce a relatively low risk of underreliance. While it may be counterintuitive, if the AICPA recommended sample sizes are used, the weight to be placed on the sample evidence should not be measured exclusively by the sample size itself since, as noted above, the AICPA sample size algorithm tends to associate higher risks of underreliance with larger sample sizes. The importance of these risks is underscored by the potential for future de facto *public* disclosures of such communications if the SEC proposal cited earlier were to be enacted in its current form.

SUMMARY, CONCLUSIONS AND IMPLICATIONS

SAS 39 and its interpretative Audit Guide concentrate on the measure and control of the risk of overreliance since it results in a potentially ineffective audit while the underreliance on controls was considered to imply an inefficient, but no less effective audit. However, the measure and control of the risk of underreliance is also an important concern in the design of compliance tests. Efficiency in the performance of the audit is, of course, one reason for consideration of the risk of underreliance. In addition, the recently issued *SAS 60* mandates communication to the audit committee of identified "reportable conditions" (including failures in the operation of the internal control structure). When combining the results of the compliance test sample with other collateral information about the operation of the control system, the auditor should consider the inherent risk of underreliance in the sampling plan when "weighting" this evidence in the overall decision to communicate a reportable condition. The importance of these matters is underscored by a recent SEC proposal that management publicly respond to these reportable conditions, which, if enacted, would elevate the auditor's decision to communicate a reportable condition to the audit committee to a potentially inaccurate de facto public report.

This paper evaluated the sample sizes published in the AICPA Audit Guide for their inherent risks of underreliance. The results showed a widely divergent set of risks ranging from a low of .1% to a high of 42.2%. In fact, the algorithm used in the construction of the sample sizes produces a risk of underreliance which converges toward 50% as the sample size and expected error rate increase.

The results of this study indicate that the auditor concerned with efficiency and the accuracy of decisions regarding *SAS 60* reportable conditions on the client's compliance with the prescribed control system should reassess the use of the recommended sample sizes in the AICPA Audit Guide. If the implicit risks of underreliance reported in this paper are deemed unacceptable, the auditor should consider revising the sample size accordingly. Additionally, if the recommended sample size is used and the sample results indicate the control can not be relied upon, then the auditor should consider the implicit risk of underreliance reported in the paper when combining the sample evidence with other information about the operation of the control system in concluding whether the perceived failure in the control should be communicated as a reportable condition under *SAS 60*.

ACKNOWLEDGMENTS

The author gratefully acknowledges the useful comments of Richard W. Andrews, workshop participants in the 1989 Mid-Atlantic Regional Meeting of the American Accounting Association and, especially, two anonymous reviewers. Financial support was provided by The University of Michigan School of Business Administration.

NOTES

1. The comment period on the proposal ended in October 1988 with nearly 200 comment letters being received by the SEC. At this writing (March 27, 1990) the SEC proposal remains under consideration and has not yet been enacted into law. Thus, *public* management responses to auditor-identified reportable conditions under *SAS 60* are not yet mandatory. Until such a requirement is enacted, the auditor's costs from misidentified *SAS 60* reportable conditions in the operation of the control system could be limited to an impaired reputation with the client.

2. *SAS 60* does not require the auditor to search for reportable conditions. Indeed, generally accepted auditing standards historically have not required the auditor to test compliance with controls which will not be relied on in the conduct of substantive tests. However, given that the auditor has elected to test compliance, in the event that deviations are noted the decision must be made regarding whether the sample results combined with additional collateral information about the control system warrant the communication of a reportable condition under *SAS 60*.

3. The texts reviewed were Arens and Loebbecke [1981, 1988], Carmichael and Willingham [1987], Grobstein, Loeb and Neary [1985], Guy and Alderman [1987], Guy and Carmichael [1986], Meigs et al. [1989], Roberts [1978], and Robertson and Davis [1988]. Robertson and Davis do provide a formula for calculating the risk of underreliance when the control is rejected on the observation of 1 deviation in the sample and the expected population rate is greater than 0% [p. 358]. However, this formula would never be applicable for the AICPA recommended sample sizes since the control is *only* rejected on the observation of a single deviation when the expected

rate *is* 0%! Roberts [1978] does discuss varying the risk of underreliance through the selection of the sample size [pp. 55-57] and discusses a computer program [pp. 184-185] designed to calculate a sample size to control both the risk of underreliance and overreliance. However, none of the texts provide complete formulas for measuring both the risks of overreliance and underreliance for a contemplated sampling plan. (Bamber and Bylinski [1984] do provide the formula for the risk of overreliance.) More importantly, none of the texts disclose the inherent risks of underreliance in the sample size tables they provide.

4. Of course, *SAS 39* mandates that "in addition to the evaluation of the frequency of deviations from pertinent procedures, consideration should be given to the qualitative aspects of the deviations" [AICPA, 1981, par. 41]. However, because consideration of the qualitative aspects of sample results is a matter for professional judgment which eludes precise statistical evaluation, it will not be considered further in this paper.

5. In point of fact, it is not the objective of the auditor's compliance tests to accept or reject the control system per se, but rather to provide reasonable assurance that the control procedures are being applied as prescribed in order to support the planned degree of reliance on the control system in the conduct of subsequent substantive tests and to assist in overall audit risk assessments under *SAS 47*. With this distinction in mind, for expositional brevity this paper will, at times, employ the phrase "accept (reject) the control" to represent the more precise terminology.

6. The sampling distribution for the observed number of errors, e, is binomial if the sample items are selected with replacement and hypergoemtric if they are selected without replacement. However, in most realistic audit sampling situations the populations are large enough relative to the sample sizes so that the differences between these two distributions are negligible. For simplicity all results in this study are obtained from a model which assumes a large population relative to the sample sizes so that the use of the binomial distribution is appropriate. This is consistent with the assumptions employed by the AICPA [1983] in the construction of the sample size tables published in the *Audit and Accounting Guide.*

7. The actual risk of overreliance is a strictly decreasing function of the true population deviation rate, p. Thus, it is greatest when the true rate is "just intolerable." Hence, $\hat{\beta}$ is measured under $p = p_t$.

8. The rules are equivalent in the sense that each accepts (rejects) for the same sample results, or:

$$p_{cul(n,e,\beta^*)} \leq (>)\, p_t \iff \hat{\beta} \leq (>)\, \beta^* \iff e \leq (>)\, e^*_{(n,\beta^*)}$$

While this is easily shown algebraically, for the sake of brevity a detailed proof is not presented in this paper.

9. The expected number of errors/critical value must, of course, be an integer and all fractions (regardless of size) are rounded up to the next higher integer.

10. The risks of underreliance reported in this paper assume the auditor's expectation of the population deviation rate is accurate. Ad hoc "conservative" overestimation of the population deviation rate would imply lower risks of underreliance. Conversely, underestimation of the population deviation rate would imply higher risks of underreliance. The actual risks of underreliance for all possible population rates (0 to p_t) are given by the complement of the *oc* curve, as shown in Figure 1. Tables 1 and 2 simply report what should be perceived by the auditor as the risk of underreliance in the contemplated sampling plan using the AICPA recommended sample sizes, assuming the "expected error rate" faithfully represents the auditor's belief about the population. This is consistent with the auditor using an expected deviation rate based upon the results of a (presumably unbiased) pilot sample or the prior year's (presumably unbiased) sample as is often recommended in auditing textbooks [e.g., Arens and Loebbecke, 1988, p. 404].

REFERENCES

American Institute of Certified Public Accountants, *Statement on Auditing Standards No. 39,* "Audit Sampling" [AICPA, 1981].

———, *Audit and Accounting Guide: Audit Sampling* [AICPA, 1983].

———, *Statement on Auditing Standards No. 60,* "Communication of Internal Control Structure Related Matters Noted in an Audit" [AICPA, 1988].

———, *Statement on Auditing Standards No. 60,* "Commnication of Internal Control Structure: Related Matters Noted in an Audit" [AICPA, 1989].

Arens, A.A. and J.K. Loebbecke, *Applications of Statistical Sampling to Auditing* [Prentice-Hall, 1981].

———, *Auditing: An Integrated Approach* [Prentice-Hall, 1988].

Bamber, E.M. and J.H. Bylinski, "Attribute Sampling: A Review in Light of SAS No. 39," *Journal of Accounting Education* [Spring 1984], pp. 83-97.

Carmichael, D.R. and J.J. Willingham, *Audit Concepts and Methods* [McGraw-Hill, 1987].

Grobstein, M., S.E. Loeb, and R.D. Neary, *Auditing: A Risk Analysis Approach* [Irwin, 1985].

Guy, D.M. and C.W. Alderman, *Auditing* [Harcourt Brace Janovanovich, 1987].

Guy, D.M. and D.R. Carmichael, *Audit Sampling: An Introduction to Statistical Sampling in Auditing* [Wiley, 1986].

Meigs, W.B., O.R. Whittington, K. Pany, and R.F. Meigs, *Principles of Auditing* [Irwin, 1989].

Roberts, D.M., *Statistical Auditing* [AICPA, 1978].

Robertson, J.C. and F.C. Davis, *Auditing* [Business Publications, 1988].

Securities and Exchange Commission, "Report of Management's Responsibilities," Securities Act Release No. 6789 [July 19, 1988].

Advances in Accounting

Edited by **Bill N. Schwartz,** *School of Business and Management, Temple University.* Associate Editors: **Philip M.J. Reckers,** *Arizona State University,* **James C. Stallman,** *University of Missouri,* **James H. Scheiner,** *University of Tennessee at Knoxville*

Publication outlets in accounting tend toward editorial poles. "Academic" journals are read by academicians, and the papers emphasize research menthods. The topics addressed in these journals generally do not interest the practicing profession. On the other hand, "Practionier" journals focus on interesting current issues but often lack internal rigor.

Advances in Accounting (AIA) aims to bridge this gap by meeting the information needs of both academicians and practitioners. AIA will include articles that both (1) address contemporary issues and/or problems in financial or managerial accounting, accounting education, or auditing, and (2) display sound analyses.

Articles will range from purely empirical to purely theoretical, from practice-based application to speculation on the development of new techniques. AIA articles will be readable, relevant, and reliable. To be readable, articles will be easily understood by both academicians and practitioners. The articles will not include an excessive amount of technical jargon or mathematical notation. To be relevant, articles will focus on current issues and/or problems currently facing the accounting and business communities. To be reliable, the articles will develop conclusions from sound evidence and/or logic. Empirical reports will present sound research designs and well-explained execution. Theoretical arguments will present reasonable assumptions and logical development of ideas. AIA articles will include well-defined problems, concise presentations, and succinct conclusions that follow logically from the data in discussions.

Volume 1, 1984, 290 pp. $63.50
ISBN 0-89232-397-3

REVIEW: "Professor Schwartz and his associate editors, Philip Reckers and Arnold Wright, have produced a new, high-quality accounting publication that contains articles from some of the most respected names in academic and professional practice. The papers tend to be methodologically rigorous but are also quite readable and relevant to the concerns of the profession today — a combination of qualities seldom seen in accounting journals produced by academics. The editors have grouped the articles into three categories: financial and managerial accounting, accounting education, and auditing. The broad range of topics in this collection will prove interesting to the average reader."

— *Journal of Accountancy*

JAI PRESS

CONTENTS: List of Contributors. PART I. FINANCIAL AND MANAGERIAL. An Intergenerational Comparison of Socioeconomic Status Among CPAs, Attorneys, Engineers, and Physicians, *Ralph Estes, Wichita State University.* **The Association Between Municipal Accounting Numbers and Credit Risk and Return,** *Robert W. Ingram, University of Iowa and Ronald M. Copeland, Northwestern University.* **Market Reaction to Corporate Environment Performance,** *William P. Stevens, DePaul University.* **A Framework for the Selection of Representative Financial Ratios: Methodology Note,** *Kung H. Chen and Albert Y. Lew, University of Nebraska.* **Effect of Different Cost Behaviors on "EOQ" (Economic Order Quantity): Practice Note,** *Mohammad A. Sangeladji, California State University, Northridge.* **PART II. EDUCATION. Accounting Accreditation and Schools of Accounting in the United States,** *Wilton T. Anderson, Oklahoma State University and Gary John Previts, Case Western University.* **The CPA Examination — Profile of the Successful Candidate,** *Park E. Leathers, James A. Sullivan, Bowling Green State University and Jerome Bernstein, American Institute for Certified Public Accounts.* **The Economic Status of Accounting Educators: An Empirical Study,** *Merrill T. Lewis, W. Thomas Lin, and Doyle Z. Williams, University of Southern California.* **The Contributions of the Financial Accounting Standards Board to Accounting Education,** *Paul B.W. Miller, University of Utah.* **PART II. AUDITING. Intent to Turnover Among Higher Level Employees in Large CPA Firms,** *Ralph L. Benke, Jr., James Madison University and John Grant Rhode, University of San Francisco.* **Evaluation of Research on Expectancy Theory Predictions of Auditor Effect Judgements,** *Steven Kaplan, Arizona State University.* **The Impact of Selected Behavioral Variables on Disclosure Decisions,** *Philip M.J. Reckers, Arizona State University.* **Observations on Needed Research in Auditing: Materiality and Audit Risk,** *Abraham D. Akresh, Laventhol and Horovath, Philadelphia.* **Decision Support Systems and Auditing,** *Jean Bedard, Glen L. Gray, and Theodore J. Mock, University of Southern California.* **Probability Elicitation in Auditing: Additional Evidence on the Equivalent Prior Sample Method,** *Ira Solomon, University of Illinois, Lawrence A. Tomassini, University of Teaxs at Austin, Marshall B. Romney, Brigham Young University and Jack L. Krogstad, Creichton University.*

Volume 2, 1985, 289 pp. $63.50
ISBN 0-89232-514-3

REVIEW: "This hardbound collection of articles contains materials on financial and managerial accounting, auditing and accounting education. Most of this year's editionn is devoted to the last two areas. There are interesting pieces on the uses of

Financial Accouting Standards Board statements and annual reports as teaching aids in the classroom and a study of recent graduates from a PhD program in accounting, which examines, among other things, the length of time necessary to complete the coursework and thesis. The section on auditing contains articles that will be of interest to practitioners, especially the work that examines the proficiency of senior auditors in evaluating their staff. All of the articles begin with an abstract and most have well-written summary and conclusion sections."

— *Journal of Accountancy*

CONTENTS: List of Contributors. PART I. FINANCIAL AND MANAGERIAL. A Taxonomic Approach to Defining Industrial Social Costs, *Martin Freedman, State Universtiy of New York at Binghamton and A.J. Stagliano, George Mason University.* **Materiality in Commercial Bank Inflation Accounting,** *Patricia A. Frishkoff and Mary Ellen Phillips, Oregon State University.* **A Theoretical and Empirical Procedure for the Measurement of the Economic Income of Corporations,** *A.J. Merrett and G.D. Newbould, Cleveland State University.* **PART II. Education. A Profile of an Accounting Doctoral Program: A Study of Recent Graduates,** *James W. Deitrick, University of Texas at Austin, C. Wayne Alderman, Auburn University and David L. Sayers, University of Nebraska.* **FASB Statement in the Classroom: A Study of Readability,** *William P. Stevens and Kathleen C. Stevens, DePaul University and William A. Raabe, University of Wisconsin, Milwaukee.* **Consulting as an Instructional Tool in Accounting,** *Mohamed Elmutassim Hussein, University of Connecticut.* **A Computer-Assisted Teaching Aid for Bayesian Variables Audit Sampling,** *Edward Blocher, University of North Carolina, Chapel Hill.* **Annual Reports: A Pedagogical Tool for Intermediate Accounting,** *Jeffrey L. Harkins, Universtiy of Idaho and John Mills, University of Nevada, Reno.* **PART III. AUDITING. Improving Auditor Judgement Through Research: A Problem and Some Potential Solutions,** *Stanley F. Biggs, University of Connecticut.* **Rating the Raters: Indications of Seniors' Performance in Evaluating Staff Auditors,** *Arnold Wright, Boston University.* **The Expectation of Accounting Errors in Medium-Sized Manfacturing Firms,** *James R. Coakley, Air Force Institute of Technology and James K. Loebbecke, University of Utah.* **The Death (Perhaps Timely) of an Audit Report: Some Empirical Results,** *Kurt Pany and Douglas A. Johnson, Arizona State University.* **An Empirical Study of the Effects of Time Pressure on Audit Time Allocations,** *George F. Kermis, Canisius College and S. Mahapatra, California State University, Long Beach.* **Bayesian Inference in Substantive Testing: An Ease-of-Use Criterion,** *Mohammad J. Abdolmohammadi, Boston University.*

JAI PRESS

and K.K. Raman, North Texas State University. **A Comparison of Financial Ratios: Historical Cost Versus Price-Level Adjusted Disclosures,** *Kung H. Chen, University of Nebraska, Lincoln.* **PART II. EDUCATION SECTION,** *Bill N. Schwartz, Associate Editor.* **Capital Budgeting Under Risk and Inflation: A Pedagogical Guide,** *Robert E. Jensen, Trinity University.* **Treatment of the Material Price Variance,** *Leonrad A. Robinson, Loudell Ellis Robinson, University of Alabama in Birmingham.* **Vertical and Lateral Considerations of Undergraduate Accounting Honors Programs,** *Mark W. Dirsmith J. Edward Jetz, Ronald J. Teichman, The Pennsylvania State University.* **PART III. AUDITING SECTION,** *Arnold Wright, Associate Editor.***Red Flagging Management Fraud-A Validation,** *W. Steve Albrecht, Marshall B. Romney, Brigham Young University.* **An Empirical Examination of the Effect of Orientation Information on Audit Judgements,** *Steven E. Kaplan, Philip M.J. Reckers, Arizona State University.*

Volume 4, 1987, 328 pp. $63.50
ISBN 0-89232-685-9

CONTENTS: List of Contributors. Part I. FINANCIAL/ MANAGERIAL SECTION. An Inquiry into the Utility of a Parallel System for Providing Insights into the Development of An Accounting Conceptual Systems, *G.A. Swanson, Tennessee Technological University.* **Non-Economic Contributors to Tax Evasion: A Replication,** *Steven E. Kaplan, Arizona State University and Philip M.J. Reckers, Arizona State University.* **The Information Content of Unfunded Pension Obligations for Municipal Bond Ratings: An Empirical Evaluation,** *Barry R. Marks, University of Houston at Clear Lake and K.K. Raman, North Texas State University.* **International Accounting Research,** *Kathleen R. Bindon, University of Alabama and Helen Gernon, University of Oregon.* **Methodological Note: Using the Repeated Measures Model in Accounting Policy Research: The Case of Segment Reporting,** *Bruce A. Baldwin, Portland State University.* **PART II. EDUCATION SECTION, An Analysis of Trends and Sources of Published Funded Accounting Research,** *G. William Glezen and James A. Milar, University of Arkansas.* **Improving the Writing Skills of Accounting Majors: One School's Approach,** *James W. Deitrick, The University of Texas at Austin and Richard H. Tabor, Auburn University.* **Consulting and Internship Opportunities for Accounting Faculty Members: Their Nature and Variables Associated with Their Attainment,** *Chee W. Chow, San Diego State University and Rebecca Todd, New York University.* **Incorporating Economic Uncertainty in Tax Planning,** *Stephen T. Limberg, The University of Texas at Austin.* **Administrative Note, 1985-1986 Contract Terms for Incoming Accounting Faculty,** *Lucille E. Lammers, Illinois State University.* **PART III. AUDITING**

ment, *A. Faye Borthick, The University of Tenneessee.* **An Empirical Analysis of Audit Withdrawal Decisions,** *Richard G. Schroeder, University of Texas at El Paso and Kathryn Verreault, University of Lowell.* **The Effect of Audit Billing Arrangement on Undereporting of Time and Audit Quality Reduction Acts,** *Timothy Kelly and Loren Margheim, University of San Diego.*

Volume 6, 1988, 276 pp. $63.50
ISBN 0-89232-892-4

JAI PRESS

Auditor and Client, *Steven P. Golen, Arizona State University, Stephen W. Looney, Louisiana State University, and Richard A. White, University of South Carolina.* **An Analysis of Auditor Judgement in Nonstatistical Sampling,** *William J. Read, Bentley College.* **Forecasting Accounting Information for Auditor's Use in Analytical Reviews,** *Arlene C. Wilson, Auburn University, William Glezen and Timothy P. Cronan, University of Arkansas.*

Volume 7, 1989, 256 pp. $63.50
ISBN 0-89232-960-2

CONTENTS. List of Contributors. Editorial Board. AIA Statement of Purpose. Editorial Policy and Manuscript From Guidelines. PART I. FINANCIAL AND MANAGERIAL. The Market for Corporate Control and its Implications for Accounting, *James E. Groff, University of Texas at San Antonio and Charlotte J. Wright, Oklahoma State University.* **The Impact of the Accounting Treatment of Leasing Contracts on User Decision Makinng: A Field Experiment,** *Bart P. Hartman, Louisiana State University and Heibatollah Sami, Temple University.* **An Empirical Examination of the Influence of Selected Factors on Professional Tax Preparers' Decision Process,** *David LaRue, University of Virginia and Philip M.J. Reckers, Arizona State University.* **The Relevance of Level of Aggregation of Geographic Area Data in the Assessment of Foreign Investment Risk,** *Timothy S. Doupnik and Robert J. Rolfe, University of South Carolina.* **New Evidence on the Accuracy of Management Forecasts and Time-Series Forecasts of Annual Earnings,** *Allen W. Bathke, Jr., John M. Hassell, and Kenneth S. Lorek, The Florida State University.* **The Prediction Accuracy of Alternative Income Reporting Measures: An Empirical Investigation,** *Jenice P. Stewart, University of Missouri.* **A Comparative Analysis of Error Metrics Applied to Analysts' Forecasts of Earnings,** *Ruth Ann McEwen, Temple University.* **PART II. EDUCATION. Assessing the Further Impact of College-Level Accounting Study on Student Performance in the MBA-Level Managerial Accounting Course,** *Mehmet Canlar, Plymouth State College and Man Chand Maloo, Towson State University.* **Participation in Software Selection: Effects on Students' Motivation and Performance,** *Dennis Murray, University of Colorado at Denver and Hugh Grove, University of Denver.* **PART III. AUDITING. The Effect of Perceived Expertise on Authors' Review Judgments,** *E. Michael Bamber, Indiana University.* **The Effect of the Length of Prediction Interval on Prediction Error of Regression Models Used in Analytical Review,** *Arlette C. Wilson, Auburn University and G. William Glezen, University of Arkansas.* **Factors Affecting Materiality Judgments: A Comparison of "Big Eight" Accounting Firms' Materiality Views with the Results of Empirical Research,** *Alan H. Friedberg, Jerry R. Strawser, and Judith H.*

Weapon, *Chris Smith, Aston University, Richard Whipp, University of Warwick and Hugh Willmott, Aston University.* **Waving Goodbye to the TWA Bus: "Paper Prophets" and the Sraffian Critique of Marginalism,** *Tony Tinker, Baruch College, The City University of New York.* **Towards a "Real" Value Accounting,** *James F. Becker, New York University.* **The Dingell Hearings and Related AICPA Initiatives,** *Thomas P. Kelley, American Institute of Certified Public Accountants.* **The Regan Administration, A New Issue with Warmed Over Ingredients,** *John E. Ullmann, Hofstra University.* **A Social Analysis of Corporate Polution Disclosures: A Comment,** *David J. Cooper, University of Manchester Institute of Technology.* **An Analysis of the Impact of Corporate Pollution Disclosures: A Comment,** *In-Mu Haw, Baruch College, The City University of New York and Byung T. Ro, Purdue University.* **An Analysis of the Impact of Corporate Pollution Disclosures: A Reply,** *Martin Freedman, The State University of New York at Binghamton and Bikki Jaggi, Rutgers University.*

Volume 3, 1990, 275 pp. $63.50
ISBN 0-89232-784-7

CONTENTS: Editorial. Intellectual Tyranny and the Public Interest: The Quest for the Grail and the Quality of Life, *Ed Arrington, University of Iowa.* **Talking About Accounting: A Comment on Arington's Paper,** *Paul F. Williams, North Carolina State University.* **Publica or Privatus: Pro Whose Bono?,** *Ralph Estes, Wichita State University.* **The Debate on Whether Client Management Should Negotiate Audit Contracts: Yuppiees Versus Puuppies Versus Guppies Versus Supplies,** *Robert E. Jensen, Trinity University.* **The Market For Poitive Theory: Deconstructing the Market for Excuses,** *Fahrettin Okcabol and Tony Tinker, Baruch College, The City University of New York.* **Sex Role Identity and Career Success of Certified Public Accountants,** *Rebekah J. Maupin, University of Hawaii at Manoa.* **The Effects of Changing Role Requirements on Accountatnts,** *Sarah A. Reed and Stanley H. Kratchman, Texas A&M University.* **The Importance of Being Ernest: Gender Conflicts in Accounting,** *Cheryl R. Lehman, Hofstra University.* **Corporate Social Disclosure Practice: A Comparative International Analysis,** *James Guthrie, University of New South Wales and Lee D. Parker, The Flinders University of South Australia.* **The State and Political Theory in Corporate Social Disclosure Research: A Response to Guthrie and Parker,** *Patricia J. Arnold, Harvard University.* **The Association Between Environmental Performance and Environmental Disclosure in Annual Reports and 10Ks,** *Martin Freedom, State University of New York at Binghamton and Charles Wasley, Washington University.* **The Accountant in the Class Structure,** *Robin Roslender, Napier College of Commerce & Technology.* **The Relevance of Weberianism to Class Analysis of Accounting: A Reply to Roslender,** *Trevor Hopper, University of Manchester.*

the ACCOUNTING REVIEW

Quarterly Journal
of the
American Accounting Association

VOL. 65 JANUARY 1990 No. 1